1.79

CORVO

BARON CORVO.

MORE "WIDE WORLD" ADVENTURES.

EXTRAORDINARY STORY.

A NOBLEMAN FROM ABERDEEN:

THE "BARON"

The world was recently startled by the discovery by the "Wide World Magazine"—a new periodical devoted to the promulgation of true statements of thrilling adventure—of a greater than Robinson Crusoe, in the person of M. Rougemont, and a little later the public were equally amused when it was shown what manner of man that great explorer and anthropologist really is. Being about done with the Rougemont affair, the "Wide World Magazine" has discovered another remarkable personage. This time it is a nobleman, and in this month's issue of the magazine he is presented with the customary editorial flourish, which, at the head of an article, is understood to give keener relish to the tale. The new writer tells a story of his experiences with great minuteness, but there are many experiences of his much more striking than the statements in the "Wide World Magazine," which it would be as well for the world to know.

THE BARON'S STORY.

The article in question is entitled "How I

Frontispiece: The beginning of the first article of the Aberdeen Attack, *The (Aberdeen) Evening Gazette,* 8 November 1898.

Donald Weeks

CORVO

'Saint or madman?'
Hadrian the Seventh

London
MICHAEL JOSEPH

First published in Great Britain by
MICHAEL JOSEPH LTD
52 Bedford Square
London WC1
1971

7181 0896 5

Printed in Great Britain by Northumberland Press Ltd.,
Gateshead, and bound by the Dorstel Press, Harlow

Bud and Julia

Brendan and Susan

CONTENTS

LIST OF ILLUSTRATIONS

ix

FOREWORD

'*Eccovi*, this child has been in hell.'

Although the critic meant these words for Francis Parkman, they also describe the life of Frederick William Rolfe, Baron Corvo. Whether he is presented as a psychiatrist's case-history or as a folk-hero, Rolfe's singular life is fascinating. Any introduction to him or his work immediately pleases or disgusts. He is never the mediocre artist of middle ground. Pronounced to be a genius by some people who knew him, his talents were all thrust into the work, which received little recognition or reward during his life.

My approach to Rolfe was two-fold: first as a reader and then as a collector. These two roles finally overlapped into that of the student, wishing to see the man beyond his manuscript and printed pages. I had come to this conclusion forty years after Rolfe had died and at a geographical distance of 4,000 miles.

No work on Rolfe should omit some dedicatory reference to Sir Shane Leslie for the preservation of Rolfe's name and work. This I acknowledge. I also wish to acknowledge one other person. My own literary-collecting life owes its conception to Elmer Williams. Critic and writer, violin-maker himself and compiler of a list of American violin-makers, Elmer knew the major and minor works of modern literature and possessed a representative collection of these works. Following his father, he was a newspaper man all of his life, moving from Toledo to Detroit. At one time in the Ohio city a young journalist was introduced to the senior Williams and his family. The young man, Russel Crouse, could not easily forget this event, for parents and children all had red hair. The Toledo family was recalled years later when Crouse and Howard Lindsay adapted Clarence Day's *Life With Father* for the stage and Crouse decreed that Father, Mother and all the younger Days should be crowned with red hair. This silent tribute to the Williams family can be extended here by me in the silent thoughts of the important things in life stressed by Elmer. Through his general introduction to The Book, I eventually became acquainted with that strange but spellbinding host of moods and words, Baron Corvo.

Belonging to The Folio Society of London, one book shipped to me in Detroit was *The Quest for Corvo* by A. J. A. Symons. I had heard of neither the book nor author nor subject. But I read with delight pages filled with sheer magic. It told the story of an embittered man who had managed to write some of the most thrilling prose of this century. Who was he and what did he write? A visit to the local library produced only *Hadrian the Seventh* and the Borgia book. At the same time I saw two other items announced in a New York book catalogue. In the next two or three years I had gathered together and read most of Rolfe's books. Through Elmer Williams, I learned of some shops in London and wrote to them. One day a London dealer offered me a holograph letter by Rolfe. Until then, I had never dreamed that I would actually see a specimen of his writing. I immediately acquired it at a fraction of the cost for a similar item today. This, then, was the foundation of my collection.

Rolfe had lived in England. He had written in England. Therefore, I thought, England was the place to seek out information and material. A number of letters travelled over the Atlantic. The first was to the late David Roth of Martyr Worthy, who had built an enviable Rolfe collection. In a spirit of friendliness, we exchanged letters, information and items until his death just before 1960, which prevented our meeting. I gratefully acknowledge the use of any material from his collection, now destined for The British Musum, I understand.

My first trip to London was in July 1960 and Rolfe's bibliographer, Cecil Woolf, and his new bride, Malya, were my hosts in London. At Oxford I was the guest of J. M. Dawkins, Prof. Dawkins' younger brother and the perfect guide to the city and the Bodleian Library, where I had my first glimpse of the Hugh Walpole Rolfe collection. The Woolfs' invitation to visit Venice was accepted and I was in the city of Rolfe's dreams on

July 22nd, the one hundredth anniversary of his birth.

Roth first had told me about the bibliographer and editor of Rolfe, who is also a book dealer and who has added many of the rarer pieces of Corviana to my collection. In turn, I have given him whatever information pertaining to Rolfe I came across.

The Reform Club was the setting in 1960 for a luncheon with the late Captain Leonard Green, another of my correspondents. He was an invaluable source of information. A nephew of a brother-in-law of John Addington Symonds, Green knew both Charles Kains-Jackson and John Gambril Nicholson. He had known Theodore Wratislaw and Edward Carpenter. At Oxford he had met T. E. Lawrence, with whom he had planned to set up a private press in a windmill, a project never realized.

As my collection and interest in the early 1960s grew, I thought about returning to London, but not for just another short holiday. I saved my money for an extensive visit and then, one day, finally decided to make the trip. My job in Detroit as Art Director of *Friends Magazine* was left in capable hands, as I turned all my thoughts towards Rolfe and England.

London was not the only home of Rolfe and I wanted to see all the places in which he had lived, richly or poorly. From the small farmhouse in Bude, Cornwall, to North Wales and Scotland, I travelled the British Isles. 'How did anyone without a penny in his pocket do so much travelling?' was a question which came into my mind more than once between the towns he had seen some eighty years before. But, then, I also thought, I must be in some of the same railway stations he had used.

As times have changed, so have landmarks. Rolfe's birthplace in Cheapside has been replaced by a modern building. The provincial schools in which he taught no longer exist and are not even remembered. The 'tin temple' at Oban was pulled down years ago to make way for the new stone building, one of the three cathedrals used for measuring and assessing the sonic boom made by Concorde on 1 September 1970. Oscott, however, is just as Rolfe had left it, electricity being the only addition. (In Rome the Sforzia-Cesarini house—'a vast barrack of a palace' (*Hadrian*)—still stands, I am told. But during World War II it was used as a German Army Headquarters and its entire contents were destroyed or removed.) Christchurch, Hampshire, looks about the same today as in 1891. Gleeson White's Caxton House has been replaced by a Woolworth's. The house in Bridge Street in which Rolfe stayed still stands and I spent a night in it, next to the room he must have occupied. It is owned by a doctor and his wife today and had been owned by doctors since the early nineteenth century, with one exception. This was about 1890, when Rolfe knew the owner and lived there for a short while in 1889 and during 1891. When I left the Bridge Street house I was asked what Rolfe looked like, just in case either of my hosts ever 'see' him. The house is haunted, apparently, but the only ghost who has been seen appears in the garden with his horse and in Cromwellian uniform. Aberdeen, the Granite City, looks both old and new, but the only remaining address dating back to Rolfe's 1893 is H. H. Champion's office and apartments in Union Street. With a map in hand, I strolled Seaton Park looking for Seaton House, the home of Cuthbert and Malcolm Hay. Not finding it, I asked a uniformed gentleman where the house was. 'You're standing on it,' he replied and told me that it had burned down to the ground only a very few years before. As small as Holywell is, progress has altered the town and the only things remaining from Rolfe's day are the church, St. Wine-fride's Well, five of his banners and the Victoria Hotel. The thrill of the hunt and the courteous reception given to me every-where combined to make a memorable, and informative, trip.

At Oscott the student archivist was my guide around the college. I saw the chapel, Rolfe's room, the museum and the library. During lunch I sat next to the rector at the high table, overlooking the students' dining hall where Rolfe once ate. Our table had Guinness in pewter mugs. Water alone was on the students' tables. In the National Library of Scotland at Edin-burgh I read letters by Rolfe and have to thank this institution for permission to include parts of them here. At Holywell the young priest who showed me the surviving Rolfe banners also introduced me to Mgr. Cashman, who, in turn, made an appoint-ment for me to see Alderman Leo Schwarz. In his office and in his home, the little Leo who carried and fetched for 'Mr. Austin' in 1896 clearly recalled the most artistic and eccentric—and, according to Schwarz, the most religious—individual in Holy-well's history. He prized two objects given to him by Austin, the name Rolfe used at the time. One was a photograph of Leo at the Well and the other was a wash drawing, each the work of Rolfe. Showing me these, he displayed a curious filing system, for each was between the pages of an encyclopedia's first volume—*A* for Austin. Yet his nimble mind flashed back seventy years as if he were only going back so many days. I had made a sketch of the Well and showed it to him. The top edge of the wall behind it had a new dog-tooth design which he had not seen. Back in London, I had a copy made and sent it to him. He thanked me in a letter which arrived but a single day before one from his son to tell me that Alderman Leo Schwarz had just died. He was buried at Pantasaph, near the crucifix cleaned by Rolfe in 1895.

At the start of my extended stay in London my hosts were again the Woolfs and I am indebted to Cecil and Malya for their hospitality and to him for all the assistance he has been kind enough to give. He naturally was eager to learn of my find-ings. 69 Broadhurst Gardens, Hampstead, the birthplace of *Hadrian the Seventh* and other books, did not survive the blitz, but there were other Corvine compensations in London. I was excited at finding letters by Rolfe at the Public Record Office, the two 1886 advertisements for a possible position placed in *The Tablet* by Rolfe, and *The Church Times* brief review of *Tarcissus* in 1881. In each case, I turned this new information over to Woolf.

Perhaps the most unexpected, and most pleasant, call I had was from Mrs. John Holden. On a visit to England, she was in London between trains and paid me a visit. I thank her for the stories she told me, relating to her late husband, the young man Rolfe knew at Holywell. When the two men parted company there, neither contacted the other again. Rolfe and Holden had collaborated on stories and had even started a novel based on the character Hadrian VII. It probably was no more than a romantic piece of pseudo-historic fiction, absolutely nothing like the book written by Rolfe himself in 1903. Holden left Wales never to return and finally settled in Belgium to teach for the rest of his life. During one of the early years of this century he was walking through the Black Forest when a sudden storm caused him to lose his way. In the dark and blinding downpour he spotted a light and ran towards it and found a small inn. Once inside, he took off his drenched outer garments and ordered something to eat and drink. Because of the weather, he was the sole patron and, while waiting for his food, he glanced around the inn. On the earthen floor he saw a crumpled newspaper. Picking it up and smoothing it out, he discovered it was printed in English. In it he read a review of *Hadrian the Seventh*, the first he had heard of the published book.

Vyvyan Holland recounted to Symons the relationship of Fr. Benson and Rolfe at a time when Benson 'was deeply absorbed in all questions concerning magic, necromancy and spiritualism'. Benson once experimented 'in White Magic, which he had carried out at Rolfe's request'. Throughout his life, Rolfe was fascinated by the causes of Magick. Young Holden at Holywell was a sceptic and remained so to his last day. Yet one evening with Rolfe was never explained. Talking to the young man on the subject of Magick, Rolfe elaborated with a demonstration. He produced from nowhere flashing clouds of white smoke which formed into a gigantic horse.

The first person I would see in London was Sir Shane Leslie. (Just before leaving New York, the artist-author Edward Gorey referred to him as the ghost-story writer and knew no more of his literary activities.) Meeting Leslie for the first time was indeed a thrilling experience. Here was a link with that first revelation of Rolfe in 1923. It was Leslie who introduced Rolfe to the world in general and to Symons in particular. With a natural Irish ability for spinning tales, Leslie delighted me, not with ghost-stories, but with stories of the book world. He had known F. Scott Fitzgerald and escorted the American and his wife Zelda on their first visit to London, proudly pointing out the locale of Jack the Ripper, among the other notable landmarks of the city. (As a girl on Samoa, the daughter of Henry Clay Ide, Leslie's first wife knew Robert Louis Stevenson.) Leslie had introduced Dr. Rosenbach to some of the private libraries of England and saw the talkative American bookman speechless one day before a shelf of Caxtons. His own literary reminiscences could easily fill a volume as long as his autobiography, *The Long Shadow.*

Julian Symons, an honest literary critic, poet, biographer, historian and master mystery writer, made available for me what he could from the remains of his brother's papers. As the detective I am certain that he must have some satisfaction in knowing that this has provided innumerable and invaluable clues for this singular task. I am also sincerely grateful to him for the permission to use anything of Rolfe's belonging to A. J. A. Symons' estate.

At times Rolfe had an extremely odd way of showing his affections. Although later letters to the Pirie-Gordons were abusive, he never relinquished an initial sense of friendliness towards young Harry; and Harry—'Harricus' or 'Caliban'—never had an unkind thought for 'Hadrian', his literary collaborator. About the last representative of an old England never to return, Col. Harry Pirie-Gordon was the complete country gentleman, living with his wife, books and immense garden near the crossroads of Yesterday and Tomorrow, Gatwick Airport. Interested in the countries at the other end of the Mediterranean, he and Harry Luke toured Arabia in 1908, during the last year which Rolfe spent at the Pirie-Gordon house in South Wales. Before the trip, he and Rolfe and Luke planned the trip with an Ordnance map, which he loaned to T. E. Lawrence a year later. Attacked in the desert, Lawrence's blood flowed over the map case. Although washed before it was returned to Pirie-Gordon, the blood is still visible today.

Pirie-Gordon's life-long friend was Sir Harry Luke, a Colonial Office official who served as Governor in Cyprus, Malta, and the Pacific at the time the Japanese waged war against the Allies. He was in his fifties when he first tasted spirits. On one day the Japanese had taken five islands from him and prompted his first glass of whisky. He was responsible for the romanizing of the Maltese language into a universally accepted alphabet. Our first meeting was over a lunch which Luke had prepared. In his travels around the world, he prized the varying menus he encountered. Both he and Pirie-Gordon died during 1969, each a vital loss. Before the end of his life, he thought of *Hadrian the*

Seventh as his 'grandchild'. This is the world-acclaimed play skilfully adapted from the novel by his son Peter. Luke's longevity I attribute to Turkish cigarettes and Pirie-Gordon's to country cider.

There is much to thank each Harry for, but I am truly grateful to Pirie-Gordon for providing me with a close association with Rolfe. In a room of his country home, lined with ancestral portraits, each looking on, he and I were two actors in a ceremony which Rolfe himself once had endured. As Grandmaster, Pirie-Gordon accepted me into the Order of Sanctissima Sophia as a Knight, the rank also held by Rolfe. The accolade was performed with a family Scottish sword of the fifteenth century.

(At a time when each was the age of Symons when he died, Symons asked Pirie-Gordon to suggest to Luke that the latter should will his Rolfe items to him. But Pirie-Gordon and Luke survived Symons by almost thirty years, for Symons was attacked by disseminated sclerosis. He may never have given away a book without inscribing it and to the doctor who diagnosed his final illness he presented a copy of his *H. M. Stanley*, in which he had written: 'Hopefully from the author'. This was written in March 1941, five months before he died.)

One clue—a letter by Kains-Jackson to Christopher Millard in the 1920s—led me to the son of Gleeson White of Christchurch, 1891. Eric Gleeson-White was living with his wife in Devizes at the time and I met them on a trip back from Bath, where I had stood in William Beckford's library. Eric recalled the men of the nineties around his father. What he said about Rolfe made him an exception. At Christchurch he and his sister took an instant dislike to the painter-photographer. Of all the boys Rolfe tutored, who did not include Eric, each thought of him as a wonderful companion and teacher. ('I cannot imagine a more delightful companion for small boys, and all my memories of him are happy and to his credit. I can remember that he was a great story teller.' 'I remember him as a man of charming manners to a child, who knew all about magic and charms, who wore strange rings and told fascinating histories.' These are but two testimonials by men who had been boys when they first knew Rolfe.) However, Eric and his wife Betty produced for me a clearer picture of his mother than found in the glimpses of her in Rolfe's writings. By pure accident I heard of another boy. An exchange of letters with several people resulted in meeting Cuthbert Hay, whom Rolfe tutored at Aberdeen in 1892. Still a forceful personality, I am indebted to him for his permission to use letters pertaining to Rolfe's Aberdeen episode in relation to Seaton House.

Wherever I happened to be, people were gracious with their hospitality and assistance. This search for the Rolfe behind Corvo brought me many pleasant and surprising discoveries. The fact that his work remains alive today speaks well for it. The popular writers of his day—Benson and Harland, just to name two—have been forgotten by the public. Yet Rolfe continues to be published. His life, however, so far has been presented only in an abridged form and he himself has been moulded into the character of whichever story was being told. In biographical essays, he now has survived half a century, but myths speak for many events of his life.

One debasing stigma placed upon Rolfe is the fact, some say, that he twice was expelled from Catholic seminaries. However, neither Leslie nor Symons endorsed this surmise. Rolfe entered two seminaries, Oscott and Scots College, in his pursuit of the priesthood. The more recent authors who advocate his discharge from the first as well as from the second base their theory on their own interpretation of Rolfe's words in *Hadrian*. Nowhere in these words is there an accusation registered against an act of expulsion from Oscott. Rolfe devotes two pages to his account of Oscott. Although he states that 'it was my first introduction to the inexorability of the Roman Machine', he is merely saying that he did not understand why his first-year sponsor 'was unable to make further plans' for him. What happened at Oscott was simply that Rolfe's sponsorship was not extended into a second year and, with no money to pay his own fees, he did not return in the autumn of 1888. The idea that his first-year sponsor should have continued in this charitable act for at least one more year may have been only a proposed reality of his own imagination. (This same imagination accused his sponsor to Rome for not paying all of his bills there.) The fierce Aberdeen

Attack first wrote of his discharge from Oscott, but this cannot be fully accepted as an unbiased document. No contemporary of Rolfe's at Oscott ever declared that he had been expelled. Nowhere in his own writings did he speak of any expulsion other than that from Scots College. If he had been expelled from Oscott, another sponsor for a second seminary would have been exceedingly difficult to find, it would seem, within one year's time. Writing parallel thoughts in *Hadrian* and in letters to Dr. Walsh in 1903, Rolfe wrote to the latter about his religious history: 'Then came Oscott, and Rome. Then came the verdict that I had no Vocation four years later'—in 1890 at Scots College, four years after his conversion to Catholicism in 1886, and two years after leaving Oscott: when he wrote to the Archbishop of Westminster in 1910 expressing his desire to renew his vow of celibacy, he reminded the archbishop that 'I am an ecclesiastical subject of Your archdiocese, expelled from the Scots College of Rome in 1890 as having no Vocation'. Rolfe was expelled from only one seminary.

As Rolfe indulged in might-have-been historical romances, so some have tried to force him into the same category. No doubt well-meaning in their appraisals of his life, a few essayists believe his life would have been much less perturbed if he had been accepted into the Church. Yet, would it have been? The human personality rarely changes beyond the first stages of maturity. The seeds of his future life and its outcome were already within him at an early age. Too, there is another of his traits to be considered. He was born with a natural inclination towards the collection of gossip which was half-morbid, half-gleeful. How would he have fared with his flock as a confessor?

In depicting his life, Rolfe has often been taken out of context, so to speak. He and his deeds have not always been related to the world around him. His eccentricities were the same as many people's but there is no denying that his were always exaggerated. Yet this exaggeration may have been the result of nothing more than the contrast between the few elaborate things in life he desired and his almost constant poverty. The age in which he existed was filled with people doing things seriously. No one dabbled. And, if he chose for himself another name, he was not alone in this act. It was a common practice. 'Corno di Bassetto' was a name gracing feuilletons on music in T. P. O'Connor's *Star* during 1888-90. When Rolfe invented his 'Corvo' by 1891, 'Corno' had been just one of the names signed at the bottom of articles by G. B. Shaw. If not the name alone but the baronial title was the cause of retaliation in others, he at least picked a title foreign to England. For just reasons, friends never forgave Harland's widow when she began to publish his work in 1917 over the undeserved title of Lady Henry Harland.

Hadrian the Seventh remains almost unique in English literature. Yet two months before it was started in 1903, *L'Oblat*, 'a continuation of M. Huysmans's Encyclopaedia of Catholicism,' appeared in France. At first Catholic reactions were favourable, until it was pointed out that certain ecclesiastical dignitaries had been caricatured in the book, thus linking it with Rolfe's novel.

Rolfe may have favoured a system of punctuation 'derived from Addison'. Lafcadio Hearne and Walt Whitman imitated Poe's style of punctuation. Rolfe created his own vocabulary and style of spelling and composition, using 'the final k, and the placing of the adverb before the verb (in Mr Henry James's manner)'. But many other authors have indulged in idiosyncrasies of style and vocabulary.

Rolfe did breathe life into his characters. He did not depict them in the patronizing way of public portraits. Rather, Rolfe used a candid mirror to capture their real images for all time. As immortal as the angels, saints and devils of his pen are the pictures of Henry Harland, Prof. Dawkins and John Lane. Neither Harland in Richard Le Gallienne's *Romantic '90s* nor Dawkins in Osbert Lancaster's *With an Eye to the Future* nor Lane in his full biography by J. Lewis May can come to life once again as vividly as each one does in the pages of Rolfe's books.

Rolfe possesses the writer's greatest gift: timelessness in expression. This is true of all of his major books, save one. In *Nicholas Crabbe* he speaks as a new author, wanting 'to do a thing which would justify his reincarnation as a crustacean'. The only book of his which has not fully escaped the date of its composition is *The Weird of the Wanderer*, whose subject is reincarnation.

A departmental mind was one curiosity of his personality. Perhaps the best example of this involves his *Chronicles of the House of Borgia*. Its publication in 1901 entirely dissatisfied him and caused his friendship with the publisher, Grant Richards, to cease. Yet four years later, in July 1905, he wrote to Richards, asking 'if I can be of any assistance to you'. He asked that the past be forgotten and added, 'if my help in any other way would be useful, I should have liked you not to be embarrassed by any false delicacy about asking, for it'. In December he made a few possible publishing suggestions to Richards. He was sincerely trying to help and said: 'Please note that I am not concerned with this. I am merely ... "voicing a felt want," in a hint which perhaps may be useful to you.' At the same time that these letters were written to Richards, Rolfe was meeting young Harry Luke at Oxford. Seeing a copy of his Borgia book on Luke's shelves, Rolfe inscribed in it: 'An insult to the public intelligence.'

Coming from a religious family, Rolfe was not the only child with devout aspirations. His brother Herbert wrote two pieces of music accepted into the Church of England services at the time and he was a local church organist for many years. Another brother became an Anglican minister in Australia. A recurring strain in the family was the reluctance to speak of each other. All the boys seemed to live their own lives apart from the rest of the family. Yet, sensitive Freddy must have felt a certain twinge of Fate's unkind hand whenever he thought of his pastor brother Alfred. Here this one brother—younger and creatively inferior, yet one of Freddy's dedicatees of *Tarcissus*—became a Church of England minister. At the same time, the Church of Rome would not accept Freddy's insistent supplications. His deepest desires 'to serve God' in the Church of his choice were never realized. The opening lines of *Tarcissus*, written at twenty, were personally prophetic:

> Listen, boys, I tell the story,
> Blazoned on the rolls of time,
> How a Boy, in bygone ages
> Died a martyr's death sublime.

Throughout his life, Rolfe became so many times a martyr to his own causes.

George Arthur Rose existed only as an interval between Baron Corvo and Nicholas Crabbe. Rolfe borrowed from his grandfather not only the name Nicholas but at least one of his traits. The son of William, Nicholas carried on the family business of manufacturing pianofortes. He also wrote music. Like everyone else, he was called upon from time to time to write his name and occupation on official documents. William before him and James after him had signed such documents as 'Pianoforte Manufacturer'. Probably weighing in his mind the more genteel-sounding position, in most cases Nicholas signed as 'Music Seller'.

Only recently it has been noted in print that a peculiar phenomenon existed during the latter half of the nineteenth century. Perhaps 'homosexuality' is the only general word to cover it, but it is not to be accepted in any clinical sense. Since about 1850 and especially in England, there was a rash outpouring of 'homosexual' expression in literature, mostly in the form of poetry. Tennyson, Swinburne, Hopkins, some of the poets of the 1890s were all represented, as well as John Addington Symonds with his own work and his translations of Michelangelo's. Added to these were a number of men who composed slender volumes in limited editions proclaiming their love for boys as argued by Plato and the Greek philosophers 'who took this educational pattern in their lives as they found it, only maintaining that the less physical it was the more philosophical, and therefore the better'. One was John Gambril Nicholson, of whom Rolfe wrote to Prof. Dawkins in 1908: 'I know one of these. Sonneteering became a regular disease with him. He certainly got the knack of form: but his matter—Lor! They were all about young males too, written from the amazingly curious standpoint of a devoutly Wesleyan [boy-snatcher]. Ha ha! And, really, the blatant *naïveté* of some of them was simply flabbergasting. Yet he has held his mastership in a big school for quite a dozen years, and still holds it, and still writes and publishes, and still buys Wesleyan ministers to his propensities.' Brian Reade develops the history of this theme in saying (Introduction, *Sexual Heretics*, 1970): 'It can be argued I think that the Roman Church had greater

attractions than any Protestant Church for the homosexual ...
in that its theology and teaching were not based on empirical
studies in the Bible. In spite of former tirades by early Fathers
against sodomy, and in spite of the Aristotelian growth of
Schoolmen in the Middle Ages, this teaching embodied elements
of Platonism, inherited as parts of the primitive philosophical
structure. Such strains permitted on the one hand, the charitable
classification of homosexual emotions as mental events, leading
to celibacy and dedication to the monastery ...; on the other
hand as mental events extending, if they extended at all in
physical expression, to venial sins.' A foundation stone for this
new concept at the time was Kains-Jackson's 1894 article, 'The
New Chivalry', which Reade says 'was an unusual essay, and
Kains-Jackson is entitled to any credit that may be due to his
originality'. This particular segment of the history of his day is
one vital part of the mosaic making up Rolfe's life.

Shane Leslie's two other literary favourites have been Swift
and Wilde. Sharing his associate's enthusiasm for Wilde, Symons
equally admired Edgar Allan Poe, without realizing any coinci-
dental link between the American genius and Rolfe. Unlike most
of the family, Rolfe's father was not born at the Cheapside
address. James Rolfe's birth was at Stoke Newington, five years
after Poe's schooling there between 1817 and 1820. Across the
way from Bransby's Mansion School was the mysterious building which inspired the setting for 'William Wilson'. The theme of
this tale—the narrator meeting himself in the form of a second
person—occurs in almost all of Rolfe's books beginning with
Hadrian. His English schooldays were referred to by Poe as 'the
third lustrum' of his life. With this same little-used word, Rolfe
had written in Venice that he had 'ardently asked to be number'd, lustrums five ago, on the roll' of God's priests. Poe had invented his own Raven, which also won for him everlasting fame,
and in his writings he adopted the Horace motto, 'Omne tulit
punctum qui miscuit utile dulci, lectorem delectando pariterque
monendo'. Adopted also by Rolfe, the latter translated this portion of *Ars Poetica* as: 'He who combines useful with agreeable
carries every point by delighting while admonishing the reader.'
As if he had the yet unborn Rolfe prophetically in mind, Poe

wrote in his *Marginalia*: 'The Crab might never have become a Constellation but for the courage it evinced in nibbling Hercules on the heel.'

'In politics Rolfe was a medieval Tory, and *Hadrian VII* contained a violent parody of English Socialism,' writes Shane Leslie in his 1923 essay on Rolfe. 'But he hated factory-owners even more, and the [Toto] tale *Why the Rose is Red* carried an outburst against "the infamous local Rose of Lancaster dyed red with the Blood of Innocents, victims of minotaur-manufacturers"! He was a fanatical Jacobite, and his eulogy of Cardinal Stefano Borgia was chiefly based on the good turn the last Borgia Cardinal was able to do the last of the Stuarts, Cardinal King Henry IX, who, we learn from a note (and this must be a profound relief to post-Jacobites), "bequeathed his right to the English Crown to the descendants of Anna Maria d'Orleans (daughter of Henrietta Stewart and the niece of King Charles I), who married Duke Vittotamadeo of Savoja, from whom descends not the Bavarian Princess of the White Rose but King Victoremanuele III of Italy".' There is scarcely anything known of Rolfe the Jacobite. 'This day, in Scotland, is kept the festival of the Blessed Mary Stewart, Queen and Martyr,' declares Hadrian-Rolfe, who 'had a very tender romantic feeling of attachment towards the Stewarts'. From 1710 until the 1850s a society founded by some gentlemen of Cheshire and Denbighshire and called the Cycle of the White Rose met continually and became the Jacobite Council of North Wales. A revival of Jacobitism created in London the Order of the White Rose in 1886, based on the former society and on the principles that 'All Authority has a divine sanction, and that the Soverign power does not exist merely by the will of the People or the consent of the governed' and that 'the murder of King Charles the First, and the Revolution of 1688, were national crimes'. Rolfe possessed a membership prospectus for the society, but it is unlikely that he joined it. (In one of his scrapbooks Rolfe had pasted a reproduction of Van Dyke's portrait of Charles I and Henrietta Maria (opp. p. 260, *Harper's Monthly Magazine*, July 1884). The beard which Rolfe grew between Holywell and London in 1899 is described in *Nicholas Crabbe.* When Crabbe-Rolfe appears without it, Eileen

Thorah exclaims, 'Do you know, Mr. Crabbe, that Mrs. Toovey used to go into raptures over your little beard and upturned moustachio? She used to say that you were the living image of Van Dyke's Charles the First.') Writing to a newspaper in January 1888, the Earl of Ashburnham drew attention to the fact that the 31st of the month would be 'the hundredth anniversary of the death of Prince Charles Edward Stuart,' a reminder followed by an announcement of a solemn mass to be celebrated at the Carmelite Church, Kensington, of the repose of the prince's soul. The Order of the White Rose, with very few Catholic members, had no connection with this affair. Before the scheduled date for the mass, Cardinal Manning prohibited it. This act revived interest in Jacobitism. The Order of the White Rose's Patron was Queen Victoria, who took the keenest pride in the history of her own Royal House of Stewart. Three magazines—*The Royalist, The Whirlwind* and *The Jacobite*—appeared in the 1890s. Henry Irving produced a revival of W. G. Will's *King Charles the First*. Andrew Lang's interest in the history of the House of Stuart manifested itself in the advice he gave to Alice Shield for her book, *The King Over the Water*. Whistler's butterfly signature and declaration, 'I affirm the principles of the Order of the White Rose,' graced the roll of its companions. In *Hadrian* the pontiff and Semphill 'talked of books' and 'His own preference was for Thackeray's Esmond,' in which the author displayed a gross ignorance of the young prince. Stevenson's *Master of Ballantrae* is largely an outcome of inspiration derived from the Chevalier de Johnstone's *Memoirs of the Rebellion in 1745 and 1746*. Rolfe had read this Stevenson novel and quoted from it—'I know no better way to express my scorn of human reason.' Before Rolfe left England, he corresponded with the Marquis de Ruvigny and Raineval, who had compiled various editions of the *Legitimist Kalendar* and who was the author of *The Jacobite Peerage*, 1904. 'Hadrian had no armorials,' Rolfe writes of himself in the novel, but adds: 'My shield is white.' The white of purity also meant to him the colour of the White Rose, the theme of the Toto story mentioned by Leslie. 'Sir, it is the supreme insult, to offer Red Roses to an Englishman,' declares Toto. In a note at the end of the story he speaks from 'personal experiences' of certain 'Lancashire Cotton Mills' exploiting their workers. One of these may have been operated by the 'cotton-waste manufacturer' mentioned in *Hadrian*.

The opening page of *Hadrian* sets the scene for the author at work—with his thoughts, his drawing board on his knee, and his cat. Walt Whitman would write down phrases on bits of papers at odd moments. When he was ready for the final composition, he would sit down with a writing tablet on his knee and wait for the inspired start of a new poem while he played with his cat. Whitman also truthfully commented on the passage of history from one person to another. Believe everything you are told, he said, but examine each thing for yourself. With this thought, I humbly apologize to two people for giving them inaccurate information. Brian Reade's *Sexual Heretics* and Timothy d'Arch Smith's *Love in Earnest* may have been otherwise faultless without the story of Rolfe painting the mural in the Christchurch chapel. At the time I gave them this information I merely repeated what I had read and heard, without having opportunity to examine this 'fact' for myself, only to discover it to be another myth.

For the chapter dealing with Rolfe's letters from Venice, I have examined their contents in comparison with all the material from the same period which survives. I was not content merely to follow the tenets of past essayists on Rolfe. who spoke of the letters alone and with no intention towards any understanding of them in the light of other documents. Long extracts from two of the letters are published here for the first time. In all of Rolfe's voluminous correspondence, the Venice Letters are unique in subject matter; and they have been used by many to blacken his character. I have formed no concrete opinion one way or the other about the activities described in these letters. I have tried only to visualize Rolfe during this period by placing these letters next to the other material written by him at the same time. Rolfe wrote begging letters, although he never admitted it. He was also a liar at times, another attribute never confessed. The truth about him in so many instances appears only after close examination of his letters to various people and of his stories. Therefore, I have set down here only what I have been able to discover regarding the period of the Venice Letters. It is only a theory, based on the accumulation of what I call 'negative evidence'. The reader of this chapter is free to judge for himself.

A small counterfoil to a ticket used by Rolfe for a Promenade Concert at Queen's Hall in 1903 uncannily survives. On the back of it he had written: 'This admitted me to search all parts.' For this study on Rolfe, I have endeavoured to 'search all parts' of his life and have done so wherever possible, utilizing—to use his own expression—'original documents'.

Other than those already named, I wish to acknowledge my thanks to the following for whatever part they played in this work:

Francis King for all his many kind and critical considerations in this endeavour; Edgar S. Brown, jr., for his prevailing urgent and American voice across the Atlantic; Dr. G. Mary Rolfe; A. (Dusty) Miller, formerly of Frank Hollings; R. F. L. Bancroft, Superintendent, and The British Museum Reading Room; John Blair-Gould; Dr. and Mrs. James Cantlie; Mgr. Cashman and Fr. Thomas Shepherd of Holywell; Marina Chavchavadze of Burrswood; H. J. Collar; Basil Cook; Fr. Crichton of Pershore; Fr. Francis Edwards and R. K. Browne, Librarian, Farm Street; Mgr. Richard Forster, Rector, and A. J. B. (Sandy) Brown, Student Archivist, Oscott; Mrs. E. Gotch and The Royal Literary Fund; Victor Hall; Mrs. Ethel Hudson; David Lodge; Douglas Matthews and The London Library; Sir Francis Meynell; Alan Munton, for a friendly exchange of information for each of our projects; Mrs. Aurelia Pirie-Gordon; Eric Quayle; Brian Reade; Anthony and Betty Reid; Timothy d'Arch Smith, for his knowledge of puzzles and for supplementing my absent library; Mr. and Mrs. Harold Swan; Margaret Taylor; Mr. and Mrs. Ernest van Someren; and Alexander Canon MacWilliam, for his data on Rolfe at Scots College.

I am further grateful to the present Marquess of Bute for his kindness in making the correspondence from and pertaining to Rolfe available to me and for giving me permission to quote from it, and to Catherine Armet, his Archivist; to Kenneth Hopkins for permission to quote from *Welsh Ambassadors*; to Chatto

& Windus for their permission to quote from *Looking Back* and *Nicholas Crabbe*; and to Cassell & Company, together with Julian Symons, for their permission to quote from *The Quest for Corvo* and *The Desire and Pursuit of the Whole.*

I thank the staffs and facilities of the Aberdeen Library; the Bodleian Library, Oxford; The British Museum Newspaper Library; the Records Room, London County Hall; Central Catholic Library of the Franciscan Friars of the Atonement, London; Guildhall Library; King's College Library, Aberdeen; Public Record Office; The City of Westminster Reference Library; The Wiltshire County Record Office, Trowbridge; and the countless people who answered my letters of enquiry.

Last, I include acknowledgements to Brendan and Susan Gregory for their critical considerations in general; to Brendan in particular for my introduction to Latakia, one blend in the Corvo Mixture; and to Susan in particular for typing one version of this study.

1

Eleven years after his death, Frederick Rolfe was the dedicatee of (Sir) Shane Leslie's *Masquerades: Studies in the Morbid*. The dedication reads: 'To the entertaining soul of that superfine writer Frederick Rolfe Baron Corvo in Purgatory'.

How long does a soul repose in purgatory? Until all the earthly accusations against the person are exonerated?

If purgatory be similar to a court of justice, then a lengthy process was due to determine the eternal fate of the new arrival in the dock. The witness of friends and enemies, counter-weighed with Rolfe's own defence, was to be sifted for an infinite decision. The outlines of his life, deeds and motives had to be reviewed. His sins of commission and omission, of thought, word and deed, those known to him and those not known, all stripped the man of his puny nakedness to unveil what faith was held in his heart. The man of many moods, of impish invention and vitriolic words now faced his Maker, the God of 'Truth and Beauty and Justice'.

'Yes! It pays to be good—just simple goodness pays. I know, oh I know. I always knew it,' he pleaded heavenward as a man. 'God, if ever You loved me, hear me, hear me. Don't I want to be good and clean and happy? What desire have I cherished since childhood save to serve in the number of Your mystics? What but that have I asked of You Who made me?' But he had to ask, 'How can I serve You? How be happy, clean, or good, while You keep me sequestered? Only he, who is good and clean, is happy. I am clean, God, but neither good nor happy. Not alone can a man be good or happy.' These words of religious sincerity were spoken by a human heart. In the face of privations, of earthly trials and temptations, he kept his faith. Yet it may

I

have been a complicated one to explain. The Truth and Beauty and Justice of God mingled with his knowledge of ancient Greek and Rome and the glory of the Renaissance, which breathed a fresh life into his Victorian mind.

The subject for this purgatorial debate was to speak on his own behalf. He was also to account for those names by which he was known at certain times during the span of his life: Baron Corvo, Frederick Austin and Fr. Rolfe. Out of an imaginative creativeness his most impressive and lasting invention was the name 'Baron Corvo'. And, if the Church would not condescend to bestow a simple title upon him, he would improvise with 'Fr. Rolfe'.

The witnesses for this case—if this be the protocol in limbo—were summoned, from the Present and from the Past. But the first question was directed towards recorded fact and not towards any one person. In his adult life, regardless of the name he may have been using at the time, Rolfe's origin and early life were rare subjects of conversation. And what was said was not always according to facts. Although he had no general love for the natives of Scotland, to some he made this land his birthplace. He said that his godfather was the German Kaiser, a claim not entirely unique. Even W. C. Fields once told a woman that the Kaiser was his third cousin and a band of critics named the German sovereign as the illegitimate father of B. Traven. An Englishman with an elementary knowledge of heraldry, Rolfe certainly knew the coats-of-arms of several Rolfe families. Most of these contain the Raven, a device employed by him from his earliest days and finally translated by him into a name, and title, for himself. In 1850 a certain Sir Robert-Monsey Rolfe, no relation to Frederick, was created Baron Cranworth. If there were one baron in the 'family', why not another?

As for his actual origin, the simple record states that Frederick William Rolfe was born on 22 July 1860 in Cheapside, London. The dawn of creation came for him on the day when the sun moved out of Cancer into Leo. This astrological fact, together with the Moon—perhaps indicating an early-morning birth—retained its significance throughout Rolfe's life.

Before any of the summoned witnesses were called upon, the

2

preliminary, and brief, history of Rolfe's immediate family was read. He was artistic and musical, an hereditary trait going back at least to the introduction of the pianoforte into England. His great-great-grandfather Robert was a parish clerk of Eltham, Kent, for many years. And in 1793 his younger brother Thomas officiated in the same parish as an Overseer of the Poor. His son, another Thomas, was a baker in Eltham and the father of five daughters and one son. Robert was a musical instrument-maker. His eldest son William, born in 1756, later became 'the founder of a most respected house' of pianoforte-makers in London. At the beginning of the English industrial revolution in the 1790s, he was a partner of Culliford, Rolfe & Barrow, a small firm publishing music and making musical instruments. He himself lived above this place of business in Cheapside. With Samuel Davis he took out a patent for improvements in pianoforte construction in 1797 and, 'By His Majesty King George III's Royal Letters Patent', established a family business. His son Nicholas continued in his steps and added his own brand of creativeness. He composed musical pieces especially for this particular instrument. Out of the forty native exhibitors of the piano at the Crystal Palace in 1851, the Rolfe company was represented. But the popularity and prosperity of the name and business did not last. It flourished under the direction of Nicholas, but his son James did not have the business acumen to maintain its success.

The section of London into which Frederick William Serafino Austin Lewis Mary Rolfe was born was decent enough.

Two and a half centuries earlier, on 9 December 1606, John Milton had been born practically around the corner in Bread Street. 61 Cheapside was almost in the shadow of St. Paul's Cathedral. Yet in the opposite direction the slums of London's East End were less than a mile away. Ten years later Dickens would die and before a second decade ended the East End would be gripped in the terror of Jack the Ripper.

Frederick Rolfe was born into the golden age of Victorian aristocracy, class-distinction, bigotry, snobbery and poverty; and the mark of his birth followed him to the grave. He was the eldest son of a poor family, without university training or degree, one of a retinue of starving artists. He never attained his one desired

3

position of priesthood within the faith of his choice. The attitudes of people placed him outside all the posts he sought. The thickest wall dividing him from the teeming populace was that of mediocrity. His domineering sense of right, as only he sometimes saw it, and his ardent claim to a few simple luxuries, seemingly eccentric to others, set him apart. He lived within his own world, within his own dreams, within his work, within himself. His life seemed to give the lie to Donne's 'No man is an island, entire of itself.'

Rolfe left no written record of his birth or early childhood. In *Hadrian the Seventh* he lists his father and forefathers, himself and his brothers as sound English people. 'No Society Gossip [of any newspaper] told of Robert and William and Nicholas and James and Frederick and Herbert and Percy and Alfred, day-labourers for a too scanty wage, who never drank nor fought nor swindled nor yelled for their rights, but who led decent noble lives under circumstances often cruelly unjust and always rigorously hard.' The collective image he painted here was of the single one closest to him in the mirror.

In a magazine review of the 1924 *In His Own Image*, Alfonso de Zulueta speaks of Rolfe's parentage. 'One who knew him during his stay in Oxford tells me that the future freak had to father a very humdrum old tuner of pianos—broken, patient, inoffensive, wearing a poverty very different from that of his snarling son, or at least wearing it in a very different way.'

Rolfe was never to know the City he was born into as a home. As a young child he moved with his parents away from the address of the family firm. William and Nicholas had prospered. In the hands of James, Freddy's father, the business began to tumble. Freddy inherited his artistic nature from his forefathers and his total lack of any business sense from his father. As the family grew, the business dwindled. Freddy was soon to have three brothers and three sisters. The family made its home at Camden Town while the firm moved in turn to Great Marlborough Street, to Orchard Street and to Lower Seymour Street. No trace of it remained after 1890.

In *Hadrian* there is a swift portrait of James, almost lost in the blinking of an eye. Written in 1903, about nine months after his father died, Rolfe, as George Arthur Rose in the novel, takes a train to Highbury, where Mrs. Rolfe and one daughter still lived. He walks down Islington Upper Street, describing several passers-by. One is 'a venerable drudge of a piano-turner whose left arm was dragged down by the weight of the unmistakable little bag of tools.' Grandson of William Rolfe, Pianoforte Manufacturer, James had turned from instrument-maker to instrument-tuner. The grandeur of birth or family position denied Freddy was borne for a while in stillness. His impetuous imagination would answer this at a later date.

A fuller portrait of James occurs in the March 1897 *Holywell Record*. Serialized, 'The Man From Texas' by 'Maurice Francis Egan' (which may have been a collaboration between Rolfe and John Holden) is set mostly in a fictional, half-Spanish Texas. The first chapter deals almost entirely with its protagonist, John Donavan. Conceived in the author's image of Rolfe, Donavan was a character Rolfe had already identified himself with three years earlier. ' "Thank Heaven," he said, "I have strength." ... John Donavan was not a particularly good-looking fellow, nor a particularly ill-looking one.... John was intended for the priesthood, for which holy calling he had neither vocation nor inclination.'

The chapter is short. Donavan's mother is pictured, but not with the same focusing delineation as the father.

'His father did not say much. He sat, in the evening, in the little back room behind the shop, silent and grim; but his old pipe often went out and the hand that held the paper—his favourite—trembled. That trembling, withered hand, in which the purple veins stood out from the sinews and wrinkled skin troubled John's heart more than his mother's pleadings. Words spoken lose part of their force, but unspoken words touch a sensitive heart like red-hot steel.... John Donavan's heart was very generous and sensitive. He had never been taught to be demonstrative; the Donavans were a silent family, and John had been long away; but he could not resist the impulse to take his father's hand in his, and cry out,—

'I can't father, I can't.'

'Who asked you to do anything against your will?' said the old man, his eyes twinkling, 'But don't say you can't, say you won't....'

Old Donavan was a man of few words. His son, with a feeling that was despair, understood that the iron had entered his inmost soul.

John's mother 'loved him still in heart', the story continues, but 'made little sign of it'. The home 'was clouded. Father, mother and son were miserable. The old man seldom spoke and his wife went about the house sadly as one heart-broken'. Donavan himself has 'a certain vague and evil odour' because he 'had failed to be a priest'.

Written by Rolfe, these few words are all that remain to document his early years at home. 'The key to all your difficulties, present and to come, is Love,' he, as Hadrian, later tells himself. In this one quick reference to his background, in *The Holywell Record*, Rolfe speaks of something which never manifested itself. As a child he was taught the A-B-C, neatness and cleanliness and the Scriptures. Each of these he later utilized to the full. But one thing was missing from the make-up of his personality. This is neither a natural nor a self-acquired quality. Together with the alphabet, the caring for property of body and soul, the element of Love has to be taught to the formative child. This one important aspect of a person's life was never taught to Freddy or any of James' children. To the end of his days he sought after the Unknowing. The Ideal or Divine Friend he called it. But he looked only for an explanation for his own being, an explanation that would not have been necessary if he could have been taught about Love.

Rolfe, the adult, never completely outgrew his boyhood dreams. Through the years of his life he identified himself with the white-garbed, dragon-slaying St. George, the protector of England. In the words found in *Hubert's Arthur*, the name of George Arthur Rose, the hero of Rolfe's *Hadrian the Seventh*, finds its origin in English history: 'When I left Duke Arthur [of Brittany, murdered by King John in 1203], he was a very large boy in his full ripe bloom, sprightly and lithe as his panthers of

6

England, clean as a wild white primrose of Messire Saint George in body and soul.' A personalized and 'unchangeable George of the Roses' marches through his books until his own 'sweet white Death'. The maidens, villains and kingdoms of legend were exchanged for young martyrs and the roots of his own history. 'Rolfe,' he said at Oscott really came from 'Rollo' (or 'Raouel the Reckless'), a common ancestor of himself and William the Conqueror. This may not have been pure fancy. Writing about 'that fierce Norse pirate, Rolf or Rollo, who was driven from his own land, Norway, as an outlaw, and who came to Normandy and founded the settlement there which afterwards became the duchy, and of which William was the duke,' R. R. C. Gregory establishes a possible ethnic relationship in his book, *The Story of Royal Eltham.*

In 1890 Rolfe acquired a 'grandmother', the Duchess Sforza-Cesarini of Rome. And the Dr. Hardy he was to know for more than twenty years may have acted as a father to his imagination. His actual family was seldom mentioned. One of the very few times he spoke of either parent was in a letter to Frederic Chapman. Rolfe asked to rearrange a 'tea-time engagement with John Lane' because he had 'a standing engagement with my father for *Friday*, which I cannot possibly break'. This was written on 20 May 1902, just two months before James Rolfe died.

The few references to his family in letters do indicate that he was a devoted son. A copy of his *Chronicles of the House of Borgia* was inscribed: 'This first copy of my second book offered with respect and love to my Father and Mother by their eldest son Freddy'. *Hadrian* was dedicated to his mother, and the dedication probably would have included his father had he lived only two more years.

The exaggerated eccentricities and innovations of his existence branded his personality. Zulueta continues his *In His Own Image* review by saying that it is not up to him 'to deny the probability of Frederick Rolfe being blest with a mother! All we can say is, that if she existed, it is unfortunate that she was unable to exert a moderating influence which might have deflected her weird offspring into the fair water-roads of fame instead of stagnating, as he did, among the sewers'.

7

The mother did exist, and out-lived the strange creature of archaic days who could find no niche for himself in the time he lived.

Leaving school when he was about fourteen, Rolfe entered the academic world as a teacher. Until his open conversion from the Anglican Church of his upbringing, his life was uneventful. He was first at Stationers' Company's School, attaining the prized position of the first Secretary of the school's Swimming Club. By 1880 he had travelled to the King Edward VI Grammar School, Saffron Walden, meeting a young boy of the town and school by the name of Nicholson. John Gambril Nicholson and Rolfe were to keep a friendship until the end of Rolfe's days in Venice, but a friendship which was neither smooth nor continuous.

At Saffron Walden, Rolfe displayed his many talents. His teaching of the youngest boys in the school was done 'thoroughly well', commented the head master. 'His questions are always simple but searching, and he never shrinks from the laborious repetition which is requisite for driving home ideas in very young minds.... He rendered valuable aid in training a young Choir, and undertook successfully a class of beginners in Drawing.'

The silent witnesses to this testimonial can verify its accuracy. Drawing and painting had already attracted his artistic nature. And the walls of his Saffron Walden den were hung with paintings and sketches. Some were his; some were done by others. Reproductions of greater work were also represented, such as Andrea del Sarto's 'Young St. John' later to be mentioned in *Hadrian*.

Coming from a musical family, Rolfe possessed a tolerable voice and the ability to play the piano. School work did not occupy his every hour. According to several numbers of *The Herts & Essex Observer* from November 1880 to June 1881, the 'Saffron Walden Glee Company ("Limited")' performed at local functions. As a member the alto voice of Rolfe was heard in solo singing 'The Chorister', 'The Distant Shore' or the humorous 'Ye Franklyn Dogge'. One programme included a skit used by the American humorist, Artemus Ward. For another the *Observer* reported that 'Mr F. W. Rolfe's song was well sung

8

and the way he handled the keys of the piano showed that he was no novice as regards music'.

In this time, which was to form the later man, Rolfe stood between Past and Future. His natural attributes were being utilized. But a streak of the future author of words and causes was beginning to show itself. The *Observer* of 25 June 1881 printed his letter-to-the-editor. 'Having lived in the town some few months, it has often struck me that Saffron Walden is priviledged above many towns of its size,' he began and named the worthy sites of the town. 'Now looking at all these privileges, I think there is one thing above all others we are greatly in need of, that is, Public Baths. As there are good waterworks here water can easily be obtained. Considering the number of young men employed in the town, and there being no place for public bathing, it would be gratefully appreciated if such a need were supplied.' In essence, this is not an uncommon plea from a young man. But this forms the first request he made for something either difficult to procure or procurable only at the expense of others.

Saffron Walden was the earliest period in Rolfe's life later to be recognized. R. M. Luckock, the school's head master, is kindly but briefly remembered in *Hadrian*. Admonishing himself while 'regarding his own image' in a mirror, Rose-Rolfe is having 'one of your bad days.... You look all your age, and twelve years more.... If you had an inch more thigh, and say a couple of inches more shin, you might look people down a little more: but with that weak subservient aspect—how Luckock used to chaff about it—no wonder everyone takes advantage of you'.

The 'laborious repetition' used in teaching the young boys which Luckock spoke about stayed with Rolfe for the rest of his life. Certain words, phrases, ideas, themes were used by him time and again. Throughout his work, drawing or writing, his mind zig-zagged between a present need and a past pronouncement. In the creation of novels, he was said to be weak in plot but magnificent in situation. This truth—the situation rather than the plot and the ever-repeated thoughts—narrowed the full scope of his work, in printed writing as well as in private letters.

A believer in some visible form of assurance for existence,

Rolfe lived with mottoes. The 'Do ye nexte thynge' motto in *Hadrian* was found in his room at Saffron Walden and stayed with him for thirty-three years.

The change-over to the Roman Church affected only his outward profession of the Church of his choice. It did not recondition anything in his mind and heart. At fifteen he had already decided on a religious life and lived accordingly. At twenty-five he proposed to himself the possible state of priesthood. The chastity accompanying such a decision was of no consequence. It automatically followed his unconscious, and religious, desires.

The disappointments which lay ahead taught him how to live—as the crab, enclosing his most tender emotions within a hard casing. Accepted by few, he had to live within and for himself. And to this end he satisfied himself in living a clean and healthy life, in body, mind and soul. White was the symbolic colour of his days. The whiteness of cleanliness and the whiteness of religion showed itself in the clean linen and the cold water he preferred. Versed in the customs of ancient Rome, he believed that white in its cleanliness and simplicity was the acme of aesthetic taste. A son of the Church (Anglican or Catholic) he added white to his daily duties. His early, and immaturely composed, poems from the 1870s and 1880s speak of 'snow-white raiment' for heavenly bodies, 'radiant vestments', saints walking 'in white', St. Sebastian's 'limbs of flaming whiteness' in the land where fadeless lilies blow, 'white robes of purity' and of laurelled martyrs and of Mary's Maids of Honour.

In the last novel, completed in Venice in 1911, Rolfe writes of himself as Nicholas Crabbe. The time-traveller of *The Weird of the Wanderer* is donned with a 'mantle of silver tissue lined with white fur'. The Rolfe who becomes pope, 'the White Father', in *Hadrian the Seventh* 'had no armorials. Years before, while discussing heraldic blazons with an aged clergyman, he had burst out with "My shield is white." "Keep it so," the other replied. And Hadrian's shield was Argent.'

The significance of this colour can be traced to the period when he began to teach. In *The Church Times*, 24 September 1880, Rolfe read of the funeral of 'Father' Charles Fuge Lowder, the

Anglican pastor of St. Peter's, London Docks. 'When the history of the Catholic revival in the Church of England came to be written,' said the paper, 'not the least honoured amongst those who won back for us her forfeited inheritance would be the name of Charles Lowder.' In a mind swaying between Anglicanism and Romanism, this statement must have been devoured with significance. But another portion of the long article drew his attention. He underscored the words speaking of the pastor's church on the day of his funeral. As Lowder was *'a celibate priest, the altar and sanctuary were vested in white'*.

At twenty Rolfe was beginning to design the exacting pattern of his future personality. He had already chosen the raven and the colour of white as symbols for his name and beliefs.

To express himself Rolfe turned, like many young men of his age, to painting and poetry. At Saffron Walden he paid for the first separate publication of his work, the little eight-page poem, *Tarcissus*. Just before the start of his academic career three years earlier, a prize poem by him appeared in the August 1877 *School Magazine*. In the nine stanzas of 'Seeking and Finding: A Sequel to "The Lost Chord",' the young Rolfe revealed his abstract notions of heaven. 'The white-robed choristers' chanting ... the choral song ... And the aureoled choir give answer/ "Alleluia" and "Amen"' are words similar to the dedication of *Tarcissus*. Percy and Alfred Rolfe and John Nicholson were included among the twenty-two dedicatees, all 'Singers in the Sanctuary here below, and I trust Choristers of Christ's Church in Heaven'. *Tarcissus: The Boy Martyr of Rome, in the Diocletian Persecution*, A.D. CCCIII, was the first young martyr of the Church honoured by Rolfe's pen. But this poetic essay is no more than a juvenile's attempt at literature.

The first review of any of Rolfe's work appeared on 1 April 1881 in *The Church Times* and was as slight as his published poem. And an error in it—in this case the misspelling of his name —set the pattern for the inaccuracies about him to appear in print for almost a century. The review read in full: 'Tarcissus, the boy-martyr of Rome, is the title of a short but well-written poem, which may be had of the author, Mr. F. Rolph, Saffron Walden, Essex.'

For two terms Rolfe, 'a nice youth', taught History, Latin, French, English, Arithmetic and Divinity at Winchester Modern School. He assisted with choir work and played the harmonium in chapel. Minor eccentricities of character did not undermine the general fondness for him of both boys and head master. He was described as neat, methodical, regular and punctual at St. Bartholomew's Grammar School, Newbury. And he excelled both as a teacher and disciplinarian here and at Balsham Manor, Cambridge.

At twenty-two Rolfe was no more than a dreamy-minded creator of sentimental poems on the theme of unending friendship. The objects of his poetic reveries were his pupils. They were, for him, the incarnations of his worshipped boy saints. And in these early years, away from home, he diligently sought an identification with the people immediately around him.

While at Winchester he edited, wrote out in longhand and probably produced the hectographed school paper, *The Wintonian*. For the number of 4 February 1882 he had written about the boys who would soon rise up to prominent places. He singled out one boy—a cricket player of 'capital style', a football player and 'one of the most popular boys in the school'. He deserved to be popular, Rolfe continued, '& I am sure that while he is away on the other side of the globe we shall long remember the name of Austin & I hope that he on his part will sometimes think of the Winchester Modern School & his friends in England'.

Austin no doubt was the initialled R. C. A. to whom Rolfe addressed at least two poems. 'Tell me if you will be as sad at parting as I shall be/Send me a hundred loving messages, heart's darling, from o'er the sea' were two lines in one. Another poem, 'Farewell', also may have been to the same person, reading, in part:

> Goodbye! from sight but not from heart.
> Though half the world may intervene,
> In love and hope and trust serene,
> We never more can be apart.

He did not let the matter stop at these poetic excursions. For at this time he made himself known as Frederick Austin-Rolfe.

For twenty-five years Rolfe conducted himself within the limitations of organized society. No doubt a model child, he grew into a model teacher. He had a genuine gift and the greatest tributes to his character come from boys of his tutelage and from his fellow masters. His one pupil at Saffron Walden, Nicholson, became a teacher, was admired by his boys and was an author of verse and fiction. But a seed of discontent was slowly taking bloom within the wayward vagabond of later life. He did not respond himself to the disciplinary acts he set out for his pupils. In his exactness a perversity was born. For him there would be just one way to do a certain thing. He would fight the world to bring his cause into being. The path he was to choose would be through a jungle of adversity. And the only oasis was within his own self.

The witnesses for the first quarter of a century of his life can say nothing against him. Yet, in a single act, his day darkened and the newer witnesses were no longer fond of him. The day that Rolfe was received into the Catholic Church was one which led to humiliation, misery, loneliness and stark privation. His mind and heart were set. The Church was his goal. But it was a determination not shared by others.

Speaking for himself, Rolfe said that he attended Oxford. Yet no records endorse his claims. He may have only sat in at lectures. There is no doubt about his being at the university city. Being born with no roots, he could adapt himself in any way. And Oxford provided him with an accent and a scholarly manner.

The pursuit and teaching of knowledge did not impinge upon his natural sense of the ridiculous. The admiration of the boys in his classes was enhanced by his humour and comic story-telling. The touch of the bizarre within him was demonstrated when the Prince of Wales visited Oxford. Some students 'got up a fancy dress ball in his honour'. With two friends, Andrew Ping and John Aubrey Thurstans, Rolfe drove to the ball in a furniture van, disguised as a raven. 'When the Prince reached the top of the steps, where the head stood ready to receive him, I edged up to him, and after having looked at him with one eye and then the other, bird fashion, I emptied a pound of whitewash through a hole in my tail.'

Grantham was his last post at a grammar school. Here he met its head master, E. G. Hardy, who was to remain his friend and mentor for more than twenty years. Here it was, too, that he finally decided to join the Catholic Church. His turning to Rome differed from the eleventh-hour conversions among the artists of the 1890s. He had 'received a Divine Vocation to serve God as a secular priest when I was a protestant boy of fifteen. I was very fervent about it. I went to confession (Stanton, St. Alban's, Holborn), said the rosary, used the Garden of the Soul for a prayer-book.... Then at twenty-four I became intensely earnest. At twenty-five I suddenly realized that, if it was "priest-hood" I was after, I was on the wrong road: the Church of England-As-By-Law-Established had nothing of the sort to offer me, for she had nothing to do with Peter, and Peter had the Key.'

The young, passive but perceptive boy of fifteen may have sensed a ruffled atmosphere within the Church of England. Francis Thompson's words, 'From almost earliest youth / I raised the lids o' the truth' (*Sister Songs*, 1895), perhaps may be applied to Rolfe during his early years. Later, in North Wales, he would be 'denied' the sacraments of the Church. In 1874 he already had experienced the Church's refusal to grant the rite of communion to its flock. On June 24th of this year the Curate of St. Alban's, the Rev. A. H. Stanton, tacked a sign on the church door: 'There will be no celebration of Holy Communion in this Church until further notice. All other services as usual.'

The Daily Telegraph reported St. Alban's Easter observance in 1874 as 'being sumptuous and joyful', but the year was to be a dark one for such ritualistic churches. On April 20th Archbishop Tait introduced the ill-starred Public Worship Regulation Bill into the House of Lords, an Act to come into force on 1 July 1875. The Prime Minister, Disraeli, welcomed it with effusion, believing the 'Bill to put down Ritualism'. The Bill was to deprive the ritualistic segments in the Church of England of any continuation in their practices and to present this Church as something new and strange. The stress created by this sudden and

dire action caused many to secede at once to Rome. The ritualis-
tically-inclined who remained did so with ever-decreasing confidence in the Anglican position. Dr. Littledale once suggested
that The Church Association, formed in 1865 to 'counteract
Popery and Ritualism', was 'quick to see much more danger in
the spread of ornate services to the classes represented in the
congregation of St. Alban's' than in some other churches.

A suit against Rev. Mackonochie of St. Alban's inspired a
Memorial to be written on 28 May 1874. The Memorial—reading,
in part, that the 'Petitioners learn with great sorrow that the
Clergy' of St. Alban's and the congregation are threatened with
a renewal of prosecutions 'with regard to certain observances
which are highly esteemed by them as exponents of the Catholic
Faith professed by the Church of England'—and a Protest were
signed by 1,918 communicants and presented to the Bishop of
London. On 13 June 1875 Fr. Mackonochie was suspended from
duties for six weeks. The wise vicar took a holiday to Italy.
The parish was entrusted to the Rev. Stanton. On June 24th the
Bishop of London directed the acting curate to refrain from all
ritualistic practices, even in the wearing of vestment. This prompted Stanton's 'no celebration of Holy Communion' notice, a rite
not returned to until 8 August 1875. This was the disturbing
undertow within the Church of England when Rolfe, a Protestant and fervent boy of fifteen, was attending St. Alban the
Martyr's Church, Holborn.

Rolfe's Anglicanism completely fell from him in 1885 when
he read two books. The first was Dr. R. F. Littledale's *Plain
Reasons Against Joining the Church of Rome* and the second
Fr. H. Ryder's reply, *Catholic Controversy*. One of the numerous
Church of England clergy to follow Newman and champion
the Catholic cause, Ryder 'had wiped the floor with Littledale'.
Rolfe's mind now was firmly set in the direction of Rome—
against all odds.

In his lectures to the Grantham boys, his now anti-Protestant
mind spoke in belittling terms about Luther and his morals.
Luther had lived at the time of Rolfe's beloved Italian Renaissance and also at the time of Henry VIII, another personage
detested by Rolfe because of his anti-Catholicism. The same

Luther wrote that 'a man might veil his own eyes and go out of the light into the darkness and hide himself and then blame the sun and the day for being obscure'—a description not too unlike Rolfe in his later days.

For two reasons Rolfe left Grantham. One was due to his open conversion to Rome. The lesser of the two reasons had to do with an article by him in the school paper, voicing his rather unconventional ideas about Henry VIII. He 'resigned my housemastership of my own free and unaided will'. Rolfe had enjoyed a pleasant relationship with Grantham. Employed by Hardy at an annual salary of £50 on 22 September 1884, he worked conscientiously in the execution of his duties. Following the dictates of his heart, he collected his last salary payment from the school on 8 March 1886. The next step was to look for a job as a Catholic.

Early in 1886 the twenty-five-year-old Rolfe found lodgings in Iverson Road, just off Kilburn High Road. His juvenile days were well behind him and he was now facing a new world and a new life. The nearest Catholic church was fifteen minutes to the south; and here he attended services and met the William Slaughter family. For several generations the male Slaughters had attended St. Mary's College, Oscott. By 1886 two of the three Slaughter boys had already been there. After two years at the school, young Edward was staying at home because of illness. Rolfe was employed to tutor him and his brother Reginald. This encounter with the Slaughters probably led Rolfe to think about Oscott for himself. The one brother returned there in 1886. Edward did not. And Reginald began at the school shortly before Rolfe himself started on a career in the Roman Church.

While tutoring the boys, Rolfe discussed some of his experiences at Grantham. Edward later remembered 'that when he was Tutor to my Brother and myself he was fond of painting in Oils and, amongst other things, did a Portrait of himself. My late Father at one time went in very much for collecting and colouring meershaum pipes, and I remember one occasion when [Rolfe] had got down to his last half crown and received a couple of guineas for, I think, an article he wrote which was accepted by one of the Magazines, he rushed off at once and expended the whole of the two guineas in a new meerschaum pipe.' Noted here are some of the traits to be found in his later life. The most marked is the one of unreality. To possess some unneeded object, he would spend his entire fortune, no matter how slight, often so depriving himself of the actual necessities of life. But the story of the meerschaum pipes is one of the few showing Rolfe as an imitator.

Convert that he was, Rolfe's life was to be filled with converts. The first one appeared in the year of his conversion. In 1886 Rolfe met the third Marquess of Bute, who offered him his first, and last, position in the Catholic establishment.

Before John Patrick Crichton Stuart was born in 1847, his forefathers had established themselves in Wales and Scotland. The first marquess began to renovate Cardiff Castle. His son risked his entire fortune to promote a scheme of docks at Cardiff. After nine years of building, the first docks opened in 1839 and earned him the title of 'the creator of modern Cardiff'. The third marquess completed the building of the docks and devoted the rest of his time to civic and personal needs. Born a Presbyterian, he studied all forms of Western and Eastern Christianity before finally going over to Rome in 1866.

The similarities between Bute and Rolfe were actually few. Each was a convert and an ardent professor of his faith. On the one side, Bute was a forceful man of action, a man with a name, a position and wealth. His programmes were intended to benefit a great number of people. He translated into English the Breviary and other Orders of Service. He restored churches in England and Scotland and erected 'tin temples'. The passive nature of Rolfe could match none of these. Selected for the position Bute offered, he had to borrow from his salary to travel from London. His influence was directed to the few. And his own literary translations of a later period were actually adaptations in an acquired erudite language of his own making. Bute and Rolfe really had little in common. But then Bute was not the easiest man to please.

One of his 'tin temples' was built at Oban and he wanted it to be the centre of the Diocese of Argyll and the Isles. A fanatic for liturgical ceremony, he envisioned the Pro-Cathedral of St.

Columba as offering daily sung services. It mattered not at all that only a few parishioners lived nearby and that priests looked upon Oban as too distant a location for them. His pent-up enthusiasm was let loose upon the bishop and the project continued. While the cathedral was being constructed, he planned 'to get the Vicar-choral (or whatever we are to call him) to take a house and keep a small choir-school of, say, six boys who would be a standing nucleus for the choir'. He rented half of the Jesuit house, 'Loyola', for a dormitory and school. All he needed now were others to agree with his designs. In the short time of the cathedral's history before Rolfe, Bute interviewed for the position several applicants who did not please him.

On 8 May 1886 he wrote to a friend in Italy:

I imagined that, the duties being light and the remuneration (I venture to think) adequate, a chaplain could easily be found; but the difficulties seem endless. Whether the cause be chronic ill-health, constitutional indolence, or an entire want of interest in the Liturgy, I know not; but so far no priest has been found in England or Scotland able or willing to celebrate the daily sung Mass. Kindly set on foot inquiries among the unattached clergy of Rome, popularly known as *preti di piazza*—many of them, I believe estimable priests, unoccupied through no fault of their own—and see if one can be found to supply our needs. Unexceptionable references would be, of course, required.

On this same day Rolfe applied for a Catholic position through the pages of *The Tablet*:

F. R. Experienced in Tuition and school keeping, will be glad to hear of a Vacancy in a Catholic School or Tutorship in a private family.

Not even being able to obtain the services of a semi-retired priest, Bute looked about for a lay master. Seeing Rolfe's announcement in *The Tablet*, he could write to the Argyll bishop that he had 'heard of a layman, formerly housemaster at King

18

Edward VI School, Grantham, a position he resigned on becoming a Catholic. I have written to him, and if he is all I am led to expect, and I secure his services, the priest will only be required for the much less responsible position of chaplain, and anyone will do who is respectable, obliging, and sufficiently acquainted with his duties.' Before the end of June, Rolfe, 'the defender of the faith' for only a few months, met Bute, a Catholic for twenty years.

The testimonials from his former headmasters were in order. To secure a job in a Catholic institution, Rolfe may also have had written recommendations from members of the Church—such as Fr. Parkinson, who accepted him into the Church at Oxford in January, and William Slaughter. Before the end of another month, Bute told him to start as soon as possible 'to make some sort of beginning'. An August 'opening' for the 'tin temple' was ardently wished for, because of the tourist and shooting seasons. His salary was settled and the aspiring and conscientious novice set off for his first independent job as 'head of the Cathedral establishment'. What Bute expected of Rolfe has not been recorded, but the young man's position was no more secure than those of the five priests who had been hired and dismissed in the preceding year.

The journey to the Scottish town on the edge of the Hebrides was made via nearby Ft. Augustus. Here he picked up four of the first boys for Bute's choir school. Together the five arrived at Oban on the night of August 3rd, finding a fifth boy in the care of the French caretakers, Albert and Charlotte Duhamel. And the following morning he began to teach the Office of Compline and the boys sang the eight o'clock Mass in the pro-cathedral.

Dutiful letters were sent to Bute, now in Europe while a house was being built for him in the Argylls, to include the first electricity in the area. Rolfe spoke of the furniture arriving for the cathedral, suggested text books and outlined his teaching programme. The inexperience of position and religion made him confess that he was 'no master of the Breviary'. And, when the new font came, he could not say 'what a Catholic font is like but the one they are setting up is just like a High Church (not

Ritualistic) one. The carvings are lovely & when it is up, I think it will be well worthy of a better building to contain it.'

Rigid discipline was part of Rolfe's daily routine. Each morning began for the boys with a cold bath. 'The boys do not take kindly' to this. 'I fancy that if warm water is put into one's morning tub the whole point of the cold bath is lost. The nearest the water is to freezing point, the more invigorating is the bath I consider. I hear that at Fort Augustus the boys were treated just like the other boys there, & I fancy it has made them rather too dainty.' He superintended the operation himself and made certain that each boy had 'a splash, a thorough ducking & a good rub'. Innocent sincerity prompted him to remark that 'these boys are very particular to wear bathing drawers when they take their morning cold bath'. The boy Tarcissus and the youths of his poems, real or now legendary, had not as yet taken concrete form in front of him. Rolfe had not begun to admit the beauty to be seen in a young male body.

The mental, physical and spiritual welfare of the boys included recreation. But this was extremely limited at Oban. On fine days there would be walks and there was one excursion to the island of Mull. The only other place for leisure-time to be spent was 'a small garden in which they run about but they seem to be tired of that'. During Rolfe's interview, Bute had briefly mentioned the subject of boating for the boys. In a letter to Bute's agent Rolfe stated that 'the charge for a boat is 1s/6d per hour or 30/- per month', but 'a boat could be purchased for about £7 & it seems to me it would be cheaper to buy one if you think his Lordship would sanction the expense'. A boat was procured, but at thirty shillings a month.

Two peculiarities at this time involved the boys. He did not allow them to speak to anyone out of the house without his leave. He had taken this step when he had discovered that the housekeeper in the other half of the double villa had 'asked one of the boys what they had to eat & other similar questions'. In addressing him in writing, he insisted upon the boys using 'Rev. Fr. Rolfe'.

'A Belgian with a huge red beard,' Fr. Francis Beurms, arrived on the last day of August. Rolfe found him a 'good companion' and a scholar and the two shared in the work at the services. A French chaplain had been summoned but had not yet come.

By mid-September Rolfe had had a 'frightful row with the Duhamels, with things said in "cool blood", but it was all a misunderstanding'. When everything was explained, 'all ended happily'. Happily for Rolfe, perhaps, but not the Duhamels. Charlotte wrote to 'Madame La Marquise' that they wished for a more strict master at the head of the school. Mr. Rolfe, she said, was unjust and betrayed their trust with his lies. She also spoke of the strained expenses due to Mr. Rolfe's invitations to people for dinner almost every day.

The appearance of the French chaplain, the Abbé Berard, solved nothing for Rolfe. He was 'shelved & completely power-less' when Berard assumed mastership of the establishment and completely altered all programmes. He would not say Mass at ten o'clock 'as it would mean too much for him to fast every day till 11.15 or 11.30'. The Belgian priest was dismissed but did not leave. He was a Flemish brewer's son and addicted to drinking with friends. He and the Frenchman consumed a noticeable amount of beer. Rolfe complained to Bute about the 'disagreeable things going on here' and that 'things were in a muddle'.

At twenty-six Rolfe found himself surrounded by forces mightier than himself.

In *Hadrian* Rolfe recalls Oban:

The school perhaps might be called a school for outcasts. But I, a young inexperienced Catholic of six months, was lured by innumerable false pretences, on the part of the eccentric party [Bute] who offered me the post, to accept what he called the Head-mastership of a Catholic Choir School. He did not tell me that he was forcing the establishment on the bishop of the diocese, nor that the Head-mastership had been refused by several distinguished priests simply on account of the im-possible conditions. I bought my experience. That I quarrelled with the chaplains is quite true. I did not quarrel effectually though. They were a Belgian and a Frenchman. They drank themselves drunk on beer, out of decanters, chased each other round the rectory tables in a tipsy fight, defied my authority and compelled the ragamuffins of the school to do the same. I naturally resigned that post as quickly as possible.

In such a setting Rolfe had his baptism into Catholic institutions.

Into *Hadrian* he sifted the ingredients of his past life. Bute—who owned property in Jerusalem and whose heart was buried on the Mount of Olives when he died in 1900—becomes the Marquess of Mountstuart and, in part, Edward Lancaster in the novel. One other person in the book derives from this short experience—one of the boys. All the boys were from Cardiff and the Highlands and were not outcast waifs. They were to Rolfe 'clever but conceited', 'bucolic', 'quite a baby', 'up to the average but good boys & good workers'. For himself there was one thing in Catholic teaching which he could never fathom. He could not comprehend the broad Roman definition of a lie. In *Hadrian* he confronts an interviewing cardinal:

Yes, Eminency: we teach little children that there are three kinds of lies; and that the Officiose Lie, which is told to excuse oneself or another—the meanest lie of the lot, I say—is only a Venial Sin. It's in the catechism. Well, naturally enough the miserable little wretches, who can't possibly grasp the subtilty of a *distinguo*, put undue importance on that abominable word 'only'; and they grew up as the most despicable of all liars. Ouf! I learned all this from a thin thing named Danielson, just after my return to the faith of my forefathers. He lied to me. In my innocence I took his word. Then I found him out; and preached on the enormity of his crime. 'Well, sir,' says he as bold as brass, 'it's only a Venial Sin!'

Danielson was Frank Daniel, one of the boys at Oban and the liar of the lot.

Whether Rolfe wrote them or not, these words ring out from *The Holywell Record*: 'Purgatory! Purgatory! Purgatory! Great lazer-house of departed souls, whose physicians are still in the flesh. The souls in Purgatory are all saints.'

Saints or not, if these souls depend on the voices of witnesses for escort, then their stay in limbo can be long. And the experience of Oban produced the first witness against Rolfe.

On 11 October 1886 a letter was sent to Bute from Ft. Augustus. Dom David Oswald Hunter Blair, in speaking of Rolfe's resignation, was eager to nominate a replacement. He knew 'a clean Cambridge man' who was 'a pleasant fellow and accustomed to teaching.... He is a man of much more solidity than Rolfe— of whom I did not augur well.'

Rolfe's stay at Oban lasted only a little more than two months. In the only contemporary reference to his termination, Hunter Blair, in the same letter to Bute, wrote: 'I had a note from Rolfe this morning saying he had resigned his post, in terror of Oban damps.'

2

Oban meant bitter disappointment to Rolfe's spiritual life. There was also a material blow. With him at the choir school were his belongings. Leaving, he packed books, paintings, personal papers and clippings from newspapers into two boxes. They were sent separately to Oxford. Only one arrived. The box which was lost contained a silver Maltese Cross, inscribed: 'Stationers' School Swimming Club. Presented to Frederick W. Rolfe, First Secretary of the Club, by the members, July 1879'.

Rolfe was already collecting newspaper articles. But he had not started to copy the letters he wrote. From London in January 1887 he sent one to Bute. Ill at the time he left Oban, he 'completed my cure with the aid of Thermo-Oxygen Baths'. He had gone to Oxford 'to talk over my future with my friends there'. His 'friends' were all Catholics, and some must have been mere casual acquaintances. This is one letter he should have copied to keep with him for the rest of his life. His accusations against 'the Faithful' were based on the treatment, not always kind, he had received at their hands. Eleven members of the Church body and two laymen made up the 'friends' mentioned in this letter, six of whom were:

Fr. Parkinson was the Jesuit priest who, a year earlier, had received Rolfe into the Church at Oxford. The incident is recounted in *Hadrian* when he, as Fr. Perkins, says of Rolfe, 'I'm afraid he's a genius, poor fellow!' Father Parkinson was to hear of the convert only once again, in 1894. During a drastic period in Rolfe's life, he tried to do whatever he could to aid him.

Fr. R. Clarke, another Jesuit, was asked to recommend Rolfe for a position in 1892. He could only answer and say that he never 'knew him personally and I am sorry to say that I have

24

no definite remembrance that would justify me in recommending him'.

Fr. Oswald was the Benedictine Hunter Blair. As Fr. Benedict in *Hadrian* he is taken to task when it is pointed out that he and 'so many worthy priests' spoke against Hadrian's moral character 'from an exceedingly casual acquaintance'. In 1934 he could write an article, 'More Light on Baron Corvo', and end it on a consoling note. He could say that he had 'never ceased to remember him and to commend him to God's mercy'. Yet his intelligence about Rolfe's past life was used for detrimental purposes in a 1907 lawsuit.

Mr. W. Slaughter, one of the laymen, was Edward's father. With both of them, until about 1904, Rolfe kept alive a friendship which had its moments of rupture. In *Hadrian* the Slaughters are 'a purse-proud family'.

Mr. Grissell of Oxford was to meet Rolfe as a student cast out of Scots College, Rome, in 1890. And he was to refuse any aid, even though Rolfe's plea for help was exaggerated. He appears in two of Rolfe's books—as Signor Gargouille Grice in *Hadrian* and as 'a fatuous Gallican, by name the Sieur Carffontaine de la Gardegrise' in *Don Renato*.

The Bishop of Emmaus was to provide a notable, if not notorious, suggestion at a vital point of Rolfe's life. He was also to deprive Rolfe of a means of secular livelihood. For the latter injury, inflicted in 1891, Rolfe never forgave him and named him a mere priest in *Hadrian*.

So, from an early day, Rolfe possessed the unfortunate knack of choosing the wrong people. Inadvertently he sought out an acquaintance whose personality, in whatever way, clashed with his own. He was blessed with the gift to see the naked character of human beings and to describe accurately their glories or foibles. But he was cursed with the unfaltering theory that any person, of interest to him at the moment, would be his Ideal Friend. The list of 'friends' in this letter to Bute proved him to be no genius in the matter of human selection.

The letter to Bute spoke about Rolfe's immediate acute position. The friends of Oxford were consulted, he said, 'to aid me in getting some work to do'. But no work materialized. Rolfe

25

offered his tutorial services through another announcement in *The Tablet*. But 'up to this time I have been unable to hear of any work' and he did not have the means to allow him 'to remain so long unemployed'.

There was a double purpose to this letter. During his interview with Bute, Rolfe had expressed his decision for eventual priesthood. His future employer had approved of this and had said that he would speak to the local bishop about possible minor orders being given to the new Catholic. This spontaneous offer on Bute's part went no further than the interview. Knowing of his connection with people of the Church and journalism, Rolfe now indirectly recalled this initial conversation. 'I long had an earnest desire to become a priest, but as I consider it my duty to contribute to the maintenance of my father & mother & sisters, I cannot yet, as I should wish, enter a seminary. It has been suggested that if I could get some employment which would bring in a salary, I might read my Philosophy & Theology in my spare time, so as to render myself well prepared when my duty to my parents has ceased, & I am free to give myself to the service of the Church.' The boldness of an inner nature broke through Rolfe's timidity in saying that he was advised 'to ask your Lordship to bring your influence to bear to find me employment of any kind'.

Asking people, and usually at a distance, to find him work 'of any kind' was to be a frequent request. This letter differed from later ones only in the person to whom it was addressed. Rolfe had met Bute, a man of wealth and position. Five years later he would begin a series of begging letters to people he had never met. As in the case of this one, many of his future letters, if answered at all, would bring no favourable reply.

During the first two months of 1887 in Kensington, Rolfe had suddenly 'undergone a modicum of persecution lately'. The first signs of paranoia slowly stirred in his mind as he was asked to leave one rooming house for another. No doubt the simple reason was merely non-payment of rent. Yet this 'modicum of persecution' was not long-lasting. 'In a few days' he left for a new home. He had been hired as a tutor near Newcastle-upon-Tyne.

At Cheeseburn Grange, Rolfe tutored one of the sons of Francis Henry Riddell for a few months. An invalid, young Arthur John died just a year later at the age of eighteen. The position with this family and the quietness of the remote estate pleased him. The history of the house also must have fascinated the ever-learning Rolfe. In monastic times the manor and its 180 acres had belonged to the Prior and Canons of Hexham, but Henry VIII robbed them of these possessions and gave the land to royal favourites. Elizabeth I granted the estate to Gawaen Swinburne, through whom it passed to the present-day Riddell family. Adjoining the manor hall is a chapel dedicated to St. Francis Xavier. The priest in residence in 1887 was Baron Rev. William.

The one characteristic to be noted in Rolfe's letters is the extreme personal touch. In writing of the same events to several people, each letter would convey a different thought. His letters were personal in that they were meant as a communication only between himself and the one person he was addressing. To each person he, perhaps only half-consciously, contrived to impart his own personal situation in the light of the other person's. When in January he wrote to Bute about contributing to the maintenance of his parents and sisters, he said that he could not enter a seminary 'as I should wish'. Since this letter was written, Rolfe was never in a position to contribute anything of importance to his family; and by October 1887 he had entered a seminary in preparation for the priesthood. Impetuous and unreliable in 1887, these traits multiplied and grew in exaggeration in years to come.

The Bishop of Shrewsbury was asked to be Rolfe's financial sponsor, with the result that he became an ecclesiastical subject of the prelate at St. Mary's College, Oscott. The records of the school read: Rolfe, Frederick (Oct. 29, 1887—Mid. 1888) (in Divinity).

Once again he found himself in the position of a student-teacher. Part of his duties as a seminarist at Oscott was to extend his past experience in teaching young boys. Popular with these charges, a certain discriminating film separated Rolfe from his fellow students. An atmosphere of genial toleration existed. Yet the instinctive artistic and creative nature of his personality, coupled with his manner of aloofness, were neither shared nor fully appreciated by the others, with one exception. The walls of his room were again decorated with paintings and designs, almost every boy in the school being employed as a model, for single or group studies of angels and saints.

The decisive individuality of Rolfe's character, his setting himself apart from others and the rules governing their society, was marked at Oscott. In the 1880s, the college students were not permitted away from the school grounds, except on Sunday and Wednesday afternoons. Then they could walk in nearby Sutton Park. But these regulations did not prevent Rolfe from visiting the town of Sutton Coldfield, to call on a certain William Wort, photographer. His interest in photography started soon after he began to paint. He had a fondness for photographing his art and taking portraits of himself. The bill he ran up at Wort's included the costs for photographs and supplies and was left unpaid when he left the school in mid-1888.

'There was no artistic atmosphere' at the college, Vincent O'Sullivan remarked. He was the one person who could discuss with Rolfe both literature and art. The only Pre-Raphaelites Rolfe talked about were Burne-Jones, Holman Hunt and William Morris. Although he never referred to Morris as a writer, O'Sullivan was convinced that Rolfe was influenced by his work. Almost twenty years earlier Morris had again turned from the decorative arts to writing. The words from his pen at this time 'were short, hard words, none of which might not have been used hundreds of years ago: the words in which legends then old would be cast by a poet of the fourteenth century,' says William Gaunt in his *Pre-Raphaelite Dream*. In his work 'he turned himself into a man of the past looking back into a still further past'. O'Sullivan read a long story by Rolfe in manuscript and compared it to 'the pseudo-archaic style of Morris'.

O'Sullivan was the first person to recommend books of interest to Rolfe, and in so doing helped him to nourish his maturing imagination. In the habit of reading, as in others, Rolfe practised extremes. In his pursuit of knowledge, he read theological works and the Greek and Roman classics. For entertainment, he was greatly attracted to women writers. He was enthusiastic about the art of Kate Greenaway in books, and one of his favourite novels at this time was *The Channings* by Mrs. Henry Wood, author of *East Lynne*. Dickens, Thackeray and Scott were in the school library for anyone to read, but he showed no interest in them. 'Newman's "Apologia" of course—but everyone at Oscott (except me),' O'Sullivan said, 'read Newman's "Apologia"—that is, of those who read anything besides school-books— a very limited number among those sons of country squires and army officers.' The lack of any artistic atmosphere 'is one reason why Rolfe stood out.'

In the exchange of thoughts on current artists, O'Sullivan's passion for Rossetti was one-sided. 'Rossetti's obsession about women would have repelled him, and the kind of women Rossetti sometimes painted, big strapping wenches with bull necks and shoulders and arms, would have repelled him too. Anyhow, I never heard him mention Rossetti, and as I liked Rossetti very much at the time I should have certainly brought him to the subject if he had known anything about it. (Wilde liked Rossetti, but then Wilde liked women, and women of the "womanly" type —Mrs. Langtry for instance).'

'Whenever they come to the horrors I stop listening and draw pictures,' was something Rolfe confided to O'Sullivan in relation to the subjects taught at Oscott. 'By "horrors",' explained O'Sullivan, 'he meant sex-questions. But he was very devout. I was told that he used to go down to the chapel late at night and stay there an hour sometimes when he could have had no notion that he was observed.'

Rolfe's physical portrait of the time emerges from the words of this one contemporary. The myopic countenance of the future author was noted. He 'wore *pince-nez* from which he was never separated except in bed'. That Rolfe smoked a great deal was an unusual feature of the day. He 'had a wonderful collection of meerschaum pipes which he had taken great pains to colour'. At this time Rolfe may have smoked pipes more than cigarettes. He later preferred cigarettes, rolled fat and squat. When in funds, he had his own special Corvine Mixture, smoking cigarettes in endless succession without inhaling. 'Cigarettes inspire me,' said Oscar Wilde, the author of *The Happy Prince* of 1888. 'They are the perfect type of a perfect pleasure.' and, as such, they must have appealed to Rolfe.

Thinking back to their days at Oscott, O'Sullivan did not have the impression that Rolfe was 'a man of strong intellect, or even of very high intelligence. But then, when I was present he was talking to school boys, and perhaps he tempered his talk to the lambs he had in front of him.' The young student-teacher was already 'a man formed' about a lot of things. But Vincent had read more and was therefore able to supply him with 'lists of obsolete words and spellings which made him prance with delight'. And it was he, at this same time who set Rolfe 'on the way of the final *k* in words ending in *ic* and of writing *shew* for the more usual *show*—forms which he kept to till the end of his days'.

Vincent could not speak of his books, 'because "Hadrian VII" is the only one I have read. When "Hadrian" appeared, I noticed the signature, "Fr. Rolfe," I wrote to R. at the publishers to ask if it was his. He replied (promptly I believe): "Yes, it's mine. But don't read it." He added: "Are you a millionaire? Send me £500 at once." ' This question illustrated Rolfe's remarkable store of personal information. Eugene O'Sullivan, Vincent's father, emigrated to the United States from Ireland and amassed a large fortune during the American Civil War as a coffee broker. Vincent did not pursue any position in the Church. Instead, he moved to London and began to write. One of his friends was Wilde, whom he befriended in Paris soon after his release from Reading Gaol. After the turn of this century, he went to live in France. His inheritance spent, he sold his collection of books and letters from his friends, from Beardsley to Wilde. He died a forgotten man. Yet he retained a philosophical turn of mind, which enabled him to see things in a cheerful light. Recalling Rolfe's question about his being a millionaire and the demand for £500, he could compare Rolfe with Wagner. 'They both asked for important sums,' he said, adding that 'perhaps Rolfe got them sometimes. I hope so.' He was not to know of a second point of similarity between Wagner and Rolfe. The composer died in Venice in the Palazzo Verdramin-Calergi. Thirty years later Rolfe was to die next to this place, in his Palazzo Marcello on the Grand Canal, in better circumstances than those surrounding O'Sullivan's last days.

In writing about Rolfe, O'Sullivan has said that 'he was born for the Church'. He was neither a great scoundrel nor a great artist, but, 'rather, a saint without patience'.

In contrast to this witness for Rolfe, Mgr. James Dey spoke about the subject from within the Church. Sharing his priestly education at Oscott with Rolfe, Dey later became the school's rector. At the end of 1898 he was the only person whose word was printed in defence of Rolfe when *The Catholic Times* reprinted the crippling attack on Baron Corvo. As a fellow creature, Dey harboured no ill thoughts towards Rolfe. As a member of the Church body, his opinions were different. He felt sure that Rolfe 'would never have passed successfully through the Jesuit mill. Nor can I imagine him ever submitting to the discipline (mental) of a Scholastic Philosophical and Theological course. He was inclined to see enmity when there was only disagreement. I cannot remember why Rolfe in *Hadrian* should have made the remark of being ashamed of myself,' Dey said. 'It referred of course to some failing of mine regarding himself—and the only thing we differed about was the summoning of a Provincial Council. You see, Rolfe never knew much of the Ordinary Church Government and he may have thought I had only to express the wish and my Bishop would have acted. R. could never have become a priest. He was far too self centred for any Bishop to ordain him as a secular priest with the cure of souls and he never would have submitted to the discipline of a Religious Order. The Catholic priesthood is a vocation, not a profession—this R. did not understand.'

At a time when Romanism was held suspect in Great Britain, it had to guard itself with a loyal strength. It could afford no opportunity for individualism within its ranks. As a regulated body it had to maintain its existence and growth in an alien field. Not a fraction of one per cent of any dissenting word could be allowed within its ramparts. The priesthood was for and of the masses. An original mind, especially one of a convert, was subject to doubt about conformity to the governing doctrines of Rome.

To speak for himself, Rolfe turns to the records in the pages of *Hadrian*:

I will begin with my career at [Oscott], where I was during a scholastic year of eight months as an ecclesiastical subject of the Bishop of [Shrewsbury], and where I received the Tonsure. At the end of those eight months, my diocesan wrote that he was unable to make any further plans for me, because there was not (I quote his words) an unanimous verdict of the superiors in favour of my Vocation. This was like a bolt from the blue: for the four superiors verbally had testified the exact contrary to me. Instantly I wrote, inviting them to explain the discrepancy. It was the Long Vacation. In reply, the President averred inability to understand my diocesan's statement: advised me to change my diocese; and volunteered an introduction to the Bishop of [Southwark], in which he declared that my talents and energy (I am quoting again) would make me a very valuable priest. The Vice-president declined to add anything to what he already had told me. A dark man, he was, who hid inability under a guise of austerity. The Professor of Dogmatic Theology said that he never had been asked for, and never had volunteered, an opinion. The Professor of Moral Theology, who was my confessor, said the same; and, further, he superintended my subsequent correspondence with my bishop. You will mark the intentions of that act of his. However, all came to nothing. The Bishop of [Shrewsbury] refused to explain, to recede, to afford me satisfaction. The Bishop of [Southwark] refused to look at me, because the Bishop of [Shrewsbury] had rejected me. It was my first introduction to the inexorability of the Roman Machine, inexorable in iniquity as in righteousness.

Some of the other Oscott contemporaries recalled Rolfe. He was 'a thin, somewhat emaciated, rather good-looking young man,' said one. 'In the course of his first week he took us by surprise one dinner-time by exclaiming aloud, in an interval of silence—"Oh! what lovely legs!" This, in those far-off days of the past, was considered a somewhat outrageous exclamation to come from the lips of a Church student .... But it turned out that the legs he was referring to were those of a small insect which was creeping towards his soup-plate.'

Another brought two points to light. 'His outstanding eccentricity was to stamp everything available with his crest, the raven (*Corvo*) [by means of a small embossing device]. But more noticeable was a *stuffed* raven which had the place of honour on his table' — imitating Dickens in this one gesture. Rolfe 'kept much to himself, and seemed more interested in art than in theology'.

The name of Oscott was attached to his in the art of poetry during this period. 'A Chante Royal, in Honour of the Most Pure Mother of God,' appeared in *The Month*, May 1888. It was by 'Frederick Rolfe. St. Marie's College of Oscott'. In the December 15th number of *The Universal Review* another poem was printed, 'Sestina yn honovr of Lytel Seynt Hew Who Was crucified by ye Jewys atte Lincoln, on ye Eve of Seynt Peter ad Vincula, in ye year of ovre Lorde MCCLV'—by 'Rev. Frederick Rolfe. S. Marie's College of Oscott.' And this one poem proves that Rolfe was an able student. O'Sullivan's archaic spellings abound throughout the seven-page sestina.

Little St. Hugh's life is told in verse. Rolfe 'must have had a grand "pull" with the editor and publishers to persuade them to so much expense,' said Vincent. The lines are set in black-letter type, which adds to the difficulty in reading it. Each stanza, printed on a separate page, begins with a large illustrative initial. Each initial letter is incorporated into a water-colour painting. In turn, this is placed within a border of decorative lettering. The paintings are signed with the heraldic *label*—a horizontal bar with three short descenders, denoting the first son—over an *R*. The first initial is a simple portrait of Hugh in Renaissance-looking garb. The last is another one of Hugh, being translated into heaven, crowned and bearing a cross. Four depict his martyrdom. The sixth initial displays the scene of little Hugh's burial, with a procession of fifty-eight mourners.

This one illustration is the first in Rolfe's life to be elaborated with an unbridled imagination. Rolfe was neither a natural nor a swift artist. He drew and painted slowly. The seven initials therefore must have taken a considerable amount of time for

33

him to execute. And when each was done, it must have been exhibited on the wall of his room. He was at Oscott for only eight months and his duties included studying and teaching. He painted only in his spare time. The first biographical note after his death appeared in 1923. 'At Oscott,' this sketch reports, 'he had caused *admiratio* by painting a translation of St. William of Norwich in which 149 reproductions of himself in varied vesture performed the ceremony of bearing a saint, who was not unlike him either!' Not only was this repeated but added to, in saying that this one painting covered three sides of his bedroom and 'even the Saint (what could be seen of him) was marked with Rolfe's nose'. Yet neither of these essayists saw the picture they described. Nor was it described—in these words—by any of Rolfe's Oscott contemporaries.

Three walls of his bedroom were no doubt covered with paintings, as were his dens in the schools in which he taught. But the largest painting he had attempted up to this time would have been no more than two feet square—hardly the size to cover even one wall. Earlier in the 1880s, while still a teacher, Rolfe did compose a poem about St. William of Norwich. This was a sonnet and no illustration for it was ever mentioned. In *The Universal Review* the initial measures 3″ x 3½″. If the original painting were even eight times this size, the largest of the heads of the mourners would be only about a quarter of an inch high. Fantasising about the size, subject matter and number of figures in the painting seems also to have extended to the sameness of their profiles. But, in any case, it is the prerogative of any artist to portray his characters in whatever fashion he chooses. In painting, an amateur has to fall back on what he knows best: his own image. If all fifty-eight mourners, and the saint, do possess the Corvine profile, why should this single fact serve to brand Rolfe? This is only the first of many occasions when Rolfe is taken out of context to be 'explained'. But, then, other men have suffered from the pious hands of biographers.

The human side of Nathaniel Hawthorne, for example, was deleted from his journals by a puritanically vigilant family. Poe will live forever through the distorted reports of his 'friend', Rufus Wilmot Griswold. So Rolfe has been torn asunder, to be

34

shown only by the fragments favourable to the person who has presented the outlines of his life. In holding him up to the world as an individual, the fact has been overlooked that he was a part of humanity. Whatever his exaggerated deeds, he was still a part of this world for fifty-three years and, as such, he was one of this earth's teeming population. After a life in which he constantly met with indifference, in death he has met with legend and myth. For fifty-three years he was merely a person, no matter how far he strayed from accepted society; and this world's tragedy, not his, is that there were, and will be, other Corvos.

Accompanied by Rolfe, who was 'good company', Vincent and his brother Percy once made a tour of Worcester, Lichfield and Lincoln cathedrals. As a cameo portrait, Vincent always remembered the ending of their visit to Worcester. Leaving the cathedral, just after the choir had sung the one hundred and twenty-sixth Psalm, the three made their way to the railway station. The entire scene reminded O'Sullivan of *John Inglesant*. Inglesant and a friend walk in the shadow of Worcester Cathedral as the sunset light reddens and dies on the towers. 'The sun has gone down,' he says cheerfully, 'but it will rise again. It is time to go home.' These words of Inglesant's were among the last O'Sullivan said to Frederick Rolfe in this world.

When Rolfe left Oscott, he never saw either O'Sullivan brother again. Percy returned to his native New York and corresponded with Rolfe. From time to time he would send the struggling Englishman sums of money. The tribute Vincent paid Rolfe, at a much later date, was never returned. Although others from Oscott are named, and elevated, in *Hadrian*, Vincent is absent. The year after *Hadrian* was written, Rolfe composed *Nicholas Crabbe*. In this novel he exclaims, ' "If we are happy asleep in bed, it must be exquisite to be dead" says that silly O'Sullivan.' This reference is to one of Vincent's verses in his *Poems* of 1896. Percy is the one to be remembered—as 'the most exquisitely beautiful boy, body and soul, (with the most exquisitely horrible voice,) I ever met'. Writing *Hadrian*, Rolfe thought of him vividly 'with ardent admiration'. Percy is Hadrian's creation, Cardinal Van Kristen.

After eight months at Oscott, and with no change in his

35

sponsor's adverse verdict—if the Bishop of Shrewsbury originally had intended to sponsor him for a second year—Rolfe spent the Long Vacation with a friend at St. Andrews. One of the few members within the Church never to be subject to his quarrels, Fr. George Angus, too, was a convert. Once an Army officer and an Anglican minister, he was eighteen years older than Rolfe. He was ordained a Catholic priest in 1876 and was stationed in Kensington before becoming the first resident priest at St. Andrews since the Reformation.

St. Andrews is south of Aberdeen, Fraserburgh is to the north. At Fraserburgh Rolfe stayed for the next six months, as guest of another convert. John Matthias Ogilvie-Forbes had been accepted into the Church six years before, after being in the Anglican ministry and a missionary to Ceylon. His Boyndlie House was the first of the country houses Rolfe later would make a topic of conversation, together with the servants who had waited on him.

The 'Lytel Seynt Hew' sestina was the first experiment of a series. During his stay with Ogilvie-Forbes, Rolfe produced paintings for his poems. Those to be illustrated included 'Sir Ralph the Page', 'Ballade of Boys and in Particular the Percies', 'Ottava Rima: The Three Ages of Love', a 'Triolet' and 'Ballade of Boys Bathing'. The success of the St. Hugh poem was not repeated. He sent poems and photographed illustrations to magazines. The only success was with the 'Triolet'. It was used in *Atalanta* for January 1890. 'Here's a little new Year pitched out of the sky' is the first of its eight lines. Hand-lettered, the poem is on one side of an illustration of a small baby sitting on a snowy porch step and rubbing one eye. Neither poem nor drawing has the merit belonging to a later Rolfe. 'Ballade of Boys Bathing' was also accepted, but without its single illustration— a water-colour of 'a mysterious group of divers in the clear of the moon' which hung on Rolfe's wall as he wrote *Hadrian* in 1903.

Rolfe wrote verse, said Vincent O'Sullivan, 'atrociously bad most of it. They were about boys and saints, generally both together—altogether objective, by-the-bye.' Rolfe's meeting with his poetic muse came at a time when most young people believe the only way to express their innermost emotions is through the medium of verse. The only criterion for any semblance of quality to the young poet is fitting words into a mechanically metered number of lines. Form is more important than natural sincerity. And, so, Rolfe's early efforts are all appallingly adolescent. Unlike most beginners the subject of a never-dying love betwixt youth and maid did not occupy his sing-songy and properly rhymed verses. The first noticeable awareness felt towards things religious was expressed in his lines. Abstract themes of heaven and angelic hosts preceded a series commemorating the youthful martyrs of the Church. Tarcissus was the first of these to be honoured in print. The boys in his care as a teacher shared space with the saints. In these poems there is no indication of the spark of genius that illuminated his future work. He wrote the ordinary type of poem at this age and nothing more. By far the best of his early endeavours is 'Ballade of Boys Bathing'. Its setting is the St. Andrews Bay he saw in the summer of 1888. It was not printed until 1890, after his first visit to Christchurch. Meeting experienced poets here may have influenced the quality of this ballade in some way. Two stanzas read:

Deep blue water as blue can be,
　　Rocks rising high where the red clouds flare,
Boys of the colour of ivory.
　　Breasting the wavelets, and diving there,
　　White boys, ruddy, and tanned, and bare,
　　　　With lights and shadows of rose and grey,
　　And the sea like pearls in their shining hair,
　　　　The boys who bathe in St. Andrews Bay.

A summer night, and a sapphire sea,
　　A setting sun, and a golden glare:
Hurled from the height where the wild rocks be,
　　　　Wondrous limbs in the luminous air,
　　Fresh as a white flame, flushed, and fair,
　　　　Lithe round arms in the salt sea spray,
　　And the sea seems alive with them everywhere,
　　　　The boys who bathe in St. Andrews Bay.

Whether consciously or not, an inner and previously stifled

37

part of his personality here began to break through the propriety of the age. As the 1880s came to a close, a new decade, a new life and a new personality were awaiting the student and teacher, still in his twenties. Ten years had passed between the saintly young martyr of Rome, Tarcissus, and the 'white boys, ruddy, and tanned, and bare ... who bathe in St. Andrews Bay'. Rolfe may not have yet recognized the fact, but the dominant theme of physical attraction in the form of the boy had been born.

The year between Christmas 1889 and Christmas 1890 was a crowded one for Rolfe. He was to travel from Scotland, through England, to Rome. And he was to travel from his pursuits towards the Roman Catholic Church and into a new career.

On Christmas Day 1889 Rolfe was still at Boyndlie House, where he was described by a visitor as a pleasant and talented young man. He was dressed as a priest, in the soutane and sandals which complemented his aesthetic features. In the new year Fr. Angus had been instrumental in providing Rolfe with another ecclesiastical subject. The Archbishop of St. Andrews and Edinburgh 'was instigated' to invite Rolfe 'to volunteer for his diocese' and then to send him to Scots College in Rome. In *Hadrian* Rolfe adds that Fr. Angus and Canon Lord Archibald Douglas assured him that, 'in return for my services, my expenses would be borne by the archbishop'. These 'expenses' may have ended at tuition and the fare to Rome. But Rolfe's literal mind always expected the fullest measure of any agreement, intended or not.

Acquiring the archbishop's sponsorship naturally took time. Before any final arrangements could be made, Rolfe left Fraserburgh. After six months as Ogilvie-Forbes' guest, Rolfe travelled south with his poetry, paintings and photographs. Part of the summer was spent at Christchurch, where he met Charles Kains-Jackson and Kains-Jackson's younger cousin, Cecil Castle, and Gleeson White and his family. But before he went to Italy, Rolfe made a short stay near Bristol, where 'he had friends'. He was here on November 4th. And on this day he wrote his last letter to Bute:

My Lord Marquess
    I do not fail to perceive, after a very careful consideration

38

of the matter, that your Lordship regards me with suspicion & disfavour; & as a person entirely undeserving of either your interest or assistance. To be a judge in one's own case is a difficult role to play, but I am constrained to say, on the evidence before me, that I have not merited the ill-opinion with which your Lordship is pleased to look upon me. And further it must be said that your refusal to allow me to rehabilitate myself in your Lordship's good graces prevents me, & is the only thing which prevents me, not only from continuing my studies for the priesthood, but from earning the bare means of existence.

Has your Lordship considered this?

My former relations with you apparently did not give you satisfaction. May I suggest my inexperience as a Catholic as some excuse for my failure to carry out your desires?

Since then I have had more experience & much adversity; & I venture to say that if you will extend your help to me a second time you will have no cause to regret it. I have already indicated the course approved by the Abp of S. Andrews, viz to send me to Rome. In writing this I disclaim all intention of giving needless trouble or of assuming a cringing attitude with a view to preying upon your purse. I desire only to remove your prejudice against me, to make known the real necessity which your Lordship has the power to relieve, & to obtain the means to enable me to finish my theological course.

I am

My Lord Marquess

Your obedient servant

Frederick William Rolfe.

There was no answer to Rolfe's plea.

3

'It was winter time & an almost incessant
"tramontana" shrivelled up the land with its
icy blast. If you know what a Scotch North-
East wind is & multiply by ten, you will
have some idea of a "tramontana".'

These words appear in the first Toto story, written by Rolfe in
June 1891. If he remembered the ill winds of Scotland, at last set
behind him as 1890 began, he was unaware of the icy blasts of an
even greater storm awaiting him. Fierce winds were to blow, not
from Scotland, but from Rome, chilling Rolfe for the rest of
his life.

'The course approved of by the Abp of S. Andrews' led to
Rolfe's second, and last, attempt at preparatory studies for the
priesthood. 'The late Archbishop Smith, of Edinburgh,' reported
an Aberdeen newspaper account of Baron Corvo, 'well known for
his softness of heart in such cases, was induced to take him up,
and sent him to the Scots College at Rome, to be trained for the
priesthood. After five months he was expelled. It was not owing
to his lack of Vocation, nor because he refused to give the rector
his dressing-case, ... but because—as is averred on authority
which the Baron is not likely to challenge—he was regarded as
a general nuisance in the place, to say the least of it. Even there
he contracted large debts, which he said Lord Archibald Douglas
had agreed to pay, but which Lord Archibald would have nothing to do with. However, Mr. Rolfe has always been characterised
by a polished manner, backed by his accomplishments as a little
music, some capacity for art, and a considerable expertness as
an amateur photographer.'

As 1889 ended, Rolfe found himself in Rome. His sudden appearance at Scots College may have been the first act on his part to create an unpopular relation with its rector and students. His inability to concern himself with any group of people was manifested here, for on December 7th Rolfe arrived at the school without any previous notice or communication. He was allowed to stay only until 3 May 1890, when, in his own words, he was 'kicked out into the streets of Rome on a Saturday night, it being alleged that I had no Vocation.'

Although this one event was branded so deep in his soul that he referred to it numerous times in his writings, *Hadrian the Seventh* and *The Desire and Pursuit of the Whole* give the most complete account of the incident as seen in Rolfe's mind.

A year after I left Maryvale [Oscott], the Archbishop of Agenda [Edinburgh] was instigated by one of his priests, a Varsity man who knew me well, to invite me to volunteer for his diocese. I was only too glad. His Grace sent me to St. Andrew's College [Scots College] in Rome. The priest who recommended me, and Canon Dugdale, assured me that, in return for my services, my expenses would be borne by the archbishop. They never were. I was more than one hundred and twenty pounds out of pocket. After four months in College I was expelled suddenly and brutally. No reason ever has been given to me; and I never have been aware of a reason which could justify so atrocious an outrage. My archbishop maintained absolute silence. I did hear it said that I had no Vocation. That was the gossip of my fellow-students, immature cubs mostly, hybrid larrikins given to false quantities and nasal cacophonies. I took, and take, no account of such gossip. If my legitimate superiors had had grounds for their action, grounds which they durst expose to daylight; and, if they frankly had stated the same to me, I believe I should have given very little trouble. As it is, I am of course a thorn, or a pest, or a firebrand, or a rodent and purulent ulcer—*vous en faites votre choix*. The case is a mystery to me, inexplicable, except by an hypothesis connected with the character of the rector of St. Andrew's College ... 'an awful little liar'.

41

Of course a man with his face and manner and taste and talent and Call ought to have been a priest.... The fault was hardly his. When he was studying for the priesthood in the Scots College of Rome, he chanced to be of signal service to Mario Attendoli-Cesari [Sforza-Cesarini], whose princely family shewed due appreciation. The Attendoli-Cesari were of royalist politics, lords-in-waiting and ladies-in-waiting at the Quirinale; and the Black Clericals (following their usual custom of pin-pricking White Monarchist patricians) quickly discovered that the friend of the Attendoli-Cesari had no vocation to the priesthood, and expelled him from college. Not to have a vocation is a misfortune: it cannot be called a crime: it is not even exasperating to anyone but the wretch who doesn't possess it.... Crabbe [Rolfe] was expelled with every sudden circumstance of rough abuse and indignity: he was flung out, at night, to penury and starvation, as the English consul of the 'nineties has testified.

These facts, set down on paper, were never forgotten, or forgiven. He never accepted the verdict of his superiors, persisting as long as he could that he had a divine vocation for the priesthood. He had 'formed the opinion that someone carelessly had lied: that someone clumsily had blundered; and that all concerned were determined not to own themselves, or anyone else but me, to be in the wrong. A mistake had been made; and, by quibbles, by evasions, by threats, by every hole-and-corner means conceivable, the mistake was going to be perpetuated.' Now, as later in his life, he faced the insoluble problem of an individual versus a machine, an established force of religion or business or society. And, as always, he thought only in terms of himself. In the long list of students for the priesthood, many are excluded from final ordination. Some decide against it themselves. Some are persuaded against it by their superiors. Although they have an entirely different meaning, some words from the New Testament may be quoted here in relation to Rolfe's case: 'Many are called, but few are chosen.'

One attribute missing from his personality was a toleration towards the men and women placed in the same world with him.

He could create and maintain a warm friendly feeling for some people; but he lacked the universal compassion necessary for a shepherd within the bounds of the Church. In his arguments in favour of his vocation, Rolfe repeatedly stated that he at least could perform the Office of the Dead. At the end of the Prooimion chapter in *Hadrian*, the finally ordained Rev. George Arthur Rose is permitted his first mass. 'My first mass must be a black mass,' he states, naming the Requiem Mass for the Dead but using an unsavoury term to express himself. His divine vocation may have summoned Rolfe to say Mass for the Dead, but how could he deal with the live people of this world?

He never envisaged the possibility that his vocation might ever be questioned by others, especially by his superiors in a seminary. Yet this one act of expulsion from Scots College may not have been wholly justified. Someone perhaps 'clumsily had blundered'. But the deed once done was never rectified.

Rolfe was a creature born out of his time—not by centuries, but, rather, by a matter of only a very few years. Mgr. James A. Campbell, Rector of Scots College in 1890, was a vain man without imagination or the capacity to fathom anything beyond his own little world. Mgr. Robert Fraser succeeded him on his retirement in 1897. After the latter's death, someone had said of him: 'What a lovable personality he was! so uniformly cheerful, so buoyant in his optimism, so infectious in his enthusiasm, so kind and considerate, so ready to help, so tolerant of the shortcomings of frailer mortals that did not reach his own high standard of efficiency, so unselfish, so hospitable and accessible to all his priests.' He might well have reacted differently towards Rolfe. But history—whether of a single man or of a nation—is composed only of actual events, be they good or bad at the time of their occurrence.

As the name implies, the Collegio Scozzese was established in Rome for the education of youths destined for the ranks of the secular clergy in Scotland. A certain number of young men are periodically selected by the home bishops from the preparatory schools and sent 'to be trained in Roman ways and habits of thought—to be made, in face, out-and-out Papists'.

The rector was an 'old boy' of the college and now presided

over the school in a 'vulgar, suspicious, and narrow-minded' way. He was described as being short and dumpy, terribly pompous and consequential in his manners, with a large head and two small malignant eyes. His favourite expression was: 'O misericordia!' He took little interest in the teaching of the students, and his choice of a superior was an unhappy one. This position was given to an uninspiring Benedictine, who only dulled young enthusiasm. The general atmosphere in the school instilled a lazy indifference.

Mgr. Campbell had no friends among the Roman ecclesiastics. There was, indeed, only one creature who entertained any affection for him, and that was his dog, Topsy—his familiar spirit, some of the students averred. When he prepared for Sunday morning Mass, 'Pio, the old College porter, who had stuck at minor orders at some prehistoric date, lit the bugia, or torch, and went through the farce of holding it close up to the book, while the Doctor scanned its page'.

Since the Monastery of SS. Andrew and Gregory on the Coelian Hill could not house all of the students for the school, a kind of hospice was established at the college. Here Rolfe had his pension.

As all men, Rolfe was more than one person in the eyes of all the people around him. A spark of tolerant understanding could discover something in him which offensive indifference could, or would, not. Two of his Scots College contemporaries thought that 'he was most amiable despite all his little eccentricities'. One recounted the fact that Rolfe always conducted himself with 'an element of mystery in and around his elusive character. The second spoke of 'his musical ability and his gift of song, his weird sermons in the refectory, with their stinging hits at our somewhat uncultivated Scottish manners, and his own rather scant treatment of respect; his saying his office in his bath; and so on. I really think it was genius on the very border.'

A third contemporary said quite the opposite. 'There was a universal prejudice against him in the College. His eccentricities of conduct made the institution a subject of unfavourable comment in other similar Colleges,' Robert (Canon) Carmont wrote. Unlike the other students, Rolfe insisted on the liberty to visit

44

friends in the city; and the rector permitted him to wear the black soutane, instead of the usual purple one, which exempted him from all but the fundamental rules of the school. He tried to mix with his colleagues. But the first impression he made was of a tendency to 'swank' in his talk about the importance of his family. A belief in the insanitary conditions in the kitchen made him a vegetarian but only in the college. He supplemented his diet with good steaks and wine in Rome.

'He possessed a large fund of stories and anecdotes—of the anti-Anglican type—a few also of a slightly Rabelaisian cast. I have heard some funny "Anglican Confession" stories in my time, but none so ingenious and ornamental as his. Some of his stories were really good—a certain "cheese" story almost challenged Mark Twain. He was wont to condemn the alleged laxity of the Roman Communion in the matter of truthfulness, and its *subdistinguishing* "the lie". He himself, brought up as a strict Anglican, had all the Anglican horror of lying and equivocation of every description. He seemed to be quite serious about it, which surprised us, as he was universally regarded as about the biggest liar we had ever met.'

The same commentator, Robert Carmont, believed that 'everything about him suggested one who dabbles'. Rolfe still had a number of his paintings and his camera with him. In his room he had a large piece of cardboard, on which was lettered a motto, an epigram or an atrocity culled from the Catholic or Anglican hymnology—such as 'And he ate nothing in those days' and 'And he lived with beasts'. He 'used to toy with triolets and fidgetty trifles of that sort. He wrote articles weekly to the long defunct "Whitehall Review",' being introduced to this periodical, perhaps, by another contributor, Fr. George Angus.

A friend from Oxford was in Rome as a tutor, and the two frequently met. It was usually this Aubrey Thurstans who paid for the meals they enjoyed away from Rolfe's seminary. His only other friend was a young man he had just met at the school. To test Rolfe's ability in his studies, a professor ordered him to read an English-into-Latin paper one day. It was the friend at the college, Duncan McVarish, who rendered the essay into Latin for him.

A triolet by him had appeared in January. And *The Art Review* published 'Ballade of Boys Bathing' in April, the author being listed in the contents as the Rev. F. W. Rolfe. This was a period devoted to writing and to an assumed title of the Church. His own Roman visiting card read: 'Rev. Frederick William Rolfe, F. R. Hist. S. / F. R. S. L. / Scots College of Rome.' The Rev. Frederick William Rolfe had been elected to the Fellowship of the Royal Historical Society in 1889. (He was removed from the Roll of Members on 21 December 1893 for non-payment of subscriptions.) The Rev. Frederick William Rolfe was elected to the Fellowship of the Royal Society of Literature on 30 April 1890. (His name did not appear on the 1892 list of members, with the implication that his subscription was never paid.) Among the 'New and Forthcoming Books' advertized by Elkin Mathews in October 1890, one, *The Story of S. William: The Boy Martyr of Norwich*, was by 'The Rev. Frederick William Rolfe, Late Professor of English Literature and History at S. Marie's College of Oscott'. The printed brochures described the unpublished book in detail, but it never appeared, and it may never have been written.

The basic cause for the 'universal prejudice' against Rolfe was one of mistrust. His aloofness and air of mystery and special privileges were enviable. Cultivating a dislike for Scotsmen at this time, he did not hesitate to express his views. The trips into the city did not stop at seeing Thurstans and visiting restaurants. W. Wort, the photographer of Sutton Coldfield, was now replaced by some new supplier of photographic equipment—to be paid at a later date. The supplies had been billed for L 156, a sum never paid. Gossip about the English student and his debts began to go around the school. Any sordid claim of the outside world on the school brought humiliation, shared by its students. The end came when a certain tailor, suspicious about payment for clothes ordered by Rolfe, 'came and annexed £20 worth of Rolfe's effects'. Of the L513.50 this Signor Luigi Giomini had charged, he saw only L 25. Saying that the students bitterly resented such a transaction, Carmont further related that Rolfe's 'general laxity & carelessness lowered the tone of the college.... And then the inevitable: "What is the man doing here?" We put our ideas regarding him before the Rector, and the Rector expelled him. He got a fortnight to look about him, a week was added to that, 3 days, one more, then his departure.'

Mgr. Campbell and Rolfe had had a stormy interview on 23 March 1890 and Rolfe was given notice to leave the college. The rector had justly accused him of habits irregular to the rules of the school. Rolfe was now thirty, older than the other 'immature cubs', and he also seemed to be unable to settle into the required regimentation of the school's atmosphere. On the evening of the interview Rolfe wrote to Mgr. Campbell that he 'had not the remotest idea that I was laying myself open to the charge of infringing any rule by using my own descretion as to my occupation in recreation hours. . . . I am not a child who requires careful supervision but a man, well able to take and with every intention of taking care of myself, both for my own sake and for the sake of that ecclesiastical habit, which, having once put on, I shall never put off [and] I can offer you the inspection of the MS. work I have done since 7 Dec., which alone will prove that my study hours have been exceedingly well spent.' The rector gave Rolfe a second chance.

At this time, it should be noted, Rolfe had not yet been accepted as a permanent student towards priesthood. When he had arrived at the Roman school, he was there for a period of trial and preparation. Abp. Smith, 'out of charity', had offered to defray Rolfe's pension fees only 'if his trial proved satisfactory'. It was during this trial period that Mgr. Campbell, perhaps considering the advice from senior students too carefully, decided that Rolfe was not prepared for further studies in the Church. Among the debts incurred in Rome, the new student owed the college for his pension. The rector had already deprived him, he later said, of his dressing case 'with luxurious fittings on the score of earthly vanity'. Rolfe insisted that the rector was 'fully paid really. He has seized a meerschaum pipe that I value at forty pounds.'

Carmont continued in his picture of the 1890 Rolfe: 'There was in him little pride, in the better sense of the term. He did not disdain to beg. In fact he seemed to consider that he had a right to expect assistance and favours from those in a position

47

to grant them. I have heard him say so. As to gratitude—less said the better. There was a sort of ruthless selfishness in him which led him to exploit others, quite regardless of their interests or feelings, or advantage.... His humour, such as it was, was of a thin and rather sardonic kind. I don't know if he could be called revengeful—perhaps not. The short descriptions of the students in *Hadrian VII* are certainly not friendly in tone, and might be regarded as a payment of old scores. I doubt it. I fancy he loathed most of them for the same reason that he apparent[ly] liked me—artistic sense.'

To this person who was later described by Carmont a final notice was given by Mgr. Campbell to quit the school—on or before April 21st. This naturally solicited a letter from the English student, which, with the others written by Rolfe to his superior at Scots College, is the earliest surviving document to record the working of his mind in such a case. These letters became the prototype for his future correspondence, containing his acceptance of the truth of reality, but hopelessly mixing it with fancy. On April 20th he wrote to the rector: 'You have expelled me for a breach of rules, knowing that it was not in my power to observe them. You have prevented me, by forbidding me to use my recreational hours for literary work, from acquiring funds to pay my necessary debts.... Having made you aware of these facts, I have nothing to do but leave my effects at the College, to obey your injunctions to the letter, and to turn out into the streets.' But he did nothing to fulfil this latter statement. Given a fortnight's grace, Rolfe stubbornly remained at the college. The manner of his actual eviction was curious in one respect. At the appointed date of his departure, May 3rd, he refused to get out of bed and was bodily deposited, mattress and all, outside the school building. (Was this same scene repeated at Aberdeen three years later or did the journalist attacking Rolfe in the Aberdeen newspapers of 1898 purposely confuse the tale told to him by one of Rolfe's contemporaries in Rome with the Skene Street affair?)

Five days later Rolfe again wrote to Mgr. Campbell: 'The British Consul is unable to give me my travelling expenses from the Relief Fund, and he suggests that it is your duty to do that;

indeed, I am advised that you, representing my diocesan, are bound in justice to place me in the condition in which I was when Abp. Smith first took me for one of his students.... I suppose the charges [for my expulsion] may be summarized as follows:

1 "never observed a single rule."
2 "Having contracted unwarrantable debts."
3 "Having deceived you about my departure from Oscott."
(These I quote in your own words.) ... Now that your sentence of dismissal has been carried out, you have refused to hear the explanations I have to offer ... in short, you and my diocesan have refused me what every Christian principle of justice demands, viz. an unbiased hearing and a fair trial ... the right of the lowest felon.... I ask once more, are you going to see me starve in the streets? You know that I have not even stamps to communicate with my friends, that I have to go about Rome begging for a meal here and a sofa to sleep on there. Is such a public scandal to go on indefinitely?'

In his report on the expelled student, Mgr. Campbell wrote that Rolfe had 'failed egregiously in his trial, and, to pass over his breaches of discipline, and his disregard of the duties required of a divinity student, contrived to contract in the space of three months debts to the ascertained amount of about £40, knowing well that he had neither the means nor the prospects of being able to pay them,' was just cause for the rector's action.

Twenty years later Rolfe, as the narrator Nicholas Crabbe, wrote in *The Desire and Pursuit of the Whole*: 'The Spalding Club of Aberdeen, an amateur literary society, published a reprint of the Registers of ... the Scots College of Rome. And Crabbe found therein only two records of expulsion ... but neither case was his. What did this portent signify? ... And so Nicholas Crabbe's record in the college register simply consists of his name, date, diocese, and parentage, inaccurately stated ... and then follow three plain dots such as are ordinarily used to signify incompletion. It is charitably supposed that the notorious details of the case being too shameful for publication....' These 'notorious details' were withheld by Rolfe himself. When the new rector, Mgr. Fraser, was preparing the registers of Scots

49

College, Rome, for publication by the New Spalding Club, the seemingly omniscient Rolfe wrote and threatened legal action if anything appeared in the book more than his bare entry.

Hadrian the Seventh is not the only novel written about Scots College in the last decade of the nineteenth century. John Crane's *Frank Baylis* tells about the same pompous rector, the same pupils and the same general atmosphere of indifference towards any non-conformist. Baylis' account of his days at the Roman college is a general one and does not list the individual fellow students and their private habits, which are portrayed in Rolfe's book. In *Hadrian* the Supreme Pontiff (Rose-Rolfe) visits his old school in Rome. In time for dinner, he sits at high table and notes the mannerisms of the young men in front of him. One of these is 'a crisp-brown-haired muscular hobbledehoy with shining grey eyes and a tanned skin,' whose name is Hamish Macleod. 'Privately the Pope wondered what in the world was the sign of this one's Vocation,' and asks him when he expects to be a priest. ' "I never will be", the creature shrilled.'

This creature, the Hamish Macleod of *Hadrian*, was Duncan Charles McVarish in actual life, who under a pen name wrote *Frank Baylis*. Four years younger than Rolfe, he was born at Kingairloch, Argyll, of a Catholic family. He dutifully attended a seminary at Lisbon before he went to Rome. It was during his stay at Scots College that he decided he was not destined for the Catholic Church. 'Being careless about the College rules and negligent in his studies, he was, with the Cardinal Protector's permission, asked to leave, on July 8th, 1890'—two short months after Rolfe's dismissal. And before another month was out he made his entry into the Anglican Church.

Rolfe and McVarish shared the same loathing at Scots College. McVarish severed all connections with the Roman Church when he left the college, but he was an object of surmise as late as 1933. Thinking he was still alive, Robert Carmont spoke of a 'rumour going that he had given up the Anglican ministry and taken up farming in the north of Scotland. This is inherently probable, as I don't think he believed in Anglican orders.' Studying as an Anglican theological student at King's College, London, McVarish was ordained a minister in 1895. As Chaplain to the Forces he was sent to the South African War and served at the Siege of Ladysmith. Remaining there for two years, he returned to England to minister to various parishes. From 1914 until his death in 1929, he was installed at Wollaston, Wellingborough.

There is no glimpse of Rolfe as a person in *Frank Baylis*, but his influence, through contemporary association, may be felt in some small way. Baylis' school is attended by young men who are coarse and common and who will make priests for the lowest of people. The rector's name is Dr. Toady Canmore—in real life Mgr. James Alexander Campbell and Cateran in *Hadrian*. Baylis-McVarish realizes his lack of vocation and discusses the future with Fr. Ferretti, confessor to the school. Leaving the school, he becomes a tutor to the three children of the Cotton-Wooles. (Mr. Cotton-Woole is 'the clever author' of *The Comedy of Canterbury*.) When the family leaves Rome, he goes back to England with them. Rolfe's only other friend at the time, Thurstans, was a tutor in Rome.

The novel was published in 1903, when Rolfe was working on *Hadrian*. How long their friendship lasted is not known. Both were in London in 1894. There is no evidence that Rolfe ever read *Frank Baylis*, even knew of it or who the author was. In the story Baylis returns to Kent. In reality McVarish went to Scotland.

McVarish was dismissed from Scots College on 8 July 1890, and on July 27th an incident involving him in Glasgow was reported in such newspapers as *The Scotsman*, *The Edinburgh Evening Dispatch* and the *North British Daily Mail*, as well as in *The Tablet*. The articles led to letters of condemnation and defence. The journalists of the day, as self-appointed moralists, exposed what they considered sham and some newspapers seized the opportunity to dilate on religion in general. McVarish had been part of an anti-Catholic demonstration and, as a result, was subjected to attack in the Catholic-controlled newspapers. With a number of letters-to-the-editor McVarish answered his assailants. The last letter appeared on August 15th in *The Edinburgh Evening Dispatch*, the same paper printing the Aberdeen Attack in 1898, with a portrait of 'Baron Corvo'.

Perhaps Rolfe had McVarish in mind when he penned *Hadrian*. Speaking of his expulsion, Rose-Rolfe says: 'Had the case been one of the ordinary type of ecclesiastical student, (the hebete and half-licked Keltic class I mean,) ... I furiously should have apostatized....'

In the Scotland of 1890 two men were holding 'Great Protestant Meetings'. The Revv. Jacob Primmer and Robert Thomson held one such meeting in Edinburgh on July 20th. A protest against the introduction of 'Popish images and liturgies into the Church of Scotland' resulted in a huge turn-out and eventual scenes of rowdyism. Police ended the 'no-Popery' day. A week later the two men carried their Protestant message one step further in Glasgow by introducing a 'converted priest'. *The Evening Dispatch* recorded that 'modern Scottish history will be searched in vain, probably, for a parallel to the ceremony which took place ... in Wellpark Parish Church, Glasgow. The unique spectacle was there witnessed of a priest publicly renouncing his allegiance to the Church of Rome, and embracing the tenets of the Church of Scotland. The convert is a young Highlander, Duncan Charles MacVarish.' In front of 1,000 people, Primmer, Thomson and McVarish marched to their seats. The latter was welcomed 'from Rome to Glasgow—from error into truth'. After the singing of the twenty-third Psalm, Primmer called upon McVarish 'to make his public renunciation'. 'In clear, unfaltering tones,' he declared 'it to be my firm conviction that a great portion of the discipline of the Roman Church is of its nature conducive to the grossest immorality and hypocrisy,' listing ten main causes in his mind which are 'monstrous doctrines ... based solely upon human presumption and depravity'. The Mass, transubstantiation, indulgences, auricular confession, image worship, the pope's infallibility, the immaculate conception of Mary, purgatory, the Roman doctrine of grace and justification, and tradition were the points outlined. 'Mr MacVarish then discarded his robes, and was "received" into the Church [of Scotland]. He expressed his joy at the day's proceedings. The steps he had taken would bring a hornet's nest about his ears. The Church of Rome was a master-hand at throwing mud.'

In the exchange of onslaughts and letters of defence, one

appeared with the heading, 'A M'Varish Mystery'. It reproduced two letters. From Glasgow, McVarish had written to Mgr. Campbell on July 16th, asking him 'to supply me with a few lines testifying to my honesty and morality during the time I spent under you in Rome'. On the 19th, the rector answered: 'In reply to your letter ... I regret to say that it is impossible for me to give you a testimonial such as you ask. My personal acquaintance with your character is limited to the time you were an inmate of this College. It is only of you as an ecclesiastical student that I am in a position to speak, and the fact that you were studying for the priesthood I cannot suppress.' No recommendation would be forthcoming from Rome for a student who was expelled and was now an apostate. In a letter to *The Evening Dispatch*, McVarish referred 'to a leading article in the *Scotsman* of May 11th, 1886, which will ... help you to estimate at [my Roman superiors'] true value.... It is very strange that my superiors in Rome should take two years to make the discovery [of my having no vocation]....'

In *Hadrian*, when Rose speaks of the judgment against his vocation, he refers to the Roman rector: 'I remember the Marquess of Mountstuart [Bute] reading a leading article about him out of *The Scotsman* to me in 1886, and remarking that he was "an awful little liar".' The same article is mentioned in a footnote in his *Chronicles of the House of Borgia*. Rolfe and McVarish were not the only ones who presented Campbell in this light. The words of two students expelled by him may not justify their severe criticism. A third picture, also by a contemporary, may add credence. At Dumfries in 1886 a 56-page book was printed. It is about the Mitchell Fund litigation instituted by the Rev. John Carmont against the Scottish Hierarchy in 1882, and is written by Charles Canon Menghini. Bringing a Church issue before a civil court, the Rev. Carmont incurred excommunication for himself, although he acted with discretion and courage and deserved all the praise given him. Acting as the deputy in Rome for the Scottish prelates, Campbell professed no personal knowledge of the Carmont case. Yet the entire case against the Scottish clergyman was enforced on the strength of a letter by Campbell. The rector said that he was merely quoting the Cardinal Prefect of Propaganda. Canon Menghini wondered if such a message really had emanated from the cardinal. 'It is painful,' he writes, 'to have to doubt the word of a person in the position of Mgr. Campbell, but there exist two *a priori* reasons for believing that he has made some extraordinary mistake in the matter.' In *The Catholic Church in Modern Scotland: 1560-1937*, Peter Anson speaks of Campbell's successor, Mgr. Robert Fraser. Campbell retired in 1897 and died in 1902, just before Rolfe started *Hadrian*. Fraser, who completed his studies at Scots College and who then became a professor at Blairs College, Aberdeen, was appointed Rector of Scots College. He became very popular and 'did much to improve the conditions of the students, which before his time had not been up to modern requirements'.

The only reference in print to Rolfe by McVarish is a silent one. In letters to *The Evening Dispatch* and the *North British Daily Mail* on 6 August 1890, he wanted 'to say a word or two concerning that much-abused term "vocation." What is meant by Roman Catholics by an ecclesiastical vocation? A friend of mine in Rome described a "vocation" thus—

(1) Money. Any man with a heavy purse has a "vocation."
(2) The servility of a dog. A man who is prepared to swallow anything, however absurd, that the Roman Church teaches, without question or murmur, has a "vocation."

There is a great deal of truth in my friend's definitions. Money forms a safe passport to the Church as well as to most professions. And, again, if a man shows that he has a mind of his own, and refuses to bow down to a lie, or bend the knee to Baal, he is judged to have no "vocation".'

McVarish's 'friend ... in Rome' was Rolfe.

Unlike Rolfe, McVarish gives the actual name of the school in *Frank Baylis*: Collegio Scozzese, 161 Via delle Quattro Fontane. As for the use of names for his characters, the Rev. Jacob Primmer was remembered thus in the novel: 'Brother Jacob Blackberry [on leaving Scots College] dressed in aggressively worldly habiliments, with Miss Julia Primmer on his arm.'

When Rolfe was finally dismissed from his pension, Fr. Mackie—'Father Dawkins—such a holy person' in *Hadrian*— sheltered him for several days. Rolfe's uncanny knowledge of people's
whereabouts was put to use. One of his 1887 'friends' from Oxford was in Rome. Hartwell de la Garde Grissell was another
convert. Since 1869 he had been Chamberlain of Honour to the
Pope; and as Knight Commander of the Order of Pius IX he
was present in Rome when 'the Piedmontese ursurpers' marched
into the city a year later. In 1898 he was to become one of four
permanent Chamberlains *di numero*. Rolfe called on him in
May 1890 and asked him for the fare to take him back to England. Of course, eating and other diversions were all to be included in the cost of the trip, he carefully pointed out just before
he was flatly refused. For his expenses Rolfe had asked Grissell
for the sum of fifty pounds, at a time when he had just refused
an offer of ten pounds by another person.

'Sforza-Cesarini, Mario, dei Conti Santa fuora (1887-   )' was
an entry in the list of Oscott students at the time Rolfe was
there. In his *The Desire and Pursuit of the Whole*, Rolfe claims
to have been 'of signal service to Mario'—and through him he
met the Duchess Sforza-Cesarini.

The actual relationship between Mario and the duchess is uncertain. He was neither son nor grandson. There was 'no mention
of a Mario Sforza-Cesarini living at the time of Mr. Rolfe's residence in Rome', wrote Francesco Tomassetti to A. J. A. Symons
in 1933. 'From Duke Lorenzo, born in 1807 and married to a
Caroline Sherley, young Francesco (1840-1899) the head of the
family, and Bosio (who died many years ago).—Francesco, who
married a Vittoria Colonna, had two boys, Duke Lorenzo (born
in 1868), who married a Maria Torlanni, and Umberto (dead not
long ago).—Lorenzo, the archeal head of the family, has a boy,
Mario (born in 1899).' Rolfe's Mario, then, may have been a
nephew.

The duchess was an Englishwoman, the daughter of Robert
Sewallis Shirley, styled Viscount Tamworth, who in 1800 married Sophia Caroline, daughter of Nathaniel Curzon, Baron
Scarsdale. The duke had died in 1866. When she and Rolfe met
in 1890, her two sons, Francesco and Bosio, were about fifty. Her

two grandsons, Lorenzo II and Guido, were twenty-two and sixteen.

The duchess instantly became fond of Rolfe and he was installed in their country villa 'on the top of a rock amid the hills'. For more than half of this year he was looked upon as a member of the family. He had the freedom of the house and of the surrounding countryside. His body and mind absorbed the warmth of the Italian sun and the colour of its history. The pageantry of Rome, the glory of the Renaissance, the lyrical pattern and sound of its people and language deeply impressed the man who had recently attended the cold Scottish college. The Abruzzi hills were delineated for the present and the future, Rolfe drawing and photographing and storing away memories for his writings sufficient to last for the next eighteen years. He wandered among the living legends of Italy. With his camera he depicted the young boys who, in fancy, were to remain with him for a long time ahead. Toto was one. He posed for Rolfe's camera and was the model for the tales beginning in *The Yellow Book* of 1895. Rolfe's artistic and sensitive eye aided his camera in taking photographs of boys in natural, classic and timeless poses.

His thirtieth birthday was celebrated in the Sforza-Cesarini house. The duchess felt inclined to treat him in as gracious a manner as she could, so that she 'filled the house all through the summer with the loveliest girls I could get hold of, any one of whom would have made him an excellent wife, and I watched to see if he would take a fancy to any of them, but no, not a bit of it. He was always very nice and kind and polite, and all that, and made himself very much liked by everyone, but he never took any interest in them....'

At the end of 'How I Was Buried Alive' he says that 'the old lady and I made an escape to Spezzia, and went for a little yachting, till we all went back to Rome at the beginning of November.' He also must have visited Florence, for the descriptions of the city's art in his later stories have a clarity that only actual contact could have afforded. He could write back to his friend of Christchurch, Kains-Jackson, that 'the Pope is about to open His Borgia Rooms, which are some of the finest apartments in the Vatican, and which have been practically closed for several years.' This note appeared in Kains-Jackson's *Artist* in September. The opening of the rooms gave Rolfe the opportunity to see the beautiful paintings there by Bernardino Betto, called *il Pinturicchio*. The 'Papa Alessandro adorando il Cristo risorto' was destined to be the frontispiece of the *Chronicles of the House of Borgia*.

The kindly duchess was aged but she came from the same country as Rolfe did and she was a convert to the same faith. She 'adopted' him and he repaid this gentle act by remembering her in his writings. In the first six months back in England, Rolfe wrote 'Two Sonnets, for a Picture of Saint Sebastian the Martyr in the Capitolone Gallery, Rome. (Inscribed to Her Grace the Duchess Caroline Sforza-Cesarini.)' and his first Toto story, in which she figures as 'the Princess of Saint Angelo'. Caroline Shirley was one of the 'Women of a Woman Hater', a series of stories he spoke about doing in a letter of 22 July 1898. At the same time she appears as the Dowager '(R.I.P.)' in 'How I Was Buried Alive'. He continued to commemorate her until 'Deinon to Thely' in 1909.

In many ways, 1890 was a decisive turning point in his life. For the time being, the decision of the Church officers had settled his career and he turned from his Roman pursuits to art. His painting now matured into professionalism. An earnest approach to photography was added to his achievements. His juvenile poetry changed into prose. The Italy he had savoured for only one short year would be injected into nearly all forms of his future art.

When he returned to England at the end of 1890, Rolfe brought back the images of the duchess and Toto; and, when the first Toto story was written in 1891, he had embarked on his long list of autobiographical writings. The duchess always remained the same grand lady: Toto, as the years passed, was idealized and appeared as one person or another. Although Zilda in *The Desire and Pursuit of the Whole* is based on an actual person of the time, the character no doubt is but another fragment of the original Ideal: Toto.

The duchess was an ardent Catholic and Socialist. She possessed an understanding but firm mind. Looking upon Rolfe as a member of her own family and knowing his past, she planned for his future. She agreed to finance him. She would grant him a monthly remittance. This aid would furnish him with supplies to produce photographs and paintings and would assist him until he could support himself from the proceeds of his own work. With this promise he returned to England and chose Christchurch as the place to settle. He knew people there, people of an artistic nature and a landlord. With money in his pocket he could live without the nagging fear of want and exercise his imagination to the utmost.

The seminary student of the previous year settled on the south coast of England to begin a new period in his life, with a new occupation and a new name: BARON CORVO.

4

'Who, then, is Baron Corvo?' asked a newspaper of the 1890s, answering its own question by remarking that 'people will look in vain in the peerage of this or any other country for the lineage of Baron Corvo.'

A shrewd mind chose the name and title. Rolfe's own name meant nothing; he was seeking an identity which would be personal and unique. For more than ten years he had been a schoolmaster and seminary student. The grandeur of Rome and the seemingly limitless beauty of Italy had made him aware of individuals in its history, many of whom had survived by assumed names. The world does not recognize any Alessandro di Mariano dei Filipepi, Donato di Nicolo di Betto Bardi or Andrea Cioni di Michele. But it does pay homage to Botticelli, Donatello and Verrochio. So, Frederick Rolfe, the nondescript teacher and pupil, was abandoned and Baron Corvo, the artist, emerged from Italy.

The origin of this title remains a part of Rolfe's enigmatic story. He himself gave three versions:

' "Baron Corvo" was a style offered and accepted for use as a tekhniknym [trade name] at a time when I, a tonsured clerk, denied Sacred Orders and eternally persistent in my Vocation thereto was forced to snatch a secular livelihood,' he wrote in 1908. 'It never was officially confirmed and I do not know that I ever shall seek some confirmation. . . . And there I think that the matter had better rest: the people responsible for the idea being dead. . . .'

The Bishop of Emmaus was in Rome at the time Rolfe was still at Scots College. One day the two were walking together and the bishop, then and there, said that the young man should have a title and made him a baron. Rolfe took the name Corvo from the small village upon which they were looking down. (Could this have been the Corvicastra in Aria, named in the colophon of *Stories Toto Told Me* of 1898?)

The third version involved the duchess. She had given Rolfe property in Italy and the title came with it.

Whichever was the true story—if all three were not mingled— 'Baron Corvo' was Rolfe's most lasting and impressive invention.

Everything told in *Hadrian* concerning Rolfe's own past life is based on facts and real people. The novel favours the title in relation to the bishop, but only in that he approved it. The Duchess Sforza-Cesarini was the person who 'conferred' this rank upon the luckless student.

There was no property attached. Later, in 1891, Rolfe tried to buy Gleeson White's business. With no money, he planned to settle the transaction with properties at Oxford and Bristol, but these were found to be already mortgaged 'up to the hilt' and not totally his. There was no mention of any property in Italy.

In the nineteenth century the heads of Roman princely families allowed certain of their titles to be used by brothers or sons, but only during their lifetimes. This infrequent habit was never passed to outsiders. 'Corvo' came easily enough. The heraldic raven he had already adopted; the new nomenclature was merely the Italian for the symbol of his English name. On one occasion when he and the duchess were discussing titles and personages, she asked him if he wished for a title. Made either in jest or in order idly to carry on the conversation, her remark was taken quite literally by Rolfe. She added that she had several titles to give away. Saying that he would like a barony, Rolfe did not hesitate to append the name of Corvo. This occurrence, during the privacy of a quiet evening, marked the first decisive stage in the bizarre life yet to be lived.

Accused of many things, Rolfe answered most with *Hadrian*. This 1903 rebuttal to the charges against him included his defence for pseudonyms:

Regarding my pseudonyms—my numerous pseudonyms— think of this: I was a tonsured clerk, intending to persist in my Divine Vocation, but forced for a time, to engage in secular pursuits both to earn my living and to pay my debts. I had a shuddering repugnance from associating my name, the name by which I certainly some day should be known in the priesthood, with these secular pursuits. I think that was rather absurd: but I am quite sure that it was not dishonourable.... As Rose [Rolfe] I was a tonsured clerk: as King Clement [Baron Corvo], I wrote and painted and photographed: ... And of course my pseudonymity has been misunderstood by the stupid, as well as misrepresented by the invidious. Most people have only half developed their single personalities. That a man should split his into four or more: and should develop each separately and perfectly, was so abnormal that many normals failed to understand it.

These words were written by a disappointed and embittered man in 1903. The causes for his retaliations began at the end of his Christchurch year. But at the beginning of that same year his creative powers were freshly developing, unhampered by the anxieties of dire want.

After Scots College, Rolfe relates in *Hadrian*, he 'made haste to offer my services to other bishops. When I found every door shut against me, I firmly deliberated never to recede from my grade of tonsured clerk under any circumstances whatever; and I determined to occupy my energies with some pursuit for which my nature fitted me, until the Divine Giver of my Vocation should deign to manifest it to others as well as to myself. I chose the trade of a painter.' And to start this new career Rolfe came to Toinham House.

While a schoolmaster at Winchester in 1881, Rolfe had become acquainted with Charles Carrington Gardner. After he had retired from the position of butler in the services of Louisa, Marchioness of Waterford, Gardner and his wife Dorothy moved to Christchurch. They bought Toinham House, a private dwelling throughout its history except for this period. The Gardners let out rooms. Well furnished, they had the walls decorated with pictures by the Marchioness of Waterford, who had become an accomplished amateur artist after the death of her husband, Henry de la Poer (Beresford), in a hunting accident in 1859. She herself died at seventy-three, while Rolfe was at Christchurch.

Gardner was fond of horses. In another part of town he had stables and let out traps. Rolfe had a passion for the outdoor air. He swam whenever he could and loved to walk. He briskly covered the combined distance of ten miles into Bournemouth and back many times. Yet he utilized Gardner's business on a number of occasions. By the end of the year Rolfe owed Gardner many pounds for the use of traps, hiring them for a full day at a time.

One of the summer residents at Toinham House was the twenty-one-year-old Cecil Castle. Renewing their friendship from 1889, they became steady companions. With his elder cousin's permission, Cecil posed for Rolfe's canvas and camera. He may have posed also for his pen. Just after an episode involving Christchurch in *Hadrian,* Rolfe mentions a 'young lover'. The description illustrates his answer to the question: 'Do you love your neighbour?' 'No,' is the emphatic reply, 'I frankly detest him, and her.... Most people are repulsive to me, because they are ugly in person; more, because they are ugly in manner: many, because they are ugly in mind. Not that I never met people different to these. I have. People have occurred to me with whom I should like to be in sympathy. But I have been unable to get near enough to them. I seem to be a thing apart. I can't understand my neighbour. What satisfies him does not satisfy me. Once I induced a young lover to let me read his love-letters. He brought them every day for a week. His love had appeared to be a perfect idyll, pure and lovely as a flower. Well—I never read such rot in my life: simply categories of features and infantile gibberish done in the style of a housemaid's novelette. It made me sick.'

Charles Kains-Jackson spent his annual August holidays with his cousin Cecil at Christchurch. Kains-Jackson was about the same age as Rolfe and the two men had a number of other things in common. They both knew Rolfe's former pupil, John Nicholson; each had become a friend of Gleeson White; and the arts interested them both. A solicitor by profession, Kains-Jackson's life leaned towards literature. In 1880 Rolfe had produced his little *Tarcissus*. Kains-Jackson was the author of the much more ambitious effort, the 112-page *Our Ancient Monuments and the Land Around Them*, published in the same year. He wrote poetry and he was an art critic. Before the end of the 1880s he had began to edit *The Artist and Journal of Home Culture*. Containing little more than poetry and art criticism at first, by the early 1890s it had anticipated the atmosphere of the Yellow Nineties with an article by him on 'The New Chivalry'.

This creative solicitor not only had his own periodical, but contributed to other magazines. In prose and poetry, he advocated Beauty for Beauty's sake—the complete and naked beauty of nature. He was one of the many minor writers of the period who were homo-erotic in their tastes, looking to ancient Greece for the ideals of both friendship and poetic expression. Lines from one of his poems indicate the source of inspiration, no less than of his literary gifts:

> Youth, standing sweet, triumphant by the sea
> All freshness of the day and all the light
> Of thy white limbs, form, bared and bright
> For conflict, and assured of victory,
> Youth, make one conquest more; and take again
> Thy rightful crown, in lovers' hearts to reign.

From Rome, Rolfe had written to Fr. Henry Westall of St. Cuthbert's Church, Earl's Court: 'May I be allowed to ask the name of the painter of the Stations of the Cross in your church …? Though I do not suppose any weight attached to my opinion, I feel bound to say that your Stations are far more beautiful than any I have seen, even here. . . .' The Stations of the Cross in this non-Catholic church are indeed beautiful and indeed original. Their attraction for Rolfe lay in the people depicted— people wearing Renaissance costumes. This fragment of artistic criticism was written on the eve of the beginning of his own career in art.

For the first time in his life, Rolfe was free, with no problems about an income. His 'grandmother' duchess had promised him an annual £200 for two or three years; and he was perfectly content to be away from the experiences of the previous five years. No longer desiring an immediate position within the Church, from a safe distance he could eye the Roman world with a certain toleration. Not everything, however, had been forgotten. Papists, to him at this time, were 'b——— fools.... Owls! They do make me sick when I think of them. Thats why I came here to be out of the way of the whole crew. I hear my Mass on Days of obligation & go to my duties but I am "Not at home" to the whole crew. Nobody believes this & all kinds of delicious myths float round about me.... But I don't care as I keep most people at arm's length. That reminds me I am trying to kick up some awful row about the way priests treat their converts in one of the newspapers. Papist ones wouldn't look at it so I've sent a letter to the Manchester Guardian.' Present security and occupation separated him from the Church.

Painting came first for Rolfe in Christchurch. The New Year's baby of the January 1890 'Triolet' was unashamedly amateurish. The initials for 'Lytel Seynt Hew,' executed with a crude naïvety, breathe a stylized primitiveness. The lettered borders achieve a meticulous, even mechanical draughtsmanship at the expense of any art. The conscious effort of the artist overshadowed any unconscious talent. The year in Italy corrected this.

'If a chap can't compose an epic poem while he's weaving tapestry, he'll never do any good at all,' William Morris once said, and Morris was an idol of Rolfe's. His art had been admired by Rolfe at Oscott—and, secretly, his literature, said Vincent O'Sullivan. The fact that the man of letters and design had now become a Socialist and laboured for the cause of the common man was not considered by Rolfe. No matter what Morris turned to, it became a success. His limited company—'the monastery, the brotherhood'—included products to meet the demand of the Anglo-Catholic revival: wall-painting, embroidery, altar-cloths, stained-glass windows, tiles and tapestries. The soul of pre-Raphaelite art breathed a warmth into these new designs, embodying nothing of the coldness of religion or aristocracy. Tapestries for the Church could be beautiful and at the same time useful as decorations and a source of income, Rolfe thought. If he did not have 'an epic poem' in mind, at least he could 'weave' sonnets.

'Inspired by one of the pictures your charming cousin per-formed for me,' Rolfe wrote to Kains-Jackson one day, 'I have put a *translation* (mind that word) unto an arras of pure flax. At 6 yards it is—hum—ha—well not bad, anyhow moonlight, Italian, etc. I call it "Canzonata". The boy is in white & black, 5 feet 8, 9, 10, 11, how do I know, in height, on a terrace of red & green tiles with a stone battlement behind him, dark blue sky & black trees in distance. There is a border of black & yellow & the whole thing will hang over a door & be a door cur-tain.' He continued that, in a desire 'to interest you in my idea of stained flax *of my designs* as a hanging for doors & walls, I want your advice as to whether I can make a living at it.'

Rolfe, it has been said, 'did not disdain to beg'. This attribute went beyond the need for daily bread. 'I want your advice' is a phrase he used time and time again. Not blessed with any talent for business himself, he forever sought his ideal counter-part: a businessman. To him, a solicitor seemed a perfect choice. A solicitor could be a businessman, to manage his affairs, and also an agent, to procure the necessary commissions. Kains-Jackson was the first of these ill-starred companions.

The solicitor-critic felt a warm attraction for the man now starting a new career, and he attempted to help him in what-ever ways he could. In his *Artist* he wrote that 'a piece of the "Corvo" Arras representing St. Michael Archangel has been hung in the Roman Catholic Church at Christchurch. The model, an Italian boy of 17 years, yellow haired and blue eyed and of the most exquisite physical development, was instantaneously photographed in mid-air, when leaping into the lake of Nemi near Rome, hence the extraordinary grace and vigour, and at the same time unconventionality of the composi-tion. We have seen the photograph from which the design was made and we can say with confidence that the fortunate operator has succeeded in snatching from nature "a grace beyond the reach of art". The Archangel is clad in Roman armour and brandishes shield and lance banneretted and bearing the motto "Quis ut Deus". We have no very high opinion of the merit of Catholic Art at the present day, which partakes too much of the sentimental and tawdry, and we are glad to notice that a really respectable piece of work has found a place in a Roman Catholic place of worship. The pity is that in a secluded village like Christchurch a design of this character should be hidden from the notice of the Roman Catholic world.'

In art and in literature, Rolfe repeated favourite themes. 'Holiness,' says Cardinal Percy Van Kristen to Hadrian, in Rolfe's novel, 'do you remember the saint You used to worship on this day at [Oscott]?' 'Little Saint Hugh? Fancy your remembering that!' is the reply. The little saint was murdered by crucifixion in 1255, at the age of nine. William of Norwich shared a similar fate, at twelve, in 1144. Supposedly a victim of ritual murder during Holy Week at the hands of Jews, his little body was found hanging on a tree outside of the town. Sebastian was another favourite of Rolfe. He possibly suffered martyrdom during the Diocletian persecution of 289-305, which also ended the lives of Tarcissus and Pancras. Sebastian was an army officer, condemned to death for his Christian faith. His fellow soldiers pierced his body with their arrows. Representation of him through the years has made him younger. The youthful St. George was included on Rolfe's list for two reasons. A martyr, he is also the Protector of the British Kingdom. The archangel Michael is one of the chief princes among the angels. Bare-legged, strong and young, he is portrayed usually as the captor of Satan or a dragon, a distinction shared with St. George since the sixth century.

Cecil Castle posed for Sebastian—collecting 'arrows literally in person'—and St. George—sticking 'a hop pole into the Dragon'. Rolfe's oil painting of St. George shows a 'liparose' and yellow-haired youth at the centre of the canvas. Six white plumes rise from his helmet. Roman armour covers his body, which rests on bare legs and sandalled feet. The arms hold a red-crossed, white shield and a red-crossed, white banner. Rolfe is revealed here as a serious artist. The figure is not easily placed in any school of art, although the colours and the general idea show an influence from the Italian Renaissance. The dragon at St. George's feet is the most striking bit of realism in the painting. With its perpendicular spikes, it crawls out from a time which is remote and dark. A scaleless body trails behind a revolting head. More than a mere portrait of a triumphal St. George, it depicts the eternal combat between Good and Evil.

Academicians in the world of English art had just received a shock. In 1885 John Millais painted 'Bubbles'. It was bought by *The Illustrated London News*, who, in turn, sold the copyright to the Messrs. Pears. It was then used as an advertisement for the soap firm. This 'degradation of Art' was inconceivable before this date. It is the unorthodox who measure time with things untried, against all the cries from the sequestered conventionalists. Concepts of purity in art were rapidly changing. Delacroix was one of the first artists to use photographic studies for his paintings. The Impressionists were to influence the character and taste of all future fields of fine and commercial art. With prophetic insight, Rolfe's ideas of originality did not agree with accepted views of the day. He thought that 'the value of art which appeals to the eye through the mind, must in fairness be judged by its effect upon the eye. To condemn it because it is a sham is to import an ethical distinction with which art is not concerned. There is no inherent reason why lath and plaster should be inferior to stone: the result is all that need be considered.'

Hadrian-Rolfe speaks of a secret many people once tried to discover. Whenever one invention appears, perfections for it and extensions to it are scheduled. The daguerreotype of the 1840s preceded the glass and flexible negatives of a later day. The photographic periodicals of the 1890s were filled with 'solutions' for the problem of colour. 'Then understand that all colours lie hidden in the black and white and greys of the negative,' says Hadrian. 'At least, everybody wants to photograph in colours: so they paint on the backs of the films; and they play the fool with triply-coloured negatives. Only one man in the world knows that the colour already is there ... stored in the black white grey negative; and that the black white grey ordinary negative will give up its colours to him who has the key.'

The invention of a number of things have taken place simultaneously by a number of people. This is true with colour photography. Different people arrived at various solutions. Rolfe was not the only one engaged in its discovery. But he did perfect his own method of producing colour photographs by 1897. *The Artist* stated that his discovery was accidental. In July, Kains-Jackson said that Baron Corvo 'has met with some curious discolourations in ferro-prussiate paper prints. These prints which should be a strong blue will sometimes come a very peculiar but beautiful grey, warmer than callitype but somewhat similar. One which he sends has come a beautifully pearly pink and it is a partially undraped figure and the colour of the flesh a charlatan might easily have produced as "photography in natural colour". Baron Corvo naturally recognized that it is a *freak*, though a charming one.'

In the following issue Rolfe replied: 'Since the publication of your notice of my experiments in colour photography I have carried my research a few steps further. The coloured prints you have were from negatives taken last summer in Italy, printed on ferro-prussiate paper produced at some Wall-paper Manufactory in Rome. I mention this because it was a much stiffer paper than used in England, and before printing, of a pale cinnabar hue.... Out of some 300 negatives, however, not more than 30 have given satisfactory colour prints. I mean by colour prints those which show other colours, *i.e.*, grey, brown, flesh, pink, green, than the natural blue and white of the paper. During the last month of hot weather I have printed from several fresh negatives made in this place. I used English ferro-prussiate paper, and conducted my operations in the sun. One negative, a child's head, taken in the drawing room, has given the pink of flesh on the face, the rest of the picture being a very delicate arrangement of fawn browns. Another, representing three children sitting on a stony beach with a background of sea and sky in full sunlight, is simply amazing. The sea has its exact values in bluish greens and yellows, while the stony beach is browning, and the children yellow and grey. Now I have not the very faintest idea of the way of all this. I know nothing, and I wish to know nothing, of formulae which are to me a stumbling block and a cause of offence. My photography is an amusement, and I can assure you that the emotion on seeing your pictures go in colours in this way is worth all the paper one has to waste.'

Financially comfortable for the moment at Christchurch, he

could express himself in these words. Before the end of the following year, this 'amusement' was to turn into an earnest pursuit of a livelihood.

Cecil Castle was Rolfe's most constant model. Writing thirty-one years later, Kains-Jackson recalled how Rolfe and Cecil would work together at Christchurch. At one time they were preparing a photographic study to be used as a guide for Rolfe's wall-hanging of St. Michael. Wearing only a knit cap, the nude Cecil would rush in from the water to be photographed by Rolfe in a 'spontaneous' pose. 'I can recall as though it was yesterday my enjoyment of the two Earnestnesses and all but realized anticipation of Cecil in his eagerness to run in from the sea not stopping in time but upsetting Corvo with his camera. But,' Kains-Jackson continued, 'Cecil was wonderful in those things & stopped dead on the towel laid down as his objective.'

The artist also asked Gleeson White's permission to photograph his son Eric. Permission was granted and Rolfe subsequently used him. (Eric's was the 'child's head' in the pink and fawn brown colour photograph and he appeared, again in a drawing room, holding a candle. 'The original photograph was taken with a flash light,' an unusual procedure for the day, and was printed in his father's magazine, *The Studio*, July 1893.) Although the boy was a model for Rolfe's camera, he acted out of obedience rather than fondness. Mrs. Gleeson White did not approve of the arrangement, and neither did the boy himself. He was about thirteen at the time and his sister Cecily was a year older; each took an instant dislike to the new baron. 'He couldn't speak with me & of my barony for quite a week after I came here,' wrote Rolfe about the boy and comparing his self of 1891 with the Rolfe of the summer of 1889, '& even now I am sure he regards me with a suspicious eye.'

In Italy, Rolfe had been closer to the glories of rich art. A few examples of Greek art were exhibited with the sculpture, painting and artefacts of the Renaissance. Here he studied 'the nude, human anatomy, generally with no emotion beyond passionate admiration of beauty'. In his painting and photography of 1899, he was approaching the ultimate. But it was not until he actually beheld the natural nude in Italian art that he felt free to express himself in the same terms. The subjects of his previous art were rendered genderless because of the requirements, and sentimentalities, of religion and society. He had assured Lord Bute that the Oban schoolboys wore 'bathing drawers when they take their morning cold bath.' But at Christchurch the male nude made its entry into Rolfe's paintings and photographs.

Kains-Jackson had sent him some verses and pictures from London. Rolfe returned all but one item. 'The photo I keep a little longer,' he explained. 'I worship the white sprawler. Such limbs never grew in this land: I know! Who is the artist & all about the picture?' This could have been his introduction to the work of Henry Tuke. 'I too worship "the decadent Roman,"' he continued. 'It is the image of a boy I had for camericke once named "Aurelio". A lovely name & a gorgeous creature. But how is that an English can look the same, such a perfect impression & should *ought* to be perpetuated.'

The London solicitor evidently disliked the tone of this letter, just as the Toto stories were later to cause concern to Henry Harland. 'I wonder whether you are making a mistake about my relations with boys,' Rolfe had to say. 'You know I never make friends of them now, I am too old [at thirty] & uninteresting. But I make them my bondslaves & then I worship their beauty. When my knees get stiff or I am bored I kick them to Gehenna or Sheol. Then I go on sweet remembrance till I find another idol. But I am not a scrap sentimental about them *to* them (though I often said to Toto "ah how lovely you are" & he replied "Eccellenza, si.") & invariably get myself abhorred by them because of my horrid tempers.'

In the same letter Rolfe was looking for a model for an arras, 'a perfectly naked boy floating in mid air perpendicularly head thrown back & arms up. I'll give him a golden bow & quiver & call him "Love". The flesh on a tan brown canvas will be heavenly. But where to find him I dont know. I haunt the bathing places but the boys are ribald & ugly. Pose they wouldnt for this live & how do I dare take a camera into their midst. Oh for Italy again where I was worshipped & allowed & had my hands kissed by everyone. (I wish I could tell you a romance about a certain "Ercole" whom I found naked & divine one day (I of course having left the camera at home) & who was never seen again though we set all the Syndices round to look for him.)'

As 1891 advanced, dark clouds began to gather over Toinham House. Establishing himself in painting and photography, Corvo rented a small studio from Gleeson White to work on future designs. 'My idea is to do things for churches saints you know, boy saints, the question is how to dispose of them when done,' he asked Kains-Jackson, who knew people of influence in the literary and artistic worlds of London. 'I can design they say & my designs are much admired in Italy & I dont see why some of the ghastly blank walls of churches shouldnt have their hangings from my studio. I dont mean expensive ones, no, but good ones yes & of so moderate a price that a church might have a stock of them & hang them up on various occasions, different ones I mean.' Such a suggestion for a possible means of livelihood would go out to his friends. Friendship for Rolfe usually meant receiving as many benefits, personal or professional, as the other could afford. 'For the rest I place myself in your hands & will do what you tell me,' an agreement soon to be shattered by his own act.

The most prominent member of the Hampshire village was Gleeson White. Author, art and music critic, magazine editor, and friend to most of the figures of the 1890s, he was born in Christchurch. In *Hadrian* Rolfe calls him 'a great friend of mine'. 340 pages later he is brought into the story again, at the point when Rose-Rolfe is defending his use of pseudonyms:

I am not the only person who has traded under pseudonyms or technikryms. Take, for example, the man whose shop I am said to have offered to buy. He himself used a trade-name. He begged for my acquaintance when I was openly living as a tonsured clerk, about a couple of years before my first pseudo-nym even was thought of.

This accusation against White was hardly a just one. Born Joseph William Gleeson White, he merely dropped his first two given names when dealing with the professional world. In any case, Gleeson had been associated with him since he was a child, not Joseph or William. Rolfe, in *Hadrian*, was the only person to take him to task.

In 1891 Gleeson White was preparing for his first move from Christchurch. Acting as his solicitor, Kains-Jackson found him a house in London, not too distant from his own near William Morris' Kelmscott House. But life in the new house would not be a long one. In 1891 he was in New York for several months as the associate editor of the *Art Amateur Magazine*. At the same time a young Englishman went to the United States and by 1893 was appointed to an editorial position on the same magazine. This young man, Scotson Clark, later wrote that 'Gleeson White was a man whose mission in life was to help the young and struggling and there are many artists of national reputation both in England and the United States who have him to thank for their first introduction to the public.' Speaking of a school friend of his, he added: 'Beardsley was perhaps the greatest.' White was the first to recognize the talent of this young artist. He asked Joseph Pennell to write an article on Aubrey Beardsley for the first number of his *Studio*, in April 1893. The artist died on the 16 March 1898, at the age of twenty-six. In the following summer White made a trip to Italy with the Art Workers' Guild, from which he returned with typhoid. At the age of forty-seven, he died on October 19th.

White's inheritance at Christchurch included Caxton House, a double-fronted stationer's shop and a baker's shop next door. When he and his family decided to move, 'Corvo actually proposed to buy the whole caboodle'. As White's solicitor, Kains-Jackson looked into this proposed transaction. Kains-Jackson had cashed the duchess's 'monthly remittances of 200 liras giving [Corvo] £8 & paying them in to my bank when I was back in town.' He knew of no other money of Rolfe's, and his investigations unearthed nothing more. 'Corvo tried to buy the stationers business lending library & two freehold houses on securities which proved to be bogus. . . . He knew—who so well!—that he had planned a fraud on White & from the hour that White brought the matter to me knew that the game was up.' This, in Kains-Jackson's words, terminated the friendship between him and Corvo. He was 'looking into' a Hammersmith house which White took on 24 June 1892. 'A complicated case in 1891 kept me in Chancery Lane till 19 September! I could not get away till 20 Sep & was at Christchurch till well into October.' This was the last time he saw Rolfe, who 'must have vanished not earlier than Dec 1891,' leaving 'debts all round,' although 'not in moral bad odour.' Kains-Jackson earned Rolfe's undying disfavour by saving £11,300 for Gleeson White.

The blackest cloud on the horizon was to come from the direction of Rome. Throughout his life, Rolfe was both auto-biographer and prophet. He wrote intentionally of what he knew. The role of prophet was unintentional. His innocent, casual writings more than once would reflect violent events to come. Commenting on the duchess to Kains-Jackson, he wrote that 'the dear old lady is inbred with Socialism. A man is not satis-factory to her unless he works for his living, ergo I have to find a way to show her either that I am selling paintings drawings designs or verse, then she is happy & pleased with me. I confess that I have somewhat of the same views myself ... very startling & unorthodox views. I want then to be in a position to say that if my little income disappeared tomorrow, if kingdoms rose & waned, & that filthy abhorrent idol of the British public, the British workman, upset thrones etc next week, I should still be able to snap my fingers at circumstances & with my hands earn my bread & cheese.'

In less than six months' time this fancied eventuality became real.

'I was just beginning to make headway when the defalcations of a Catholic ruined me,' Rolfe states in *Hadrian*. He continues:

I took advice about adopting [pseudonyms]: for, in those days, I used to take advice about everything, not being man enough to act upon my own responsibility. Also, the idea of using pseudonyms was suggested to me; and the first one was selec-ted for me.... [Later] the Fathers of Divine Love [in London] refused me shelter for one night in 1892 at the very time when they are said to have 'charitably maintained' me. They did suggest a common lodging-house at fourpence, though; and I flung back the suggestion in their faces and walked the streets all night. But all these people knew all about me and my pseudonyms. In fact, the very priest who suggested the common lodging-house, was the man on whose advice I adopted my first pseudonym. It was invented by an old lady who chose to call herself my grandmother: she was the priest's patron and penitent. It was approved by him and adopted by me. And there you have the blind and naked truth on that point.

The 'defalcations' of people within the Roman Church continued to ruin Rolfe's life. Oban, Oscott, Scots College came to an end for him. In part, he may have been to blame in these cases. But he was entirely innocent in the Christchurch episode. In writing *Hadrian*, Rolfe did not settle old scores. The characters were presented in the story as he saw them in their natural poses. Fr. Beauclerk received the most blunt treatment. But almost all of the people he once knew who were brought into the novel were elevated in position. If any old score had to be settled, Rolfe did it with only one person. For only one person is demoted in *Hadrian*.

One of his Oxford 'friends' of 1887 was James Laird Patterson, the Bishop of Emmaus and rector of St. Mary's, Chelsea. A favourite with Cardinal Manning, Patterson frequently was sent to Rome to conduct the more delicate business between Westminster and the Vatican. On such a trip, the bishop and Rolfe, the seminary student, walked together when, for some reason, and perhaps only humorously, Patterson thought that Rolfe should be a baron. When Rolfe finally left Italy, the duchess, as has already been indicated, undertook to assure him of £200 a year for at least two years. 'Papists ... make me sick,' he said to Kains-Jackson in 1891. 'Thats why I came here to be out of the way of the whole crew.' But he could never move far enough away from their reach. Before this first year was up, clerical pressure had been brought to bear on the duchess to discontinue her aid to Rolfe. The 'friend' of 1887, the bishop who suggested his barony, the 'priest' of whom the duchess was a patron and a penitent was responsible for this unexpected, and unnecessary, blow. The Church would not even let Rolfe live in peace in a secular world. The Bishop of Emmaus died in 1902. A year later he was demoted to a mere 'priest' in *Hadrian the Seventh*.

'Not earlier than Dec 1891' Corvo vanished from Christchurch. The end of his allowance from Rome and current debts caused his departure. The act of a Catholic within the Church had suddenly left Corvo derelict.

A moment of jest on the part of a Roman duchess resulted in the name by which posterity has identified Rolfe. Then, as posterity began to take form around him, myths were created and added to the name of Corvo. In one segment of his history his biographers have been generous.

On Purwell Road, an extension of Bridge Street, Christchurch, there is the Roman Catholic Church of the Immaculate Conception and St. Joseph, bearing the same name from the time Rolfe first visited the village in 1889. In this little 132-seat chapel, the only Roman Catholic church at Christchurch, there is a large mural which has been claimed to be Rolfe's work.

Did he paint it?

'Rolfe ... settled at Christchurch, Hampshire, where he commenced to live on his wits and indulge alternatively in expenditure and asceticism. He painted the wall painting in the local Catholic Church.' With these words (Sir) Shane Leslie sketched a portion of Rolfe's history in his article, 'Frederick Baron Corvo,' in the September 1923 *London Mercury*.

This same title was used by A. J. A. Symons in a talk to Ye Sette of Odd Volumes in 1926. 'I have never seen one of [Corvo's] mural masterpieces for Catholic churches,' he says, 'but I know that draughtsmanship was his weakness, and that it was ingeniously overcome by photographs of suitably posed and draped models projected by magic-lantern on the painting area. The Byzantine eikon was his ideal, and his oil-paintings were enhanced with fur and feather, and spangled with sham gems.'

Eight years later, in *The Quest for Corvo*, he writes: 'The local Catholic church [at Christchurch] had been liberally adorned by his brush in a fresco of figures still to be seen by the curious, and it was said that churches elsewhere also rejoiced in his work.... The Byzantine eikon was his ideal, and some of his oil-paintings were enhanced with needlework, and spangled with sequins.... The fresco at St. Michael's, Christchurch, though damaged by damp, is still, in its way, impressive.'

With the report of Symons' death in 1941, the *Bournemouth Daily Echo* asked if anyone remembered 'Baron Corvo'. 'According to Mr. Symons, Corvo lived at Christchurch [and] devoted most of his time to art. He executed a number of frescoes in the Roman Catholic Church of St. Michael's, and Mr. Symons hints that other local churches may have been similarly adorned. It would be interesting to learn if this is so, and whether these other paintings can still be traced.'

During the centenary year of Rolfe's birth, a photograph of the mural and a letter by M. Littledale of Hastings appeared in *Country Life* for September 29th. 'Corvo's fresco' is still 'at St. Michael's,' the letter said. Two later photographs of the mural appeared in the centenary booklet of The Church of the Immaculate Conception and St. Joseph. In a one-page article, entitled 'The Mural', the painting 'is thought to be the work of Frederick Rolfe'.

The painting in question is a mural—painted on canvas and then tacked to the wall—and not a fresco—painted directly on the wall. And the church is not St. Michael's, a name misinterpreted from the facts given by Kains-Jackson.

When Fr. Foley prepared the little chapel for its anniversary, he called upon two artists to look at the mural. Years of damp had deteriorated it. The artists examined it and advised on its restoration. Bernard Hammond Davis, believing the myth about the painting's creator, drew up a report on ' "The Assumption" by Baron Corvo'. The restoration was reported in the *Christchurch Times* a year later: 'Some of the most recent local research into Corvo's story was carried out last year when restoration work was started on a mural in St. Joseph's Roman Catholic Church.... The mural is unfinished and it now seems likely that he left it when pressure from his creditors became so great that he left the area.'

Three questions should be asked about the mural and the possibility of Rolfe's painting it.

First, are the drawing and design elements of the Christchurch mural consistent with the known works by Rolfe?

The Assumption mural shows Mary beginning her ascent into heaven from a horizontal pedestal. Twelve people are at her feet, four of whom are fully viewed. On either side of her outstretched arms is a winged and haloed angel. This illustration forms the horizontal arm of a great reredos cross. The base of the cross is the church's altar. The vertical extension depicts her coronation in heaven at the feet of Christ the King. Two kneeling figures in the upper corners of the cross, but outside of the original design, were added at a later date by a second person.

Davis' report on the mural says that 'the medium is linseed oil and turpentine and the method of painting ... is the old process of painting with very thin oil-starved paint much thinned with turpentine at the early stages proceeding on to thicker paint at the final stages and finalising with a transparent varnish; the whole process being known as the "glazing technique".' The mural must 'be taken seriously as the work of a talented painter.' It contains 'many corrections and counter-corrections clearly seen ... in the form of corrected under-painting, in some cases very close, indicating an eye not easily satisfied, and a hand that does not tire at work.'

The purity of pigment in Rolfe's oil painting of St. George differs greatly from the church mural. The surface of the mural was smooth and the palette was varied and bright. (The colour and design have been faithfully followed by Davis and his wife in their restoration.) The St. George is rather sombre. The mural figures are photographically life-like. Rolfe, favouring the 'Byzantine eikon,' preferred single studies. The perfection in his painting is more mechanical than the natural and experienced art of the mural. Of the two, Rolfe's figures are fixed in space and pose for eternity. The St. George paint was applied on the canvas in an opaque method, thinned just enough for blending purposes. Metal and chain mail are depicted with touches of jammy paint. And the painting is unvarnished.

77

The size of the mural poses a problem if Rolfe were the artist. There are two tiers of life-sized figures, by far larger than anything else attempted by him. If he, as it has been suggested, utilized sketches to make lantern slides for projection, he needed a large studio to extend them to the size on the mural's canvas. Neither in his Toinham House room—where oil painting would not be permitted—nor in the small studio rented from Gleeson White would he have enough space for this projection. The St. Michael wall-hanging was probably no larger than twice the size of the St. George painting, which measures 13" × 25".

Secondly, if he painted the mural, when did he do it?

On 25 June 1891 he wrote to Kains-Jackson about a finished arras or wall-hanging, which 'is laying out in the fields in the rain to drag the canvas. Where shall I send it. You were going to introduce me to some firm who will hang or exhibit my work. Something ecclesiastical you know for I have a really good St Edmund just ready. There is a St Martin coming & now what I want is a perfectly naked boy floating in mid air....' In the 1 November 1891 issue of his *Artist*, Kains-Jackson spoke of Rolfe continuing 'his good work in church decoration. The success of his arras of St Michael has led him to attempt a larger piece representing the five warrior saints of the Catholic Church.' November 1st was close to the end of Christchurch for him. An arras is not a mural and the Assumption group contains no St. Michael or warrior saints.

The painter of the mural had to execute it in a studio and had to work on it for at least six months. During the single year at Christchurch, Rolfe, from documented evidence, spent his time working with photography or painting wall-hangings. When he was commissioned to do ten banners for a church a few years later, he spent two years on the project.

Thirdly, and most important, why is there no mention of this mural in any surviving piece of writing by or pertaining to Rolfe?

In no letter or published work is any church mural mentioned. In the one work in which he lays himself and his past history naked before his jurors, *Hadrian the Seventh*, no wall-painting is credited to him. If he were doing the mural at the

78

time when the duchess' allowance stopped, he would have had another source of income, or at least, a temporary sanctuary. 'Chased from the priesthood, he painted arras,' he says of himself, as Crabbe, in *The Desire and Pursuit of the Whole*.

When he wrote to Wilfrid Meynell from Aberdeen in 1893, he pleaded for his work to be given a chance to be seen and appreciated. 'My turn of mind is nothing but ecclesiastical,' he said. 'I want nothing but to know that I am devoting my talents to the Church.' He spoke of three oil paintings on display in the Scottish city. And these three are the only paintings noted in the Aberdeen Attack a few years later.

Kains-Jackson knew Rolfe for several years and learned a great deal about his past from him. The two possessed a small number of mutual friends. In none of Kains-Jackson's surviving letters, from 1891 until his death in 1933, is there any mention of any fresco or mural by Rolfe. He wrote that the Rolfe of 1891 'was an agreeable colourist & great at arranging drapery [and] thus obtained considerable verisimilitude & action.' Speaking further about the Rolfe methods of painting, he said that Rolfe reverted to the convenience of sketches, photographs and 'a lay figure from Lechertier Barbe.' The striking contrast between the figures in the church mural and a group of figures actually drawn by Rolfe can be seen in his illustration for 'Ballade of Boys Bathing'. The more than forty boys in this are evidence of that fact that 'his lay figure was somewhat disjointed.'

A galley proof of the Christchurch episode for *The Quest for Corvo* was sent to Mrs. Gleeson-White, who now hyphenized her name. For accuracy, she 'wanted to consult Mr Kains-Jackson,' just before he died in December 1933, 'as well as my children.' When all four had seen the proof, she sent it back to Symons. The galley had printed: 'The Byzantine eikon was his ideal, and some of his oil-paintings were enhanced with fur and feathers, and spangled with sham gems.' 'Fur and feathers' was now crossed out and 'needlework' was added in the margin. 'The local Catholic church had been liberally adorned by his brush in a fresco of figures....' ran the galley. 'Fresco' was crossed out and 'banner' was substituted by the person who saw Rolfe's work in the studio on her property.

Two days after Davis submitted his recommendations to the little church for restoration, the *Christchurch Times* reported on the mural's mysteries. When Davis and his wife had cleaned the painting they found a date: 1910.

Even though Rolfe left behind him no concrete evidence of his stay at Christchurch, he brought something with him out of the village. The end was caused by Kains-Jackson's 'ghastly blunder,' he continued to think, which he never 'attempted or desired to set' right. During the earlier portion of the year life had been pleasant. He delighted listeners with his fertile tongue and tales of foreign places and times. He joined musical gatherings either with his voice or at the piano. But his gifts of amusement did not please all people. There was something in his make-up disagreeable to women, and Mrs. Gleeson White found little in his favour.

Speaking of himself in *Hadrian*, he says that he is 'frightened of all men, known and unknown; and of women I go in violent terror: though I always do say superb and hard things to the one, and all pretty gentle soft things to the other, while writing pitilessly of them both:— for I'm frightened of them, frightened; and I want to avoid them; and to keep them off me.' In the same novel he includes Mrs. Gleeson White and her two children.

[Mrs. White and her daughter Cecily] spoke as though they were alone. Alaric [Eric] went quite unnoted. He folded his napkin and rose from the table.
'A—and, mother,' he mooed, slowly, with a slight hesitation, in a virginal baritone voice, resonant and low; 'if you go to Rome, don't be nasty to Mr. Rose?'

In the years that followed, Eric enjoyed a full career with the Bank of England. Since he had inherited his father's interest in art and music, his mother was disappointed in his choice of occupation. To her, he possessed all the qualifications of a music critic. He loved music too much, was his defence. If he were a critic, he said, he would have to endure hours of torture listening to works which did not interest him, for the few which did.

Cecily chose a musical career and had started singing lessons by 1891. Her father had been one of the first admirers of Wagner in England and she had been brought up from the cradle on his music. Her father heard her sing in only one opera, *Don Giovanni*, before his early death. *Hadrian* amazingly, and amusingly, reflects Rolfe's passion for information about people. At the time he wrote the story, she was singing in concerts in London and other English cities. The later operas in which she appeared included some productions by the Carl Rosa Company at Covent Garden. Her first appearance in Rolfe's book is when she flows 'into the room in a pink wrapper, finishing a florid cadenza.' When her mother speaks of a trip to Rome in the novel, Amelia-Cecily asks, 'But what about the cost? I'm sure I can't help you as long as I only get these three-guinea engagements.'

Unlike the young Eric of 1891, Alaric stands up for Rolfe in the novel.

'A-and he [Rose-Rolfe] taught me to swim.'
'So he did me. At least he tried to. And what of that?' snapped the girl.
'A-and I don't think it's fair. I liked him. A-and father liked him.'
'Yes indeed, he's just the sort of man your father would have liked, unfortunately. He liked that sonnet-man, too. A pretty kind of person! All I can say is, Alaric, if I were to let you see the letters I've got of his and the albums full—: but there, you don't know as much as I do about your father!'

'That sonnet-man' is the only reference in *Hadrian* to John Nicholson. The 'letters' probably were no more alarming than those between Rolfe and Kains-Jackson. The 'albums' easily could have been collections of drawings, prints and photographs of Roman and Greek youths. Such an album was not uncommon at that period and may have included the efforts of others, such as the painter Tuke.

In an exuberant mood of colourful description, Rolfe pens Mrs. White's portrait in *Don Renato*. As 'the widow of Tyrant Bianco di Correale' who 'collects curials and litterates,' she fits into this exotic and most singular book. She is 'an erudite virago, to the extent permitted by her sex,' who 'tries to shine in the light deflected from these others, seeing that, by cause of her said sex, she cannot attain litterary eminence in her proper person.' She is painted 'as a proper lamia; with a total defect of hair, not concealed by a wig of fulvine colour; with a dry and withered cuticule, not disguised by minium and cerusa, nor adorned by semicircular asymmetrical supercilia depicted in sepia; very in-pudent, very passionate, very vain; a hypocrite who, nevertheless, is maternally beneficent to a proterve daughter, and to a very docile tender juvencal son, for whom she had no love.'

On this point, Rolfe was mistaken. Mrs. White was a remark-able woman and was accepted by the people who knew her with affectionate respect. She was justifiably proud of her daughter's achievements. And she soon became reconciled to Eric's de-cision to work outside of the musical world. Cecily and her brother were equally adored by their mother. Rolfe may have seen the finer aspects of her nature at one time. In a letter to his brother Herbert he listed Mrs. White as one of the 'Women of a Woman Hater' he was preparing to write about. She, then, was one woman he at least tolerated. The letter to Herbert was sent on 22 July 1898, less than four months before 'Baron Corvo' was attacked in several newspapers. When Rolfe re-covered from this blow he naturally tried to detect the person or persons responsible. Hunter Blair's name came to his mind as one possible perpetrator. In these articles Rolfe also saw the hand of a woman and probably none other than Mrs. White's. In Appendix III, suppressed from the Borgia book in 1901, he writes 'to impeach the credibility' of historians who, with con-temptuous whispers, had accused the Borgia of crimes without establishing their truth 'by unbiased evidence'. 'For the man, or woman, who would make use of such a weapon for the gratification of spite or grudge ... must be held to be devoid of any moral principle,' he continues. Speaking of men in history, Rolfe's words reflect a future phrase in *Hadrian*: 'At one or another time, they inadvertently have trodden upon some human worm ... they have made an enemy, have scorned a woman, flouted a priest, offended the vanity of an inferior....' Rolfe was writing his Borgia book before the full effects of the newspaper attack against him had subsided. He still imagined Hunter Blair as the priest. The scorned woman must have been the same person of whom he wrote to Grant Richards in April 1899. One of Rolfe's July 1898 'Women of a Woman Hater' was no longer tolerated.

For reasons of his own, then, he remembered Mrs. White in his writings. *Hadrian* records a unique encounter in his life:

About fourteen years ago, I dined with a woman whose husband was a great friend of mine. Her two children dined with us—a girl of fifteen, a boy of thirteen. Her husband was away on business for a few months. Soon after dinner, she sent the children to bed. A few minutes later she went to say good-night to them: she was an excellent mother. I remained in the drawing-room. When she returned I was standing to take my departure. As she entered, she closed the door and switched off the electric light. I instinctively struck a match. She laughed, apologising for being absent-minded. I said the usual polite idioms and went away. A fortnight later, I dined there again by invitation. All went on as before: but this time, when she came back from saying good-night to the children she was wearing a violet flannel dressing-gown. I said nothing at all; and instantly left her. Afterwards, I gave her the cut direct in the street.... Her husband was a good man, a martyr, and I immensely admired him. He died a few years later. I have no feeling for her except detestation. She was wickedly ugly. Vague thoughts ensued from these incidents; thoughts not connected with her but with some sensuous idea, some phasma of my imagination. They never were more than thoughts. I think that I must have delighted in them, because they returned to me perhaps twelve or fourteen times in as many years. I confess these sins of thought. Also, I think that I ought to confess myself lacking in alacrity after the final switching off of the electric light; and that I never ought to have remained alone with that woman again. I was ridiculously dense: for, only after the second event, did I see what the first had portended.

The length of this narrative in *Hadrian* is significant in the life of its author. Gleeson White 'was away on business for a few months' as associate editor for the *Art Amateur Magazine* in New York. From there he wrote a column, 'Art in New York', for Kains-Jackson's *Artist* for the February, March, April, May and August 1891 issues. Rolfe later wrote a letter to Grant Richards on 6 April 1899: 'All tales of the "Gleeson White" order are false. *He remained on friendly terms with me for some years after the Episode of the Woman Scorned.*'

Speaking of Mrs. White in *Hadrian*, Jerry Sant says that George Arthur Rose had 'borrowed twenty-pound notes of her.' Remembering back to 1891, she was later to speak of Rolfe as 'a clean imposter living on his wits & condescending to insisting on a conceited plan of *fraud*, even to renting our property from us, as well as owing us £20.' Knowing Frederick Rolfe before he had become Baron Corvo, she sent him a letter soon after he departed from Christchurch. Reproduced in the Aberdeen exposure of the baron some years later, it spoke in part about her advice to the baron 'to re-adopt [your real name of Rolfe] for the future, for the very fact of your assuming a new and foreign title has, I find, now given rise from the first to suspicions here and elsewhere.' In the Aberdeen article, it was said that Rolfe was now following her sensible advice about dropping the barony. If she were responsible for this reversion back to the name of Rolfe at this time, then he later had his revenge, if only on paper. The name (Corvo: raven) which she discouraged him from using was given back to her. In a vulgar, incorrect form, in *Hadrian* she becomes Mrs. Crowe.

5

'I was just beginning to make headway when the defalcations of a Catholic ruined me,' Rolfe continues as his own witness to his exploits, in the words of *Hadrian*. 'All that I ever possessed was swallowed up. Even my tools of trade illegally were seized. I began life again with no more than the clothes on my back, a Book of Hours, and eight shillings in my pocket.' Thus began the wanderings of a wearied soul, who would find little recognition or security during the next twenty years.

The 1891 paintings and manuscripts were substituted for money in meeting his unpaid bills at Christchurch. In this way only his 'tools of trade illegally were seized.' The monthly allowance from Rome was no more than the nominal sum of 200 lire— approximately £3 or $8. It covered basic needs, but more was spent, in the expectation that his paintings would sell. Wrenched from this sole security, Rolfe was totally abandoned. And, with no money, no credit, not even an immediate means of support, he was forced to leave the village. The only direction to travel was north—to London. In violent contrast to the previous year, he faced 1892 with nothing.

He returned to a familiar neighbourhood. As a Protestant boy of fifteen, he had attended St. Alban's, Holborn. No more than four blocks away is St. Etheldreda's, Ely Place, the oldest church in the Archdiocese of Westminster and the house of the Fathers of Charity. Fr. William Lockhart, an ex-Anglican and the first of Newman's Littlemore Community to 'go over to Rome', presided over both. His energies were divided between the duties of his church, needed social work in the Holborn slums and interests in literature. He also opened the doors of the house belonging to the Fathers of Charity to young Catholic men newly arriving in London. Here Rolfe stayed for a little, perhaps only for a few days. His other address in London during the early months of 1892 was merely 'West Hampstead'. The street, the number, the house, are not known. From here he tried to earn a living.

The Pope and The New Era was published in 1890. Its author was W. T. Stead, one of London's most enterprising magazine editors, a Socialist and spiritualist. One chapter of his book was entitled 'Is a Humanised Papacy Possible?' It was much too early at this time for the future author of *Hadrian the Seventh* to answer the question, or even think about it. But he did call on the progressive editor, who willingly listened to his artistic and journalistic schemes. Rolfe's being a Catholic was in his favour for once and he had humbly dropped his Italian title. To aid this newcomer in whatever way he could, Stead loaned Rolfe art and photographic materials. But this, in no way, was to be any assurance of employment. It was only one more piece of experience for the artistic novice. The short association with Stead was to give Rolfe a glimpse of two worlds, the natural and the supernatural. Forever delving into such unnatural sciences as astrology himself, Rolfe later came to abhor spiritualism. Perhaps his one contact with it had made a lasting impression.

In the middle of April, Rolfe visited Stead. The editor was engaged in one of his many bits of 'spookery'. He would ask callers to place some small object at his disposal for a few minutes. He would then go into the next room and give the object to his favourite medium, Julia, who would say what manner of person the visitor was. When Rolfe arrived on this particular day, he was subjected to the experiment. The object provided by him was given to the medium, who said that the owner of the object was untrustworthy and had a hole in his head. In the words of (Sir) Shane Leslie, 'Mr. Stead thereupon chased and seized Rolfe until he could feel his cranium, when behold there was a perceptible hole to be found in the skull! He was accordingly dismissed as a blackguard, and for once Rolfe was baffled by powers more sinister than his own.'

(The hole, the result of an operation by a Bournemouth doctor, was mentioned by Rolfe in one of his novels. Hadrian

86

and Nicholas Crabbe are exact copies of Rolfe, Dom Gheraldo Pinarj in *Don Renato* only resembles him in some particulars. In the Epilogue of *Don Renato*, the author discovers the priest's skeleton beneath the old palace of the Countess of Santa Cotogna (the Duchess of Sforza-Cesarini). 'In that part of the crown of the skull where a clerk would wear his tonsure, a gold-hilted dagger was inbedded.')

The 'spookery' incident coincided with Stead's waning interest in Rolfe. He asked for the return of his supplies. On April 25th Rolfe sent a letter to the editor. The materials were going back, it said, and went on to speak about an enclosed drawing. 'I also send a small preliminary design which I have been able to do, representing a funeral procession in the Catacombs.' To effectively show it, the finished drawing would have to be quite large. Dismissing any tone of urgency in Stead's letter, he wrote that he was also 'doing a "Felicitas and Her Seven Sons before the Prefect". It is awfully good; but I am sending all the drawing materials of yours which I have had the use of. I cannot afford to buy them of you yet, and I wish you had not recalled them.'

The letter demonstrates Rolfe's usual lack of concern over another's money. On one point he had to agree with Stead. 'I acknowledge that the Steoroscopic Company is an awfully expensive firm to deal with, and if I had been able to conduct matters in my own way the result would have been altogether different, and more pleasing. You would have had to lay out more as a beginning, but you would have had more than enough for your money.'

A sharp reminder had to be sent by Stead before he received the items loaned to Rolfe. On the 28th a letter by Rolfe said that he 'should be glad to know that' everything had arrived back at the editor's office. It ended: 'Did I tell you that I have an opportunity of getting photographs of the Doré engravings? The Kyrle Society will be happy to pick my brains, but they do not pay for doing so.' Nor did any one.

At this same time Rolfe had cause to contact an old pupil. John Gambril Nicholson's book of verse, *Love in Earnest*, was published in March, and one of the poems was 'St. William of Norwich. (Painted by F. W. Rolfe.)' In the early 1880s the master had shown a rough example of this poem to his pupil. Nicholson suggested a way to improve it, a way approved by Rolfe. Their continuing friendship was never smooth and a rupture in 1887 ended correspondence between the two. This book taught Rolfe what had become of his poem. He was not pleased with the manner of its appearance.

From Colwyn Bay, North Wales, Nicholson sent a letter to Kains-Jackson, asking his friend's advice as a solicitor. 'I was going to write you soon to tell you about my work,' he started, 'and to ask you where you intended to review *Love in Earnest*. But I must confine myself to-night to a point which causes me considerable anxiety.' He had just heard from Rolfe's solicitor, who had conveyed an injunction to stop the sale of the book, 'as it contains some literary property of their client, viz: this Sonnet in question'. Rolfe's puzzling mental attitude was demonstrated here. Struggling for recognition in April 1892, the publication of this old poem threw him into rebellion. In the 1880s he had written about it to Nicholson: 'I send you an uncut diamond: you send back a polished crystal. No thank you!' Seeing this poem in print made him react against stealthy ingratitude. In answer to Nicholson's question, Kains-Jackson advised the most practical solution. The publisher took out the offending page and substituted another with a poem by Nicholson.

London, for all its size and opportunity, proved to be little better than Christchurch. A lack of money, materials to work with and prospects made Rolfe move once more. The 'well-to-do Roman Catholic' of Boyndlie House had been a genial host three years earlier. Why not visit him again?

Travelling to Scotland, Rolfe was not as welcome as he had been in 1889. The house was now shared by more people. Ogilvie-Forbes had married in 1890 and a mother-in-law and a new baby now crowded out any singular consideration for the English guest.

Rolfe's host was related to the late James Gordon Hay of Seaton. Born in 1815, Hay married late in life. He died in 1883, when the younger of his two sons was only a year old. Their mother died in 1891. Cuthbert and Malcolm, older by a year, were placed in the charge of their father's sister, Miss Georgiana Hay. A stern and serious Catholic, she was deeply concerned about the educational and spiritual welfare of the two young boys. Until the time of their mother's death, they had been taught by various tutors. Now they were just completing their first year away from home at St. John's, the preparatory school to Beaumont College at Old Windsor. With the summer holidays approaching, Miss Hay looked for a tutor. Ogilvie-Forbes suggested Rolfe.

'I can testify to his having been a sound Catholic, gentleman-like in his manners, & I should think him the sort of man who would take well to boys & make their education interesting,' Ogilvie-Forbes told Miss Hay. Cautious in any matter pertaining to the boys' interests, she did not accept merely one person's approval for a proposed tutor. Knowing Catholics from Aberdeen to London, she wrote to the Jesuits of Farm Street. Fr. R. F. Clarke, whom Rolfe had listed as a 'friend' in 1887, answered. It was a long time since he heard anything of Rolfe, he said, and continued, 'I do not think I ever knew him personally and I am sorry to say that I have no definite remembrance that would justify me in recommending him.' But events worked out to Ogilvie-Forbes' advantage.

Once back from school, the boys were invited to Boyndlie House. When they returned to Seaton House, Rolfe accompanied them as their tutor. In a most proper, and polite, way, Ogilvie-Forbes rid himself of his guest.

The short summer was pleasant and disappeared all too rapidly. But the memories of it clung to the boys' minds for a very long time. All other tutors had been either good or bad and nothing else. None had been so harmoniously enjoyed. And none, perhaps, was so vigilantly watched by the boys' guardian. What she could not understand herself was questioned. She had spied some books in Rolfe's possession and wrote to the Bishop of Aberdeen about their nature. 'Voltaire & Rousseau are certainly not reading for your nephews,' he replied, 'nor indeed for general readers of any kind. But as such books are *occasionally* needed for reference, & to refute the false teaching contained in them, they can be kept in large libraries. In a

Catholic Library they would be under lock & key.' The new tutor taught neither Voltaire nor Rousseau, but he let the boys engage in an even greater sin. Miss Hay and the bishop were aware that Rolfe was a heavy smoker. But neither knew that he was permitting Cuthbert and Malcolm to smoke cigars.

The weather allowed tutor and boys to spend a good portion of time outdoors. Rolfe's romantic innovations delighted the boys who were with him. He could change the course of an ordinary drain to form a stream filled with an imaginary history linked in some way to their lessons and christen it the Malcuth Dew. He and the Hays were not alone in their summer rambles. The five Burnetts, sons of a widow who all later occupied honoured positions in life, were their companions. Robin Burnett was even immortalized by Rolfe's camera as St. Sebastian, tied to a tree in a loin cloth.

Though he wished to be as correct as possible in his manners, Rolfe's means restricted him. For example, he had no change of clothes for evening wear. But to this problem he had a simple solution. He made the adjustment by merely putting on a priest's collar. This mode of dress added an authoritative touch to the remark he made each evening. At meals with Miss Hay and the boys, he would always say, 'Let Father Rolfe say grace.'

The two months with the Hay boys passed too quickly. Life at Seaton House could be endured for a longer period of time. He suggested a plan to remain, as the boys' permanent tutor. In turn, this would mean that the boys would not go back to their Jesuit school. The scheme was ignored. The boys started their second year at Old Windsor, and Rolfe was dismissed.

By the time the boys left Aberdeen, an incident had severed all relations between Miss Hay and the tutor. She did not want any association between him and the boys to continue. She even instructed the Jesuit fathers at the boys' school to intercept any letters to them not from their uncles and aunts. Unaware of such restrictions, Malcolm tried to find out Mr. Rolfe's whereabouts. His aunt had written to him that 'Mr Rolfe left Seaton on Monday without leaving any address.' In a short schoolboy's note, he wrote back to his 'Dear Auntie

Georgie', saying that 'we had a little snow last Thursday week, I have received a letter from Mr. Ogilvie Forbes. Will you please send me some money, also some jam and my crucifix.... I suppose you dont know Mr Rolfe's address yet.' Ogilvie-Forbes sent him a letter about 'the Water Kelpie' being well and wanting 'to know how you are getting on, & how Cuthbert is getting on, at Beaumont, & what you would both like when you visit her again. The baby is flourishing & so are Mrs Ogilvie Forbes & Mrs Vaughan. I don't know Mr. Rolfe's address, indeed I seldom do, he moves about a great deal & I don't often hear from him.'

Neither Cuthbert nor Malcolm ever found out what had happened to cause the decisive break between their aunt and Rolfe.

The rift between their tutor for the summer and the female head of Seaton House occurred suddenly; and each had just cause to remember the other.

On September 19th Rolfe moved from Seaton House.

Fr. Gerry of Strichen kept him for a few weeks, until he decided to go back to Aberdeen. On his last day at Seaton House, Rolfe still was asking to be allowed to stay, if only for a little while. The excuse was a photographic one. 'I have not yet been able to find lodgings,' he said to Miss Hay in a letter, 'and I am very anxious to complete some photographic work which I have in hand for the coming Exhibition in Aberdeen, which ... will be of service in the way of getting my secular work known to the public.' The Home Industries Exhibition was held on October 13th and 14th. For this civic occasion, the main streets of Aberdeen were decorated. Venetian masts and spars were used in honour of two royal guests, the Princesses Beatrice and Louise. The photographic section of the exhibition was judged by the president of the Photographic Convention of Great Britain and several men from the city, including John Wilson of Messrs. G. W. Wilson & Company. Of the seventeen awards, none went to the ex-tutor of the Hay boys.

Rolfe's dauntless stamina faced an uncertain future many times. Resorting to his wits and manufacturing his own opportunities, he became a boarder at a lodging house at 162 Skene

Street in October. And by the first of November he had applied for a position with Messrs. G. W. Wilson, photographers.

Approaching this company, one of the largest makers of lantern slides in Great Britain, he said that he wished to study the practical details of photography. Money was no concern, he added. He wished only for a chance to perfect his own work. No 'improvers' were employed, he was told. He insisted and a boy's place was found to be vacant. If he cared to take this, he could, submitting himself to the ordinary rules of the company. He accepted. 'For fully three months he was in Messrs. Wilson's works ... at 12s 6d a week ... coming and going when he liked, pretty much doing what he liked, telling enormous yarns to his fellow-workers of his father's property in England and abroad.' Most of the company's 250 employees were women, and Rolfe tried to impress them with his learning by scribbling Latin phrases in chalk on the walls.

Three months' association with Rolfe was enough for the photographic company. He was given his notice. But this did not prevent him from going to their place of business every morning. A formal statement of separation was sent to his lodgings. It was answered. Rolfe acknowledged the note and asked 'whether one would be allowed to invest a small sum, say £1,000, in your business.... Perhaps it is inopportune now, but I think I had better mention it.' Informed now that the police would eject him when next he came, he found a solicitor to act for him. He claimed that the firm had retained £300 worth of his property. One letter from the company was enough to satisfy the solicitor. He dropped his client's claims.

His strong pride outweighed any sense of business. In no way could he comprehend the normal day's work and its wage. Impossible schemes were the fibres that held his life together from day to precarious day. After his departure from the Wilson company, Rolfe registered vows, duly attested and subscribed, to Our Lady of Lourdes, Our Lady of Eternal Help and other benevolent saints. If he were given property 'absolutely, within a week from the offering of this vow, which will give me at least £10,000 a year,' he would have one Mass said each day, as well as build and endow a church.

The Church to him was always a treasure store of material goods. It was, he thought, merely to be asked for. But financial aid from the Church was never in the amount he desired. (And when he received any, even as the fictitious Hadrian VII, he gave it all away.) He appealed to the Bishop of Aberdeen and was given one pound. To this he answered, 'I regret that I have made a mistake as to the funds at your Lordship's disposal, but I was informed by the curate at St. Margaret's, Aberdeen that a sum of £4,600 had been inherited by the Catholic clergy "for the relief of the Catholic poor". This information,' he stated, 'was derived from the "Free Press". I repeat my apologies for having troubled your Lordship about a matter on which I have been misinformed.'

This same Bishop of Aberdeen, Hugh Macdonald, conferred the name 'Serafino'—after 'Frederick William' and before 'Austin Lewis Mary'—on his profession in the third order of St. Francis.

Rolfe's adoption into the worldly order was performed with the sincerity which first brought him into the Roman Catholic Church. From childhood he understood only one basic way of living. He envisioned for himself 'the one thing needful,' the religious life. The economic government of the Church would have simplified his daily routine, for his religiously slanted mind left little room for ordinary necessities derived from the world of business. He could not comprehend these facts of existence. His childlike faith extended to a childlike acceptance of people and business. He was an innocent trying to survive in a commercial world he never understood. The 'certain pleasures, certain luxuries, cleanness, whiteness, freshness, and simplicity,' he dreamed of formed a part of the teachings of St. Francis. The third order of St. Francis demands of the professor more fervent and austere acts, as he denounces, as much as he can, his relationship to a worldly life. Rolfe followed this moral principle. As he adopted measures to live by in this world, he adopted ways to associate himself with the Church. By meagre claims, he clung on to both lives. The tonsure, with its almost meaningless title of clerk, was given to him at Oscott. With all other attempts to gain entry into the Church body failing, he joined the order of St. Francis as a citizen of the world.

The austerity of his dress during most of his life was due more to necessity than to choice. In Aberdeen, in the top-floor room on Skene Street, he wore a dressing gown. The one suit he owned had to be preserved. Yet other tenets of St. Francis were not fully kept. He had hired a piano and had acquired a complete set of photographic equipment. He did a little photographic work for a nearby hospital. And in his room he made pencil and crayon drawings of religious and classical subjects. A few of these he sold.

His singular life and his treatment of his fellow creatures placed him apart. The warmth of Italy and the mild climate of southern England may have been kinder to his lone personality than the Scottish north. His loneliness may have chilled and fevered here, to the breaking point of despair. In the dead of night he would open the window of his little room and thrust his head out. Piteously and piercingly, he would yell into the darkness of the universe, during the time when no sign of man or of this world could be seen. His beseeching screams into the night perhaps worked as the only solacing outlet for his emotions, pent up by the loneliness which froze his every day. This outburst of mind and soul refreshed him for another day, a day in which he could persevere to yet another one.

Rolfe was always a heavy reader. The ancient classics and volumes on religion were balanced by works of current literature. Italy and certain families from its past fascinated him. 162 Skene Street was near a public library and he constantly used its facilities. He may have read two novels, *Valentino: An Historical Romance of the Sixteenth Century* (1885) and *Sforza: A Story of Milan* (1889). Each was written by William Waldorf Astor. The American capitalist and journalist later became a British citizen and was granted the title of Baron Astor of Hever Castle. At the death of his father in 1890, he inherited $100,000,000, and in 1892 he bought *The Pall Mall Gazette*. Rolfe sent a letter to Astor in London. 'I am not a begging letter-writer,' it began, 'but a couple of thousand would be my salvation just now. I have been a Catholic for seven years, and am cast off by my parents in consequence. I had to give up all my chances in life, and try as I will I cannot find a situation of any kind. So I have learnt

94

a trade—artistic photography—and have invented a portable light by which I can dispense with the sun.' There was, of course, no reply.

Surprisingly, at this time another person in London wrote his first letter to Rolfe, enclosing a cheque. Fr. Lockhart of Ely Place had died in May 1892, four months after the death of Cardinal Manning. In the mid-1870s Wilfrid Meynell had lived with him at Ely Place and the two had become close friends. Meynell's literary and editorial efforts were of special interest to Fr. Lockhart. He had spoken to Meynell about the artistic convert now in Aberdeen; and Meynell, ever eager to help people in need, then wrote to Rolfe, who immediately replied:

> I can only say that your letter was a great surprise to me and that I am deeply touched by its headlines. Perhaps you may remember that 22 years ago Fr Lockhart (on whom be blessing) wrote you very earnest recommendations on my behalf. I do not think now that you know that I called 8 times without ever being able to see you. As you are good enough to say that you are willing to be of use to me I will trouble you with the following particulars. I have been honoured with unusual powers of design and the faculty of creation & criticism to no small degree. I am learned in art and literature ancient & modern. I am entirely original. My turn of mind is nothing but ecclesiastical. I want nothing but to know that I am devoting my talents to the Church. To descend I am a photographer & have learned all the technique as a factory 'hand' at Wilsons. My inventiveness has stood me in good stead & I can do things which no photographer has ever done. My speciality is instantaneous work & flash light. All ecclesiastical & artistic work. I have incubated a scheme which has a distinct business value. I am powerless to work these things because my goods are in pawn. Therefore it is necessary either—
> 1   To release my goods and give me capital to start with.
> 2   Or for some capitalist to back me up by taking me and my devoted services.
> Will you advise me?

One of Rolfe's complaints was that no one ever agreed with

him on the sum of money needed. No matter how large the amounts he asked for, only small quantities were given. He had an inborn horror of alms. His industry was never rewarded and he could not understand why. The quest for an answer is outlined in *Hadrian*:

Idle? Idle? When I think of all the violently fatuous frantic excellent things I've done in the course of my struggles for an honest living—ouf! It makes me sick! Oh yes, I have been helped. God forgive me for bedaubing myself with that indelible blur. I had not the courage to sit-down and fold my hands and die. A brute once said that he supposed that I looked upon the world as mine oyster. I did not. I worked: and I wanted my wages. When they were withheld, people encouraged me to hope on; and offered me a guinea for the present. I took the filthy guinea. God forgive me for becoming so degraded.... But one can't pay all one's debts, and lead a godly righteous sober life for ever after on a guinea. I was offered help: but help in teaspoonfuls; just enough to keep me alive and chained in the mire: never enough to enable me to raise myself out of it.... My weakness, my fault was that I did not die murdered at Maryvale, at St. Andrew's College. The normal man, treated as I was ill-treated, would have made no bones whatever about doing so. But I was abnormal. I took help, when it was offered gently. I'm thankful to say that I flung it back when it was offered charitably, as [with] John Newcastle of the *Weekly Tabule*.

As author and literary adviser to Burns & Oates, Wilfrid Meynell also edited various Catholic periodicals. One of these was *The Weekly Register*. In addition he wrote himself under the name of John Oldcastle. Both he and his wife, Alice Meynell, were converts to Rome. Wilfrid was a kind and charitable man. Francis Thompson was one person he assisted. He tried to do the same for Rolfe. Thompson responded to the gentle, humanitarian treatment. Rolfe remained adamant.

At the beginning, however, Rolfe welcomed a new chance and, four days after his first letter, he again wrote to thank Meynell 'for your kind letter and enclosure. The latter I shall immediately lay out in the printing & publishing of some photographic studies & in the endeavour to get my work known, & I beg you to convey my respectful thanks to the donor.' He continued, 'One would certainly think that with my talents there would be no difficulty getting employment, but the horrible misery I have endured during the last 7 years has only proved to me the impossibility of doing anything without either capital or a backer-up.' He proposed two ways in which he could be helped. One was for him to be taken on to Meynell's staff at Burns & Oates, where 'there are 100 ways in which the originality and versatility of my mind could well be exercised.' A second plan involved 'the use of some columns in your paper to plead my own cause. I have in MS a series of letters intended for a public character illustrating my wants & the exact and easy thing it would be to correct them. Let me have the use of your columns to explain myself for a few weeks & I have a faith to move mountains. The condition of converts ought to be interesting to Catholics ought it not?'

A month later he was still asking for 'a fair chance of making my living by the use of my undoubted powers.' And he again emphasized 'the dreadful suffering, mental as well as physical the deprivation of all refinements & almost of all the necessities of life, the distracting humiliation of my Catholic life, added to my weakness of character, *knowing perfectly well that it is only a prolongation of my agony & can effect no permanent* good, (I allude to sums of money similar to those you have sent me) [which] have all reduced me to the condition known as madness.'

By the first of May, Meynell had arranged an interview between Rolfe and a publisher in Aberdeen. Rolfe replied that he would gladly go along but only 'on the understanding that I am merely to discuss with Mr Thomson my ideas for the future. I am glad to call upon him though I have not the slightest hope that any good will ensue because I know from past experience how my appearance is against me. However it shall not be said that I have neglected any opportunity.... I shall see Mr Thomson then as soon as possible and let him know what

I can do and what is necessary to enable me to do it. I should be obliged if you would say whether you wish me to place myself under his *direction*, or to receive his advice only.'

'Oh I admit that I have been helped—quite brutally and quite uselessly,' Hadrian says. The episode of Rolfe and Mr. Thomson appears in the novel:

I'll tell you more about [John Newcastle-Meynell]. He said that, being anxious to do me a good turn, he had deposited ten pounds with a printer-man, who would be a kind friend to me, and would consult me as to how that sum could be expended in procuring permanent employment for me. I took seven specimens of my handicraft to that printer-man. He admired them: offered me a loan of five pounds on their security.

To Meynell he wrote: 'You may know what Mr Thomson thinks of my powers of design from the fact that he jumped at lending me £5 on the security of a set of capital letters for Good King Wenceslas.' But the brief story had a bitter ending:

Then I consulted the printer-man, the 'kind friend.' He proposed to give me a new suit of clothes, (I was to do without shirts or socks), to accept my services at no salary, and to teach me the business of a printer's reader for three months; and, then, to recommend me for a situation as reader to some other printer. But, I said, why waste three months in learning a new trade when I already had four trades at my fingers' ends? But, I said, what was I to live on during those three months? But, I said, what certainty was there at the end of those three months? But, he said, that he would 'have none of' my 'lip, for' he 'knew all' my 'capers'; and he bade me begone and take away my drawings. Those were ruined: he had let them lie on his dirty office floor for months.

If the situations were ideal, there might have been poetic justice in Rolfe's refusal of this proposition. Five years later two Aberdeen newspapers would expose Baron Corvo. But, alas,

Mr. Thomson was not the owner of the Aberdeen *Daily Free Press* or *Evening Gazette*. The chief owners of these two newspapers during the 1890s were Henry (who edited the *Free Press*) and William Alexander (who edited the *Gazette*), nephews of Henry McCombie, the founder. W. and D. C. Thomson operated newspapers in Dundee and their only periodical in Aberdeen was the *Aberdeen Weekly News*.

A month passed since Rolfe's last letter. There had been no word from London and Rolfe presumed 'from your silence that you will do nothing more in my case.' Four days later he was saying that 'I am always ready to take off my hat to my superior & I must do so to you now, for I can never hope to equal you in the graceful art of letter writing.' This same letter finished without any thought of Meynell. The rest of it pleaded Rolfe's case. He appended six notes, each stressing the points of his schemes. Note V spoke of not degrading 'myself to take tips. I have good goods to sell & the money I shall make by them will secure for the capital on which I can do all that is necessary for myself & by myself. I want no one's alms.' Note VI added to this by saying that 'I will not take up a fresh trade because I have already a good one at my disposal & I am too wearied with my struggles & starvations to give my attention at 33 to a new and *uncertain* occupation.' His joint occupations of painting and photography were financially just as *'uncertain'* at this time as anything new would have been. The impossible logic was too much for Meynell. Nothing could be done in person. 400 miles separated the two and his attempted aid through Thomson had no result. He did not even answer Rolfe's letter.

For a possible source of income, Rolfe continued with his painting. In June there were 'three pictures of mine in monochrome, St Michael & the Dragon, St Gabriel & St Edmund K.M. at Gifford's Galleries, Aberdeen. I have also here a design for a window St. Raphael nearly finished. The price of these is seventy guineas each & I am prepared to furnish from each a working cartoon for a window or a panel of tapestry.' Writing these facts to Meynell, before the Thomson interview, he added : 'Find me a purchaser for these works that will pay my debts, enable me to put on clean clothes & to make my living *by the*

99

use of the powers & materials I have.'

Meynell was not the only person approached. The Marquis of Huntly, the Rev. Dr. Cooper, Sir Walter Dalrymple, the Duke of Norfolk (known to Meynell) and Sir John Knill, the Lord Mayor of London, each received a beseeching letter about the paintings' merits. Only the Lord Mayor considered the idea, suggesting to the City Fathers of Aberdeen 'their appropriateness as a gift in connection with the Royal wedding, especially as they are the work of an artist who has settled in Aberdeen because of its exquisite suitability for his work.' Even this failed to sell them.

When the Bishop of Aberdeen refused to make a purchase, Rolfe recounted the incident in a letter: 'The Bishop stamped his foot at me and told me there was no room for "high art" in Aberdeen, and offered to pay my fare to London.' In the end, the three paintings brought him twenty pounds. A lawyer accepted the pictures as security for a loan to Rolfe, a loan never paid.

At the same time Rolfe was also experimenting in two new fields of photography: colour and submarine. He produced the usual black-and-white photographs—and these at least were approved by the Bishop of Aberdeen. The patient bishop sat for five photographs. Rolfe thought that he might be able to dispose of prints of these as a source of livelihood. Prints were made 'to send to London for copyright,' but nothing more materialized.

For his underwater experiments, he went to an electrical engineer and a firm of iron workers and ordered a diving bell built to his specifications. This was begun in a belief in his good faith, but the work came to a sudden halt when his true financial status was discovered. Rolfe was better treated by Commander Littledale, who gave him special facilities for photographing the Royal Naval Reserve at drill aboard H.M.S. *Clyde*. The commander even tried to bring Rolfe's submarine photographic schemes to the attention of the United Services Institution.

A national disaster struck on 22 June 1893. On a clear day the misinterpretation of commands during a routine run in the Mediterranean caused a collision. The six-year-old 10,470-ton turret ship H.M.S. *Victoria* sank within minutes. Rolfe immediately sought out individual people and periodicals to let him photograph the sunken ship. But no one employed his services.

While he was working on these experiments in Aberdeen, Gleeson White published three of Rolfe's photographs in *The Studio*. The photographer had already written to Meynell about his colour work. 'I have just discovered the secret of colour photography. It is wonderful. Mr H. S. Tuke the painter of "all Hands to the Pump" writes me "If you can get those colours otherwise than accidentally it ought to be worth something." I have communicated with the Patent Editor of Pearsons Weekly who offered to secure me a Provisio nel Protection for 9 months for £4.4.0. I said that I could not afford anything & this morning they have written offering me the same for £3.3.0. I have given no particulars of my discovery to anyone.' But submarine photography was the subject of his last letter to Meynell.

Rolfe was a careful reader of the daily news. Lord de la Poer Beresford had commanded H.M.S. *Undaunted* since 1889. He had just returned to England in June 1893. On July 3rd a sheaf of letters was posted from Aberdeen. They were addressed to Meynell, Gleeson White, W. T. Stead, the Duke of Norfolk, the Bishop of Shrewsbury and the Bishop of Aberdeen. Each said the same thing: 'I have this morning received a letter from Lord Charles Beresford expressing his interest in my invention for *submarine photography* & inviting me to go to see him at Chatham July 10th about it. It is an absolute necessity that I should be financially backed up before I can do this. Can you do anything?' With each letter he enclosed a self-addressed, stamped envelope. None was returned to him.

The frustrations of his work in this one field were rewarded. In 1895 the British Admiralty added to their files the fact that Frederick William Rolfe invented submarine photography.

The few people who knew him well at Aberdeen could later comment on his personality. One was a doctor. He found Rolfe a good companion and a pleasant talker, but in his opinion as a doctor Rolfe was not a normal man. The second spoke of his industry, stating that he was a genius at doing useless things. The third person was willing at any time to pay his single fare back to London.

The incidents of his life were both pathetic and humorous. The fact that he had a roof over his head did not prevent him from having hungry days. In one letter he reported his condition, saying that he had 'eaten nothing but four biscuits since Friday last (Sunday 4 p.m.).' His life must have been summed up in the autobiographical, although untraced, story, 'A Pickle I Have Been In'.

From October 1892 until the following August he lived in Skene Street. The first fortnight's rent was paid when he moved in. But the longer he stayed, the less he earned and the less he had to give to his landlord. After ten months he owed £37 2s. 9½d. One evening the landlord, with the aid of a fellow worker, entered Rolfe's bedroom. He was given ten minutes to dress and leave. When the ten minutes were up, the Aberdeen newspapers later said, 'he seized hold of the iron bedstead and clung for dear life. He was dragged forth, wearing only his "pyjamas", out to the staircase, where he caught hold of the balustrade, and another struggle ensued. Thence he was carried down the long staircase and was shot on to the pavement as he stood, to the wonderment of the passers-by. His clothing was thrown after him, which he ultimately donned—that was the last of [Rolfe] in that particular locality.'

The Bishop of Aberdeen provided enough money for a meal and induced the Poor Sisters of Nazareth to shelter him for one night. Reduced to 'sleeping in the street and living on bits of bread,' he called at the Royal Infirmary to see Dr. Thompson, one of the Residents. He asked to be certified to enable him to enter the Asylum as a voluntary patient. He would at least be given food and lodging if he were an inmate. But the doctor's reply was that he could not do so without evidence of insanity. He told Rolfe to go out and 'qualify' and then return. The Association for the Improving of the Conditions of the Poor in Aberdeen came next. They assisted him. The sums of money given him totalled £5 19s. od. If the Aberdeen newspapers are to be believed, these sums were distributed over a period of sixteen weeks—with a weekly average of 7s. 8d.

This meagre figure is not surprising in the light of the facts of the day. The city was suffering from dire unemployment, resulting from a depression of the early 1890s. In the winter of 1892-3 almost 1,500 people were without jobs. The majority of this number turned to the Poor Association. It was not fully aware of the tremendous role it was called upon to play. It did not realize the extent of distress in the city and one newspaper assailed it for 'almsgiving'. Rolfe's case was merely one of hundreds. But his appeal was different in that he asked support not for himself but for his work. The Association's Secretary, George Milne, 'submitted for consideration the case of Frederick Wm. Rolfe who desired to be assisted in his efforts to utilize his inventions of colour photography, Flash Light Photography & Co., either by providing him with the means of supplying specimens required for the various directions, or by purchase of pictures painted by himself so as to place the means of self-help at his disposal. The Secretary stated what steps he had taken to demonstrate the success or otherwise of the coloured photography and Flash Light Photography, but that the trials had not been successful. The Committee while approving of what the Secretary had done for him hitherto, was unable to comply with Mr. Rolfe's request or to offer any suggestion in the circumstance.' This concluded the relationship between the Poor Association and Rolfe on 20 September 1893.

His next home was a sandhill.

Progress and Poverty would be an excellent title for a biography of Frederick William Rolfe. His progress did not lift him from the poverty haunting him throughout his life. But, however apt this title might have been for the subject, it already had been used for a book written in San Francisco and published in 1860. This one book, in an indirect way, was responsible for Rolfe's genius expressing itself through literature. He had no doubt heard of it, but it seems unlikely that he had ever read it. Henry George, its author, dedicated it to the people for whom he wrote it—'to those who, seeing the vice and misery of wealth and privilege, feel the possibility of a higher social state, and would strive for its attainment.' Henry Hyde Champion read George's book and was converted to Socialism by it. The printing press and journalism were the means he employed in striving to attain a higher social state. He, in turn, 'converted' Rolfe to literature.

The Labour leader had a military and Scottish background. The same age as Rolfe, Champion was fearless, outspoken and politically unorthodox. While in the Royal Artillery he had read George's book. He resigned his commission in 1882 and started his vocation of attempting to correct the wrongs committed against the working class of the day. Setting up the Modern Press, he was the first person to promote the policies of the new Labour movement in print. In 1884 he began the first British Socialist newspaper, *Justice*, aided by Edward Carpenter's money. A Socialist monthly, *To-day*, followed and was the first to print G. B. Shaw's work. It serialized both his *Unsocial Socialist* and *Cashel Byron's Profession*.

The only Socialist organization in England at this time was H. M. Hyndman's party. Champion joined it and soon became the Secretary of the Socialist-Democratic Federation. He dedicated himself to the formation of a more concrete movement by joining new groups, addressing audiences, contributing to periodicals and organizing demonstrations for the unemployed. He was the *bête noire* of a section of sincere fanatics who fondly hoped to die on the barricades, like the heroes of the Paris Commune, of an impossible English Revolution or go to the gallows chanting some Socialist hymn. Though Champion played an important part in establishing the Fabian Society, the S.D.F. received his first considerations. But his manner and suspected Tory leanings were fatal. On 6 November 1888 he was expelled from the S.D.F. In a day when a man must be on one side or another, Champion was that anomaly, a 'Tory-Socialist'.

The years 1887-90 were his most successful. He had begun to build a Socialist party in England. He kept the unemployed foremost in his thoughts and preached the Eight-Hour Work Day. At twenty-eight he was an important political leader.

Concentrating on parliamentary by-elections, he solicited funds to start both Keir Hardie and John Burns on their political careers. Most of the money came from a soap manufacturer who wished to remain anonymous. Secrecy at the time was synonymous with betrayal of the cause and Hardie refused further financial help from Champion. He was eyed with suspicion and the funds he gathered were labelled 'Tory gold'. In this one connection, Rolfe came closer to wealth than at any other time in his life. The Aberdeen Labour party members suspected that the eccentric Baron Corvo supplied Champion with his funds.

The Socialist had gone to Australia in 1890-1 and his reputation suffered drastically. Suspicions against him were enhanced when he publicly predicted a strikers' defeat among the Australian shearers. Back in London he was assistant editor of the *Nineteenth Century*. By 1893 he had moved to Aberdeen. Here he was on better terms with the local party leaders. He began another newspaper, but his outspokenness and impulsive acts had made him a joke in the eyes of other members by the end of 1893. Broken in health, he made his last public appearance at Liverpool before he sailed for Australia early in 1894.

He was away in September 1893 attending the Trades Union Congress at Belfast when Rolfe called at his apartments, 255 Union Street, on a chilly evening. The Frederick Rolfe of his early period at Aberdeen had once more become Baron Corvo. With the re-adoption of this title his fortunes began to rise. The Labourist's co-worker had just sat down to a tea of smoked haddock, scones, toast and butter. When Rolfe discovered Champion was not present, he turned to leave. He did not wish to transact business with an 'underling'. The 'underling' was fascinated by the guest's weird appearance. His garments sparkled in the lamplight. In a cultured voice he introduced himself, bowing and flourishing a sombrero-type hat. He wore glasses with huge rims. A faded black cape hid his jacket and trousers, which were a mass of tears and patches held together by multitudes of pins, meticulously interlaced. He wore sandals and carried a camera and a bag containing all of his belongings. A sand dune was his present home, an hour and a half's walk from Aberdeen, with access to it only during low tides.

The 'underling' persuaded Rolfe to stay for tea. But Rolfe agreed to this only if the fish were removed. Fish, he explained, affected him and he had a special dispensation from the pope to eat meat on fast days, even on Good Friday. The haddock was replaced with eggs and bacon, 'almost my favourite dish'.

When Champion returned, Rolfe was introduced to him. The two personalities instantly complemented each other. The baron was tactfully asked to evacuate his sandhill and move into the Union Street lodgings. Champion had a profound instinct for evaluating people. To assist Rolfe, he did not in any way hint at charity. He offered the baron the position of his secretary and gave him nominal work on his newspaper.

The time the two were together was short but full. As soon as they met, Rolfe must have sensed Champion's dynamic influence—one that was to remain with him for the rest of his life. Henry Hyde Champion probably was the one man who moulded Rolfe into the literary personality he later became. Until 1890 Rolfe had been an aspiring cleric and poet. He then attempted to live by painting and photography. In each profession he knew others had succeeded and he tried to emulate their fame and fortune. The one thing lacking in his literary efforts up to this point was the stamp of individuality. Association with Champion changed this. Just to study one of the Socialist's periodicals, the *Aberdeen Standard*, is to see the man himself. It is attractively written, showing signs of his intellectual dominance and containing scathing references to prominent Liberals. Yet it was less the organ of the Aberdeen Independent Labour Party than of Champion himself. The paper contained his thoughts, the thoughts of a political outcast, the most hated and distrusted man in the ranks of the advanced politics of the days. He had made political enemies, but he had lost no self-respect. Adversity only inflamed his powers. Working as closely as they did, Rolfe saw the way in which the other operated. Champion was one man against the world, as was Rolfe. Yet the baron's myopic eyes could see things only in one light. Champion worked for a universal cause, embracing all men. Rolfe's future work was to be solely the claiming of his own personal rights.

'The Architecture of Aberdeen' was the only piece in the *Standard* signed by 'Corvo'. Another article written by Rolfe demonstrates his unworldly attitude to the needs of the day. Entitled 'A New Local Industry,' he suggests that the unemployed of the city turn to something new for their income. They can become, he said, artists' models. The fantasy of such an idea was not beyond his serious proposal. But the article brings into print for the first time the name of his Toto. Describing the means used to identify models, Rolfe says that a register is kept with names, addresses and best features noted in it. Four examples are given. Three are:

Yvette Guilbert, aged 23, head, golden hair, hands, 75 Rue MacMahon.

Toto Menichini, age 15, figure or costume, curly hair, 15 Piazza di Spagna.

John O'Donovan, age 32, figure or costume, priest's face, 55 Little Gum Street.

This is also the first appearance of 'O'Donovan' or a variation. He was later to speak of himself as John Donavan in *The Holy-well Record* story, 'The Man From Texas'. Rolfe's curious translation of names is also seen here for the first time. A constant reader of *The Tablet,* he was well aware that its publisher was James Donovan and that it was published in Wellington Street, London.

(One of many literary coincidences occurred at this time. The *Standard* article appeared on 9 December 1893. In the January 1894 number of *The Bohemian Magazine* an article was printed on artists' models. Each spoke of the registers of models, but stressed the fact that models should visit studios. The wage was the same in each. Instead of giving a printed example of models, *The Bohemian* used illustrations. They were not by Rolfe, of course, but two showed 'A Fin de Siècle Model' and 'An Italian Model'. The 'Art Centres' of the *Standard* were London, Antwerp, Paris or Rome. In *The Bohemian* the model 'hails from Damascus to New York, from Camden Town to Fulham.' Until he was seventeen, Rolfe lived in Camden Town and during the 1886-7 winter he stayed in London on the edge of Fulham. 'In the first place, the model is as indispensable to the artist as the Thesaurus to the journalist,' said *The Bohemian* in its article signed 'Amateur'.)

The Labour leader appreciated Rolfe and his work. The colour photography had advanced to the stage of near-perfection. Without the use of foreign pigments or coloured lenses, Rolfe was able to produce vivid blues and greens in his prints. Bright reds and yellows were at times washy and flecked with mauve. Even so, the results were marvellous for his day. Champion tried to interest people in this work, but without success. Rolfe's insufferable vanity and rudeness made him impossible in any business dealings.

In their many conversations, Champion vividly impressed upon Rolfe the wrongs committed by the economic and industrial society of the day against the working man. The extraordinary mentality which produced the short article on artists' models and, later, *Hadrian the Seventh* saw a solution. Few rays of practicability ever filtered into the maze of abstract reasoning and intention in Rolfe's mind. The problem could come to a simple, if fantastic, end, he said, in an amalgamation of Leo XIII's epic-making Encyclical on Labour and Socialism and the tenets of *Das Kapital*. This, Rolfe said with all serious intent, could easily be brought up to date and a New Message of Redemption be launched in the form of an encyclical as soon as he achieved his ambition and became Hadrian VII.

Leo's decree already had inspired one 'solution', but not the one emanating from Rolfe's mind. Professor Pedrazzini of the University of Fribourg was the actual author of Leo's *Rerum Novarum* ('On the Conditions of Labour'—called 'the Magna Charta of the working man'). It appeared on 15 May 1891 and was published to promote the Church's decision 'in a democratic age to seek popular in place of princely support,' wishing to establish 'a kind of truce of God in the industrial world, all towards a new organization of society based upon some conception of equality.' To assure its place of recognition in the changing course of social and economic events, the Catholic Church issued this statement to combat any onslaught of new thinking upon members of its fold. The great enemy of 'On the Conditions of Labour' was not Marx but the American author of *Progress and Poverty*. The encyclical proposed by Corvo was not in Henry George's mind when he wrote his reply to the

Vatican, *The Conditions of Labour, an Open Letter to Pope Leo XIII*. George appreciated 'the many wholesome truths' in *Rerum Novarum*, but vigorously stated that the encyclical 'gives the gospel to the labourers and the earth to the landlords.' Every precaution was taken in the publication of George's answer. The pope received the first proof, the first American edition and a handsome copy of the Italian edition. There was, of course, no reply from the Vatican to George's *Letter*. But American Catholics took exception to it. Archbishop Corrigan proclaimed 'that all Catholics are bound by the Encyclical as well as by a well established doctrine of Holy Writ.' In a letter George bitterly complained, thinking that 'Catholic priests seem so thoroughly bulldozed that they are afraid to openly deny this teaching. I cannot but despise and hope for the downfall of a hierarchy that teaches so slavish a doctrine [and I] wish that the spirituality of the Church could in some way be separated from its political and corrupt machine, which turns into merchandise the efforts and sacrifices of men and women who are really God's servants.'

George's *Open Letter* did not coincide with any of the theoretically abstract ideas Rolfe formulated from his discussions with Champion. Yet George's personal opinions perhaps were not unlike Rolfe's, each being a solitary individual pitted against the vast structure of the Roman Church.

Rolfe and Champion met, worked and lived together as equals. The respect and debt owed to the Socialist was never forgotten. On 25 July 1897 Rolfe wrote to John Lane: 'I havent spoken to an intelligent creature since Feb. 22nd 1894!'

H. H. Champion sailed on the *Orient* from England to Melbourne on 23 February 1894.

6

Also, it was remembered that a certain Comrade Dymoke, the only capable fighting man ever possessed by socialism, had been sponged upon for fifteen years by socialistic cadgers, sucked dry, ruined, and cast out, a victim of socialistic jealousy and treachery. In the plans laid for a Social Revolution, towards the end of the nineteenth century, that man had been named commander-in-chief. Now he was not available; and his place was vacant: for a military expert rarely errs into the purlieus of socialism.

So, nine years later in *Hadrian*, Rolfe could give the name of Dymoke, the Champion of England, to the man he met in Aberdeen.

The mind of the future author stored away personal knowledge at each place he visited. Before 1890 there was nothing to recall but his conversion and the days of schooling for the priesthood. In Rome he met Toto and the duchess. Cecil Castle and the Gleeson Whites contributed to his fragments of memory. In the Scottish city Rolfe saw the men and the machinery of the new Labour movement. And everything about the working of this new definition of democracy was repulsive to him, with the exception of Champion and his one co-worker.

When he was changing over to Rome for a new life, a social unrest in England was taking place. Stirred by the new world-wide religion of Socialism, labourers demonstrated. Paving stones were thrown through the windows of the Carlton Club, one of the symbols of the English capitalistic class. During the winter of 1886-7 Champion addressed a meeting of working men in London Fields. If the whole propertied class had but one throat, he said, he would cut it without a second thought. In direct contrast, Rolfe had talked about 'that filthy & abhorrent idol of the British public, the British workman.' Coming from a management family and being an artist, Rolfe had no use for the common labourer. In his writings he derided Socialism and unionism. He saw in them a type of people and mentality indicative of some evil. In a strange way, he compared this new doctrine with certain inner functions of the Church. Each had areas to be exposed and cleansed, and each housed men who did not tread the same paths as humanitarians. Because of his understanding nature and intelligence, Champion was placed high in Rolfe's *Hadrian*. This was not so with another man from Aberdeen: the character Jerry Sant in *Hadrian*.

Sant is more than a mere portrait of a man. He embodies all the fears and distrusts Rolfe's mind had collected against unionism and labourers. As an individual character, Sant personifies ruination. In outlining *Hadrian*, Sant's model was picked from the Aberdeen of 1893. He and Mrs. Crowe are the two main background figures in the novel. Each knows something about Hadrian's past. They band together in a plot to destroy him.

Sant's picture is fully drawn in *Hadrian*. '[Sant] had the haggard florid aspect, the red-lidded prominent eyes, the pendulous lip of a sorry sort of man. He stood up and began to speak, sometimes dragging a sandy rag of moustache or fingering shiny conical temples, but generally holding on by the lapels of a short-skirted broad-cloth frock-coat, protruding black-nailed thumbs through the button-holes in a manner acquired during a week in Paris.'

Physically, the word picture can be compared to an 1893 photograph of the actual man elected as a Member of Parliament in the previous year. He had scandalized the House of Commons by wearing the 'short-skirted broad-cloth frock coat' in which he had arrived from Scotland. It was a working man's suit and with it he wore a cap, the first to appear in the Parliament buildings. The 'black-nailed thumbs' refer to his beginnings as a coal miner. The 'week in Paris' took place in 1889, when he attended the Second International Conference in the French city. Even

the colour Rolfe names may not have been unintentional, allud-
ing to 'red-lidded prominent eyes'. When this person was preparing for his third Parliamentary session in 1895 and appealing
for funds to begin a national unemployment agitation, he was
labelled 'a little splotch of red from West Ham'. In *Hadrian*
Rose-Rolfe had worked for Sant's newspaper, the *Social Standard*.
Rolfe combines the *Aberdeen Standard* with *The Labour Leader*,
founded and edited by Champion's rival, the original of Sant.
Speaking of Rose-Rolfe in *Hadrian*, Sant says: 'When I knew
him first he was pals with the traitor Dymoke—.... Don't someone remember I was the one that stopped the traitor's letters
and give information of his treachery? If it hadna have been
for me he would have bought the bally show with his Tory gold.
It was me as put my spoke in his wheel and got him expelled
in time. Well, as I was remarking, when I knew Rose he was
gey thick with Dymoke.'

Champion's expulsion from the S.D.F. was never fully explained to him. But he was suspected of trying to buy the new
Labour Party for his own interests with 'Tory gold'. The opposing
leaders carefully watched his every movement. Letters addressed
by him and sent to the Labour Literature Department in Glasgow were opened. Copies of them were made and sent to the
original of Sant, as well as to the editors of *Justice* and the
Workmen's Times. Sant's original also received advance proofs
of the *Standard*, sent to him by a boy in the printing plant.
If any material in an issue were thought to be a conspiracy
against the masses, it was printed in one of the other Labour
periodicals, damning Champion.

Although all the descriptions of the Jerry Sant in *Hadrian*
apply to Keir Hardie, the two are not entirely identical. Financially supported by Champion at the outset of his political
career, Hardie turned on him in 1893. Believing him to be a
Tory spy, using 'Tory gold', he openly denounced Champion. In
protecting the memory of Champion's personality and cause,
Rolfe picked his last rival for an enemy. At Aberdeen, Rolfe saw
and heard Hardie, but he did not actually know him. Whatever
he learned about him was through Champion or the newspapers
he read. Sant, as Dymoke's enemy in the novel, is only a travesty

of Keir Hardie; yet Rolfe draws the portrait with power and depth. Rolfe was aware of the fact that Hardie was Champion's enemy in 1893. At the end of the novel it is Sant who shoots Hadrian; and this action parallels Hardie's character assassination of Champion in the last year of his political life in England.

On 25 November 1893 Champion left Aberdeen for London. His years of work for Socialism went unrewarded, and he decided to leave England. For three months he was a busy man. He had to settle all of his affairs before the final day, but he did not forget Rolfe. He sent for him and invited him to his house in Kilburn. He intended to introduce him to certain literary people in London, but the pressure of his last days prevented him from doing so. The job was given to a third member of the Kilburn household, a person who was not enthusiastic about Rolfe. When Champion sailed for Australia in February 1894, he left Rolfe 'certain monies to be used for clothes and things ...

I —— £5 —— before he went away
II —— £2 —— from "TODAY"
III —— £3.3.0 —— from the British Weekly
IV —— £10 —— cheque due March 4th
V —— £10 —— cheque due April 15th
VI —— £40-£50 —— proceeds of the book [Champion left the third party] to sell.'

Rolfe regarded these sums as a loan, although he did not see them all. By the end of March he had received only £5 5s. od. The money was actually sent to the third person to be given to him 'from time to time,' thinking this 'would be better for him.' From the first three items, Rolfe realized only four pounds. The third person at the Kilburn household kept Rolfe after the Labour leader left England in February; but in less than a month's time he, too, left—for New York. Corvo was handed the final payment of Champion's money—£1 5s. od. 'to start on my hook.' Nearly all the promised calls and introductions to members of the literary world were unfulfilled. Champion's successor had no time for Rolfe. On his own, Rolfe found a lodging house in Beaufort Street, across from the House of Expiation.

'*Extra Special!*' were the words which rang out in the streets of London from February 13th to 17th. *The Sun* had unmasked Jack the Ripper. 'The Story of Jack the Ripper. Solution of the Great Murder Mystery. His Personality, Career and Fate', its pages screamed. Divided by official conflicts and public opinion, the police had failed to track down this criminal. But *The Sun*'s reporter had 'solved' the case. The 'murderer' was an inmate at Broadmoor, the asylum for the criminally insane. This reporter told the asylum's Medical Supervisor, Dr. Nicholson, that one of his detained patients was Jack the Ripper. His name, as given in the newspaper, was 'W——— K———'. In fact, the suspect's name was Thomas Cutbush, a relatively harmless man of thirty. By an odd twist of fate, his name defined a personal fetish. He followed women and ripped their skirts from behind with a knife. Apprehended, he was sent to Broadmoor, where he was named by *The Sun* as Jack the Ripper.

In one of the very few illustrations of current events appearing in Rolfe's work, Jack the Ripper—and the one 'named' by *The Sun*—is mentioned. In a four-part story in *The Holywell Record*, Geoffrey Lygon (Rolfe), trying to secure a possible position in Fleet Street journalism during 1894, meets 'an Editor, a big Editor.' Lygon is handed cuttings from the morning's newspaper and is asked if he recalls 'that last White-chapel murder'. The cuttings state that the murderer 'turns out to be a mad boy who had just escaped from a lunatic asylum.'

In the story Lygon is offered a job to tutor the ward of a Mrs. Maltravers. The 'dear young boy' is at a 'medical school at Windsor' and the tutor will have to stay there as well. Lygon discovers that the position would rank as 'an Officer of the Asylum'. He refuses the offer which would deprive him of any liberty and wonders how he can rescue the boy from the place. The editor he meets asks him for information about this boy. This child, Lygon explains, 'who, though perfectly sane, is confined in that very asylum [housing *The Sun*'s Whitechapel murderer], consorting with dangerous criminals.' But he says no more. Although he possesses 'a very damning character against this lunatic asylum,' Lygon refuses to reveal his information to Fleet Street.

Parts of this story are based on facts, but it is not as auto-biographically clear as *Hadrian the Seventh*. The lunatic asylum spoken about in the novel reaches close to Rolfe's inmost life. In a moment of dread horror he remembers it. 'Once, when they told me at the hospital that I was on the verge of a nervous collapse,' Rose-Rolfe recalls from the latter part of 1894, 'a Jesuit offered to help me. He would procure my admission to a certain House of Rest, if I would consent to go there. By the Mercy of God I remembered that it was a licensed mad-house, where they imprisoned you by force and tortured you. Fact! There had been a fearful disclosure of their methods in the *P.M.G.* Well: I refused to go. Rather than add that brand to what I had incurred through being a Catholic, I made an effort of will; and contrived to escape that danger: contrived to re-cover my nerves: and I continued my battle.'

This same story, 'Temptation,' recounts Rolfe's life in London after the departure of his two Kilburn hosts. As Geoffrey Lygon, he is facing a world wearing 'a very serious aspect for him just then. For, nine years before, his conversion from high Angli-canism to the Catholic Faith, had blasted his career, deprived him of his relations and friends, and brought ruin, utter and complete ruin upon him.' He has 'the advantage of inherited culture of cultured sires, the training and polish of Oxford and Rome.' He is 'an artist by temperament,' but he 'lacked *technique*, the conventional *technique* of the schools, or the blatant impertinence of the nineteenth-century black and white work. But among two widely-divided classes, the *cognoscenti* and the utterly-cultured, he met with appreciation.' Although these classes are poor, he refuses to degrade his art into a money-grubbing business. 'At rare intervals, people did buy' his occa-sional magazine articles and 'he managed to just live and no more.'

With insufficient food, 'his brain absolutely refused to work at anything requiring consecutive thought. His few remaining goods and chattels went, one after another, to the pawn-shop; and then his clothes followed.' With only 'direfully shabby' clothes to wear, he earns 'a scone or two and a cup of tea a day, by haunting press agencies and picking up odds and ends of work. Fleet Street was like hell to him: the rush, the clamour, the pettifogging sententiousness, the hypocrisy, the dishonourable dealings, were like sword-thrusts to his sensitive soul.' One of these 'odds and ends of work' is gathering information at inquests for a press agency 'which had engaged him for the job at eighteen pence' for each report.

The third party of the Kilburn address wrote to Champion in Australia that Corvo had been sent '5 cheques in care Colles [a literary agent] selling La Vie.' In a letter to this person, Corvo admonished him for doing nothing with 'the Bassi notes ordered by you' and for leaving 'the round of studios unmade; ... the introductions, particular to Jerome anent my Catholic stories....' The only known piece by Corvo printed in 1894 is 'An Unforgetable [sic] Experience' in To-Day. It was then edited by Jerome K. Jerome and it was to contribute to Baron Corvo's exposure in 1898. 'My Catholic stories' may not necessarily mean his Toto stories. 'An Unforgetable Experience' is a Catholic story, dealing with Rolfe's life at the beginning of 1892. The author 'had been expelled from the college where I had been making my studies for the priesthood.' Finding it 'impossible, with my mental constitution, to live out of ecclesiastical atmosphere,' although he spent 1891 as an artist in Christchurch, he 'went to board in a house of priests who were simpatici.' This was the house at Ely Place which Fr. Lockhart opened to young men with no other place to stay in London. The author and Fr. Serafico visit a poor man in Maltravers Alley whose wife had just 'died,' but their suspicions save her from a premature burial. At the story's end, 'you can see Mrs. Flanagan any day you like at the seven o'clock Mass at St. Arabella's [St. Etheldreda's].'

As the decade began Rolfe was still sending poetry to magazines. But none of it was accepted. What stories he wrote also went to editors. The first Toto story was written in June 1891. When the others were composed and how many periodicals saw them are two unanswerable questions. 'About San Pietro and San Paolo' and 'About the Lilies of San Luigi' were printed in the October 1895 number of The Yellow Book. At the time of their appearance Rolfe was no longer in London, but they may have been written here. Rolfe once told (Sir) Harry Luke that it was difficult for him to find publishers for his work at this time. After several vain attempts to attract the attention of Henry Harland, the editor of *The Yellow Book*, an idea came to him. During one of his 'periods of homeless destitution,' he wrote the first set of the stories in one of London's public lavatories, on the paper supplied by the establishment. When relating this story to Luke, Rolfe maintained that it was only by means of its unusual format and appearance that his manuscript at last caught the editor's eye.

For any possible income, Rolfe did not rely solely on literature. In the spring of 1894 he obtained 'from a certain prelate ... a commission for a series of pictures to illustrate a scheme which he had conceived for the confounding of Anglicans. He saw specimens of my handicraft, was satisfied with my ability, provided me with materials for a beginning and a disused skittle-alley for a studio; and, a few weeks later, (I quote his secretary) he altered his mind and determined to put his money in the building of a cathedral.' Hardly more than this brief revelation in *Hadrian* is known of this incident.

The 'certain prelate' was Herbert Henry Joseph Thomas Vaughan, Archbishop of Westminster. Coming from one of the oldest Catholic families in England, founded by William Vaughan in 1605, he was the eldest of thirteen children and born at Courtfield. At the death of Cardinal Manning in January 1892, Vaughan became the new archbishop. Almost immediately he began to carry out his predecessor's plans to build a new cathedral. By May 1894 he had several people pledge themselves for funds. The Duke of Norfolk, to whom Rolfe had written at least one begging letter, was down for £10,000. But Lord Bute had not promised anything as yet. On 29 June 1895 the foundation stone was laid for this 'pea-soup-and-streaky-bacon-coloured caricature of an electric-light station.'

The commissioned 'series of pictures' no doubt were to be in the style of the wall-hangings of Christchurch. How the new cardinal and Rolfe met is unknown. Vaughan often appeared at the Sardinia Street Chapel, connected to Ely Place, and may have heard of him through Fr. Lockhart. At the time of the commission, Rolfe was staying across from the Beaufort Street

House of Expiation. Fr. John S. Vaughan and Fr. Kenelm Vaughan were both resident priests and Cardinal Vaughan's brothers. The House of Expiation was also part of Bishop Patterson's St. Mary's Church. From the early 1870s the Bishop of Emmaus had beatified his church in a way never attempted before, or since. He 'Romanized' it by introducing paintings. His interest in paintings and church decoration may have influenced Vaughan to seek out Rolfe's work. Ironically, these artistic decorations of Patterson's were not lasting. On his death in 1902, his successor replaced them with his own ideas.

The recording angels in the halls of purgatory read the full account of Rolfe's life, more complete than any earthly document which survives. The enigmatic year of 1894 can only be pieced together in some way from Rolfe's own words, and most of these appear in *Hadrian*.

It wasn't that I *couldn't* stop working: but that I *wouldn't*. The fact is that I long, I burn, I yearn, I thirst, I most earnestly desire to do absolutely nothing. I am so tired. I have such a genius for elaborate repose. But convention always alleges idleness or drunkenness, or lechery, or luxury, to be the causa causans of scoundrelism and of poverty. That's a specimen of the 'Eidola Specus,' the systematizing spirit which damns half the world. People never stop to think that there may be other causes—that men of parts become rakes, or scoundrels, or paupers, for lack of opportunity to live decently and cleanly.... I courted semi-starvation and starvation. I scrupulously avoided drink, I hardly ever spoke civilly to a woman; and I laboured like a driven slave. No: I never was idle. But I was a most abject fool. I used to think that this diligent ascetic life eventually would pay me best. I made the mistake of omitting to give its due importance to the word 'own' in the adage 'Virtue is its own reward.' I had no other reward, except my unwilling cultivated but altogether undeniable virtue.... I slaved as a professional photographer, making (from French prints) a set of negatives for lantern-slides of the Holy Land which were advertised as being 'from original negatives'.... I did journalism, reported inquests for eighteen pence. I wrote for magazines. . . . I invented a score of things. . . . I was very ashamed to ask for help to make my invention profitable: but I was quite honest—generous: I always offered a share in the profits—always. I did not ask for, and I did not expect, something for nothing. I had done so much; and I wanted so little: but I did want that little,— for my creditors,—for giving ease to some slaves of my acquaintance. I was a fool, a sanguine ignorant abject fool! I never learned by experience. I still kept on. A haggard shabby shy priestly-visaged individual, such as I was, could not hope to win the confidence of men who daily were approached by splendid plausible cadgers. My requests were too diffident, too modest. I made the mistake of appealing to brains rather than to bowels, to reason rather than to sentiment. I wanted hundreds, or thousands—say two: others wanted and got tens and hundreds of thousands.

'I don't know how I kept alive until I got my next commission,' *Hadrian* continues. 'I only remember that I endured the frightful winter of 1894-5 in light summer clothes unchanged. But I did not die; and, by odds and ends of work, I managed to recover a great deal of my lost ground.' Having nothing by the end of 1894, Rolfe's naïve faith persisted in keeping him alive. In another story he tells of the beginning of this winter. 'During a three months engagement with an Association, formed for the purpose of providing every child who was a member, with a fair sum of money on attaining the age of 21, with which to start business life in real earnest,' Rolfe had spent every penny 'of his money in developing the work of the Association. His first quarter's remittance was due and was applied for, but instead of receiving a cheque he had notice to say the Association was bankrupt, and there was no hope whatever of getting a penny. Pawnshops had to be visited, while trying to obtain work. For six weeks he did not know what a real meal was. Many nights had to be spent in the open air, in the month of November. For four successive days and nights he was without food or lodging. A crust of bread was discovered on the pavement, very muddy but exceedingly welcome. It kept body and soul together. The following day a shilling borrowed on an umbrella, the only article of any value which remained, seemed like untold wealth. The feast that followed lingers in the mind and will never be effaced.'

But before November was over, Rolfe remembered three people.

Rolfe wished once more to contact Bute. But he did so through two other people. Edward Bellasis was a man once met at Ely Place. This Catholic layman was a benefactor of St. Etheldreda's and worked with Fr. Lockhart in beautifying the small church. Being so close to Rolfe in London, perhaps a letter from Bellasis would more convincingly promote the assistance he was after. Bellasis, the Lancaster Herald, knew Bute, because of his interests in heraldry, religion and Scottish history. The two had corresponded on these subjects and Bellasis had written for Bute's *Scottish Review*. But he did not write directly to Bute. Following Rolfe's instructions, his letter went to Fr. Parkinson, the person who had received Rolfe into the Church. Rolfe 'has talent,' Bellasis began his letter, '& it seems so sad to see him in such a strait. I know of him a little; & he may be a little difficult to understand, but he seems very gentlemanly & very willing to work. For 8 or 9 years his career would appear to have been very chequered, & this must naturally affect his mind in certain ways, & account for a sort of angularity & sharpness at times. It may not be an easy case,' the letter ended.

In a second letter Bellasis wished Fr. Parkinson to ask Bute about purchasing something from Rolfe rather than ask for an outright gift for the unfortunate man. The subject of his letter, Bellasis continued, 'had consulted a specialist of great repute here; & he is *unfit* for new work; the strain has been too much on him; & it is my impression that he is at the last extremity of nervous prostration, with, however, considerable recuperative powers. Whatever his defects, he seems to be a sufferer for the Faith. He has decided talent, & I think your Reverence might with propriety ask Lord Bute to take (say) 3 of the pictures, which run in sets; while briefly explaining the excellent qualities of our poor young houseless friend running to waste; & how the fault is not his own in reality.'

The aging Fr. Parkinson was no longer at Oxford. From Bury St. Edmunds he sent his letter to Bute. 'The first fact in connexion with' this man's case, he wrote, 'is that he is starving. He has devoted himself to art & from a testimonial that I have received as to his knowledge of photography he has a fair prospect before him as soon as he can undertake any work. He seems even capable of opening up a new line of the business that carries a fair promise with it. Unfortunately a specialist of repute has pronounced that he is unfit for work.... In this case, absolute rest is required for a time. A friend of his in Australia [Champion] has offered him a home till he can meet with work; but the difficulty in the way of his acceptance of the offer is passage money. And, again, possibly any money that could be raised for him might be better spent ... to go to the South Coast for a time & then use what may be left for furthering his plans. Mr Rolfe was most anxious that I should mention a set of pictures for lantern work to your Lordship, in the hope that you might be tempted to take them.... I will only add that, though I have seen nothing of him for years, from all I hear he has kept himself straight & steadfast in the faith, & from what Mr Bellasis says, he suffered at the hands of his family because of steadfastness.'

Rolfe's financial salvation could never have come from a few lantern slides. An underlying purpose of his indirect request to Bute may have been a hopeful expectation of generous assistance. If so, he was to be disappointed. Lord Bute 'had given him a bonus of £100 when he left Oban & he is not a person' Bute 'wishes to have anything more to do with.'

Neither the fierce winter of 1894-5 nor utter privation ended Rolfe's existence. The 'considerable recuperative powers' and an indomitable perseverance fed his spirit from day to day. If the fall of each sparrow be recorded in heaven, then the footsteps of a human will be watched most carefully. The swelling of Rolfe's pride made him far more important than any of God's lower creatures. Unexpected relief welcomed him in his darkest hour of need.

On the streets of London he met Champion's co-worker from Aberdeen. This meeting was much the same as the first. The other man had to rescue Rolfe from destitution. The man from Aberdeen was not alone, but he engaged Rolfe in friendly talk. Everything was again the same. Rolfe was homeless; he was shabbily dressed; and he carried with him all that he possessed. Knowing of his photographic work, the friend asked Rolfe if he had been able to continue his work. To answer this question, Rolfe showed him some remarkable photographs of the Thames Embankment and of Electric Avenue, Brixton, by night. They were shown to the third person, who thought they were extremely impressive and could be used for advertising purposes. An appointment was made for Rolfe to call at the other's office for a further discussion of the idea. On this night Rolfe refused an invitation to dinner, but he did accept a pound. At the appointed time the next morning he was in the other person's office, looking white with cold. His explanation for his appearance was simple enough, he said. When he had left the other two, he walked up Wardour Street and noticed an antique pipe in a window. He went in and bought it. Once having it, he needed tobacco and matches. The change he gave to a beggar. With no money left, he spent the freezing night on Hampstead Heath. To forget the cold, he concentrated on the study of the moonlight effects on the snow. The advertising scheme went no further. It was impossible to talk business with him.

But the Aberdeen friend introduced him to another person. A fabric mercers' establishment had opened in London in 1883 and its owner invited Rolfe to his country house, Brathay Hall, Ambleside, about forty miles north of Lancaster. Rolfe was to continue his colour experiments here, but his stay was not long. *Hadrian* condenses the episode into a few lines:

A cotton-waste merchant could not risk fifteen-hundred on my work, although he liked me personally and said that he believed in the value of my inventions: but, at the same time, he cheerfully lost twelve-thousand in a scheme for 'ventilated boots.' I myself was wearing ventilated boots, then: but the ventilated-boot man wore resplendent patent leather.

7

'What impulse, or indeed what conveyance,' took Rolfe to North Wales could not be answered by A. J. A. Symons. As in the life of any wanderer, it was a combination of chance and design.

Rolfe had learned of Holywell in the late 1880s, through his visits to the Bishop of Emmaus' Chelsea church. An old chapel designed by Edward Pugin had been removed bodily to the new St. Mary's Church. For its 1860 opening, John Francis Bentley was invited to create interior architectural decorations. He designed the new High Altar and the pulpit for the chapel and, in a prominent spot near the entrance, placed a statue of St. Winefride of Holywell.

It may have been during December 1894 that Rolfe went to Ambleside, about one hundred miles north of Chester. He was a guest here only until the first of the new year. Leaving the comforts of Brathay Hall behind him, he was reluctant to travel all the way to London, even if he had the fare; so that his next retreat, if only temporary, was to be with an intermittent friend. John Nicholson was teaching at the Arnold House School and played host to the homeless schoolmaster of another day. His resources were limited, but his generous nature may also have been checked by a completely different reason. Their friendship was still strained because of the 'St. William' poem in his book of 1892. So, Rolfe was off for Pantasaph between January and February 1895 to ask the Capuchins for shelter.

Both Pantasaph and Holywell are only about fifteen miles west of Chester, and he had heard of the Capuchins in Wales in relation to Wilfrid Meynell. For reasons of body, mind and soul, the London editor had sent Francis Thompson to this place in 1892.

The Pantasaph Capuchins 'have a little hill behind their convent, with the *Via Crucis* along a winding path; and at the summit, a large Calvary of bronze, which, they pretend, can be seen from a distance of fifteen miles.' Here he solicited food and lodging. He was willing to pay for anything given him. The bronze crucifix was 'rotting away,' the damp air cutting into its unprotected surface with a grey-green rust. He explained this to Fr. Sebastian, the Superior, asking to be allowed to repair the damage. This would be his payment for staying with the friars. The Superior wanted Rolfe to give him 'the secrets of his handicraft as a free gift.' There was no need for an outsider to undertake repairs, the Superior explained, once the friars knew the necessary ingredients. Rolfe complied. He wrote out the formula and handed it to the friar. But he did not lose his opportunity to stay and clean the crucifix. The formula had been written in Greek, in archaic terms known only to himself.

Although Francis Thompson was at Pantasaph at this time, neither he nor Rolfe ever mentioned the other in any writing. The poet had come in 1892, living at first in Bishop's House at the monastery gate. Before he left in 1896 he had been staying in a cottage behind the monastery. In a community as small as this it seems unlikely that they never even heard of one another. Yet no record exists of any meeting at Pantasaph, if there were one, between Thompson and Rolfe. The poet was a sincere Catholic and he also was grateful for the benefits afforded him by the Capuchins. For their hospitality towards Rolfe, they were used as uncomplimentary models for several of his Toto stories.

'On the hill above Holywell', Rolfe stayed with the friars 'for two or three months previous' to his coming to the home of St. Winefride's Holy Well.

The theory of design for his journey to Holywell is as strong as the one of chance. It has been stated elsewhere that he read 'a Kingsley novel instead of the edifying book provided by his spiritual director.' Rolfe did read at least one thing 'spiritual' at Pantasaph and this was the Catholic periodical, *The Month*.

'The year 1894 will probably be long remarkable in the history of the little Welsh town of Holywell,' began an article in the February 1895 issue. 'Yet, to St. Winefride's Well, large type and a prominent place have frequently been accorded in the columns of leading English newspapers [the *Pall Mall Gazette*, the *St. James Budget*, the *Daily Graphic*, the *Lancet*] during the past year [reporting] the supernatural character of the incidents [of healing] which have taken place at Holywell,' it continued. 'There is perhaps no better representative in England to-day of what is styled as advanced journalism, no editor of a review gifted with keener and quicker discernment of the tendency of public tastes, than Mr. Stead,' *The Month* introduced its chief supporter in this case and quoted him. 'As Mr. Stead truly says ' "Lourdes is but of yesterday, whereas St. Winefride is older than the British Constitution, and centuries older than Canterbury Cathedral." ' The article also reported that Holywell was observing 'a steady growth ... in the respect with which the events at the Welsh shrine have been discussed throughout the last six months.' And the single person responsible for this campaign of promotion was Fr. Charles Sidney de Vere Beauclerk, S.J.—the person Rolfe next saw with a proposal to benefit himself and the Catholic church at Holywell.

The pilgrimages to St. Winefride's Shrine link modern Wales through its mediaeval past with the Ages of the Saints and the founding of the Welsh nation. In the seventh century Gwenfrewi lived in Tegeingl (Flintshire), according to common legend. Her uncle was St. Beuno and she had her parents' consent to become a nun. One Sunday, while her parents were at Mass, she was visited by Caradoc, son of a prince living at Penarlag (Harwarden). Finding the girl alone, he tried to seduce her. Escaping from the house, she fled towards the church. Enraged by her action, he followed her, sword in hand. As she reached the threshold of the church, he cut her head from her body. When the head touched the ground, a fountain of water gushed forth, flowing to this day. Seeing the poor body of his niece, St. Beuno approached Caradoc and called upon God to punish the murderer. The prince's son was struck dead. The uncle then prayed to God on Gwenfrewi's behalf and she rose, head in place, and lived the rest of her natural life as a nun. She became St. Winefride and the flowing fountain is her Holy Well, the place of miracles.

The Holy Well is the only place of pilgrimage in Britain that survived the Reformation. The small Welsh town prospered under the guidance of Fr. Beauclerk. Rector of the local Catholic church, he built buildings in the town and introduced new means of education. For a number of years he leased the Well from the district council and combined the pilgrimages with daily services in his church. 'Attracted by the fact that the Shrine was booming,' Rolfe went to the Jesuit priest to solicit work. He entered the town about Easter, April 14th, 1895. But it was neither Frederick William Rolfe nor Baron Corvo who walked from Pantasaph to Holywell. It was Frederick Austin.

To those who noticed him, Austin-Rolfe's face 'was a pale smooth oval face, tanned to the colour of honey. It had the very high brow of a student & thinker, crowned by short hair of a reddish chestnut slightly silvered. The nose was daring—straight, with sensitive nostrils. The mouth also was straight—thin & firm & recondite as to the upper lip, with a tinge of gentle tenderness lurking in the slightly fuller modelling of the lower. The eyes were dark-brown & rather long, limpidly bright in the pupils, & the white of a most wonderfully pure candor.... The eyebrows were darker brown, authoritively drawn across the brow from temple to temple. The chin was the chin of a Jesuitical machiavellian autocrat, like (say) Caesar Augustus, cloven & fine & compact. As for the expression—I hardly know what to say.... There was vivid serenity, gentleness & ruthless ferocity, quiet fastidious disdain, immense knowledge of good & evil, fancy, wistfulness, extreme sensibility & ineffable indifference, indomitable tenacity, reserve, courage, enormous & inexhaustible force, all deliberately matured & mastered & governed by grave simple self-control. In short, it was the face of a man who has attained what Aristoteles quite luminously (& quite untranslateably) calls *Kyria Arete*.' This was the man who was to make his home in Holywell for the next four years.

Rolfe proposed to paint wall-hangings for Fr. Beauclerk's church. The scheme was agreeable to the Jesuit, and he housed the newly arrived artist with a local landlady, gave him space and materials and blessed them before the work began. Austin was fortunate. With little exertion he had found a patron and security for the immediate future. Part of the school was turned over to him for a studio. Here he painted and continued his experiments in colour photography.

The town and his work pleased him. He was not restricted to church painting alone. If other work were offered, he was free to attend to it; and no time limit had been placed on the wall-hangings or banners. When a satisfactory design was created, he would spend endless hours on the banner, tying cloths soaked in water and vinegar around his head to prevent exhaustion.

Working in the schoolroom, he met his first Holywell friend, apart from Fr. Beauclerk. Leo Schwarz was about fourteen. A member of a large family and a crowded household, little Leo came to the school building to do his homework. Meeting 'Mister Austin' was a grand experience. He carried and fetched for the Catholic artist. In return, Rolfe helped him with his homework. He taught Leo the elements of drawing and photography; and he spun countless tales of enchantment to the small boy of the small town.

Leo's grandfather was an optician, who had left Germany to settle in Holywell. His father and he were to follow the same profession. But it was not the only business in Holywell bearing the Schwarz name. During Rolfe's first days, two Misses Schwarz opened a confectioners' shop next to the optician business, and for them he produced an advertising drawing. His design showed a man putting up a placard giving the name of the shop, and this was also printed on the bags for carrying away cakes and pastry.

Rolfe's second friend was John Holden. Older than Leo, Holden had never known a child's existence. He had been brought up in a strict Catholic school and from his earliest years he had had to wear adult garments. So, the carefree days of childhood escaped him, in dress, manner and nature. He was a brilliant scholar, but he lacked the necessary experience to participate in the outside world. Illness finally caused him to leave school. After his recovery, he went to Holywell for a rest.

Here he visited his aunt, Mrs. Richardson of The Greyhound, who was Rolfe's landlady. The town seemed small and dull, but knowing Rolfe—by any of his names—made Holywell livelier.

Holden was immediately invited to the studio. The older man's 'manner was impressive'. Recalling their first meeting, Holden said that 'he walked and spoke with great deliberation, and seemed to be unaware of the existence of those about him. (Later I told him he reminded me of a priest returning to the sacristy after he had celebrated mass.) The immobile mouth and the extremely powerful glasses, the glint of which hid his eyes, made his face almost inscrutable. Most people went in awe of him. My aunt's servants were terrified.' The young man himself found Austin 'less repellent' after his first visit to the studio. But he always treated the other with a certain reserve.

Rolfe was widely known in Holywell, but only as a man of mystery. He confided in Holden and admitted that Austin was not his real name. He was actually Baron Corvo, related to several illustrious Italian families. He was almost blatant in reciting this noble history, but any further hints about his real origin were vague. Holden once mentioned reading about the German Kaiser and Rolfe exclaimed: 'So my godfather has been at it again, has he?'

More and more the artist had been thinking about literature. Meeting Holden was the opportunity of a lifetime. The young man was just the person he had 'been waiting for' and he proposed a literary partnership. For their *nom-de-guerre* Rolfe suggested John Blount. Rolfe's first Toto stories had just been accepted by *The Yellow Book*. 'That's our beginning,' he said. A number of Holden's books were moved to the studio and the two spent the evenings reading and discussing literature. As the banners progressed, Rolfe and Holden exchanged ideas for stories. 'Corvo' would be the signature for the better ones and 'Blount' for the others.

Rolfe's self-control when he was in a rage was Holden's despair. 'One Sunday afternoon after a little skirmish,' the younger man later recalled, 'we both sat reading. The door and windows were closed, and the stove was burning full blast. I opened the door and he shut it. I opened a window and he shut it. I shut the door of the stove to diminish the draught and he opened it. (Neither of us had spoken.) I felt that I was losing, and I was fast losing my self-control. What could I do next? My eye fell upon a jar of water in which the brushes were soaked. I picked it up, and, lifting up the lid of the stove, poured the contents over the red-hot cinders. There was an explosion and I was half-blinded by the steam and ashes. When I recovered my sight, I looked at [Rolfe]. He hadn't budged. He only interrupted his reading from time to time to blow the ashes off his book. I had lost again. To keep up appearances I read on for another half-hour, but I went home with murder in my heart.'

These quarrels between the two lasted only until their fury was spent. Austin possessed an inexhaustible craving for letter-writing. He would never speak a word if he could write it. 'He seized upon every opportunity for writing a letter,' Holden said, 'and every letter, whether to a publisher or to a cobbler, was written with the same care. When closing a letter to some insignificant person about the veriest trifle, he would say "And that's literature, Giovanni, that's literature." I have never seen him happier than when he had to answer an unpleasant letter.'

While the two were living under the same roof, a number of virulent letters passed between them from time to time. An extremely sharp one was sent to Holden on one occasion. Thinking he would have the last, and sharper, word, he answered it. Within fifteen minutes a reply arrived: 'Gorgeous! Drop whatever you are doing and come round at once. I've a bottle of nectar awaiting you.' Holden went and found Rolfe 'prancing about the room, my letter in his hand.' Rolfe welcomed him with tobacco for his pipe and a glass of Chartreuse, a present from Fr. Beauclerk. He read the last letter aloud and said, 'It's splendid, Giovanni. I couldn't have done much better myself.' He 'really was delighted. We had a jolly evening.'

In time Holden became aware of Rolfe's 'insatiable . . . appetite for gossip' and his singular attitudes towards women. To him they were 'superfluous'. 'What you can see to admire in the female form I don't know. All those curves and protuberances that seem to fascinate you only go to show what nature intended her for—all that she's fit for—breeding.' Yet, Holden added,

Rolfe would tell him of his adventures at Manchester or Rhyl. At the beginning of a banner Rolfe would leave Holywell for 'inspiration'. At Rhyl he would have a Turkish bath and lunch and then be wheeled in a bath chair before going to look for a 'chance romance of the street.' Such, at least, were the stories Rolfe told the young man when he returned to paint.

Rolfe's horror of reptiles was verified by Holden in recounting an incident during these days. Rolfe had told him that he had once fallen into a trance after stumbling over a lizard 'and had very nearly been buried alive. (This he worked up into a story ... under the title *How I was Buried Alive*.) ... One Sunday we had taken a walk down to the river, and when we got back we found the house empty, it being church time. I climbed over the yard door and got through the kitchen window, then I opened the house door for [Rolfe] and went upstairs. Suddenly I heard a blood-curdling shriek, and on rushing downstairs I found him in the kitchen, his face as white as chalk, his mouth twitching. He was staring fixedly at something I did not at first see. I followed his gaze, and under the table I saw a little toad. I spoke to him, shouted to him, but he did not answer. I got a chair and pushed him into it, and he sat there for more than an hour quite motionless except for the working of his mouth. When he had recovered enough to stand and walk, I accompanied him to the studio and laid him on his bed. He fell at once into a deep sleep, and when I went round early the next morning to see how he was, I found him still asleep. I didn't wake him, and he slept on till eleven without stirring once. When I questioned him later, he told me he remembered nothing after first seeing the toad.'

In Holywell, Rolfe had lodgings and friends. He was feared and admired, and he had no worries. What little money came to him was spent on himself and his friends—there was never enough for large expenditures. Fr. Beauclerk noticed this and contributed a new suit, one that was to last a long time. It was still Rolfe's only suit when he wrote *Hadrian* in 1903. It was a 'blue suit such as is worn over all by engineers,' the recipient wrote about it in his novel. 'He had an impish predilection for that garb since a cantankerous red-nosed prelate, anxious to sneer at unhaloed poverty, inanely had said that he looked like a Neapolitan.' The 'red-nosed prelate' was none other than the Vicar-Apostolic of Wales, the Rev. Francis Mostyn, the friendly Dr. Talacryn of *Hadrian* and relative of both Holden and Edward Slaughter. The suit was described in more detail in *The Holywell Record*. Fr. Beauclerk 'had a fit of princely generosity, and commissioned the purchase, from a designated slop-shop, of a half-crown blue linen jacket, and two pairs of two-and-eleven-penny trousers of the same sumptuous fabric.' The visiting bishop, Mostyn, saw him on the street and 'asked who was that extraordinary person' who 'looked like a Neapolitan.' But the suit was new and needed.

Fr. Beauclerk's patronage provided him with the primary reason for staying at Holywell. The banners were begun soon after his arrival in the spring of 1895. A year later at least four were done. When the new bronze Sacred Heart statue arrived in the summer of 1896, the procession carrying it to St. Wine-fride's Hall included a 'large banner, representing the arch-angel slaying the red dragon; banner of St. George; new banner of St. Winefred.' Decorating the wall of the platform receiving the statue 'was placed a large new banner, representing St. Wine-fride, and a number of other saints standing in a row. At the top of the banner are the words "Christus Vincit, Christus Regnat, Christus Imperat,' and at the bottom, 'For God, Our Lady, and the Catholic Faith"; on the left hand side are the words, "Jesus, Anglian Converte", and on the right 'Jesus hujus gentis miser-ere".' 'The new Holywell banner of St. David' was completed in the spring of 1897, at the time Rolfe's mind started to rebel against the kindnesses offered him.

Of the banners painted, only five survive, each as fresh in colour and design as they first were before the end of the last century. Yellow-garbed St. Augustine of Canterbury stands with staff and open book in front of a background scene of monks and soldiers. St. Gregory the Great, in white, red and gold, holds a stylus and St. Peter's keys. In the form of a dove within a golden disc, the Holy Ghost is on one side of his head. The people behind are enveloped in a misty blue. Dressed in the same colours, St. George leads a procession of faithful followers. The only banner not portraying a stylised setting is St. Winefride's. The maid is being chased by Caradoc. Vigorous in approach, it is the only one in which the figure proportions are inaccurate. In front of Caradoc, the golden-haired, white-robed St. Winefride is smaller than her pursuer. But the most startling figure is St. Ignatius Loyola. With a scroll and an orange orb, he is all in black and not totally unlike a narrow-bearded Rolfe. Each banner illustration is surrounded by a lettered border, an essential part of the artistic design.

Most of the banners were painted in the schoolroom. Little Leo mixed the paint and Holden assisted with the border lettering. Rolfe, the master artist, at times worked too close to a particular banner to notice any error. The St. George banner is likely to offend any person well-versed in heraldry. The saint is depicted with a sword in one hand and a staff and flag in the other. The flag is divided into four fields. Three are blank. The fourth one, showing the four countries of Britain, is away from the staff. This escaped criticism, probably because no student of heraldry saw it at the time. But the St. Winefride banner did provide a means for provocation. It was completed in a small cottage just north of the town and it was physically damaged. Rolfe placed it outside when he painted the grass and flowers. A gush of wind blew it over and his palette knife went through it. Although this accident was skilfully remedied, something worse occurred. A local joiner by the name of Lloyd came one day to do some work at the cottage. Rolfe had just finished the banner and was excited. He asked the joiner what he thought of it. Lloyd studied the scene of Caradoc chasing Gwenfrewi for a few minutes before he remarked that he never knew Caradoc was left-handed. Never having realized while he was doing it that Caradoc's left hand wields the sword to strike off Gwenfrewi's head, Rolfe was furious. The banner, which had taken so long to paint, was finished. He would not do it over. But he could, in a sense, disclaim it. His work at Holywell was signed for the first time in the form of a raven, but this is less apparent on this particular banner, since the raven is hidden and indistinct, almost part of the castle facade in the background. Instead of being on a prominent niche in a corner, the bird is perched on a distant branch of a tree.

A year after he had first come to Holywell, Rolfe wrote to Fr. Beauclerk one day, thanking him for a letter and several postal orders. He had been elated at the outcome of his own work, but he still strove for a certain goal.

I NEVER SHALL, for the goal goes higher always. I only mean that I have gone up *one* little step. Nor do *I* claim the smallest credit for that. It is the saints who have designed to impart some modicum of their radiance. As I correspond more closely with the graces they impart so much the more beautiful will my work become. The difficulty is for a worldly wretch like me to detach myself entirely. There was a hypnotizer once who could not hypnotize me and from whom I rose from the cataleptic trance solely on account of my strong selfishness.

Nor is it for want of diligence that I fail if continuous work is diligence. But I do not concentrate all the time and so I fail. Faces? Yes. They are only the shadow of what I have seen. And I fail to reach the reality for the reasons of hurry and human respect and worry. And really dear Father Beauclerk my worldly worries are very bad indeed and lately I have felt that I must shriek or burst. Also I have developed a violent and raging temper, blazing out at what I suppose are small annoyances, and overwhelming people with a torrent of scathing and multilingual fury. I make amends for it afterwards but it leaves me weak in mind and body. It's the Mr. Hyde surging up....

I think if I had a clear mind I could do better. Well I *know* that. But perhaps it would be more creditable to do better for all my obstacles! I will try. There's a Retreat at Manresa in Holy Week. I made my first and last one there in 1886.

Understanding the peculiarities of his nature never prevented the violent outbursts. Just before he took a hostile stand against the Jesuit priest, the April 1897 number of *The Holywell Record* reported that 'the new Holywell banner of Saint George the Martyr, Protector of the Kingdom, which will be used during this wonderful year of the Diamond Jubilee of Her Most Gracious Majesty the Queen, combines the spirit of Piety with the spirit of Patriotism.' Such sentiments were soon to be dropped from his letters to Fr. Beauclerk. 'Blessed are those who nought expect, / For they shall not be disappointed.' These words from John Wolcit's 'Ode to Pitt' never formed a part of Rolfe's philosophy. In his mind, the ills of the universe were loosed upon him; he was his sole support, and alone he had to battle against the world. Contentment only meant stagnation. From this mire he had to free himself. So it was that on 20 April 1897 he wrote to Fr. Beauclerk:

Since you so command me, that I should myself demand and put a price upon my work, as tabulated in my statement dated Apr. 8th, 1897, which demand you will submit to the Rev. Fr. Provencial, I would humbly entreat you that you would give me, for my incessant and very painful labours during twenty one months, all that may appear most pleasing to your profound and most discreet judgment. Whatever it may amount to, coming along with your gracious good wishes, it will be held amply liberal; and much more to my satisfaction than by demanding any sum, though I might receive much more than my demand.... I declare that had I to execute such a work for any other patron, I would not do it for fifteen hundred gold sovereigns; and, of a surety, no other man would contemplate, much less be enabled to achieve, such a work. Knowing, however, that, at the rate of the Preston banners, from which mine differ in being absolutely original unique designs, the value of the Holywell banners would be five hundred and sixty pounds, excluding the value of the numerous other pieces,—knowing also that, at the rate of Mr. Hanmer's banner, the value of my work would be eleven hundred and two pounds and ten shillings, and here, also, no account is laid for the other things,—but being, nevertheless your reverence's devoted and loving servitor, I will confess myself content with seven hundred pounds in gold paid straightway; and I will undertake to make an immediate offering to St. Winefride of two-sevenths of this sum, together with the sacrifice of the value of everything else that I have already done in her honour. This, because I am resolved to spend the rest of my life in the service of Saint Winefride and your reverence. And if it should be thought that I have done great things in enduring my life so far, and in producing such work under such conditions in this, my first, what may not your reverence expect in my second attempt for you.... Notwithstanding this, I would rather receive a single six shillings and eightpence at the hands of your reverence, than a whole fortune from any other patron; and am, at the same time, ever worrying Heaven with prayers for your reverence's preservation.

For two years Austin had been housed and fed, in obedience to the verbal contract between painter and priest. But now the valued friendship and patronage of Fr. Beauclerk turned to bitterness in Rolfe's mind, as he demanded payment in hard cash. Fr. Beauclerk told him that he could not give away any such sum named by Rolfe, who retaliated by saying that the Society of Jesus had plenty of money. On May 5th, Bromley & Llewelyn-Jones, solicitors for Rolfe, presented his claim to the priest under the heading 'Without Prejudice'. 'Mr. F. W. Austin Rolfe,' it said, had painted 105 figures at ten guineas a figure or £1,102 10s. od. Fr. Beauclerk had already paid him £120, leaving a balance of £982 10s. od. The claim said that Rolfe was ready to accept £700 'in settlement'. The price set by Rolfe was based on an individual banner. A woman had commissioned one banner from him and had paid him nine pounds for it. There was only one figure on it. The Church, Rolfe then thought, could afford a little more.

'And note the madness of the man!' Fr. Beauclerk later said, in a letter to Symons. 'When I asked him how he calculated up the £1,000 he charged me with? he replied, "I have counted the figures on the banners, which I have painted, and find the number one hundred. I charge them at £10 a head." Now the facts are these. There were some ten banners painted, some a single figure: but he had executed a large banner in which was portrayed a crowd of people in the background. Their heads the size of a thimble!!'

During his years at Holywell, Fr. Beauclerk was responsible for many good actions. With services and in building, he greatly improved the mission, but he may have been a better priest and planner than an accountant. Soon after his departure, his successor was writing letters concerning the matter of money handled by him. 'Fr Beauclerk borrowed £400 from an Madmoisell Degoils at 4% This Lady has sent me a legal letter 18 months ago to return the capital. I did it out of the mission money.' 'Fr Beauclerk had to overdraw the bank during his last 2 years to the amount of £500 each year.' 'Fr. Beauclerk boasted of it, that during the 8 years he was in Holywell, he received £20,000.... Fr J. Gerrard ... & Fr Mich. King ... asked him, how he spent the money & how it was that he left the place in debts? Both told me, he could not give an explanation. Unfortunately the Bishop [of Menevia, Francis Mostyn] got to hear of it & got very exaggerated ideas of the wealth in Holywell.'

The peaceful town of Holywell in 1897 had become entirely antagonistic, Rolfe thought. He had already laid the foundations of enmity and his strategy would now bring about open warfare. His ammunition was the written and printed word. When his bill for almost £1,000 arrived, the rector 'put the case into the hands of a Liverpool lawyer. This man offered Rolfe £50 for himself and £10 for his council; and to my surprise Rolfe accepted it.' He accepted it, but he immediately gave the much-needed money to a local charity.

'He then declared open war. A local magazine had been started by a speculator, named Hockheimer, and Rolfe attached himself to the concern, his writing ability gaining him ready acceptance. He let loose in this publication all his views and grievances. He built up a wildly illusioned tale of my supposed hostility,' Fr. Beauclerk wrote, 'which indeed only began and ended in my refusal to go beyond our first agreement, viz that I would find him in everything essential.'

Before this break with the Catholic priest, an English society had offered to send Rolfe and Holden to the Gobi Desert. Brown paper was tacked up on the walls of the studio and Arabic characters were painted on it to be studied. Rolfe even suggested a third person for the expedition: Leo Schwarz. But, before a decision could be made on this, his parents had to be consulted. They never were, for they already had planned another trip for little Leo. He was packed up and sent off to Glasgow as an apprentice in the profession his grandfather had started in Holywell. He neither saw nor heard from Rolfe again.

The break included Holden. The gossip which Rolfe relished included some facts about Holden's private life, and Rolfe was not now loath to spread them around the town. Harmless as they were, they were private, and the young man was furious to hear that people knew of them. He stopped Rolfe on the street one day and threatened him with assault, which was never carried out. A few days later he left Holywell for good and never saw his literary partner again.

Since June 1896 Rolfe, as Baron Corvo, had been corresponding with the publisher of *The Yellow Book*. The editor had bought his Toto stories, but Rolfe wished to contact the head of the firm. His first letter asked for payment for his two stories which appeared in the April issue. By July 1897 he was telling John Lane about 'having executed certain works of art at the commission of a Jesuit of note (whose own estimate of their worth was £1102 10s;) who promised to pay me generally, and buoyed me up with promises, [and then] I was flabbergasted when at the conclusion, he turned round & said he couldn't pay but would give me a few pounds in charity.' In his letters Rolfe spoke openly of his very personal life and troubles, though they might mean nothing to the other party. Lane was a busy person, a man of business hundreds of miles away and one whom Rolfe had never met. He could not be bothered with the seemingly trivial matters in the daily life of a budding author. He only was interested in the work of his authors and its success in terms of profit.

The six Toto stories in *The Yellow Book* established Rolfe as a writer and it was as a writer that he continued to live in Holywell. He had neither the money nor the inclination to leave. His mind told him that he had been financially cheated out of a fair wage in painting the banners. That portion withheld from him would be gained, not in the form of cash, but through public exposure. His short apprenticeship at Champion's *Aberdeen*

Standard could now be put into practice. If his brushes could not bring in gold from a patron, then the same patron would smart under his pen. 'Then I began to write, simply because of the imperious necessity of expressing myself. And I had much to say.' Writing on the only theme he ever was to know, he began his fight for his personal cause in *The Holywell Record*.

The 'speculator' from Blackburn, Frank W. Hochheimer, may have met Rolfe in Holywell early in 1896. He also may have been convinced by Rolfe that a monthly periodical could succeed in the town of St. Winefride's Shrine. The first number appeared in May, giving little more than local church news and Rolfe may have written the introduction. Reference to 'Mr. Austin's beautiful banners' in the October number must have been written by Rolfe himself. In the December issue an article on 'Christmas Customs' included: 'At the courts of Italian Princes there prevailed an ancient custom called Ropata, the Spanish word for "shoe". At Christmas time presents were concealed in the shoes or slippers of favoured courtiers, in imitation of St. Nicholas's gifts to the three maidens of Patara.'

It was not until March 1897 that Rolfe became a regular contributor, as well as the magazine's art director and nominal editor. As 'Al Siddik' he wrote 'An Open Letter to the Editor' in this number and the first chapter of 'The Man From Texas,' by 'Maurice Francis Egan'. His pieces were executed under various pseudonyms, but most were recognized as Austin's work by the few who figured in the stories. Cut off from Fr. Beauclerk's benefits, Rolfe shifted to the magazine his hopes of an income, however small. Through his own deeds, he was obliged to turn from a friendly community to the very small circle of 'the only Catholics, the Hochheimers, who have kept their senses.' From these humble surroundings he peered at the vistas beyond him through the medium of literature.

Well endowed with powers of observation and a remarkable memory, the latter half of his Holywell days created a new world for him. In 1891 Rolfe had written to a newspaper 'trying to kick up some awful row about the way papists treat their converts.' Two years later he was begging Wilfrid Meynell to 'give me the use of some columns in your paper to plead my own cause.' Now *The Holywell Record* presented the opportunity. Paper, pen and printer's ink were his weapons for the rest of his life. The theme of his own cause emanated from his abnormal mind and dominated almost all of his future writing. 'When I had been expelled from college' were the opening words of his first published short story. Rolfe made his first appearance in *The Holywell Record* as John Donovan, 'a gentleman, with his head full of Greek and Latin, [who] was out of place among [the business world],' and who had 'a certain vague and evil odour' attached to him because he 'had failed to be a priest.' At the end of his life he was still writing that 'a man with his face and manner and taste and talent and Call ought to have been a priest [but] he was not [and] the fault was hardly his.' Thus, the failure to be a priest was never admitted to be possibly a fault of his own. In his eyes, the fault rested with his superiors, who had failed to acknowledge his vocation. For twenty-four years he fought the singular fight to be recognized by the Catholic Church. For seventeen of these years he did this by continuous writing.

The power behind the written word transported any physical hardship into oblivion. Letters and prose received the same attention, each sparkling with fragments of timeless wit. John Holden had said that Rolfe was never happier than when he had to answer an unpleasant letter. 'Your latest contribution to the gaiety of nations is a bill which I do not intend to pay because it is unjust' were the opening words of one letter at this time to a landlady. But the unconscious wit quickly turned into sarcasm as he wrote: 'All of this is a matter of common knowledge to the various persons who observed the disgusting conditions you expected me to pig in; and whom you scandalized beyond measure, by that very naughty temper which I suppose you are now too old to cure.'

Through the pages of *The Holywell Record* he vividly recorded his grievances. Holywell was a definite turning point in Rolfe's history. Until now he had regarded the Church and its members with a stand-offish disdain. His efforts to gain entrance into the Roman body met with no response. But the individual people who helped him and his new career dismissed from his mind, at least temporarily, the fact that the lifeline between him and the Church had been sharply severed. Here at Holywell he was once again separated from a representative of Mother Church; and all others forsook him—because of his own actions. He now had nothing to compensate for this general loss, except this new career: journalism. Here, at least, was a calling in which he could practise retaliation; but for the present he was content to abuse only one person. The Battle of Holywell was between him and Fr. Beauclerk. The two most searingly scornful stories in the *Record*, which painted the Jesuit priest as the blackest of villains, are 'The Saint, the Priest, the Nowt, the Devil' and its sequel, 'Examples of Sewers End, No. 2.'

The Saint at twenty-two was John Holden. The Priest, the Vicar of Sewers End (for Holywell had no drainage system at the time) was Fr Beauclerk. The Nowt, 'a Mystery [who] dropped down ... from "the back of beyond", settled there, worked like a slave, spoke to few, and made no friends,' was Rolfe. The Devil was just that, the devil. The Nowt 'was proud and reserved in manner, though he could hold a roomful attentive when he chose to speak. And the meticulous delicacy of his habits, together with his voice and accent, stamped him as a person of culture and consideration.' Romances were invented about him, some saying that 'he was a "gentleman who had come down"; and, though he told some few the truth about himself, he was not believed. The bumpkins could not bother their beery heads simultaneously with a truth and their own patent romances; and, consequently, the Nowt practised the gentle art of answering fools according to their folly, and became a holy terror by reason of the reticent mysterious modesty of his demeanour, combined with a fashion of speech so plain, that it was undeniably ugly.' He 'put his back into this business' of the banners, 'and laboured early and late, leading the life of a pig at his patron's direction and expense, hoping for better things bye and bye: and, after nearly a couple of years, he had produced a series of ecclesiastical paintings of a kind which everyone admitted to be something above the ordinary.' The Vicar refused to pay for the work. No legal contract existed and he 'acknowledged no obligation to pay an honorarium, but was willing to give a few pounds in charity.' The affair was the subject of letters to the Vicar and solicitors. After a month the Vicar 'climbed down very suddenly indeed; and, pleading poverty, offered a sum of fifty pounds as honorarium. The Nowt took it, in accordance with his promise; and paid it straightway to an institution of the diocese; for, having gained his point (honorarium *not* charity) he wished to act disinterestedly; and then, without more ado, he joined the staff of the local paper, intending to get a living by journalism till the dawn of brighter days.' The Vicar is then accused of carrying out 'his threats of ruin and revenge'. The Rites of the Church are denied the Nowt and the proprietor of the magazine and his wife, and finally the parishioners of the Vicar withdrew their advertisements. 'And the Nowt preserved an equal mind and demeanour,' taking neither notice of nor action against 'the Vicar, or any of his gang.'

The bitter enmity against the entire Church body had been slowly building up in Rolfe's mind over the years. The events at Holywell unleashed this dammed fury. After his seminary days, Rolfe did nothing to reconcile himself in the eyes of the Church. In the unpleasant incidents of Oscott and Scots College he merely recognized lying, thieving, blundering fools who would not listen to him. The saints of his choice—models for his literature and brush—were well selected. Each had been a martyr. And Rolfe's life, beginning with Holywell, would be a self-made martyrdom. His body would be tortured by days of penury and starvation, and his mind would undergo persecution. But, at Holywell, his words of condemnation were directed against only one person : Fr. Beauclerk, who was to become the personification of all Jesuits.

Rolfe's unfailing memory, especially of people who had caused him wrongs, kept alive the fires of contention. The written abuse against Fr. Beauclerk did not end in *The Holywell Record*. He was similarly attacked as Padre Dotto Vagheggino in the fifteenth Toto tale of *In His Own Image*. In *Hadrian* he becomes both 'that detestable and deceitful Blackcote' and 'the Prepositorgeneral of Jesuits ... the English Black Pope'. Hadrian states that, 'with the word "Borgia" and the word "Nero", the word "Jesuit" perhaps was the eponym for all that was vilest in the world.' In 'The Armed Hands' Rolfe's poisoned imagination struck all Jesuits. As the Grey Man in this story, his hands are armed with 'monstrous platinum-coloured rings.' One of these 'was perhaps the most appallingly ferocious. It was a plain heavy circle; & the bezel was the sharp-pointed revolving rowel of a spur.' The Grey Man attacks Jesuits 'like a kitten, one pace backward; & instantly' rebounding forward, 'launching a lightning-like right-&-left double knock—ping-pang, pong-pung—across the ... foreheads,' with blood splashing out in the most extraordinary manner.

The most personal and vile affront Rolfe could give to Fr. Beauclerk was in 'The Saint, the Priest, the Nowt, the Devil'. In *Hadrian* Rose-Rolfe 'had made a point of mastering Martinucci, practice as well as theory.' Rolfe was speaking of his seminary days, during which time he read whatever he could about the moral practices within the Church. Pius Martinucci's great contribution to the scholarly literature of the Church is his *Manuale Sacrarum Caeremoniarum in libros octo diagestum*. In *The Holywell Record* story Rolfe had written: 'I question whether [the Vicar of Sewers End] had ever even heard of Martinucci.'

The bizarre nature of Rolfe spilled over from the deeds of his life into his writing. He possessed a genius for exactitude when dealing with people. Yet there were occasions when the practicability of a suggestion was questionable. To promote the advantages of advertising in the *Record*, on 15 January 1897 he wrote to the Mother Superior of St. Winefride's Convent: 'It is announced that Mrs Isabella Craigie, who, under the nom de plume of "John Oliver Hobbes", is the author of ... yellow, fin de siècle literature, has entered the Convent of the Assumption in Kensington Square, not for the purpose of taking the veil, but "to have peace and quietness for writing her new story". It will be obvious that a fashion, created by a person of Mrs Craigie's quality, is bound to have its imitators.' He then suggested an advertisement listing the convent's 'exclusive merits' as a retreat 'to mitigate the boredom of a dull winter by the introduction of a parcel of feminine writers.'

The Aberdeen article about artists' models did nothing to relieve the unemployment situation of the city. (How many artists were there in Aberdeen to use models?) Francis Thompson did live at Pantasaph for four years. But 'a parcel of feminine writers' at the Holywell convent could have been a product solely of Rolfe's imagination.

'I cultivate the gentle art of making enemies,' he once told Holden. 'A friend is necessary, one friend,' he added, '—but an enemy is more necessary. An enemy keeps one alert.' And this theory became real at Holywell. At first, Rolfe lived with the Hochheimers with little financial complaint. But the one-penny magazine never brought in enough to sustain three people. Rolfe recognized in the periodical an instrument to promote St. Winefride's Shrine and endeavoured to increase its circulation. From the March 1897 number he was responsible for its physical format. As art director his measures produced a magazine more attractive in typographical appearance. He designed letterheads for The Record Publishing Company, as well as advertisements in art and type. Holden's books in his studio—the Bible, Cellini, Chaucer, Pepys, *The Cloister and the Hearth*, W. S. Gilbert, *The Yellow Book* and books illustrated by Beardsley—added their share to Rolfe's imagination. The young artist genius of *The Yellow Book* inspired him. His design and technique flowed over on to Rolfe's drawing board. Rolfe was fascinated by the mechanical perfection of the work, without seeing its erotic undertones. The solid white and solid black areas utilized by this new artist were to form Rolfe's basic design pattern for the rest of his life. Another artist's innovation of the period was borrowed by Rolfe: Whistler's signing of compositions with a device instead of a signature. Rolfe began to substitute the raven for his name.

Although he was to continue to draw, his photography came to an end at Holywell. The experiments in colour had progressed to perfection. The secret of his final process was an emulsion with which both plates and paper were coated, without the use of any foreign pigment or coloured lenses. One remembered example was a photograph of a girl in a yellow straw hat with a red tartan band. But his first joy at seeing his pictures appear in colour at Christchurch had faded. His primary occupation now was to state his position and to demand retribution.

The outcast sent a flow of letters to the Jesuit. In June he wrote about Holden's threatened assault and added that he would try to prevent the priest 'from making these ignorant Irish your tools for the carrying out of the revenge you have said you will have upon me. To this end, I have notified the Superintendent of Police of the threatened assault; giving him an insight into the motives which have caused it.' The fury against Fr. Beauclerk reached its climax in 'The Saint, the Priest, the Nowt, the Devil' and 'Examples of Sewers End'. These articles produced only the opposite effect from that intended by Rolfe. The 'Vicar of Sewers End' was debased only in one person's eyes. The Catholic community of Holywell reacted to the condemnation of their priest in the *Record* by stopping their subscriptions. In turn, there was no money to print further numbers. The two stories about Holden, Fr. Beauclerk and Rolfe were in the 31 August and October 1897—the last two—issues of *The Holywell Record*.

The worst blow to Rolfe's spirit naturally came once again from the Church. His twisted mind believed that the rites of the Church were withheld from him. The first apparent signs of his deep-rooted paranoia made him a self-imposed victim of ex-communication. When the banners had been paid for, he left his lodgings, goods and clothes. Two days elapsed before he again had money for food. Two days had gone by with cigarettes as his only nourishment. He then went to Hochheimer, 'a Prus-sian' and 'a drunken sot.' The Hochheimers and Rolfe moved into a tiny house at 3 Bank Place, a house of neither luxury nor comfort, with packing cases for furniture. At the beginning of each venture, Rolfe besought the beneficial graces of the Catholic Church. For his painting at Christchurch and Holywell, his brushes were blessed. And for this new house, the office of the *Record*, he asked Fr. Beauclerk for the Rite of Benediction. How-ever the request was made, it was not answered. And this was his 'excommunication'. This unanswered request for a blessing was 'a serious matter for . . . if a small thing like a Rite be denied, most certainly a great thing like a Sacrament will also be denied' and for seven months he was 'forced' to live without confession or communion. In his words, this was 'Excommunion *latae sen-tentiae*, i.e. deprivation of the Sacraments without pronounce-

144

ment of a formal sentence.' This was Fr. Beauclerk's 'curse' upon him.

The loss of the magazine bound the three inhabitants of Bank Place closer together. The Prussian took refuge in his beer and neglected any further business schemes. Food was scarce. In July, John Lane was told that he and the Hochheimers were living on tea, bread and butter. This diet was only supplemented by the natural nourishments gleaned from country walks. They gathered and ate blackberries, mushrooms and nuts. Rolfe tried to smoke 'an evil-smelling twist (ouf)' before he turned to dried tea leaves mixed with wild thyme. Thinking that the Prussian and his wife were suffering on his account, Rolfe left Holywell in September. The last issue of the *Record* had been prepared for the printer, but no future was seen for the magazine. He went to Aberdeen for a short stay, but returned to Wales by December. He came back to potatoes and stewed tea leaves, shivering in the cold with only summer clothes to wear. He wrote again to Lane in London, asking to be taken 'on your staff as a reader, or even as Editor of *The Yellow Book*.... All I want is to be picked out of this hole where I am buried, and to be given a chance to use myself.'

The coming of Christmas was unbearable to him, a true Catholic, because of his excommunication and the denial of the actual necessities of life. A new appeal was sent to Bishop Mostyn. The maze of Rolfe's logic was difficult to appreciate, but an answer did arrive. Fr. Beauclerk sent an associate priest to confer the Rite of Benediction on 3 Bank Place. And on Christmas Eve, Rolfe went to confession to his 'Jesuit Persecutor', and was given absolution and a petty penance. On Christmas morning he partook of his first communion in eight months.

1898 began with a hand-to-mouth existence. His tools of trade had been 'stolen', but he was never without his pen, 'nor have I allowed that pen to rest.' 'You have got to do things that make people love or hate you' was a policy he followed for the rest of his days. As the new year wore on, 'exiguous patient toil began to win reward.' His six Toto stories in *The Yellow Book* had been acclaimed. 'The "Baron Corvo", of The Yellow Book,' was 'one of its most individual writers [and] Mr. Corvo has a new and eclectic method. He is at once classical and colloquial, early Italian and old English, Cockney and Athenian. Caprice is the *motif* of his work and his figures are admirably chosen for his purpose ... the bizarre, the graceful, and the gay,' read a review of the stories in *Literature*. (Almost thirty years later in his American *Golden Book*, Henry Wysham Lanier spoke about these tales and their author: 'Rolfe is not so much as mentioned in any of three great encyclopaedias, or in the two largest literary anthologies ... though he seems to me to have a secure seat among the Great Ones.') In February 1898 he sent a letter to Lane, who had informed him of the possibility of a separate edition of the stories. They would be put together into a Bodley Booklet, the first publication of the series being *The Happy Hypocrite* by 'that gorgeous Max Beerbohm'. In May he was writing to London:

I laugh at your wishes for my recovery: but, all the same, I am obliged. No one will ever believe my pickle. That I know. But, when you have time, just try to conceive a naked little thing, sitting at the bottom of a mud-hole, with pen, ink, paper, copying-book, & diurnal in one hand, and Mr Lane's onion-top in the other: the edges of the said mud-hole being lined with Maxims, manned by 2 Cardinals, 1 General of Jesuits, 2 Archbishops, 3 Bishops, some Monsignori, & 2 few odd Jesuits, whose tails the naked little thing has been twisting! Oh yes, as mad as one of the rabbits of San Guiseppe!

In June a relative died and left Rolfe '19/6. for a mourning ring! I shant buy one: but I had laid in a stock of stamps, Tobacco, Hovis, & V-Cocoa & intend to live a little longer.' Twenty days later a letter to Lane reported that 'I have existed since 8 a.m. June 15th on tea, 4 lemons, one Hovis loaf, and cigarettes (and nothing else upon my honour).' Perhaps with the payment from the Toto stories, he was able to leave the Hochheimers by the end of July, to make his next home at the Hotel Victoria. An offering of peace to Fr. Beauclerk fell through, and the 'Jesuit jackal' ever remained in Rolfe's mind and writings. As 'the bad priest' in *Hadrian*, 'he ruined himself, as We

146

predicted. He persisted in his career of crime till his bishop found him out. Then he was broken, and disappeared—Maison de santé or something of that sort.' The Jesuit was, in fact, neither 'ruined' nor 'broken', though he was recalled from his missionary work at Holywell.

Rolfe's first journalistic exercises in print warmed him with a satisfying sense of power. His imagined persecutions were aired and remedied, if only by making them known to the world. He asked nothing more than the chance to expose the cunningly connived breaches of Christian decency against him. He had no secrets of his own to hide and he kept back no secrets of others. His pen, he thought, would bring enemies to penitent knees. Throughout his life, the dynamic power of a personal letter brought the desired result only once—and at Holywell. A 1,500-word letter was sent to Fr. Beauclerk's Father General in Rome, detailing Rolfe's numerous complaints against the priest. It was on the basis of this single letter that the Jesuit was removed from Holywell at the end of 1898.

When the congregation learned of Fr. Beauclerk's fate, it drew up an exceedingly long petition to reinstate him. Accompanied by individual letters, copies of it were sent to the Reverissimo Padre Generale at Rome, the Reverend Father Provincial at London and the Right Rev. Mostyn, Bishop of Menevia. In part, it read: 'We, the subscribers to the MEMORIAL, received with painful surprise, on New Years Day last, the unexpected announcement of the removal of the Reverend Charles Sidney Beauclerk of the Society of Jesus from Holywell.... We therefore, with deference to your Paternitys superior judgment, humbly request that you will condescend to give your earnest consideration to this Prayer of your Petitioners.... We are of opinion that Father Beauclerk's presence here in Holywell is beneficial to our souls [and] that Holy Well is an Extraordinary, not an Ordinary, Mission and requires an Extraordinarily endowed ... Priest as Superior.... But what a howl of indignation went up from the shallow minded members of his congregation, and how diligently the ears of those in high places were assailed with importunities for the removal of one who had fallen so low as to do his duty to God, openly and unashamed, by doing his duty to weak fellow men.... We do not complain that it is any other than right and proper that there SHOULD be slanderous tongues wagging—that the devil SHOULD be busy in Holywell— his reverences very goodness demands it.... [One member of Holywell in particular], apparently virtuous and full of zeal, strove hard to incite the flock to rebellion against their pastor by various pretexts.... May your petitioners not hope that they will have an opportunity to usher [1899] in with a welcome home to Father Beauclerk such as shall be worthy of the name and glory of the great Welsh Thaumaturga? ... Festo S. Gregorii Magni. 1899.'

The storm created by Rolfe could not restore the damage already effected.

Rolfe outlasted his Vicar of Sewers End only a few weeks. This one triumph of the written word was accepted with a weary mind. By the time Fr. Beauclerk was summoned to leave, Rolfe was temporarily broken in body, mind and spirit. His mental and physical sufferings since mid-1897 had shaken him; and now, at the end of his Holywell stay, the worst blow of his life fell. On 8 November 1898 the Aberdeen *Daily Free Press* and *Evening Gazette* began a three-part exposure of 'Baron Corvo'.

The efforts of his pen had been rewarded, for once, by having Fr. Beauclerk withdrawn from Holywell. Yet, from another source, a pen denounced him. The 'world' to which Austin unmasked the priest's 'treachery' consisted solely of his flock around St. Winefride's Shrine. 'Baron Corvo' was exposed to the whole Catholic community in Britain. *The Catholic Times and Catholic Opinion* immediately reprinted the Aberdeen Attack. The Faith of his allegiance had turned against him, leaving him a pauper in so many ways.

'The Saint, the Priest, the Nowt, the Devil' was prophetic in two ways. It was written at a time of determination: literature would be his only future career, and through it he would claim his rights. In the Holywell story the Devil plays his part through the hearts of humans. After the Priest's refusal to pay for the banners, a bitter argument takes places between the Nowt and the Saint. Enraged at this point, the Saint buys a gun with the intention of shooting the Nowt. One morning he follows the Nowt to early service and shoots him on the steps of the church. In literature this predated the ending of Hadrian VII. In actual life it began Rolfe's paranoic and self-imposed martyrdom.

From the North Wales town Rolfe's name spread to the pen of another artist, to achieve another notable niche for him. Before he died in March 1898, Aubrey Beardsley had written a novel; and the tenth from the last paragraph of *The Story of Venus and Tannhauser* reads:

> Sup, the penetrating, burst through his silk fleshings, and thrust in bravely up to the hilt, whilst the alto's legs were feasted upon by Pudex, Cyril, Anquetin, and some others. Ballice, Corvo, Quadra, Senillé, Mellefont, Theodore, Le Vit, and Matta, all of the egoistic cult, stood and crouched round, saturating the lovers with warm douches.

'My Old Man of the Seas' was Fr. Beauclerk's name for Rolfe. More than thirty years later he said that 'my experience of the two or more years of Rolfe's company in Holywell gave me some queer insights into human nature.... Rolfe was a remarkable genius—and his a wasted life.' In his letters to A. J. A. Symons in the early 1930s, he spoke of Rolfe, but he stressed greater concern for another writer: Shakespeare. He ended one letter, 'As a de Vere—I claim kinship with Shakespeare!!' As a de Vere he championed the cause promoting Edward, the seventeenth Earl of Oxford, as the author of the plays and sonnets—a theory to which, incidentally, Sigmund Freud subscribed.

'One child has been forbidden to speak to or accept help in his lessons from me,' Rolfe wrote to Fr. Beauclerk at the time of the break. The child was also sent a letter, but a polite one. Little Leo, it said, should not try to contact Rolfe in any way. Even if they were to meet on the street by accident, Leo should not recognize him. This precaution was unnecessary, for the boy's parents were then sending him to Glasgow. But the time spent with Rolfe would prove unforgettable: for the boy Rolfe was a person to hold in awe. This friend remained a constant companion in his mind throughout the seventy years of his life that followed. In Glasgow he spoke of him to his young acquaintances, and it was here that he learned Mr. Austin's real name, when he read the Aberdeen Attack. Mildly shocked at first, he soon recognized the deceit of a cheap newspaper story. To him Mr. Austin would always remain the learned and charming man in the painting-photographic studio, who could answer all questions and tell the most wonderful stories. Of all the things little Leo could credit Rolfe with, one overshadowed the others. Alderman Leo Schwarz lived in Holywell to become a respected member of the community and the Church, and through all his life he never forgot the fundamental principles transmitted to him by the artist of the Shrine. This man had taught little Leo the true meanings of the Catholic faith: he was the most devout person Leo had ever met; Mr. Austin had instilled within him the true interpretations of the mysteries of the Roman belief. This primary admiration for his teacher never faded.

8

'I'm to be buried alive by *The Wide World*,' Rolfe wrote to
Frederic Chapman on 16 July 1898 with his unconscious knack
of using words in jest which later proved to be actuality.

In April 1898 a new periodical was introduced in England:
*The Wide World Magazine, An Illustrated Monthly of True
Narrative: Adventure, Travel, Customs and Sport.* 'Savages at
Play', 'How The North Pole Will Be Reached', 'How Wild Ele-
phants Are Trapped', 'How I Escaped From Siberia', 'A Brush
With a Sea Lion', 'How Vernon Fought the Gorilla', 'How a
Girl Climbed Fujiyama', 'Into the Pickling Vat' and 'Aban-
doned!' were only some of the many titles to sate the news-
hungry appetites of the day. One continuous story fully lived up
to the magazine's slogan, 'Truth is Stranger Than Fiction'. Beginning with the August issue, it serialized 'The Adventures of
Louis De Rougemont: Being a Narrative of the Most Amazing
Experiences a Man Ever Lived to Tell'. At the age of nineteen
M. de Rougemont left France for Singapore. Joining a pearl-
fisher off the south coast of New Guinea, he began a weird sequence of breath-taking adventures. Hardly anything imaginable
was omitted from the story of this nineteenth-century Robinson
Crusoe, which was accompanied by numerous vivid illustrations.

In June, Rolfe had written to John Lane about 'an MS.,
Buried Alive; and begged for its return if you did not want it.
Now, the Editor of *The Wide World Magazine* has got on its
track: and urgently asks to print it.... Therefore I want you
to give me a definite answer as to ... whether you, as my publisher, think it advisable to publish such a thing in a way which
may make people stare at me. I mean, is it advisable to get oneself known as a man who has been buried alive?'

Rolfe's story tells of an incident from 1890, while he was living at the Cesarini-Sforza house in Rome. Having a genuine fear of reptiles, contact with frogs causes him to go into a cataleptic trance. He is pronounced dead and is buried in the family vault. At the end of his trance he wakes up, on a high shelf in an open crypt, soon to be closed by masonry. He lets himself down to the ground by means of a rope and is happily welcomed back by the Roman family.

'How I Was Buried Alive' was published in early November. The article is illustrated with a photograph of Rolfe and six line drawings 'done under his own supervision.' In all but one ('The Procession to the Grave') Rolfe is shown. In three of these he is in the religious habit of 'the Cappucini' and in only one does he wear glasses, low on his nose. The artist was Alan Wright, whose drawings appeared in the magazines of the 1890s and who lived and worked near Kains-Jackson and Gleeson White.

The story was published innocently enough. But it touched off a powder keg of derision against its author. The shock from the explosion numbed Rolfe mentally and psychologically for a long time.

Writing from Holywell in May, he was 'as completely isolated and impotent as though I were, once more, in my coffin.' Seven months later the chain-reaction of personal abuse resulting from the published story certainly must have made him wish he were 'in my coffin.' 'I believe, from the illustrations which I have just seen, that *The Wide World* will make me an awful gibe in October.' He was made 'an awful gibe' but only because of the article's signature: 'Baron Corvo'.

The 'Truth Stranger Than Fiction' in *The Wide World Magazine* proved offensive to the staid, uninventive minds of newspapermen of the 1890s. These self-appointed guardians of public morals devised their own criterion of truth. To preserve life as it should be, no matter how stuffy, no matter how Victorian, was the main design of any public journalist. Anything beneath this standard was branded as deceitful sham. Stories from unknown parts of the world could never bear the stamp of truth; and critics of the magazine denounced the truthfulness of the Rougemont adventures and called him a fraud. Also, people were not buried alive, at least not in the way of one Englishman courting a foreign title. In December 1921, six months after his death in the Kensington Infirmary, M. de Rougemont was rehabilitated through corroborating statements by members of a government expedition. The only vindication for Rolfe's story was its separate publication at ninepence by the London Association for the Prevention of Premature Burial.

As soon as the November number of the magazine was printed, the periodical, this story and its author were assailed. These attacks first appeared in the Aberdeen *Daily Free Press* and *Evening Gazette* on November 8th, 12th and 26th. They were immediately copied by other British newspapers, as well as by *The Catholic Times and Catholic Opinion.*

The attack was written under the headline: 'Baron Corvo. More "Wide World" Adventures. Extraordinary Story. A Nobleman from Aberdeen.' The picture of Baron Corvo in the magazine was 'a very good photo, and has been recognized by many people in Aberdeen and neighbourhood, who can tell something regarding him vastly more interesting than what appears in the *Wide World Magazine* under His Excellency's signature.' The magazine had been under ridicule for its devoted 'promulgation of true statements of thrilling adventures,' but this was a personal attack against one individual person. The Baron's enemy had been dormant, waiting for the right opportunity. This was it. 'Who, then, is Baron Corvo?' was the question asked and, without hesitation, answered savagely, in an exposure of Rolfe's life and person from 1886.

In *Hadrian,* Cardinal Ragna thrusts a newspaper into the Pontiff's hands, snarling, 'See what a scoundrel you are! ... Fly! All is discovered! The *Catholic Hour* is exposing you finely!'

[Hadrian] took the paper ... and looked at the sheet. As He read His pontifical name and His secular name, His blood began to tingle: for He still loathed publicity. As He read on, His blood began to boil. It was a frightful tale which He was reading—frightful, because He saw at a glance that it was quite unanswerable. It was unanswerable because there are some things of which the merest whisper suffices to destroy

—whose effect does not depend on truthfulness. It was unanswerable because it was anonymous. It was unanswerable because He never could bring Himself to condescend.... He read the article on the *Strange Career of the Pope* again and again, till His head swam with the horror of it. This was the worst thing which ever had happened to Him.... It depicted Him as simply contemptible. Inspection of the image of Himself, which the *Catholic Hour* with such ferocious flocculence delineated, brought Him to the verge of physical nausea. But it was not true, real. It was not Himself. No, no. It was an atrocious caricature. Oh yes, it was an atrocious caricature. Everybody would know it for that—Would they? How many had known the previous libels for libels? How many had dared to proclaim the previous libels for libels? One—out of hundreds.—Oh how beastly, how beastly! He read the thing again;—and dashed the paper to the ground. If it only had made Him look wicked—or even ridiculous! But no. He categorically was damned, as despicable, low, vulgar, abject, mean, everything which merited contempt. Only a strenuous effort kept Him from shrieking in hysteria. 'God, God, am I really like that?' He moaned aloud, with His palms stretched upward and outward and His eyes intent in agony. He lost faith in Himself. Perhaps He was such an one. Perhaps His imagination after all had been deluding Him, and He really was an indefensible creature. It was possible. 'Oh, have I ever been such a dirty—beast? Have I?' He moaned again. And then all the being of Him suffused—and whirled—and outraged Nature took Him in hand. The blow to His self-respect, the shattering onslaught on His sensibilities, were more than even His valid virile body could bear. He lay back in His low chair; and swooned into oblivion.

The attack's author primarily resented 'Baron Corvo' and his 'patent of nobility'. This was the only reason for the exposure. The 'folly' of using the title personified for the author of the articles the 'folly' of Rolfe's life for the past twelve years. And to define this 'folly' Rolfe's life was openly ransacked. When Hadrian is handed the newspaper, he quickly reads it for the first time, noticing 'a clear chronological error' and a number of 'gratuitous or ignorant misrepresentations of fact, in a column and three-quarters of print.' 'In progress, He counted aloud "One, two,"—up to "thirty-three absolute and deliberate lies...."'

Only the undesirable and blackening aspects of Rolfe's life were catalogued in the Aberdeen Attack. The presentation of most of the facts was in the form of half-truths, purposely letting the deed fall into a debasing light. These half-truths, and in some cases actual lies, were built up into a delectable tale for gossip-mongers. The 'thirty-three absolute and deliberate lies' counted by Hadrian may have included the half-truths of the article.

(1) Outlining the *Buried Alive* story, the attack's author notes the time of it, November 1890. He writes that the Baron 'was at this time struggling for life as best he could in England.' In November 1890 Rolfe was still in Rome and did not have to struggle for his life until the end of 1891. (2) At Christchurch 'what does Baron Corvo do but propose to purchase the property [from Gleeson White], costing several thousands of pounds.' £1,300 was the figure of the sale stated by Kains-Jackson. (3) Corvo 'was lent money, given goods on credit—for the Whites had a business in Christchurch.' The attack does not clearly say whether the Whites or others lent him money. Gleeson White was away for a great deal of 1891. When Corvo left the village, he certainly owed a number of people for goods obtained on credit and for rent. (The money from the duchess was sufficient for him to use without borrowing money, but he did exist on credit.) (4) Before his conversion, Rolfe was 'an undermaster at Grantham School.' Rolfe 'was an under-master' he says in his defense in *Hadrian*. 'That is true in substance and absolutely false in connotation. I was an under-master: but as I also had charge of the school-house, I was called the house-master. You also perhaps may be aware that there is only one head-master in a school; and that all the rest are under-masters. But, when slander is your object, "under-master" is a nice disgraceful dab of mud to sling at your victim for a beginning.' (5) On becoming a Roman Catholic in 1886 Rolfe 'had to leave his mastership.' Rolfe resigned his post. There was mutual agreement for the

resignation and the head of the school, Dr. Hardy, remained his friend for twenty years. (6) The Oban episode is summed up in three sentences—Bute and his 'small school for outcast boys'. The boys were not outcasts, but came from Cardiff and the Highlands and developed into model citizens of the Church. The attack implies that Rolfe's conduct was the cause of his short stay at Oban, giving, of course, no further light on the situation or the people involved. (7) Rolfe was then discharged from Oscott after only 'a few months' and, 'after more "starving in London", he came across Mr. Ogilvie-Forbes ... and stayed at Boyndlie for three or four months.' The 'few months' at Oscott again conveys a flippant person. Rolfe spent a full school year of eight months at Oscott and his conduct, as student and teacher, was in no way undesirable. When he was 'discharged,' he visited Fr. Angus at St. Andrews before spending six months with Ogilvie-Forbes. There is no surviving evidence that he was starving in London at this time. A photograph taken of him at Christchurch in 1889 showed 'the tall angular figure of "the Baron"' but nothing was noted about a man in need. (8-11) The attack states various possible sums that the duchess was supposed to send to Christchurch, doing so with an air of disbelief. In the village, it says, 'he lived as if he were actually in receipt of the money.' The duchess was approached, the attack continues, over the pending sale of White's property, but she 'declined'. In fact, Kains-Jackson, a practising solicitor in London, handled the cheques from Rome for Rolfe, and, when he dealt with Rolfe over White's property, no mention was made of the duchess or any help coming from Italy. When her allowance to him stopped the attack declared that he was supposed 'to write letters to her begging for aid,' the letters continuing for years. Rolfe certainly must have written to her when the allowance was discontinued, to ask the cause, and he may have written about his adverse conditions at the time; but he did not continue to do so 'for years'. This term implies a long period of time, yet 1891 was only seven years before the attack appeared, and during this time the duchess had already died. (12) 'It may just be noted in passing that the title which the Baron selected is of the following signification— ... English, crow!' Its proper interpretation is, in fact, raven.

(13) Leaving Christchurch, Rolfe went to London and lived with the priests at Ely Place. The period may have been short. He 'was charitably maintained' at Ely Place, the attack states. Yet Rolfe denies this in *Hadrian*. (14) Up near Aberdeen, 'he was given the post of tutor to the young Laird of Seaton.' He was given the post of tutor to both of the Hay boys of Seaton House. (15) 'For a brief space he lived in clover' at Seaton House, 'driving out and in to the city, being able to invite friends to lunch, and so forth, all as becometh one with lordly aspirations.' He may have driven to and from the city, but he did not invite friends to lunch, because, for one reason, he had no friends: his only 'friends' at the time were the Hay boys and their playmates, the Burnetts. In all of the time he spent at Aberdeen, he had three adult friends. One was Dr. Cruickshank and the other two were Champion and his co-worker. Another reason would have been Miss Hay, who would not have allowed guests. The two Hay boys recalled no strangers at their meals during the 1892 summer. (16) Continual reference is made to Rolfe's life at Aberdeen under the title of Baron Corvo. Workers at Messrs. G. W. Wilson were shown *The Wide World* photograph of him. 'On being asked if they have ever seen that gentleman before, the remark in every case was—"Oh yes—the Baron".' From the time Rolfe arrived in Aberdeen, he lived through this period and conducted his business under his own name. It was not until he met Champion that he reverted to the Italian name and title. (17) When his three oil paintings were on exhibition, he naturally tried to sell them, even though his asking price was high. One prospective patron is quoted in the attack as having said that he 'found the anatomy, in particular, sadly out of joint.' In all of the surviving examples of his art, his anatomy is unexceptionable. (18) 'He was offered work by Mr. Thomson, printer, but that was one of the things the Baron would not accept.' This affair is treated in *Hadrian*.

(19-20) 'He was a vegetarian and a perfect Epicure in the matter of his diet, making out each day from a cookery book which he possessed the recipes for the day's meals.' These recipes included ingredients of 'an expensive character,' it is stated. 'They say that I ate daintily, and had elaborate dishes made from a cookery book of my own,' Rolfe answers in *Hadrian*. 'The recipes (there may have been a score of them) were cut-out of a penny weekly, current among the working classes. The dishes were lentils, carrots, anything that was cheapest, cleanest, easiest, and most filling—nourishing—at the price. Each dish cost something under a penny; and I sometimes had one each day.' (21) At the time when Rolfe, as Corvo, went to see Champion, the attack reports that he was living in King Street. After his ejection from Skene Street, the attack says that he found quarters in King Street, 'where he stayed for a couple of months.' He may have found new quarters, but he did not stay for 'a couple of months.' The attack is at fault in its statement of times. Only one month elapsed between the Skene Street incident and his going to Champion's apartments. And at this time he was living in a sandhill away from the city. (22) Just before he did go to Champion's he sought refuge in the local insane asylum. According to the attack he requested Dr. Cruickshank, whom 'Rolfe had known in other days,' to certify him insane. In fact, though the doctor was still his friend, he was not the one Rolfe approached. This was Dr. Thompson. (23) The attack lists the dates (from September 2nd to 16th) and aid (from one to ten shillings) given him by the Poor Association. The society declined further help, according to the attack, because 'the Baron was a hopeless case.' Careful consideration was given to Rolfe's case before their last grant of ten shillings, but the overwhelming cases of unemployment in the city could not be dealt with satisfactorily for each person. There were about a thousand people out of work. This number, multiplied by the figure of Rolfe's aid, £5 19s. 0d., would have come to a grand sum. (24) 'They offered him the final test—the workshop, which the Baron indignantly refused.' Here again the attack stresses the shiftless nature of its subject. The Poor Association discontinued their assistance, but there was no offer of a workshop. (25-27) On a Saturday afternoon Rolfe called on Champion. The Labour leader and a friend were at dinner. Rolfe was 'dressed in a knickerbocker suit, and wearing, generally, a pretty respectable appearance.' So states the attack. It was, in fact, an evening; Champion was away; and Rolfe was wearing tattered rags. (28) The attack interrupts its sequence by stating that 'while living in lodgings in the city he received £1 from a friend. He went up to the Palace Hotel in the evening, had a costly dinner, stayed overnight in a luxurious bedroom, and had a breakfast in the morning, which carried away the remainder of the pound!' 'They say that I gorged myself with sumptuous banquets at grand hotels,' Hadrian continues in his defence. 'Once, after several days' absolute starvation, I got a long-earned guinea; and I went and had an omelette and a bed at a place which called itself a grand hotel. It wasn't particularly grand in the ordinary sense of the term; and my entertainment there cost me no more than it would have cost me elsewhere, and it was infinitely cleaner and tastier.' (29) On the day that he called on Champion, the Labour leader was so moved by his story that he 'went to King Street and paid the Baron's bill for board and lodgings, and gave the Baron a spare bedroom in his own apartments.' Since Champion was in Belfast on this day and Rolfe's home was a sandhill, the attack is not altogether true on this point. (30) 'He had come to Mr. Champion in the middle of November,' is the attack's dating of the beginning of the relationship. Champion left Aberdeen on November 25th. This would leave hardly more than one week for the two men to become acquainted. Rolfe's only signed article in Champion's *Standard* is dated November 30th, but he must have been working for it for some little time. There is also the testimony from Champion's opposing Labour members in Aberdeen. Eyeing him with suspicion as they did, they assumed that his 'Tory gold' was coming from Baron Corvo. This knowledge of the association between Champion and Rolfe could only have taken place over a period longer than one week. Rolfe no doubt called at his address soon after his last aid from the Poor Association in mid-September. (30-31) 'Shortly before the New Year Mr. Champion announced his intention of returning to London. Mr. Rolfe was nothing loth to accompany him, providing Mr. Champion would pay the fare. And so it was agreed. They were to leave one evening by the Caledonian train. Mr. Champion purchased both the tickets, and with the tickets in his pocket both he and the Baron took their seats in the carriage. "By the way, Rolfe," said Mr. Champion, "go and get some papers and magazines. You've plenty of time yet." Rolfe accordingly went away to the bookstall—but he never returned. Later in the evening he called on some friends of Champion's in the city, and with the woeful intimation that he had missed the train, asked from one of them the loan of a £5 note. This was a little too much. However, the gentleman in question took the Baron down to the station, actually bought a ticket for him, and did not leave him until he saw him off with the train to London.' Whenever Champion may have 'announced his intention of returning to London,' he left in November. Although the attack presents a colourful story, the actual departure of Corvo from Aberdeen was a simple act and involved no gentleman friend of Champion's to buy him a ticket and to see him actually off on the train. All through the attack, the name used is Corvo, not Rolfe. Yet in this one episode Corvo is referred to as Rolfe. (33) As for Rolfe and his pseudonyms, the attack writes about 'Baron Corvo—otherwise Frederick William Rolfe, as well as otherwise certain other names.' What other names—at the time of Aberdeen? When the attack was written Rolfe had been using the name of Austin for four years in Holywell. So, the attack's author must have kept a close watch on the subject of his articles.

Of course, among these smears there were some true revelations. Trying to conduct business without money and Rolfe's wild financial claims and schemes were cited. Also reported was the writing of begging letters, an occupation Rolfe never admitted.

Anyone confronted in such a menacing fashion would resort to some form of defence. But, if the attack be on a grand scale, the victim may be defenceless. This was the situation here. The Aberdeen Attack was the most cruel blow in Rolfe's life. It drained him of almost every ounce of compassion he had ever held for his fellow creatures, leaving him with an everlasting look of suspicion in his narrow but piercing eyes. The attack appeared so suddenly and for no apparent reason. The shock wore off in time, but it had changed him into an entirely different person. The brand of the moralizing journalist had touched him. But, worse for Rolfe, the Roman Church was on the side of the Aberdeen Attack.

The Church, in the form of Bute and Oban, caused his expulsion from his first Catholic job. The Church, in the forms of Oscott and Scots College, denied him his God-given vocation. The Church, in the form of a 'friend', deprived him of the duchess's allowance. The Church, in the London of 1894, offered no assistance. The Church, in the form of Fr. Beauclerk—although Rolfe was at fault this time—did not agree with him on the value of his work. The Church, the one refuge for him in this life, now pointed an accusing finger at 'Baron Corvo'. The last thread of hope he had in the Church was snapped when *The Catholic Times* reprinted the Aberdeen Attack. Only one person came to his defence—the Rev. James Dey of Oscott; and *The Catholic Times* garbled his letter in print to fit their, and not Rolfe's, cause.

1898 had a sudden and ironic end. Rolfe had triumphed over his Holywell priest. But he himself was utterly defeated.

Who was the author of the Aberdeen Attack? 'Who could have attacked Him with such malignant ingenuity?' Hadrian wonders. 'The names of half a dozen filthy hounds occurred to Him in as many seconds: but He was not able to recognize any particular paw' when he first saw the articles.

When it first appeared, and for some time afterwards, he thought the author had been Dom Hunter Blair of Fort Augustus. The Benedictine composed endless articles for the Catholic periodicals, including *The Catholic Times,* and in *Hadrian* he is mildly rebuked for this occupation. At the end of 1898 Rolfe had just reason to suspect him. Hadrian refers to the 'series of libels which were directed against' him 'in the newspapers, especially the Catholic newspapers—dirty Keltic wood-pulp' as accountable to 'the Erse clergy' who held 'the Catholic press in the hollow of their hand.' The press and Hunter Blair were present, in print, in 1890 when his friend McVarish was being attacked.

Rolfe's friend was assailed in *The Tablet* and Scottish newspapers when he converted to the Anglican Church. But he immediately answered back. One of his letters was published in the Edinburgh *Evening Dispatch* on 6 August 1890. 'You quote a passage from the *Tablet* this evening, concerning which kindly permit me to make a few remarks,' McVarish began. 'The quotation, in which I can clearly detect the paw of an old "friend" of mine—a fellow-novice at Fort Augustus, now on the *Tablet* staff—bristles with inaccuracies.' This 'friend' was Hunter Blair, who first attended Fort Augustus as a novice in 1878. He became a deacon on 25 March 1886 and was ordained a priest on July 11th of the same year. A month later, on August 18th, he assisted in the official opening of Fort Augustus for the National Council of the Scottish Church. This was while Rolfe was at Oban. In his printed letter, McVarish continued, 'The writer begins by informing the public that I was first "discovered" by Fr. Jerome Vaughan [the abbey's first rector], who, treating me with invariable and constant kindness, gave me a chance of testing a vocation which I declared it to be my earnest wish to pursue—received me as a postulant and then as a novice at Fort-Augustus, &c.' *The Tablet* had declared that his vocation was becoming 'steadily unfavourable.' McVarish's noviciate was over in November 1885, but he did not leave the abbey until February of the following year. 'The community would have admitted me to monastic vows had it been my own wish to take them,' he added, 'in the same way as they admitted the scribe of the *Tablet* to them, who afterwards discovered that his "vocation" was to journalism, although at Fort-Augustus, he had gone under a pall, with death candles burning around him, bells ringing his knell, and other tomfooleries to signify his death to this world and all its vanities.'

But, studying the attack more closely and thinking clearly about it over a period of time, Rolfe decided against Hunter Blair as its author. By 1903, when he was writing *Hadrian*, he could answer the attack and could say to himself that he knew who wrote it.

'Who in the world could have collected such a mass of apparently convincing evidence?' Rolfe asks in the novel. 'At some time in His life, He (perhaps inadvertently) must have trodden upon some human worm; and the worm now had turned and stung Him. He sought for a sign, a trace;—and found it—Of course;—and the motive simultaneously leaped to light. It was payment of a grudge, owed to Him by a detected letter-thief, a professional infidel, whom He had scathed with barbed sarcasms about ten years ago [1893-4]. There was something more than that. Again He studied the paper for corroboration.... And the letter-thief resides at [Aberdeen]; engaged in job-journalism: also, he had access to more than much of the information here misused.... Here and there in the article, Hadrian's literary faculty enabled Him to perceive a change of touch.... The Pope, of all men on God's fair earth, was qualified to recognize "the fine Roman hand"—the fine Roman hand at least of one of His Own contemporaries at [Scots College], whom He had afflicted with a ridiculous label, a harmless jibe simply composed of the man's initial and surname joined together—the fine Roman hand of a pseudonymous editor with whom He had refused to have dealings. Yes, and there too was the obscene touch of the female.'

'The fine Roman hand' belonged to a fellow student at Scots College, 1890. At dinner in *Hadrian* this student is 'the blubber-lipped gorger who mopped up gravy with a crumb wedge and gulched the sop.' And the 'ridiculous label' of 'initial and surname joined together' was 'Peagreen'.

Fr. Patrick Green was born in Ireland seven years after Rolfe's birth. He first attended Blairs College, Aberdeen, before moving on to Douai and then Scots College in 1887. Returning to Scotland, he was ordained by the Bishop of Aberdeen in 1891. He later served in a number of parishes within the Edinburgh Archdiocese before he semi-retired in 1925. He died in 1950. His first appointment after his ordination was on the staff of Blairs College, where he remained until 1897. He therefore knew Rolfe at Rome and at Aberdeen. One of the students at Rome who was offended by Rolfe's presence, he must have kept an eye, and an ear, open when his former fellow student was in the Scottish city. Ogilvie-Forbes, Miss Hay and the Bishop of Aberdeen were all associated with Blairs College and its staff. The 'ridiculous label,' the 'harmless jibe' of 1890 had not yet worn away.

Moreover, Rolfe 'refused to have dealings' with 'Peagreen' during the 1892-3 period. So 'the fine Roman hand' was not averse to making its tantalising contribution to the Aberdeen Attack.

The 'obscene touch of the female' was most certainly Miss Georgina Hay's. The joint authors of the attack were all at Aberdeen during the time Rolfe lived there. If at first she had felt kindly towards him, she soon had reasons to dislike him. Her two recently orphaned nephews were her chief concern. Every aspect of their upbringing had to correspond to her high standards. When they were at home, their tutor had to maintain the moral and religious levels of the Jesuit fathers of their school. Any layman was, in any case, suspect. The two months of the 1892 summer did not pass quickly for her. She consulted the Bishop of Aberdeen and the rector of Blairs College about Rolfe's methods of teaching. She corresponded with a certain Vincent H. Jackson of Staffordshire about Rolfe and his duties. Now that the summer was over and the boys were returning to school, Jackson suggested a tutor for their next holiday in a letter sounding like Hunter Blair's to Bute when Rolfe left Oban. The proposed tutor was 'a young man—26 ... studying for the Church and a person very opposite in disposition to Mr Rolfe.'

At the time of his dismissal from Seaton House, the estrangement between Miss Hay and Rolfe was wide and unbridgeable. The most severe letter between Jackson and Miss Hay concerning the departed tutor was written a week after he had left. Jackson was 'very sorry to read what trouble you had had with the boys and Mr Rolfe and very much annoyed to find what a blackguard—no other word will suit—the latter had turned out to be. After the trust and confidence reposed in him his conduct was most mean and contemptible. It is fortunate that Malcolm is young and will no doubt forget him before long. At the same time we cannot know what harm has been done to the boys mind.'

Neither Malcolm nor Cuthbert could ever recall any action on Mr. Rolfe's part to have him branded a 'blackguard'.

Ogilvie-Forbes' mother-in-law wrote to Miss Hay hoping 'you are trying to amuse yourself, and to forget all unpleasant matters. Above all, dear friend, excuse me if I repeat to you the advice not to write about a certain person. Not that I have heard anything, on the contrary, I hope your trouble in that quarter is ended. Father Gerry understood him to say he had friends at Bristol, a good long way off. But don't write, above all, and don't even speak, except when you are sure of your audience. I am so anxious that all this shall not fall on your head, and he, perhaps, came forward to say you had been speaking about him....' Whatever was the cause for the contents of these letters, it engendered a positive dislike for Rolfe, enough to aid in the newspaper attack.

One more letter to Miss Hay two years later re-ignited the flame of wrath. Written at the end of Rolfe's year of privation in London, a member of an Aberdeen company of advocates spoke about an account incurred by 'our friend Rolfe.' An enclosed letter from a lawyer 'alleged that the account [to Mr. Adam, Bookseller & Stationer here] was incurred by "Mr Rolfe, Tutor to, and acting on behalf of Mr [Malcolm] Hay of Seaton, for goods supplied for Mr Hays use." This is evidently some more of his nice work. The account only commences of 23 Sept 1892 and you will see goes on to 16 Sept 1893. This is cool impertinence with a vengeance.' This was one way in which Rolfe obtained his photographic supplies in Aberdeen—from the week after he left Seaton House until the day the Poor Association aided him for the last time and when he sought out Champion. This final revelation was the concluding blow to the relationship between Miss Hay and the former tutor.

Knowing the identity of two of the contributors does not answer the question of why the attack was written. With the exception of a fleeting visit in 1897, Rolfe had not been in Aberdeen for five years. For what purpose, then, was it written? Why should Rolfe, who was in no way a public figure and did not even live in the city at the time, be made a victim of such a vicious newspaper attack? The reasons behind certain deeds of the 1890s must be sought in a world far removed from our own. The Rougemont story was published when the public was sceptical about the parts of the world not yet openly explored. The journalist of the period deemed it his moral obligation to defend his public by exposing anything or anybody who might be a fraud. Yet the perpetrator of the attack may have had more in mind than a simple denouncement of a bogus baron.

The 'diatribe in a key of depreciation' is summed up in *Hadrian*:

> Material Cause. Information, possessed ... by the detected letter-thief and the female. Opinions, collected from ... Spite desirous of stabbing Scorn in the back.
> Formal Cause. Calumny, that is to say Slander which is false.
> Efficient Cause. The pontifical treatment of the representatives of the Liblab [Liberal-Labour] Fellowship now in the City.
> Hadrian sat back in his chair; and blamed—Himself. His mind went straight to the root of the matter. It was His Own fault. He had not loved His neighbour. He had been hard, unkind, austere. He had cultivated His normal faculty for rubbing salt upon His neighbour's rawest and most secret sore,—salt in the shape of biting words, satire, sarcasm, corrosive irony, labels which adhered.... Like all men, He had been trusting in Himself, not in the Maker of the Stars.... He pleaded guilty. He had not loved His neighbour.

If we connect the authorship of the newspaper articles with a letter-thief, a job-journalist and a socialist, we can see how they came into being. The Roman Catholic Church was an enemy to the Socialist movement. In choosing Scotland for the place to release the story about Baron Corvo, two purposes were fulfilled. In the country of 'No Popery!' and a low opinion of foreigners, especially Italianate Englishmen with assumed titles, both Papists and a seeming foreigner could be discredited.

The actual writer of the attack for the Aberdeen newspapers —who himself may have reported to the other newspapers which used it—has as yet no definite name. In *Hadrian* he is a 'diabolic brute' who once said to Rolfe, 'If I had your brains I would be earning a thousand a year.' Rolfe calls him 'a fatuous liar. I mocked him: caught him stealing my correspondence ... and he wrote these anonymous calumnies in long cherished revenge.' This 'letter-thief' may have been a person who was forced to live with Rolfe. He lived in Aberdeen and, if he had to share quarters with Rolfe, it could only have been in Champion's apartments. At Seaton House, at Wilsons', to all other people Rolfe remained Frederick William Rolfe until he met Champion. As Baron Corvo he was assisted by the Labour leader and acted as a member of his newspaper staff. The Aberdeen Attack was a bitter denunciation against Rolfe's use of the baronial title— which he used only from September 1893 until he followed Champion to London.

When Champion and Rolfe were reunited in London, again the two lived with a third person, which may have been the same man from Aberdeen. 'At some time in His life, He ... must have trodden upon some human worm; and the worm now had turned and stung Him.... It was payment of a grudge, owed to Him by a detected letter-thief, a professional infidel, whom He had scathed with barbed sarcasms....' The third person at Champion's London house was entrusted with the task of introducing Rolfe to literary people after Champion's departure for Australia. A month later he himself set sail for New York. In a letter addressed to him only as 'Dear R,' Rolfe admonished him for not doing the things he was asked to do.

One proposed introduction was, as we have seen, to Jerome K. Jerome, the editor of *To-Day*. Although this did not take place, the magazine accepted one of Rolfe's stories. Jerome and Champion were friends and the Socialist had written for the editor. The magazine itself was divided into a number of departments, each signed by a journalistic pseudonym. In 1898 a certain 'Major' on the magazine knew Gleeson White. After the second instalment of the attack had appeared in Aberdeen, *To-Day* printed an article, ' "Baron Corvo" and "The Wide World Magazine" ' on November 26th. The story was about Rolfe's relationship with W. T. Stead in London early in 1892. An advance copy of the issue was sent to Aberdeen and the attack's third article appeared on the same date.

No doubt 'Dear R' wanted a last word with Rolfe before he left for New York, but they did not see each other. Rolfe's letter began, 'Nor was it my fault that your letter didn't reach me in time to come to the club. I did not blame you, and I cannot see why you should write so snappily about it. There are circumstances over which neither of us have any control, and this eagerness to emphasize your perfection and to scold people, is neither admirable nor impressive.' Part of the letter dealt with the monies Champion left behind for Rolfe. 'Dear R' kept him at Champion's house until he was 'kind enough to tell me that I was a drag upon your movements.' The association lasted until 19 March 1894, when Rolfe was given £1 5s. 0d. 'to start on my own hook.' 'And now you are free to think even more of your own affairs,' he added, 'nor will you be worried about the different promises voluntary made to me' about 'the rounds' of editors and studios all unkept. In closing, Rolfe wrote that 'there is nothing to prevent your whole attention being devoted to the contemplation of your own navel, and no doubt you will be henceforth perfectly happy.... Ad multos annos.'

'Dear R,' or a person very similar to him, was forced to keep company with Rolfe and despised him. For five years the resentment lingered dormant, waiting for an opportunity to be unleashed.

In *Hadrian the Seventh* 'the letter-thief' and the possessor of 'the fine Roman hand' are fleetingly mentioned once more in the same book, but the female with 'the obscene touch' finds no other niche in the novel. Yet it may be she who appears in *The Holywell Record* story, 'Temptation'. Although certain factors in this serial pertain to Rolfe's life, not everything in it is as clear as it would have been if he had written it all by himself. Being a collaboration with Holden—as, no doubt, 'The Man From Texas' was—it contains elements of pure fiction. Holden had no background of experience to draw upon and contributed only from his imagination. The two may have talked about certain incidents before Holden wrote them up. However 'Temptation' was pieced together, there may have been some thought on Rolfe's part pertaining to his Aberdeen days.

Early in 1894 *To-Day* published a story by Rolfe dealing with London of 1892. While at Ely Place, Rolfe accompanies a priest to a poor workman's flat in a slum down Maltravers Alley. Maltravers had an evil connotation for Rolfe. In *Hubert's Arthur*, he writes: 'Sim himself was slain; and Sir William

Malthravers ... carved his feet and hands and all his limbs.' And in 'Temptation' there is a Mrs. Maltravers. Could this be Miss Hay?

In this story Mrs. Maltravers is the guardian of young Johnny Palmer. The boy is at a medical school at Windsor—a lunatic asylum, Lygon-Rolfe claims. The persons in charge of this place are Dr. and Mrs. Thompson—it was a Dr. Thompson that Rolfe saw in Aberdeen in 1893, for the purpose of being committed to an insane asylum to enable him to have food and shelter. In his *Holywell Record* story Rolfe hints at the asylum being Broadmoor, but this is at Wokingham and not close to Windsor. The only mental institution near Windsor in the 1890s was Holloway Sanatorium, officially opened on 15 June 1885 by the Prince and Princess of Wales. But the asylum for the boy may have been as fictitious as the married state of Mrs. Maltravers, if she were actually Miss Hay, If he named the doctor in charge after Dr. Thompson of Aberdeen, then other people in the story could come from the same episode of Rolfe's life. Windsor as a geographical place can be correct for the purpose. Malcolm and Cuthbert Hay went to a Jesuit school near Windsor. As Malcolm was Miss Hay's ward, so the name Mrs. Maltravers could have been substituted for hers.

This is the only possible reference to Miss Hay at any length in any of Rolfe's work.

Such subtle touches could have been easily supplied by Rolfe without ever telling Holden or indicating their purpose. If indeed he alluded to Miss Hay, then, once through with her, he silently comments on Nicholson.

Rolfe can never be accused of plagiarism. Yet in this story he places himself in a position to take credit for another person's writing. At the end of 'Temptation' a Big Editor of Fleet Street is very pleased to meet him. 'Now look here, Mr. Lygon ... I know you're the soul of honour and all that, and I'm sure I shall be able to persuade you that even in Fleet Street we're not so black as you paint us. I read your article on "Press Ethics" in the Carlton Gazette, and a very smart bit of writing it was.'

The *Carlton Gazette* is *The Pall Mall Gazette*. The events of 'Temptation'—dealing with Lygon-Rolfe's life in London—take place during 1894; and the only contributions in *The Pall Mall Gazette* at this time about 'Press Ethics' were two long letters-to-the-editor. Each appears under the heading, 'The Ethics of Journalism'. Each was written by Oscar Wilde.

T. P. O'Connor's *Weekly Sun* of 5 August 1894 printed a poem, 'The Shamrock', over Wilde's name. Public reference was made to this poem appearing in the *Cork Weekly Herald* in the early 1880s. And on September 16th *The Weekly Sun* ran an article: 'Is It Plagiarism? What Saith Mr. Oscar Wilde?' Receiving no satisfaction from *The Weekly Sun*, Wilde wrote a letter to the editor of *The Pall Mall Gazette*. Printed on the 20th the letter spoke of 'a very interesting example of the ethics of modern journalism.' The poem was printed without Wilde's knowledge; he was not asked if it were his; and then he was accused of stealing it. On the 22nd *The Weekly Sun*'s assistant editor feebly attempted an answer in the *Gazette*. And on the 25th Wilde concluded the incident by hoping that his letters-to-the-editor 'will have the good result of improving the standard of journalistic ethics in England.'

Curiously enough, an asylum was indirectly connected with this affair. 'The Shamrock' was first published about 1881. The real author was Helena Callanan, an inmate of the Cork Blind Asylum.

Rolfe, in his own subtle way, here saw an opportunity to compare *The Weekly Sun* with John Nicholson. Each had published a poem without consulting the real or supposed author.

Did Rolfe have the attack in mind when he penned the following words? He wished that people, especially Catholics, would not 'upset their own equanimity by the perusal of gasped and snipped and hiccoughed canards, or torpidify their divine-donated faculties by reading feuilletons of great dramatic power, vilely and cheaply printed.... For such matters are of the earth, very earthy in fact, inevitably tending to dull dirtiness.'

He had nothing in mind when he first wrote to Chapman in July 1898 about being 'buried alive by *The Wide World*.'

Whenever he later referred to the Aberdeen Attack, whether in *Hadrian* or elsewhere, Rolfe always spoke of 'the columns of your issue of 18th November.' This was not the day of its appearance in Aberdeen. It was the date of its reprinting in *The Catholic Times.*

9

On 9 January 1899, the date of his entry, Rolfe wrote the same words to several people:

> ... my address for the future will be at the *Holywell Work-house* where you must address me as F. Austin.

The Aberdeen Attack had stripped him, mentally and spiritually; and Holywell had exhausted him, bodily and financially. He posted all his pawn tickets to himself in care of the main London Post Office, St. Martin's-le-Grand, and fled to the workhouse.

Fr. Beauclerk's gift of the blue linen suit was worn as his only outer garment. A corduroy skull cap made from patching material covered his head. His feet were clothed in black slippers and 'socks of Corvine purple.' His soul was naked. The bitter battle of Holywell and the unexpected blow from Aberdeen numbed him into a temporary bewilderment. Regaining his reasoning faculties, he was discharged after breakfast on February 3rd 'at his own request.'

The distance between Holywell and Euston Station was travelled in five hours in 1899, for the price of 16s. 4d. But this could not be afforded. His friend Nicholson was no longer at Chester. The nearest friend now was Dr. Hardy, at Oxford. To go to him, Rolfe walked the 140 miles from North Wales in his 'jute-soled canvas shoes frayed and stained and amorphous with a thousand miles of walking, the withered cloak, the dreadful cap' and grew a 'chestnut-hued moustachio' and beard. Once he was in Oxford, his former master received him, befriended him and paid his fare to London—the city which gave birth first to Frederick William Rolfe and then to his individually doctrinated books.

At the age of thirty-eight Rolfe was seeking an entirely new life. The sensible ways of a daily business world were not to direct him, but the stars and their signs. Author of horoscopes for himself and others, he could never change the nature within his own self. In the October 1893 issue of W. T. Stead's *Borderland*, 'Some Horoscopes of Notable People' were listed. Of seven dates named, one was for 'a person born 8.30 A.M., July 22nd, 1865.' The exact time of day for Rolfe's birth is not known, but the month and day are correct here, if not the year. 'These are poor, ill-starred people,' the article said, 'and life is a continual struggle and hand-to-mouth existence. Some have died in actual want and misery.' Believers or sceptics of this art can only compare these words with Rolfe's life.

Now, damned forever in the eyes of Catholics, there was only one solace for him: literature. With Hardy's aid, he settled in London and immediately made his way to his publisher. In September 1898 *Stories Toto Told Me* had been published by John Lane. Correspondence between Holywell and London included suggestions for further Toto stories to be included in a larger volume. With this in mind, he had 'dug himself out of the nethermost hell' of North Wales to come 'back to town.' And his beginning in writing was assured with this commission from Lane.

Before the end of February, Rolfe met his publisher for the first time. This meeting with the pompous maker of popular literary names is recorded in *Nicholas Crabbe*:

On Monday morning, he presented himself to his publisher. Slim Schelm [John Lane] (a tubby little pot-bellied bantam, scrupulously attired and looking as though he had been suckled on bad beer,) was both interested and afraid. The two had never met before. The publisher had a curiosity to see the writer whose first book he had published; and, knowing the past, he also had his qualms. The writer, on the other hand, took no more interest in the publisher than one takes in the chopper which one seizes at random for hewing out steps to fortune: and he had no fear at the back of his mind: and he had something quite definite to say. Slim Schelm expressed in words his pleasure at the meeting; and he put on a mask which was intended to represent sympathetic commiseration. Crabbe [Corvo-Rolfe] brushed all veils aside.

Schelm-Lane asks Crabbe if he has met Sidney Thorah (Henry Harland)? 'No,' Crabbe replies. 'But I am going to see him to-day. He wrote a year ago, when he was publishing those stories of mine in *The Blue Volume* [*The Yellow Book*], and said that (if I ever wanted a man to talk to) he would like to be the man.' Told that Thorah thinks highly of the stories, Crabbe inwardly glows. 'He had been buried in a desert; and never a word of praise or encouragement had come to him so far. But he kept his satisfaction in his shell, merely poking out his inquisitive eyes.' This first interview is short. Schelm makes apologies because of another important meeting and puts a sovereign into the grim figure's mackintosh pocket as the new author leaves. Crabbe's first impulse is to dash it into the gutter. 'His second thought led him to pouch it: for Schelm actually owed him £3. A year before, the editor of *The Blue Volume* had told him he was to have ten pounds for his last contribution; and the publisher had sent seven. Besides, he was come to London to make money—fairly, if possible: but to make money. It was no good to be more difficult than was necessary. So he pounced on the coin as a bit of flotsam....'

And 'to make money' meant seeing people to his advantage in the literary world. Another person he had exchanged letters with but never met was the editor of *The Yellow Book*. Rolfe's next call was at Henry Harland's South Kensington house.

Nicholas Crabbe describes the encounter between the man from Holywell and the popular author of *Grey Roses* and *Comedies and Errors*, now meeting each other for the first time.

Crabbe waited a couple of minutes in a large and very dainty drawing-room. There were a couch and a piano and lots of weird and comfy chairs, and a feminine atmosphere. Sidney

Thorah suddenly fell in, with a clatter and a rush; and began to talk-on-a-trot. He was a lank round-shouldered bony unhealthy personage, much given to crossing his legs when seated and to twisting nervously in his chair. He had insincere eyes, and long arms which dangled while he sat silent and jerked and waved when he spoke. He spoke a great deal, in eager tones inlaid with a composite jargon which was basically Judisch but varied with the gibberish of newly-arrived American students of the Latin Quarter. He wore a fawn-coloured dressing-suit and a silk handkerchief; and Crabbe, noting the big jacinth on the little finger and the wide upturned nose, suspected an apostate Jew.... He never looked his guest in the face; but made play with his eye-glasses, fiddled with his slippers and the fringes on carpets and chairs, provided cigarettes, and finally settled down with one leg tucked under him and the other dangling in a manner which indicated mitral regurgitation. He evidently was a hard man on trousers. All the time, he was darting side glances; and his shrill clamour lashed Crabbe like sleet. He talked of books and people. His conversation was amazingly witty, pleasant, ephemeral, and insincere. But he seemed to be a man of power; and Crabbe deliberated to give him a chance of being useful.

There was no more *Yellow Book*. Harland now lived by his novels and as literary adviser to Lane. He created his own social world and his house was opened twice a week to major and minor celebrities of London's publishing circles. Harland had admired the Toto stories and he and Rolfe became friends. He listened to the story of Holywell and Rolfe's work on the additional tales for Lane. 'I don't know the ethics of publishers,' Rolfe says in *Nicholas Crabbe*, 'beyond that "Barabbas was a Robber": but I opined that a man of business would be likely to take advantage of necessity. I had no friends upon which to lean. All my goods were pawned. I had no money, and no prospects beyond that book—.' And in the novel, Harland interpolates, 'I've read it. It's going to bring you £700 in six months,' referring to the second series of Toto.

The elation produced by this statement was short-lived. At the second meeting with Lane, a different financial arrangement was suggested and accepted. 'At eleven o'clock, [John Lane] presented a silver cigarette-case containing a single cigarette. [Rolfe] took the latter; and lighted it. They were sitting in a little dirty-green room full of framed drawings in black and white [by the art editor of *The Yellow Book*, Aubrey Beardsley]. A clerk brought in the precious MS. [of *In His Own Image*]; and reverently laid it by the publisher. [Lane] tapped it. "I have been thinking what I can do for your best interests ..." he said. "I should like very much to publish your book, you know; and what I mean to say is I'm willing to give you twenty pounds for it—ten now, and ten on publication. If you consent to accept those terms, I'll send it to the printers at once."'

Harland had just said that the book would be worth £700 in six months, but Rolfe could not wait that long. The urgent need for immediate money made him accept Lane's offer. To his question of accepting the offer, Rolfe could only reply, 'It's not a matter of "will I". You know I must.' But he never forgave Lane for this meanness, although the publisher was forced to add a final ten pounds to the figure.

According to *Nicholas Crabbe* John Lane mentioned Grant Richards' name at the first interview and told Rolfe to go and see him. 'Tell him I sent you. Show him your book. He's a very pushing young publisher; and I'm sure he'll be only too glad to give you some MSS. to read.'

'No man who has put his own individuality into his work has leapt immediately into success,' Richards once told another author. If he had heard these words, Rolfe would have paid little attention to them. He had his own opinion of his talent and its worth.

Lane and Richards were deadly rivals and the first may not have named the second to Rolfe as a prospective employer. The association between the new author in London and the unmet Richards may have gone back to Gleeson White. Before his death, White was the art editor for George Bell & Sons. The firm also employed a scholar by the name of Isaacs, now working with Richards. This may have been the common ground of introduction to the publisher. Isaacs, changing his name to

Temple Scott at this time, became a close friend of Rolfe. When he moved to John Lane's firm he recommended Rolfe's work and tried to sell his stories when he settled in New York. Whoever instigated the introduction, Rolfe did take along a copy of *Stories Toto Told Me*. This was given to the young publisher, inscribed and dated 'March xxiiij 1899'.

In less than two months in London, Rolfe found himself in a pleasing situation. One publisher was going to bring out a book immediately; and a second publisher would soon commission him to write a History of the Borgias.

The experiences of the immediate past had left him with a suspicious mind. An inborn paranoia broke through the surface at Holywell, malignantly spreading and colouring all of his future actions. Rolfe's personality at this time is revealed in *Nicholas Crabbe*:

Crabbe's main characteristic was a most retentive memory. Living, as he did, entirely in himself and in the past, gave him an old-fashioned habit of mind. Consequently his progression was always lateral and somewhat slow. At the same time he was sure: for nothing could exceed his tenacity. He yearned for sympathy; and he would have purred to proper appreciation. He was timid in most things, reserved, fearful and impatient of ridicule and disapproval; and, hence, he was conventional in his dread of publicity. If he had had his will, he would have elected to live alone (with a few slaves). Forced into public life, he was in difficulty. He encased himself more or less in a carapace of secrecy and mystery, watching the world and waiting for an opportunity. He had found his natural predilection for a gregarious existence to be a complete failure; and he was resolved to ally himself to no person and to no company any more. With the development of his individuality had come a remarkable development of his imagination. With the growth of his personality had come a fastidiousness which was composed of boredom, aloofness, contempt, and fine feeling. He was a bundle of inconsistencies. Keenness of sensation, carefully cultivated, made his tender core easily accessible to wounds; but his proud hard (not to say) crusty demeanour concealed them. To his enemies he was enormously exasperating; he never let them see that they had drawn blood. Psychically, he was quick of perception: he could sum up a person or a problem in a minute, and generally accurately. Physically, he gave the impression of being phenomenally obtuse, indurated, ferocious. In the matter of money, he was extravagant, chimerical, quixotic, noncurant, to a degree: but he collected and hoarded odds and ends, books, papers, gems, facts, under all circumstances, even impossible. He was very conservative. Radicalism and dissent filled him with scorn and contempt beyond utterance: the fierce and mordant pungency of his comments on the methods of methodists were quite unequalled. Yet he himself unscrupulously would part with his own cherished illusions or opinions when new light came to him.... He never attacked for the mere sake of attacking: but people who poked at him, or trod on him, had reason for bewailing the cruel violent unexpected inevitability of his crunching grip. He never let go; and he never ceased to persecute and harass. He never forgot anything at all.... He was beginning to understand the necessity of selfishness for the protection of his individuality; and, on these lines, he was becoming self-possessed, self-reliant, strong, and potent. He fully realized that a success would be obtained by tenacity; and that failure would attend hyper-sensitiveness.

This concrete determination to succeed was not the only thing brought into London. When they first saw each other, Harland looked over Rolfe's well-worn clothes, 'but he noted that the socks and the finger-nails were clean, and that the whole arrangement was concise. He revolted at the thin unkempt beard and hair, wondering what the face would look like after shaving.' At his first opportunity, Rolfe had the beard trimmed 'in the Vandyke mode.' His poor clothes were always neat and clean. As a charming speaker, he was invited to Harland's afternoons and met the other guests. Avoiding publicity, he did not often mingle with the others. Yet, when called upon, his compelling personality could hold any audience. The majority of Harland's guests did not figure highly in his estimation. He did meet, however, one person whom he admired: 'that gorgeous Max.'

Of course, fame was one-sided, and Max had no reason to remember the struggling baron. But something in Rolfe's person left an enduring mark on most people coming into contact with him. (Sir) Max Beerbohm did recall him as 'a not tall man, with a red small beard and with spectacles that magnified his eyes in a peculiar way.' To maintain contact with the critic and witty essayist, Rolfe wrote to him, but no more than two letters. 'Both of them in bright *green* ink,' Max remembered in a letter to Symons. 'The first was a request that I would advise him as to the suitability of some very arcane word which he thought of using as a description of something; and the second was a very courteous demur to some (probably idiotic) alteration that I had suggested.'

(Could this brief encounter have instigated anything immortal? Could the 'insistently celebrated critical caricaturist in a frayed waistcoat' have unconsciously used Rolfe, albeit in a most gentle manner, when he drew the portrait of Enoch Soames?)

The small aid from Oxford, the little support by Lane and the occasional sale of the article—to *The New York World, Sunday Magazine,* for instance—kept Rolfe alive, but hardly more. The locations of his rooms for this initial period remain a mystery. The letters he wrote at this time came from business addresses, clubs or the British Museum. It was not until September that he found a permanent home.

Over the years Rolfe had kept in touch with the boy he tutored in 1886. In London, Edward Slaughter had become a solicitor in his father's firm. The first letters to Lane from Wales used Slaughter's business address as a calling post for his mail. Again the solicitor was engaged by Rolfe. Slaughter acted as a semi-literary agent for him.

The young man had moved away from his parents' house and was staying only a few blocks north. Meeting Rolfe one night in August, he brought him to the lodging house and introduced him to a fellow boarder, H. C. Bainbridge. Excusing himself to go out to confession, Slaughter asked his neighbour to entertain his friend. Bainbridge had been playing the piano and Rolfe asked him to continue; he did not wish to interrupt. While Bainbridge finished a composition by Tchaikovsky, the stranger rolled a fat cigarette and lit it. He wore an old mackintosh, a muffler around his neck, carpet slippers on his feet and heavy spectacles covering his 'eagle eyes.' He was silent. When Bainbridge stopped playing, he spoke of an odd story he had recently read in a magazine, a magazine he was able to produce. The stranger asked him to read it. At the end of the article, 'How I Was Buried Alive', the stranger said, 'I wrote it.'

In a week's time Rolfe sent Bainbridge a letter. He was temporarily staying with a person who could not put him up any longer. In Slaughter's absence, he wished 'you would invite me to stay with you, because I'm stony broke. *My book must be finished at once, without delay....* I've no money to go anywhere and that will be fatal to my book. So I wish you'd ask me to stay with you. I only want to sit tight—and write— morning, noon, and night.' Bainbridge told him to come, and on the *'Feast of St. Partridge,* 1899,' Rolfe said 'I'll come on Saturday some time. I shan't be any trouble to amuse, I want to shut myself up in a bedroom and write AND WRITE, eating bread and butter and drinking milk.'

On 2 September 1899 Rolfe moved into 69 Broadhurst Gardens.

At the end of his first day in the new home, 'he sat in his easy chair by the open window of the big bare room, gloating over ... the trees and the frusky splendour of the sunset sky. At last he had a place of his own.... The house beneath him was empty for the night. He was alone with his soul within shut doors.' And behind the same shut doors his lone soul was soon to be joined by the souls of the Borgias, Umar Khaiyam, Meleager, Dom Gheraldo, Nicholas Crabbe and Hadrian VII.

The landlady was 'a Mrs. Griffiths a widow with one small Son,' Slaughter related, but he did not think that she owned the house, merely leasing it. He 'never knew definitely what Rolfe paid her when he was there' and he saw little of his new neighbour in the attic room 'eleven feet square.' Engaged in his father's business, he left the house about nine each morning and did not return until seven at night. Rolfe 'put in most of his time writing, and occasionally going to see publishers and newspaper editors.'

In June, Rolfe had written to Lane, urging him to use his influence 'to get me *regular, and adequately paid, work* upon which I can live while I am producing the literary master-pieces which I have in hand,' referring to the new Toto stories. 'I prefer that the work should be in the nature of a *travelling commission;* and I make the following suggestion. From infor-mation which I possess, *and which I do not intend to disclose,* I am convinced that a literary man, residing for a year in *Persia,* would find the very rarest field.... I have been agitating this for some months: and last week *The Times* announced that the French Government had despatched Capt Viaud (PIERRE LOTI) to Persia. *Verbum sat.*' His second suggestion re-ferred to an expedition to the remains of Magna Graecia, the Greek colonies of Italy. But the unanswered requests confined his wanderings to London for the time. The Toto 'master-pieces' were 'ready on Sept xxviiij' and his contract to write the Borgia began on November 20th.

With the hope of seeing his first thick volume in print in the near future, Rolfe was eager to begin his second book. Payment for the Borgia history seemed adequate. He was to receive one pound each week for eight months and then ten pounds on publication. At least it was an assured income for almost a year. By the end of November he had acquiesced 'in the agree-ment' and was given his first payment of one pound. 'I have got through the first week on 18s. 10d., which I think is a bit of a triumph:' he reported to Richards. 'It was achieved by the simple expedient of cutting dinner: and it has left me furious for work. Now I find the evenings intolerable after the B.M. closes; and think you might let me have something to read by way of change. Mss. for choice, *for which I shall not expect you pay unless you like.* It's *reading* I want *hic et nunc.*'

The required research for the Borgia book came as a hallowed treat after his years of exile into Scotland and Wales. Rolfe revelled in the unearthing of forgotten facts. The fragments of truth had to be pieced together from the printed leaves of thoughts set down in the period of his study. He would not be content with mere mummers' age-old mutterings. The Borgia book would be a stunning and accurate history. In a year he would be singled out as a historian. Everything finally was taking its organized place in his life. Yet 'the Lord in His infinite wisdom has made the world that no one is so poor that he cannot be robbed by another.'

A Christmas present from Harland paid for his simple luxuries. Bainbridge cashed the two-guinea cheque and Rolfe delightfully recited the things it acquired. He first had a Turkish bath, he had his boots soled and then he bought tobacco. For a while Harland's generosity did not end here. Rolfe would walk from Hampstead, through Hyde Park, to South Kensington to breakfast with the man from John Lane's. Harland heard bits of the Borgia past as they were fitted together into Rolfe's history. Bainbridge was an audience to most of the same history and parts of *Hadrian*. Two other listeners were Temple Scott and his wife.

Scott visited Broadhurst Gardens every Saturday and watched Rolfe's 'monster genealogical tree of the Borgia family' grow. In turn, Rolfe would go to Welbeck Mansions, 'where he was a welcomed guest at all times by my wife and children as well as by myself. When he was suffering from hunger he came to us as often as five times a week, and read to us some of his new stories Toto Told Me and what he had written of his Chronicles of the Borgias. We were deeply sympathetic because of the pitiful stories he told us of the wrongs that had been done him by people, especially by certain members of the Roman Catholic Church of which he was a devout and even passionate adherent.... This went on for nearly a year, but he still continued to call on my wife after I had left England for America to take charge of John Lane's publishing business in New York. On these later visits he would read the stories which were later published in the volume In His Own Image and his version of Nicolas's Omar Khayyam.'

Speaking of the Rolfe he knew in London at the close of the century, Temple Scott continued in his letters to Symons: 'In

London I had found him deserving of pity and charity. In his letters to me in New York I found him ungrateful and bitterly misunderstanding of kindness and friendly help. I have never been able to account for this strange conduct, except to put it down to a nature tortured by disappointment and a megalomania that could not be satisfied with what the world had to offer it by way of value, either in money or praise.... His intellectual vanity was colossal. But apart from that I found him a most pleasant companion with a store of archaic lore that was at times weird in the form in which he imparted it. He was childishly superstitious and childishly romanticist.... He may have been a natural liar but he was a harmless one so long as he dealt with the things of his imagination. When it came to human relations, this expression of himself brought him many troubles. He was his own worst enemy. I am afraid there must have been an impish malice in his spiritual make-up. I cannot otherwise account for his sufferings. For he received, so far as I know, many encouragements and much material help. Indeed, I found, that it was irritating to help him. He curdled the milk of human kindness by an acidity of nature he was unable to sweeten, however he might desire to sweeten it. And I am sure he did so desire it.'

At Broadhurst Gardens, Slaughter had become his general agent. Rolfe placed his affairs in Slaughter's hands and even asked him to handle some of his uncommissioned literary work. But the solicitor had two disadvantages: he was kind and he was a Catholic. In April 1899 Rolfe had written to Grant Richards about his own character reference. He referred the publisher to Slaughter, who 'remained my friend after 13 years and in direct opposition to the will of his cousin, the Bishop of Menevia!!' In exactly two years' time, however, he was dismissing the young man. 'You will rejoice to learn that the Bishop of Menevia [Francis Mostyn], of his own volition, and personally, has restored my Rites to me,' Rolfe wrote to Richards on 16 May 1900. 'The Bishop of Menevia told Slaughter two weeks ago, that I was really very good and had been hideously maligned,' he said in a letter to Frederic Chapman two months later. In March 1901 Slaughter left Broadhurst Gardens for the

Boer War. Within three months Rolfe was writing to Richards about his confidence once more having been 'abused by a stupid and dishonourable Roman Catholic: though I have no doubt but that Mr E. J. Slaughter's aboriginal instincts and casuistick breeding, will enable him to pitch some such elaborated and delicately distinguished, yarn into his hebdomadal confessor, or will justify his treachery to me, or at least reduce it from the category of mortal, to that of venial sin; and so maintain the integrity of his idiotick selfconceit.'

Rolfe now was completely dependent on his writing for an income. Half of the twenty pounds he made in 1898 came from the reprinted Toto stories. The following year his total income was approximately £70. It reached £90 in 1900, a weekly average of about £1 14s. 7d., his highest rate of pay since Christchurch. Besides his commissioned work, he did one new Toto story, 'About What Is Due to Repentance', 'about Judas Iscariot of 2,500 words ... an afterthought, done to cleanse his clogged and slimy pen. He delivered the sheaf to [Grant Richards' *Butterfly Magazine*]; and expected guineas. None came' from the young, monocled publisher, whose dreams of Monte Carlo were realized through poorly paid authors and bankruptcies. Several articles appeared in *The New York World*, pieces 'contrived ... to excrete rot of the kind which is dear to the magazine-editor, to wit:— *The Romance of a Raphael, The Confessions of a Carnation, Alligator-hunting in the Andaman Islands, Burke's Stranded Gentry*, 800-1000 words each.'

From the time Temple Scott landed in New York, Rolfe besieged him with entreaties to sell his work. As manager of Lane's American house, Scott had no authority to spend money on authors, 'but Corvo thought I had. The short stories Corvo sent me were unsaleable here and I could do nothing to help him in that way.... The *Smart Set Magazine* would have none of them, though I tried again and again with its editor [Arthur Grissom] who was a friend of mine.... What help I gave him was at my own expense.' When the Borgia book appeared in New York in 1900, Corvo seemed to think that Scott could promote its sale, which he could not do as John Lane's agent. Earlier in 1900 Scott 'ordered a story on a special subject at £25 for serial rights.' It took Rolfe two months to write the story and then Scott 'refused to pay.' At the same time an American newspaper asked him to do an article on Prebendary Wilson Carlile, founder of the Church Army, depreciating his character and work. Thinking of refusing the commission at first, he finally did the piece. But he wrote it according to his own beliefs. He extolled the man and his mission. The article was not accepted and he lost the much-needed payment.

Rolfe's first two substantial books were published in 1901, and each was the subject of contention. The volume of Toto stories was ready in September 1899. But, without any adequate explanation, Lane delayed publication. This withheld the final payment for it and any publicity for the new author. Another point of irritation was the title. Rolfe had named it '*A Sensational Atomist* (term of logick, meaning *one to whom all knowledge is atoms perceived by the senses*—Locke for instance,' a title 'which means something.' One of Lane's suggestions was *Mortal Immortals*, but finally he chose *In His Own Image*, which was 'forced' upon the book against Rolfe's 'will' and which 'means nothing and is blasphemy as well.' Postponement of publication did not leave him idle. On 23 May 1900 he delivered 'the Translation of the Umar Khaiyam after Nicolas.' 'Forced' to complete this in three months, 'in order ... to publish in July 1900,' this book for Lane was also delayed for publication.

Seventeen months after the manuscript was delivered to Lane, *In His Own Image* was published on 5 March 1901, forty-two days after the death of Queen Victoria.

These tales present Corvo-Rolfe at his delightful best. Each is a fraction of a large and colourful panorama of saints and sinners, the pagan past intermingled with the reverent present. The glorious sun of Italy warms and illuminates all things. The bizarre but cunningly calculated stories depict saints, angels, 'the Padre Eterno on His Great White Throne,' peasants, Cappuccini and Jesuits, his boy 'slaves' and Corvo himself as 'la sua eccellenza' or 'dear Don Friderico'. Traditions of the Church are interwoven with ancient legends and created myths in a language as refreshing as a day in the Abruzzi hills. The boys who serve Corvo could have waited upon the Caesars or the gods before them. They are not mere youths but the time-less personification of Life itself.

Begun in the trying days of privation in the London of 1894 and added to during the starving, belligerent period at Holywell, they convey none of Rolfe's later bitterness. Here and there touches of intimate personality show through. In 'About Some Friends' Rolfe writes:

People are very cruel to me in the way of neglect. No one ever loved me well enough to take trouble to find out that which would give me pleasure. No stranger in the street ever said to me, 'O, sir, why are you so utterly sad?' Friends do not to me, as they would that I should do to them. There is some impenetrable mail of ice around me, which only one dead heart ever has been warm enough to melt. Sometimes, very rarely, when I speak long and late at night, the ice wears thin. Then, kind eyes look at mine, astonishingly unlidded; and kind voices say, 'Oh, if only we had only known!'—Well! why don't confounded people try to know: and know? This is not difficult, when one desires.

In giving the title *In His Own Image*, Lane had no idea that this is a faithful description of the book's chief personality. Although Rolfe is in the stories, he is not the central figure. This part is given to Toto. As the story-teller Toto is moulded in Rolfe's image and as narrator he demands the centre of the stage. The tales revolve around him, a person more real to Rolfe than anything else in them. 'I mean that Toto was, thank God & all His Saints, an uneducated peasant. No school board had ever defiled him; and hence his exquisiteness.' Instead of a character merely from Rolfe's mind, Toto emerged from the inner regions of his very soul.

Not only did the publication of this book postpone the final payment, it severed a friendship. This late friend, a Catholic, was soon to appear in the pages of Rolfe's books, beginning with *Hadrian*. Repeating his own history just after 'a series of libels ... were directed against me in the newspapers, especially in Catholic newspapers—dirty Keltic wood-pulp,' Rose-Rolfe, 'not to do any man an injustice, and that no one might call me rash or precipitate in my decision, ... waited two years—two whole years.' The first person to come to him 'in this period of isolation' was Bishop Mostyn. The 'one other Catholic' was 'a man of my own trade. Later, that one betrayed me again, so I will say no more of him.' But he does say more of him: 'Once upon a time We used to know a certain writer of amatory novels. The sentimental balderdash, which he put into the mouths of his marionettes (he only had one set of them), influenced Us greatly. He had a living to get. He thought he could get it by recommending the Temporal Power. He was a very clever worldly Catholic indeed: but the arguments, which he produced in so vital a matter as the earning of his living, were so sterile and so curatical, that We summed up the Temporal Power as negligible.'

This 'writer of amatory novels' was Henry Harland and he had been selected by Rolfe as the Ideal Friend—the first of several such Ideal Friends in a very short time. When published, *In His Own Image* was dedicated merely to an unnamed 'Divo Amico Desideratissimo'. The generous friend, the host, the provider of breakfasts and literary introductions had become a symbol of admiration. For Rolfe he was 'Viro Integerrimo Henrico Harland Scriptori Venerabunde Cogitabunde d d d' and, as such, he should be honoured as the dedicatee of the Toto book. This honour was fully appreciated and accepted by Harland. Yet the book was printed without any dedicatee's name. In an interview recorded in *Nicholas Crabbe,* Corvo speaks of the mean payment and treatment of the book by Lane. Harland answers:

'I didn't make the bargain.... And as for publication—it's simply delayed because the opportune moment hasn't arrived yet. And look here, while we're talking of [*In His Own Image*], take a word from me as a friend. There's a flavour about that book which I don't like. Cut it out.'

'Silly man. The book's in print; and I'm halfway through the first proofs already. But what's this flavour which you've only just discovered?'

[Harland] named it. It came upon [Rolfe] like a clap of

thunder, or the blast of some malignant star. His fierce claws quivered. He flamed in the face; and went out icily and incisively.

'That's quite gratuitous. What a frightfully degenerate imagination you must have. Now mark me: I won't make, or permit to be made, a single alteration—.'

Harland, who had bought and raved about the first Toto stories and had urged Lane to publish more, pronounced his own doom in this interview. Whether he himself had 'contrived to sniff ... this savour' or whether some other person had warned him, his words revealed a strongly suspected taint of homosexuality in the tales. And, if Rolfe was 'a fool for your pains,' he added, if he persisted 'in publishing that book as it is, I shall have to close my door to you; and all my friends will do the same.'

Harland no doubt gave this word of caution with the best intention, but it was repaid by a mind recognizing only broken faith. Harland thus was written into *Hadrian* and *Don Renato* and was perceptibly parodied as Sidney Thorah in *Nicholas Crabbe*. In *The Desire and Pursuit of the Whole* he becomes 'a scribe of a single theme, four time repeated.' A review of his *Lady Paramount* in *The Outlook* for 10 May 1902—(was it written by Rolfe?)—said that 'Mr. Harland only tells one story.'

Impelled by poverty to accept any offer, stamped as a novice and made to wait on the whims of his publisher, Rolfe now was branded a deviate, not from the laws of society, in his mind, but rather from the laws of his faith. And branded so by another Catholic. The satisfactory beginnings of 1899 had now turned sour.

The book, in some small way, presents Rolfe as an Illustrator. Corresponding earlier with Lane about the Bodley Booklet, Rolfe supplied verbal ideas for illustrations. But the only one utilized was placed on the title page of *In His Own Image*. This represents his heraldic device: a priest's hat over a shield on which are a raven and a cross potent, signifying Religion and Fame. Surrounding the achievement is the motto, 'All Will Be Well,' in Greek. The whole is drawn in a vulva-shaped lozenge.

('The freshness of Toto, with "his calm eyes (which) glittered like diamonds in the brown robe of his skin", blows through the book, and adds an element of living life to the mythology. For mythology it is, and here lies Rolfe's great achievement. He has written the Tanglewood Tales of Christianity. He had given to English Literature a Catholic Olympus.' So wrote Alfonso de Zulueta in his review of the 1924 edition of *In His Own Image*. And to this he added a fanciful story about the book's history. 'These stories, first published in the "Yellow Book", as "Stories Toto Told Me", ran into two editions under their final title "In His Own Image",' he said. 'But the second edition,' he explained, without naming his authority, 'was bought up by a fanatical female who piously made of it a bonfire in her back garden.')

After Holywell, John Holden never saw or corresponded with Rolfe. Years later he remarked that 'a friend showed me Rolfe's *How to Write Begging Letters*. I remember that on the first page was a sketch of Rolfe, evidently done by his own hand.' This referred to a curious article which may be considered another, although minor, attack against Rolfe's person. In the August 1901 issue of *The Harmsworth London Magazine* a six-page, illustrated article appeared, 'Begging Letters'. It speaks of the impossibility of inspecting 'the records of the Begging Letter Department of the London Mendicity Institution without being struck by the number of instances of the amazing credulity of those who are rich and charitable.' The victims are robbed by professional letter-writing crooks, operating either singly or in gangs. Illustrations of the begging letters, a Certificate of Registry of Death and a Second Notice to Quit are reproduced. And seven portraits, no doubt imaginary, show the author of each appeal. Some of the writers are unmasked and sent to jail, the article states, only to come out and start all over again.

Recalling this article and its first sketch, Holden added that he could 'never understand this.'

The style in which the article is written is not Rolfe's. Neither is the manner in which the subject matter has been gained. The author's name on the story is 'Frank Holmfield', which may be as fictitious as the pseudonyms used by Rolfe from time to time. Under the title is a drawing of a man at work on a begging letter, a man who looks surprisingly like Rolfe. The face, almost in profile, has the Corvine outline. There are glasses and an eye-shade. Holden saw Rolfe wear an eye-shade while painting at Holywell; and visitors to Broadhurst Gardens saw the eye-shade.

The sketch, like the text, does not bear the stamp of Rolfe's talent. From the reproduction, it probably was done as a wash drawing. Yet, since his Holywell days, the only surviving pieces of art by him are in line or in solid blacks and whites. In January 1903 he wrote a letter to a young nephew which he illustrated and which can be compared to this magazine illustration. The head in the sketch is stooped over a high table, on which the letter is being written. Rolfe preferred to use a drawing board, set on his knees. *Hadrian* opens with this position and it is illustrated in the letter to his nephew. When Mrs. Ragg first saw Rolfe in Venice, 'a writing board spread with thick white paper was on his knees and he wielded the tallest fountain pen I had ever seen before or have seen since.' A similar fountain pen is in the letter to his nephew, but *The London Magazine* drawing shows a meagre pen, almost lost between his fingers. Rolfe was always honest about his sparse hair. Yet the magazine man has a liberal amount. Rolfe may not have been a natural artist, but he tried to be mechanically accurate. He knew perspective and allowed for the angles of planes. The one lens of the man's glasses, in semi-profile, is almost a perfect circle, something Rolfe would have noticed and corrected.

Artists of limited experience, and even some who are professional, have favourite methods, and find that certain poses or styles are more convenient for them. This is true in drawing profiles. Rolfe favoured the left side of the face. The magazine illustration shows the right side. But the strongest point against this sketch being by Rolfe is its position on the page. It appears at the top of the 'Begging Letters' article and just above a line of text which seems to act as a caption for it. Rolfe never admitted to the writing of begging letters. And he never would permit his own sketch, if he did one, to appear at the beginning of such an article. Nor would he agree to place the sketch just over the 'caption' which reads: 'With Facsimiles and Fancy Sketches of Their Writers.'

Was the purpose of this article as innocent as any other in the periodical? The appearance of the Rolfe-like person on its first page is bewildering. Some one may have had a score to pay off and this was one way of doing it. Did Rolfe himself see it? The attack in the Aberdeen newspapers took him four years to answer, in *Hadrian*. In November 1908 Rolfe had 'done the Excommunication of Harmsworth and the new Order for damning him is an Order of Chivalry.' This is *The Bull Against the Enemy of the Anglican Race*. Written by Hadrian VII, it violently attacks Lord Northcliffe and his *Daily Mail*. 'It is the finest sequence of Corvine prose. . . . It represents his dislike of the cheap Press and all the developments in Fleet Street during the nineties. His wrath took pontifical form and it is doubtful if the Latinists of the Roman Bullatium could have composed anything so sustained, furious, and magnificently medieval. It should figure in all future Literature of Hate.' This was written by Sir Shane Leslie, but without the suspicion that Rolfe had any personal motive to blast Northcliffe.

Although he himself was plying the trade of books, there were times when he argued against the wisdom of the invention of the press. In this *Bull* he states:

Since the three-times and four-times accursed invention of the art of printing, and its application by the turpilucricupidous (baronial or otherwise) primarily for gain of gold and secondarily for gain of power, both by means of the concupiscence of human nature ever (as Saint Paul says) avid of some novelty, it has been the custom of Our apostolic predecessors (from Alexander the Sixth, the Paparch, of magnificent invincible memory) to muzzle these devils of powers by censures, maledictions, excommunications, interdicts, and all commodious anathemas, whose example We are not slow to follow; and We will make a mild beginning, while reserving far more awful fulminations for the reduction of incorrigibility.

In the *Chronicles of the House of Borgia* he both condemns and praises the work of the printer:

Yet, by means of ambulant printers, who printed only one

page at a time on a hand-press in a mule-cart (and who were the pioneers of that curse to real civilization, the printed book), before 1500 no fewer than 4987 works had been printed in Italy alone. Here again the fifteenth-century passion for perfect workmanship came into play. Look at an Aldine Classic, and mark its exquisite form. Messer Aldo Manuzio of Venice set a great artist, Messer Francesco Raibolini (detto Il Francia), who painted the dulcet Pieta in the National Gallery, to cut a fount of type after the lovely handwriting of the poet Petrarch. This is the Aldine, or original Italic type; the script of a fourteenth-century singer. Can the twentieth century, with its manifold appliances, its labour-saving machinery, better that handiwork, or approach that design; or would a Royal Academician condescend to cut types for a printer?

A month after the *Chronicles of the House of Borgia* was published, Rolfe wrote that 'the history of the Borgias was proposed to me by Grant Richards as a subject for a piece of hackwork. Because of poverty, I accepted the task at a wage of £1 a week and £10 on publication. I had no part in the initiation.' Three months after the agreement, he suggested to Richards 'the desirability of increasing that amount to thirty shillings— a sum which would save me many petty worries,' but the proposal was ignored.

At the start Rolfe was highly pleased with Richards' wish to have him write a history of the Borgia family, 'one of the most attractive subjects in history.' He knew the period and the people and where to find the facts. The research and the writing occupied him from 20 November 1899 until 30 July 1900. On September 24th he commented on the reader's report, which spoke of deletions and frowned upon his outmoded style of spelling. 'I was denied access to original sources of information, and forbidden to write from the stand-point of the serious historian. I was commanded to write vividly and picturesquely to suit the Library Public, and to confine myself to the Brit. Mus. Thus restricted, I conceived the idea of casting my work in the form of a *satura* or picturesque gallimaufry. I studied the subject, and wrote the book ... by contract. During this time, I frequently was summon'd to read portions of my m.s. to Grant Richards. They were applauded. Certain alterations, of which I could not approve were required to be made in my m.s. in Sept. 1900. In consequence of these, and there being no stipulation in my contract obliging me to sign the work, I prohibited its being issued under my name. This prohibition was dated XXVII Sept. 1900.'

Rolfe agreed with the reader that the first version was 'loose', 'clumsy', with the spelling 'incorrect'. He would have the final version completed on 'Saturday, Nov. the third' and in Richards' hands 'on Monday, Nov. the twelfth.' In the meantime he said that Richards should 'invent a man of straw, John Brown or James Black or St. George Gerry, and put him, in those lists of which you wrote in July, as the author of the *House of Borgia*.' Doing a second version of the story did not concern him. What did irritate him were the affronts to his scholarship. The facts had to be compared with original documents, or those at least printed at the time. To make the history authentic he used the original spelling and phraseology. These, at the beginning of the twentieth century, formed the reader's chief objection. But to change them would spoil the whole effect. Richards, the publisher, listened only to his reader. The heated, one-sided argument was carried on by letters between Broadhurst Gardens and Richards' office. But they did not weary the young publisher. He still maintained friendly feelings towards his 'historian'. Early in 1901 he sent an invitation to Rolfe for a meeting, which was promptly answered: 'It was extremely kind of you to say that you look forward to meeting with pleasure a person who naturally is antipathetick: but the gods alone know what we shall find to say. I don't.'

Priding himself on visual and factual accuracy, Rolfe saw the first page proofs of the Borgia book and objected 'to the insufficient spacing of the astericks; and to the diversity of numerals, here a figure, there a word. My MS. is perfectly uniform; if you gave your [Scottish] printer instructions to abide by that, I fail to see that you incur expense of over-running.' But he saw only the proofs to page 112. 'My corrections of deviations from my m.s. in the proofs of pp. 1-112 in many cases were disallowed.

I did not correct proofs of pp. 113-375,' probably because he did not see them. Richards was an adventurous publisher, indulging in expensive enterprises. The Borgia book was issued at one guinea, a lot of money in 1901. The book was costly to produce and Richards wisely did not expect a great profit from it. There-fore, once set, any additional work would diminish its scanty profit. Rolfe knew nothing about printing plants. Type-setters have their own individual codes for blocking-in areas and spac-ing. The numerous spelling errors in the books were due to the type-setter misreading words not familiar to him in Rolfe's manuscript.

Not as artist but as art director, Rolfe planned the illustrations for the history, choosing portraits and medals. For the frontis-piece he selected Il Pinturicchio's 'Pope Alexander Adoring the Risen Christ' and he berated Richards over the way it was repro-duced, saying that 'this is a carefully mutilated *piece* of the square picture named on p. 160.' But Richards 'mutilated' it to its advantage. The whole painting shows the risen Christ above an open tomb, with three watching soldiers to one side and Alex-ander VI on the other. In this setting, Alexander certainly is not the chief figure. As hero of Rolfe's history, Richards cropped the picture to show nothing but his kneeling figure. However, the picture's credit placed it as 'From a Portrait in the Vatican Library.' This mistake Rolfe was careful to point out and to correct to 'Borgia Tower.' (The complete and triangular painting is reproduced in Arnold H. Matthew's *Life and Times of Rodrigo Borgia*, 1924. An even more closely cropped portion of Alexander VI than the one which appears in Rolfe's book, showing only his profile, acts as a frontispiece for *The Borgia Pope* by Orestes Fer-rara, 1942, in which the author writes of Rolfe's *Chronicles of the House of Borgia*: 'This is a very original book, which con-tains some errors, but many fewer than other books which are more celebrated.')

A few days after the book's publication, he wrote to Richards, saying that 'the author of "Chronicles of the House of Borgia" notes that the usual Author's Copies are withheld from him, after publication.' Three days later he acknowledged receiving 'six mutilated copies ... (English edition: none of the American). They will serve to contrast Henrietta Street [Richards' office address] with Vigo Street [Lane's address], against the eighteen copies of "In His Own Image" which John Lane, and Mr. Temple Scott, courteously sent me at the proper time.' One of these 'six mutilated copies' was inscribed: 'This first copy of my second book offered with respect and love to my Father and Mother by their eldest son *Freddy xxiiij Oct. 1901.*'

Before the end of the year Henry Harland was to write to 'Dear Corvo' about this book: 'Your Borgia is GREAT. To say nothing of the labour and the learning of it—the historic imagination, the big vision, the humour, the irony, the wit, the perverseness, the daring, and the tremendously felicitous and effective *manner* of it!! It is like a magnificent series of tapestry pictures of the XV Century. Of course, I think you are *advocatus Diaboli*, but *what* an advocate. In any land save England, such a book would make its author at once FAMOUS and RICH. It is GREAT.'

'This letter gains point from the fact that Mr Harland thus spontaneously exploded in a shriek of admiration after a personal and acerb disagreement of two years' duration,' Rolfe remarked at the time.

'Frederick William Serafino Austin Lewis Mary Rolfe (Frederick Baron Corvo) (Tonsured Clerk.) Writer. Celibate' made application for financial assistance to the Royal Literary Fund early in 1902. To support his case, he listed his annual incomes since 1898. For 1901 he had earned thirty shillings. To this figure he added: 'During 1901 my affairs were directed by Stanhope Sprigge, Literary Agent, at a commission of 25%. I dismissed him, on account of his Roman Catholicism, i Jan. 1902.'

To support his application as a writer, Rolfe sent along copies of his three books and the recent letter of praise from Harland. 'I do not know whether you will consider Mr Henry Harland's weird appreciation of my work to be *ad rem*,' he wrote; 'but he is in Italy at present, and I am unable to procure further testimony from him till his return.'

For character references, the letters going to the Fund in his favour were written by Henry Newbolt, Dr. Richard Garnett, Maurice Hewlett, Edmund Gosse, J. M. Barrie and Dr. Hardy, 'an experienced writer of testimonials.' The choice of Barrie was an unconscious revelation by Rolfe of his nature. The man of letters no doubt was chosen primarily because of his relationship to Ogilvie-Forbes; but it is interesting to note some parallels in his life to that of the man who asked him for a testimonial. Although the successful author and playright enjoyed a reward unrealized by Rolfe, on arriving in New York he stated in an interview—using words which Rolfe could have spoken—printed in *The Author* for December 1896: 'Silver and gold have I none; go ye to my publishers.' This same Barrie created Peter Pan; Rolfe was a youth who, in some ways, never grew up. In *Dear Brutus* Barrie quotes Shakespeare:

'The fault, dear Brutus, is not in our stars,
But in ourselves, that we are underlings.'

—a premise to which Rolfe could not subscribe. Yet in the same play Barrie borrows one of Lamb's 'Dream-Children' and casts her in the part of Margaret, crying out: 'Daddy, come back; I don't want to be a might-have-been.' For all the recognition bestowed upon him during his life, Rolfe easily could have posed as a 'might-have-been'.

Rolfe wrote 'slowly and with difficulty,' he said in a letter accompanying his application to the Fund. 'Medical assistance alone enables me to work at all. My wardrobe is reduced to rags. I am burdened with debts.... I am on the verge of ocular and nervous collapse.'

On two of the fly-leaves of the Borgia history sent to the Fund he had written his Author's Statement. With this Statement, written when the book was published, he denounced it as a product from his hands and imagination. Copies of the Statement were sent to libraries and he asked that they be pasted in copies of the book. In the book itself, the Fund read, marginal notes were written about the 'mutilations' and 'deletions' by the publisher. A note at the top of the 'Kindling' chapter said: 'After writing the book, I made the acquaintance of Conte Cesare Borgia. From him I learned of many errors in what I had written (e.g. that these two pages are all wrong. I offered my new knowledge to Grant Richards, who refused it.' But not all

of the notes were deadly serious. One printed sentence reads:
'Now, [Michelangelo] was in Rome, "art-adviser" to the Terrible
Pontiff, eating his own heart in inactivity, burning and yearning
to work with his own hands, with all the passionate excruciating
torture suffered by any artist who may not put his talent "out to
the exchequers".' Opposite this, Rolfe's marginal note reads:
'did I write this'.

On April 11th he could send a letter to the Fund saying that
'I really am at a loss adequately to express my most particular
and lively sentiments not only of satisfaction for the delicacy
with which my affair has been managed, but also of gratitude
for the generosity with which a temporary provision has been
made for my necessity.'

On the previous day the Royal Literary Fund had granted
him £50.

After the publication of *In His Own Image*, Trevor Haddon
took the place of Harland as the Divine Friend. But what Rolfe
sought in people he could never express. He had a most retentive
memory and a splendid knowledge of ancient lore, but he lacked
common foresight. His goal was always the unobtainable, for
the ideal is never real.

In fact, *In His Own Image* produced two 'friends' for the one
lost in Harland. Each was introduced to the author by a letter
of admiration for Toto. The story of the first 'complete outsider'
is told in Chapter Twenty-four of *Nicholas Crabbe*. This letter
came from a painter, who 'wrote rather tackily, with wonderment, not without taste and discrimination. He called [the book]
an achievement; and sympathized with the personal tempera-
mental trouble which it portrayed. He offered his hand, with his
heart in it; and willingly would be a friend.' So Trevor Haddon,
another convert to Rome, was introduced to Rolfe.

In *Nicholas Crabbe*, Crabbe-Rolfe is already befriending
Robert Fulgentius Kemp-Sholto Douglas as a lodger in his spare
room. If he replied to Haddon's invitation of friendship, 'it
would be no disloyalty to' Douglas. For a week he 'perpended'
and then 'deliberately responded' with a letter, ending: 'I dedicated my book to the Divine Friend, Much Desired. I do not
know whether you are he—or another.' Soon after its reply Corvo

visited the painter's Westminster studio, finding him 'to be a man who (in a previous incarnation) must have sat for Moroni's celebrated Portrait of a Tailor'. Conversation travelled, ideas were exchanged 'and sympathy seemed to be in the air.' Rolfe was 'desperately frightened, horribly afraid of blundering: he poked out both eyes, and waved his feelers, being violently anxious not to miss any sympathetic sensations. He made a clean breast of his frightful (but not abnormally blameful) past. The painter said, "If I had suffered what you have suffered, I should have gone out of my mind".' The other 'described his present life, acts, hopes, fears. Indeed, in the knowledge that a friend is one soul in two bodies, he made the wildest and most frantic effronts to correspond with the graces which were offered to him.'

On Haddon's part, Rolfe was not the person his imagination expected. His character was shadowed by a 'cold shyness,' which was due to fear and mistrust of people. Rolfe's straitened circumstances evoked a suggestion from the new friend. Haddon recently had read of a literary agent by the name of Stanhope Sprigge, and he now offered to see Sprigge on Rolfe's behalf. Rolfe consented. But when the painter and the writer next met Rolfe was perturbed. He had discovered that Sprigge was a Catholic and he was suspicious of him and of Haddon because of the recommendation. Yet the loneliness within Rolfe's soul called out towards any answering person.

When he visited the painter's house in Elms Road, Clapham, a wife and three children were presented. Rolfe was a gracious and entertaining guest. Haddon enjoyed his company, his stories and his music. But his wife instinctively disliked this stranger, who, years later, made her husband destroy a large collection of Rolfe's letters 'of the deepest interest from a psychological point of view.' But the end of the Divine Friendship was caused indirectly by Sprigge. In their transactions one of Rolfe's manuscripts ultimately was missing. 'Then the fat was in the fire.' Haddon 'was a Jesuit spy surreptitiously enticing him into the net. There was always a catch somewhere. If through some personal influence an opening was offered it proved to be an equivalent on incarceration. Anything to silence and sequester him.

In the end [Rolfe], having asked me to let him have a statement of the various small sums I had advanced him sent me a post-card in green ink "When your accomplice S. S. has returned me the MS he purloined I will consider settling the amount of your bill." ... Praeterea nihil.'

The third of Rolfe's Ideal Friends from this period was Sholto Douglas. Although Douglas posed for Kemp in *Nicholas Crabbe*, the friendship ended as quickly and as disastrously as the one with Haddon. But Rolfe was to profit from this association in one way.

Douglas had been searching for the story about Fioravanti and Guerino for a long time. Rereading the collection of Toto stories one day, a thought came to him. He wrote to the author to 'ask him to help me. It seemed such a brilliant thought. On the one hand it might lead me to some intercourse with a de-lightful author; on the other it might give me that tale which ... I had been seeking so long. So I wrote.' A short but charming letter was sent on 10 March 1902, addressed to the publisher and enclosing a 2½d. stamp. 'An answer came promptly ... in Latin, and affected the archaic spelling of the "silver" period ... and fascinated me. I determined to go one better as I replied at length in Greek. I expected this would bring a note at least in Oscan or Hittite.... There are hellenisms innumerable in [my letter]. But I was to be disappointed: he answered in English to say he could not understand my letter and to ask for a transla-tion. To this I wrote,' on the 16th, ' "I lie down before your feet and kiss the ground, and there I try to think of all the apologies that all the parts of all lands have ever made, in the hope that among them you may find one, one little, little, obscure apology which you will deign to accept. The charm of your first letter to me, and the kindness which prompted you to charm me with your most excellent gift of language, were so intoxicating that I was led away by them into the devious forest where I per-petuated those four foolish sheets of paper, now, I hope, cast for ever away".' In a flowery gush of words Douglas explained as much as he knew of the tale of Fioravanti and Guerino and stated that he knew a young Italian with the name Fioravanti.

The reply brought only 'some meagre information' about a

certain Fioravanti who had nothing to do with the legend. But it was accompanied with numerous questions, including, 'Who are you?' Douglas answered that he was 'no doubt somewhat older than you—I can say that because you aged quickly between your first little book and the coming of ["In His Own Image"].' To this Corvo commented with a note on the letter: 'Senile.' Douglas was in his late twenties, more than ten years younger than Corvo. He was a private tutor 'doing sufficient work to reduce my poverty to the tolerable minimum.' He was not a Roman Catholic and he was a Scot.

After the exchange of six letters, Rolfe spoke about a possible meeting. Douglas 'enjoyed the delicious and clever letters. I also enjoyed writing answers to them. I felt sure that we ought to rest content with these joys. However I had left it to him to decide whether I was to go or not. And of course he decided that I was to visit him. So I journeyed from Piccadilly into the furthest suburbs; further, I believe, than any human being has ever journeyed, into one of those regions at which one looks from the trains as they draw clear of the vistas of London. As I came near the necessary street I passed a tall dark young man of about twenty. I came to the conclusion that it was [Rolfe]. I was wrong. I only mention it to show how mistaken was my pre-conceived notion of the man. At last I found the house, a horrid semi-detached little villa, with an advertisement card of board and lodging in the window. I was shewn into [a] room filled with all the abominations that every landlady of such a house seems feted to acquire. After keeping me waiting for five minutes [Rolfe] skipped into the room. Skipped is the right word. I was utterly surprised. I had expected a tall, dark, young man, with long hair and large eyes. Instead of that I saw a little man of forty, very thin, rather bald, wearing spectacles. He was carrying a bundle of papers under his arm, giving the idea, no doubt in-tentionally, that he had just torn himself away from his task of book-making. I have seldom seen a man of his age so nervous and ill-at-ease. Our conversation was hopelessly dull. I do not think that it was my fault. I soon saw that he was really pleased to meet me, but I could not make him talk. There is no doubt that it was a very dull interview. And yet as an author and a letter-writer I know no one who was less dull.'

That evening Douglas wrote to Rolfe, saying that he 'had absolutely failed to expect that very human kindliness, which twinkles so charmingly behind your spectacles' and invited him to his place 'on Wednesday afternoon.' The interview resulted in a flow of letters from Rolfe, who 'lavished envelopes upon me in an exuberant extravagance which I have never seen surpassed.' The letters which went from one to the other spoke of dreams and friends, books and art, of the past, present and future. On May 4th Douglas wrote about having 'great thoughts, but I cannot express them in words. But you have intuition, and can see what I have not written.' Some articles written and forgotten about were unearthed, sent to Rolfe and a strange collaboration began.

Douglas supplied the original manuscripts and Rolfe re-worked them in his own inimitable style. On May 12th the first articles were named in a letter. 'I wrote several "Studies in Unwritten Literature", such as "Plato's Dialogue Concerning the Music of Wagner", "On Shakespeare's Tragedy of King Charles", "Petronius Iter in Britannicum"....' Rolfe's moulding them into a new form 'damaged them' in Douglas's opinion, 'but I admit he sold them.... And he took no money for them: I got it all.'

Nine 'Reviews of Unwritten Books' appeared in *The Monthly Review* between February and June 1903. Fifteen additional 'Reviews' were returned to Rolfe. Not all emanated from Douglas, and Rolfe in each case had been the final author. For the rest of his life Rolfe was to suggest to publishers the possibility of using them together in the form of a book.

The happiest moment in the collaboration came when Rolfe discovered that Douglas had once completed a translation of Meleager. Here was a rare opportunity. FitzGerald had created a popularity for Omar Khayyam, with dozens of translations and adaptations appearing at the turn of the century. Why not do the same thing for Meleager? Rolfe had already done an adaptation of Omar for Lane and his 'silver decadence' would perfectly match the words and thoughts of the Greek poet. By the first of May, Meleager was in Rolfe's hands, to be carefully read. Before the end of June, Douglas' fury passionately struck

out at Rolfe's work. 'A detailed study of your version only con-
firms my first impression, that you have failed to find the soul of
Meleager, that your ear frequently plays you false, leads you
into complexity where a failure for the sake of simplicity would
be excusable, that my version as a whole is much better than
yours as a whole,' Douglas sadly admitted. The final parting
came with the young man's written words: 'What a fatal mistake it was of mine to send you those MSS. I would give much
to go back to that day and refrain from having sent them.'

For £25 Rolfe did one more book for Lane. Harland warmly
supported Temple Scott's recommendation to let Rolfe do a
translation of Omar from the French of J. B. Nicolas, which is
based on the original Persian. 'Forced' to complete it in three
months' time, it was another book delayed in transit between
author and public. 'The Translation of the Umar Khaiyam
after Nicolas' was delivered on 23 May 1900. It was published
in January 1903.

The work originally was promised for publication in July
1900. Six months later Rolfe suggested 'a little glossary, to be
placed at the end of the book, explaining more recondite Persian
words (e.g. medresseh, gadjadeh, noorous, etc.).' But the idea was
not considered. Temple Scott had first been selected to write an
introduction. But Lane had accused Scott in New York of taking
money from the business and brought an action against him.
The case was heard in New York and Scott was exonerated of all
charges, but he was dismissed from the Lane company in September 1901. This cancelled the original plan. An American,
Nathan Haskell Dole, composed the one used.

Nicolas had lived in Persia and familiarized himself with the
language. This Frenchman, Dole says, signalized 'the first complete translation of 'Umar Khaiyam into any modern language
by discovering in every reference to wine a symbolical and
wholly spiritual significance'. He continues with a note on
Corvo, who 'shows that he is a masterly translator. He often
penetrates through the decorative filigree of the French style to
something approaching 'Umar's own marvellous concentration,
condensation. Where, for instance, M. Nicolas, with a humorous
lack of humour, declares that the nightingale speaks *dans un*

langage approprié à la circonstance, the English reads elegantly "Whispers me with fitting tongue".' Dole's piece ends with Corvo in mind: 'He shows us in terse idiomatic English, full of original and often startling flashes of intuition, just what he thinks 'Umar himself meant, as interpreted by the Chief Dragoman; and he has given us a masterpiece, absolutely justifying the discretion of Mr. Henry Harland and Mr. Kenneth Grahame, at whose solicitation the work was undertaken.'

Of course, Temple Scott's name could no longer appear in any book by John Lane. But the inclusion of Grahame's name was a mystery.

Grahame never met Rolfe; and Rolfe had written to him only a very few times about 1900. Grahame visited Harland's household, but never for afternoon tea. Instead, he 'preferred to frequent the pleasant Saturday-night orgies—perhaps I ought to say symposia—whisky and baccy—at Harland's flat, and at these the Baron never turned up.' He was not acquainted with Nicolas' translation and 'Fitzgerald was always good enough for me.' The connection of his name with the 1903 *Umar Khaiyam* was as mysterious to him as to anyone else. 'Why the American introducer to Corvo's English version of Nicolas' Rubaiyat dragged me in, I never found out.' It may have been one of John Lane's methods of advertising one of his authors.

The book was dedicated to 'Guilhelmo · Eduardo · et · Margaritae'—the Slaughters. The glossary, never commissioned, was never written. 'This new and elaborate version of Omar fell flat in England, and was stillborn in the United States.'

Yet one person saw it, read it and marvelled over it. He had already admired Corvo's work, ever since *In His Own Image.* Across the Atlantic, in Washington, D.C., Ambroise Bierce hailed this new author to his friends.

Counterbalancing the continual disappointments, life in London had certain compensations. The errant Anglican was near his family. His two younger brothers had left England. Alfred James, an ordained Anglican minister, had emigrated to Australia and eventually became headmaster of a school in Sydney. Percy Hamilton joined a well known merchant shipping line in Hong Kong and later was promoted to the position of commander. Herbert and his family lived in London. Closest to Rolfe both in distance and in artistic temperament, he felt for him an admiration that Rolfe reciprocated. From about 1890 Herbert was a church organist. As a Fellow of The Royal College of Organists, he composed two pieces of music which were used in Anglican Church services in their time. When not seeing each other, these two brothers sent each other letters.

Making an engagement for tea with John Lane, Rolfe wrote a quick note on 20 May 1902 to say that he 'entire[ly] forgot ... that I had a standing engagement with my father for *Friday* which I cannot possibly break.' Seventy-one days later—and eight days after Rolfe's forty-second birthday—his father died.

The event may have opened a secret door once confining hidden things. In a letter to H.C. Bainbridge on 3 March 1903 Rolfe spoke of keeping the bailiff out 'with a post-dated cheque. Just after it was due. I got an instalment from the *Monthly Review*, which met it and left me naked.' In the same letter he wrote that 'my Mother has collapsed at last.' In his 'Corvo the Enigma', Bainbridge comments: 'I don't think anybody knew that Corvo had a mother living at this time. Certainly he never talked about her, and this is the only mention I ever heard of her; but it is evident that she was much in his thoughts.' And a year later Rolfe told a literary agent, Leonard Moore, that 'I always dine with my Mother on Fridays; and tomorrow I am taking her to St Leonard's.'

James Rolfe died without providing for his widow in any way. One daughter, Nellie, remained with her mother at the Highbury Hill address. Freddy took over all that was left of the once-profitable Wm. Rolfe & Sons business. This consisted almost solely of twenty-eight old clients who relied on James to keep their pianos in tune, at a cost ranging from 10s. 6d. to one guinea. The entire material estate of the business on 30 July 1902 amounted to 17s. 6d. This amount was turned over to Freddy's mother. In a letter soon to be written to his young nephew Claud, Rolfe mentioned Miller Street. It was not likely that this had any significance to the young boy. But it must have meant something to the letter's author. In 1902 there was only one Miller Street in London. This short street in Camden Town housed only

five businesses. One was William Chivers, pianoforte key manufacturer. Another was Henry Ward, pianoforte manufacturer.
Perhaps the last of the Wm. Rolfe & Sons pianos were stored at
one of these two addresses. To aid his mother in whatever way
he could, Rolfe was able to sell two pianos during 1903—one for
£3 4s. 6d. and one for £5 10s. od.

From Hong Kong, Percy sent his little son back to England
for his education. He was still quite young at the beginning of
1903, when Uncle Freddy wrote to Claud. The letter of January
26th was printed in capital letters and illustrated.

Mother wrote to me the other day, and told me all about you.
And I thought you would like a letter from your Uncle
Freddy. So first I get a big piece of paper like this [illustration
of Freddy standing behind a scroll taller than he] and then I
get a big pen like this [Freddy wielding a pen twice his size]
and then I sit in my armchair and write on a board on my
knee like this [illustration]. Well you see I never have seen
you, or spoken to you, and you never have spoken to me, so
I do not know what to say to you now, because I dont know
what sort of things you like. But most boys like to hear tales
so I will tell you a true tale about another man whose name
was Claud like yours, eighteen hundred and forty eight years
ago. He had a lot of other names besides Claud. In fact his full
name was almost as long as Miller Street. It was *Tiberius
Claudius Drusus Nero Germanicus.* When he was a little boy
he was always ill, and no one looked after him. So instead of
playing and running and swimming and jumping like you he
used to shut himself up and read books. When he grew up
the people made him King. His crown was not like King
Edward's, but just a wreath of laurel leaves made of gold. This
is his portrait [illustration]. Because he read many books he
was very wise, and when the people were unhappy he knew
what to give them to make them happy. It was very hot where
he lived, and all were very thirsty, but the river was full of
yellow mud, and not fit to drink. But up in the hills 15 miles
away there were some lovely springs of water. King Claud had
read in a book that water always runs down hill if you make

205

a place for it to run. So he told stone-masons to build a big piecy wall chop-chop slanty all the way from his house up to the hills where the water was. And he told them to build a stone pipe on the top of the wall for the water to run in, and to cover it over to keep the blacks out. So this was done, and the water ran down hill along the top of King Claud's wall, and when it got to his house it became a fountain where everyone can get pail-fuls of it to drink, and the water was so good, and King Claud's wall was so well built that it is there even now, and some day I hope you will go and see it and drink some of the lovely water. They call it Aqua Claudia. And they call the wall the Claudian Aqueduct. And that's all about King Claud.

Now if you take this little piece of paper to Mother she will change it into money for you at the post office, and then you can buy what you like as a present from me.

Well so long Claud. Come and see me some day, and write to me when you can. Give my word to your sister, old man.

And believe me

      Your affectionate

                      Uncle Freddy [illustration of Freddy finishing the letter with his pen].

10

'I have tried my best and I have failed.'

With these words Rolfe ended his fourth year as a writer in London. They were included in a letter to Bainbridge, which started, 'I am quite done now.' Lane had given him a promise 'to publish "The Rubai'yat" early in January. I have those 24 articles accepted by the *Monthly Review*. And two completed books to follow. But I have no means of living ... till I get payment for this work. I have just 8/- left, no prospect of more, and not a soul in the world to help me.'

Regarding Lane's final promise about the book's appearance in January, he wrote to the publisher: 'The only thing I beg is that you will not publish on the 3rd or 4th day of the moon's age: both of those days being excessively unlucky.' But, when the book came out, the stars paid little attention to the writer cramped in his Hampstead attic. Hoping that it would be ready before the end of the year, another letter to Lane asked if he could receive 'my presentation copies of Rubai'yat *now*, instead of later? I should like to give one to my Mother for a Christmas present....' But this complete prose translation of the *Rubaiyat* had not been fully bound and was not ready until January 26th. The author's copies were sent to Rolfe in March.

Since the Royal Literary Fund had assisted him, he had produced a number of things. He had written but, with the care of a proud parent, kept adding to *Don Renato*. The collaboration with Sholto Douglas produced 'Reviews of Unwritten Books', the Meleager and *Thirty Naughty Emperors*, brief studies of thirty Caesars from Hadrian to Diocletian. In December he noted that Lane had 'publish'd "little phrases of Sappho each one a rosebud": but why have you never put me to edit a *complete* edition of the Greek Anthology with an English version and the few obscure bits in Latin? Now there is something that never has been done before, and which would have a great vogue (certainly in America), I happen to know.'

Any affirmative answer from Lane would depend on the profitable prospects of the *Rubaiyat*, which never came; and Rolfe no longer had the support of Harland or the dismissed Temple Scott.

As 1903 began Rolfe received £10 when the *Rubaiyat* was published. He was paid £1 8s od. a month for book reviews in *The Outlook* and £3 6s. 8d. every two months for the 'Reviews of Unwritten Books.'

The dominant, determined dream in his mind created the broadest role for him to fulfil: Hadrian VII. 'Still,' in Orson Welles' words, 'at least a dream is never an illusion.'

A month before assistance reached him from the Royal Literary Fund he wrote to Maurice Hewlett that 'the thing immediately in hand is called *Hadrian the Seventh*, a modern and simple psychology, deliberately written for the many.' But the final manuscript was not started until one year later. Hadrian, as a character, was not new with Rolfe. He talked of himself as the future pontiff, after the usual ordination, of course. And at Holywell he and John Holden had written alternating chapters for a novel based on him.

After the publication of *In His Own Image* he had read George Meredith's *Adventures of Harry Richmond*. 'Things printed can never be stopped, Richie,' says one person. 'Our Jorian compares them to babies baptized. They have a soul from that moment, and go on for ever!' The 'things printed' which 'can never be stopped' meant for Rolfe the damning articles in the Aberdeen newspapers. He could never erase the printed and re-printed words of this attack, but he could counterattack. For four years he had weighed the matter and now decided to retaliate, to answer these defamatory and scandalous accusations. This was the underlying purpose of *Hadrian the Seventh*.

Another passage in *Harry Richmond* was noticed. 'I am a God, sir, inaccesible to mortal ailment!' his father says to Harry. 'Seriously, dear boy, I have never known an illness in my life. I have killed my hundreds of poor devils who were for imitating me. This I boast—I boast constitution. And I fear, Richie, you have none of my superhuman strength. Added to that, I know I am watched over. I ask—I have: I scheme—the tricks are in my hand! It may be the doing of my mother in heaven; there is the fact for you to reflect on. "Stand not in my way, nor follow me too far," would serve me for a motto admirably, and you can put it in Latin, Richie.'

Rolfe did just that. On the 1901 title page of *In His Own Image* the motto reads: 'All Will Be Well'. Following Harry's father's advice, the quoted motto first appeared on the title page of *Hadrian the Seventh* in Greek and Latin ('Neve Me Impedias Neve Longius Persequaris'). And it remained as his written standard throughout the rest of his life.

Harry Richmond was not the sole contributor to his work. An avid reader not merely of current novels, but of classical literature, Rolfe cherished certain phrases, dissecting and then translating them into the experiences he wished to express. He read and marked:

Dr. Johnson's letter to the Earl of Chesterfield: 'Is not a patron one who looks with unconcern on a man struggling for life in the water, and when he has reached the ground encumbers him with help.'

Horace Walpole: 'Life is a comedy to those who think, a tragedy to those who feel.'

Lord Randolph Churchill: 'Your "good authority" is, I fear, some evil-disposed person who was anxious to gratify a little private malice. Allow me to point out a few trifling inaccuracies.'

Cardinal Newman: 'Catholicks abound in noble gifts, and are unable to use them religiously.'

Sir Walter Scott: ' "The rude man," says the critic, "requires only to see something going on. The man of more refinement must be made to feel. The man of complete refinement must be made to reflect".'

Edna Lyall: '(What helped to bring that fellow to atheism?) "The un-Christlikeness of Christians".'

Victor Hugo: 'Never let anyone do you a service. They will abuse the advantage it gives them. To be obliged is to be sold.

The happy, the powerful, make use of the moment you stretch out your hand to place a penny in it, and at the crisis of your weakness make you a slave of the worst kind, the slave of an act of charity. A slave forced to love the enslaver! What infamy, what want of delicacy, what an assault on your self-respect! The slime of a good action performed towards you bedaubs you and bespatters you with mud for ever. An alms is irremediable. Gratitude is paralysis. A benefit is a sticky and repugnant adherence which deprives you of free movement. A benefit implies an understood inferiority accepted by you. By force of disdain they are polite. Sometimes they even know how your name is spelt.'

Havelock Ellis: 'It would not be easy to maintain that the English curate begetting his 14th baby on the body of a worn-out wife is a more elevating object of mental contemplation than Harmodios in the embraces of his friend Aristogciton—that the young man sleeping with a prostitute picked up in Piccadilly is cleaner than his brother sleeping with a soldier picked-up in the Park.'

F. Marion Crawford: 'His mind was of the sort that is satisfied by suspended judgment, that dreads the chillingly triumphant phrase of reason "which was to be forced," as much as the despairing tone of a reduction to the impossible.... Anything might be, or might not be; and decision was hateful: it was delicious to float on the calm waters of meditative indifference, between the great rocks, Hope and Despair, in the straits that lead the sea of life into the ocean of eternity.'

Edward Carpenter: 'Give away all that you have: become poor and without possessions—and behold you shall be lord and sovereign of all things.'

Kipling: 'No, I have never wearied the gods. They will remember this and give me a great place.'

Rolfe's first modern novel is a personal treatise. It catches him on the first page, as George Arthur Rose, at 69 Broadhurst Gardens. In a mixture of religious faith and a justification for his position within the Church and within life, his history is outlined. The opening soliloquy is one of loneliness, of physical, mental and spiritual weariness. Into this emptiness come Dr.

Above: Wm. Rolfe & Sons, 112 Cheapside, London, where Frederick Rolfe was born, 22 July 1860. (*Tallis's London Street Views*, 1839.) Right: Rolfe, North London Collegiate School, Camden Town, c. 1874. Rolfe: 'All the education I ever had took place in third-rate schools and terminated on my fourteenth birthday.'

Above: Rolfe, 1883, a provincial schoolmaster. Right: Interior, St. Columba's Pro-Cathedral, Oban, c. 1886.

Rolfe's first reproduced art: one of seven initials for his poem, 'Lytel Seynt Hew,' *The Universal Review*, 15 December 1888. The poem and the art were created while he was at Oscott. This particular scene of the burial procession of the young martyr, or one similar to it, hung on the wall of Rolfe's room at Oscott. Below: The 'mysterious group of divers in the clear of the moon' was painted by Rolfe to accompany his poem, 'Ballade of Boys Bathing'. The locale of the poem and painting was St. Andrews Bay, which he visited in 1888. The poem was published in 1890, but without any illustration.

Marcano Ricci

Tito Biondi

Photographs of boys by Rolfe, Rome, 1890.

Tito and Guido, Toto's brother

Nella Vigna

Left: Toto,
Rome, 1890.
Photo: Rolfe.

Left: This photograph
by Rolfe of Cecil Castle
(Christchurch, 1891)—on
which he drew in
pencil a spear, shield
and wings—was used
as a model for a
wall-hanging of
St. Michael, decorating
the local Catholic church.
Right: Pen drawing by
Rolfe, Christchurch,
1891.

" Toto "

by Baron Corvo

" Yes, excellency."

" And now, speak to no one, but send your mother to me, & tell her to bring ten or twelve respectable women who can sew. Say that I shall want them to stay in the palace for 3 or 4 days or that I will give them 20 lire apiece."

" Yes, excellency." And the lad went off with a graceful stride.

Toto was the gardener's son. He lived in a little cottage just outside the gates. He was nearly 15 years old, a beautiful brown boy with long muscular limbs, hardy & strong, & the devoted slave of the House.

The Princess was an English woman, proud as Lucifer of her own country, & devoted to Italy, in which she had lived since her marriage 30 years before

First page of the manuscript of Rolfe's first Toto story, Christchurch, 1891.

Oil painting of St. George and the Dragon by Rolfe, Christchurch, 1891.

Three designs by Rolfe,
c. 1897: (above) two
letterheads and (right)
an advertisement for
The Holywell Record.
Rolfe used the symbol of
the raven for his
signature in his art
for the first time
at Holywell.

THE "RECORD" PUBLISHING CO.

DESIGNERS,
ENGRAVERS,
PHOTO
ZINCOGRA-
PHERS, &c.

Paintings, Drawings,
Photographs, etc.,
REPRODUCED BY EITHER
Wood Engraving, Half-tone, or Line Process.

DESIGNS of every description
for Artistic Illustration.

POSTERS, ETC., BY OUR OWN ARTISTS.

Street procession, Holywell, 1896, showing some of the banners belonging to the local Catholic church and community. The last three banners in the background were painted by Rolfe. (Photo courtesy of Farm Street Library.)

Right: The St. Augustine
of Canterbury banner
painted by Rolfe,
Holywell, c. 1896.
(Courtesy of St. Winefride
R. C. Church, Holywell.)
Below: Rolfe, John Holden, Leo
Schwarz, Holywell,
1896. Photo: Rolfe.

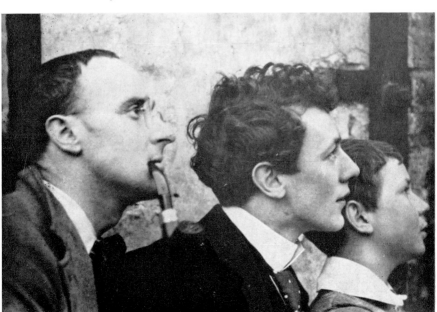

69 BROADHURST GARDENS. HAMPSTEAD.
LONDON. ENGLAND.   26 JAN. 1903

MY DEAR CLAUD.

MOTHER WROTE TO ME THE OTHER DAY, AND TOLD ME ALL ABOUT YOU. AND I THOUGHT YOU WOULD LIKE A LETTER FROM YOUR UNCLE FREDDY. SO FIRST I GET A BIG PIECE OF PAPER LIKE THIS

AND THEN I GET A BIG PEN LIKE THIS   AND THEN I SIT IN MY ARMCHAIR AND WRITE ON A BOARD ON MY KNEE LIKE THIS

WELL YOU SEE I NEVER HAVE SEEN YOU, OR SPOKEN TO YOU, AND YOU NEVER HAVE SPOKEN TO ME, SO I DO NOT KNOW WHAT TO SAY TO YOU NOW, BECAUSE I DONT KNOW WHAT SORT OF THINGS YOU LIKE. BUT MOST BOYS LIKE TO HEAR TALES SO I WILL TELL YOU A TRUE TALE ABOUT ANOTHER MAN WHOSE NAME WAS CLAUD LIKE YOURS, EIGHTEEN HUNDRED AND FORTY EIGHT YEARS AGO. HE HAD A LOT OF OTHER NAMES BESIDE CLAUD. IN FACT HIS FULL NAME WAS ALMOST AS LONG AS MILLER STREET. IT WAS TIBERIUS CLAUDIUS DRUSUS NERO GERMANICUS. WHEN HE WAS A LITTLE BOY HE WAS ALWAYS ILL, AND NO ONE LOOKED AFTER HIM. SO INSTEAD OF PLAYING AND RUNNING AND SWIMMING AND JUMPING LIKE YOU HE USED TO SHUT HIMSELF UP AND READ BOOKS. WHEN HE GREW UP THE PEOPLE MADE HIM KING. HIS GROWN WAS NOT LIKE KING EDWARD'S, BUT JUST A WREATH OF LAUREL LEAVES MADE OF GOLD THIS IS HIS PORTRAIT.

First page, Rolfe's letter to his young nephew Claud.

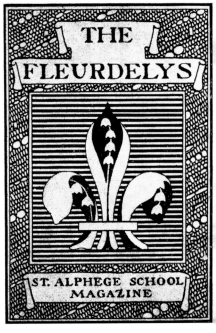

UNCLE FREDDY

The illustration for 'Begging Letters,' *The Harmsworth London Magazine,*
August 1901, which has been reputed to be a self-portrait by Rolfe. Above
right: Rolfe's self-portrait, part of a letter to Claud. Two cover designs
by Rolfe: (below left) *Hadrian the Seventh,* 1904, and (below right) *The
Fleurdelys,* December 1904, the first and only number.

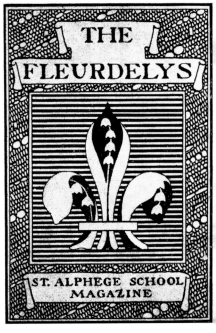

Left: The final cover design by Rolfe for his *Don Tarquinio*, 1905, was only slightly modified from this drawing.

Right: Rolfe's cover design for *Don Renato*, 1909 and 1963.

Frederick, Knight-Founder, Knight-Magnate, General of the Title of Saint Sebastian & Saint Pancras, Provost of the Comity of Flamens,

to James, a Doctor of Medicine, Law, & Philosophy, Greeting.

A writ of faculties issues from the Congregation of Inquisition, under date xv Mar. 1908, signed by the Praefect & Promaester of the said Congregation, enabling me with full power in your case.

I therefore, hereby admit you to the Noviciate of our Order of Sanctissima Sophia, from that date.

Your Domicile being in America, where our Order has not a Noviciate, I constitute myself your Master until further notice. Kindly advise me as to the possibility of your being in England this year.

Meanwhile, accept the following admonitions.

i. Add to your prayers, & say before all working, the following.

V. Seat of Wisdom: R. Pray for us. O Wisdom, Which camest out of the Mouth of The Most High, & reachest from one end to another, mightily & sweetly ordering all things, come & teach us the way of prudence. Let us pray: Give me the Wisdom Which sitteth on Thy throne, O God, & reject me not from among Thy children: for, though a man be never so perfect among the children of men, yet, if Thy Wisdom be not with him, he shall be nothing regarded. Through Jesus Christ our Lord. Amen. O Wisdom &c. V. R.

ii. You are admitted to the Noviciate of our Order, that you may the better seek after Wisdom. I require you therefore, to keep me informed of the steps which you are taking in this direction. And such assistance as you may need, & such as our Order is able to afford you, is at your call.

iii. Although you are not (as yet) a member of our Order, the grace is conceded to you (as an aspirant thereto) of wearing the badge which accompanies this letter. To wear it honourably, you must shew Loyalty, Reverence, Obedience, Patience, Diligence, Perseverance, with the convenient exercise of good faith & lively wits.

iiij. Lastly, know that your advancement in our Order depends entirely upon your own efforts to merit the commendation of (at present) your Novice-Master.

Farewell. Illuminet te Sanctissima Sapientia.

Given at Gwernvale, Crickhowel, South Wales,
under my own hand & seal, this xij day of
May, In the Year of the Lieutenancy, In the
Year of The Lord 1908.

An example of Rolfe's 'wonderful fifteenth-century script'. This document was sent by Rolfe to Dr. Walsh, New York, admitting the latter into the Order of Sanctissima Sophia. The device at the head of the page was designed by Rolfe, with the assistance of Pirie-Gordon, c. 1906.

Rolfe's first residence in
Venice from August
1908, Hotel Belle Vue et
Russie. Although the
building still stands, it is
no longer a hotel.
(Pen drawing by Donald
Weeks, 22 July 1960.)

Rolfe's final residence, on
the Grand Canal, Venice,
1913. At the left is
Palazzo Vendramin-Calergi,
where Wagner died,
to the right of which is Rolfe's
'Palace' Marcello, where
he died, 25 October 1913.
Photo: Wade-Browne.

Above: Piazza San Marco, Venice, Easter Sunday 1913. Photo: Wade-Browne. Left and right: Two pen drawings by Rolfe, Venice, 1908. Below right: pencil drawing of a boat by Ermenegildo Vianello or Zildo, Rolfe's Venetian counterpart to Toto.

Above: Rolfe sitting to Covelli for his portrait, Venice, 1913. Below: One of Rolfe's three boats, Venice, 1913. The sails were hand-painted by Rolfe, the large one bearing his motto, 'Stand not in my way: nor follow me too far,' in Latin and Greek. In the boat are Rolfe's dog, Wade-Brown and Rolfe. Rolfe's 'best ship' was wrecked during the summer of 1913 nearing the Lido.

Courtleigh and Dr. Talacryn, summoning him to an interview. Their enquiries into his present religious beliefs, based on his past life, are defiantly answered. And, to his surprised satisfaction, he is ordained the Reverend George Arthur Rose.

Accompanying Talacryn to the Conclave in Rome, in a moment evoking wonder he is offered the Throne of St. Peter. When he realizes that he has been chosen to be the Church's representation of Christ on earth, he immediately exclaims, 'I will.' The only previous English pope had been Hadrian IV, so 'the present English Pontiff is Hadrian the Seventh.' Without delay, he sets in motion reforms within the Church and in the Vatican's relationship with the rulers of the world. He sells the treasures of the Church and admonishes the money-grabbing schemes of its prelates.

For almost twenty years Rolfe had been a Roman Catholic, but certain basic elements of his Anglican teachings had unconsciously stuck with him. With no authority higher than his own, he cleansed the Temple of its stifling government. One man was the Head of the Church and one man would direct its affairs. 'We wish you to act upon the sum of Our words and conduct, in order that England may have a good and not a bad example from English Catholics. No more than that. We may call Ourselves Christendom till We are black in the face: but the true character of a Christendom is wanting to Us because the great promises of prophecy still lack fulfilment. The Barque of Peter has been trying to reach harbour. Mutiny within, storms without, have driven Her hither and thither. Is She as far-off from port today as ever? Who knows? But the new captain is trying to set the course again from the old chart. His look is no longer backward but onward,' declares the new pontiff.

The story of Hadrian at work is simple but dramatic. Yet, outside of his kingdom, an evil force germinates towards his destruction. A Socialist from the north of Britain joins forces with 'the Woman Scorned' from the south. They leave for Rome to blackmail Hadrian. When their demands are disregarded, Jerry Sant exposes the former Rose in the newspapers. Hadrian answers these charges to the cardinals—as Rolfe is here given the opportunity to answer to the whole world the charges against him in the Aberdeen Attack. Once this is done—the climax and purpose of the novel—the end swiftly comes. Mrs. Crowe and Sant are still shunned. Receiving no satisfaction for his pains, the Socialist assassinates Hadrian during an outdoor procession. The dying pontiff pardons his executioner, as the life of George Arthur Rose ebbs away to the words: 'Pray for the repose of His soul. He was so tired.'

'It is, moreover, certainly no mere chance that the death of the last great traditional Popes should continually have prompted Catholic writers from their various standpoints to sketch the portraits of ideal Popes. Barely a year after Pope Leo's death there appeared in England *Hadrian VII* by Frederick Rolfe (Baron Corvo), with its sparks of prophetic intuition, many of which were destined to wait a century before being realized.... Hadrian VII ... saw at least eight of the conflicts now involving the Roman Catholic Church, among them the question of celibacy, the possession of untaxable property, the dogma of canon law.' (Carlo Falconi, *The Popes of the Twentieth Century*.)

Rolfe was a student of literature, history, religious doctrine and language. He was also an astute observer of current affairs. Minor glimpses of this are caught in letters and articles, but *Hadrian* provided for him the scope for prophecy in the affairs of the world. The political unrest of major powers, terminating in a world war and revolution, is predicted. But the threads of upheaval do not end here. In a sense, Rolfe can be compared with Hitler. The doctor who diagnosed the disease which killed A. J. A. Symons in 1941 wrote to him about *Hadrian* during his last months: 'Hitler's Neuordnung bears an astonishingly close likeness to the ethnological settlement of Europe which Rolfe fathers on the Kaiser.' This parallel is not unfounded. Rolfe, as Hadrian and as himself, deplored Socialism. At the time he first became aware of it, Leo XIII had already embarked on his campaigns against the new 'religion'. Yet he lived to see Socialism and Communism spread across Europe. So heavy was its gain at the expense of Catholicism that, some years later, Hitler found himself in a position to defy the Church, after he had, with the pope's aid, secured power.

Each character in the novel is a real person or some one Rolfe knew about in some way. Trevor Haddon appears as Alfred Elms, 'an English Catholic painter' arriving in Rome to set the pope's image on to canvas. 'Hadrian knew him for a vulgar and officious liar: detested him.... Also, He loathed the cad's Hercomeresque-cum-Camera-esque technique and his quite earthy imagination: from that palette, the spiritual, the intellectual, the noble, could not come.' Rolfe himself needed no camera to perpetuate the images of others. He needed nothing save his memory and the glowingly colourful words at his command.

Hadrian's first act in the story is to give the Blessing to the people of Rome, anticipating Pius XI by eighteen years. He consorts with world powers, prays in Greek, designs his own crucifix and lives on a few shillings a day. His thoughts are put down with his 'beloved Waterman.' When at last he is shot, one of his first thoughts is of Flavio, his little yellow cat. Reminiscent of the Nowt's assassination at Sewers End by the Saint (John Holden), Hadrian speaks to Sir John Devine (Holden again): 'Dear John, take this cross—and Flavio.' By the end of the book, Rose-Rolfe's *saison en enfer* has been unfolded with sparkling brilliance. The bright sunlight 'on warm grey stones, on the ripe Roman skins, on vermilion and lavender, and blue and ermine, and green and gold, on apostolic whiteness and the rose of blood' then becomes subdued in the hues of death. 'The bloodstain streamed down the Pope's white robes with the red stole of universal jurisdiction. The slender hand with the two huge rings ascended. The shy brown eyes fluttered; and were wide, and very glad.'

With all its blemishes, *Hadrian the Seventh* presents a truly living and breathing personality. With an embarrassing stutter at times, suddenly shrill-voiced or emotionally spouting as a man possessed, Rolfe never ceases to have something to say. The unevenness in the story is the natural unevenness of any one person's day-to-day life. Written at a time when Rolfe was employing make-up to appear younger than his forty-two years, Rose strikes out at his reflection: 'Strip, man, strip stark.' And in *Hadrian* Rolfe lays bear his naked soul.

The years he had known of disappointment and bitterness were summed up by Horace: 'Sed tacitus pasci si posset corvus:

habaret plus dapis, et rixae multo minus invidiaeque'—'But if the raven could have fed in silence, he would have had banquets and much less quarrelling and envy.' But the raven now had been discarded. George Arthur Rose stands between Corvo and Nicholas Crabbe. Corvo had died with the publication of *The Rubaiyat of Umar Khaiyam* in January 1903. The raven has no role in *Hadrian*, but another symbol is chosen to represent his name. Rose is compared to a 'martyr who, while yet the pagan pincers were at work upon his tenderest internals, [he] beheld the angel-bearers of his amaranthine coronal.' With these words a new man arises and, as Nicholas Crabbe, Rolfe walks through the rest of his literary life.

Aware of more than one nature within him, Rolfe wrote to Fr. Beauclerk in 1896 about his 'violent and raging temper,' admitting that 'it's the Mr. Hyde surging up.' With *Hadrian* he introduces an individual type of double personality. The book is not intended to present the separate personalities of one being. Rather, the idea lies closer to Poe's William Wilson, although executed in a much less dramatic style. Rolfe's first adventure into this field of self facing self comes in *Hadrian* when he revisits his old Roman seminary. He lists the inmates from the rector to his fellow students of 1890. Hadrian-Rolfe, now twenty years older, talks with a student in a poignant scene. This 'fastidious person,' born in England in July, mocked by the other students and whose one ambition is priesthood, is William Jameson, the Rolfe of 1890 at Scots College.

The death of Corvo was prolonged with the delay in publishing the *Rubaiyat*, but there was one last flutter of his name a year later, with the first introduction of Nicholas Crabbe. In the 13 February 1904 number of *Notes & Queries* Crabbe asked about 'the spirited phrase of Corvo, "here came my Lord the Sun,"' quoted in Harland's *My Friend Prospero*. Three weeks later Corvo answered, saying that the phrase was from 'one of my stories of the Abruzzi which appeared in the *Butterfly* for August 1899.'

Rolfe is merely the narrator, or 'tralator,' of *Don Tarquinio*, which immediately followed *Hadrian*. For his secondary role in this he becomes a commentator through the means of footnotes,

214

a method repeated in *Don Renato* and *The Weird of the Wanderer*. Written about the same time as *Hadrian* and *Tarquinio*, *Nicholas Crabbe* resurrects George Arthur Rose. Asked about him, Crabbe says that he has 'lost touch with him. I suppose he still potters about somewhere. He's just another lonely devil who can't find his proper niche in this world. He wanted to be a priest: but they wouldn't have him—didn't like his auburn hair.' To the question, 'What's he doing now?' Rolfe, as Crabbe, gives his only humorous reference to this event: 'Running for Popedom, I suppose.'

Not all of these dual roles have the same impish quality. At times this method is used for striking emphasis. His first piece of writing in Venice was Hadrian VII's *Bull Against the Enemy of the Anglican Race*. In it '*Nicholas Crabbe*, a student of human and divine affairs, a lover of his Motherland, excellent in reverence toward his King and toward the Roman Office of the Blessed Peter Prince of Apostles,' exposes to the Paparch the baron of Fleet Street, 'an hyteriamonger and enemy of the Anglican race.' *Hubert's Arthur* is mostly Pirie-Gordon's book, but it does show signs of Rolfe, as in the sentence: '*Every Crab has his own Moon*.' In the story 'The Armed Hands' the narrator (Rolfe) meets the Grey Man (Rolfe). In *The Weird of the Wanderer* one sentence contains a thought—'the World of the Knight of the Crab ... and of the Ravens both Black and White'—connecting Nicholas Crabbe with the Corvo of old. And in another sentence Crabbe lists the comrades 'in my various lives; and, among them I will name ... the unchangeable George of the Roses.'

A reader of *Don Renato* suddenly encounters Rolfe in the full Italian costume of 'Messer Francesco Berni, an urbane pensive litterate, with fatigate eyes and aulick gate; very ingenious, very subtile, reputed erudite; who, under the name Gandolfo Milosj, has indited versicules most amoene, of which a *Capitolo d'un Ragazzo* and *Capitolo sopra un Garzone* already are laureate.'

(The description here fits Rolfe, yet he uses the name of a real person. This is listed on two or three pages between others bearing the aspects of people he knew, coupled with sixteenth-century names. Mrs. Gleeson White appears several paragraphs ahead under the guise of Veronic Gambara (1485-1550). In *Renato* she is the widow of the Tyrant Bianco di Correale. The Renaissance poetess, praised by Bembo, in fact had married Gilberto X, Lord of Correggio, and was the mother of two sons, points which are found in Rolfe's *Chronicles of the House of Borgia*. In the paragraph following the introduction of Berni-Rolfe, Henry Harland poses under the name of Giacinto Musca. (Written during a breach of their friendship, was Musca based on an actual person from history or on Volpone's parasite?) And in a following paragraph comes the stuttering Hartwell de la Grissell, who was a 'friend' in 1887, who ignored his pleas for aid following the Scots College expulsion, and who, in league with Hunter Blair, assailed Rolfe during an Oxford University Dramatic Society meeting in 1899. On 16 April 1908 Rolfe spoke of books and authors in a long letter to Dawkins: 'The Bergamo *V Carmina* contains Francesco Berni's (*pseudonym* Gandolfo Milosio) *"Capitolo sopra un Ragazzo"*. (Evans!) Do hunt for it.' Berni (c. 1497-1535) was the principal burlesque poet of Italy and his death did him more honour than his life. Neither layman, politician nor churchman was safe from his stinging pen. One example of his critical wit involved an 'outsider'. Because he was not an Italian, the poet ridiculed the Dutch Hadrian VI.)

'On July 20th, 1903, Pope Leo XIII died. Now was Corvo's opportunity,' writes Bainbridge in his chapter on Rolfe in *Twice Seven*. 'He who had been deprived of his Vocation, he the despised and rejected of men, would by his own consummate art be elected. Fact and fiction would be welded together as they had never been done before.... Leo the Apostle of Liberty and Humanity, would be followed by Hadrian, Hadrian VII, the Apostle of the Personal Responsibility of the Individual, the Overthrower of that Phantom Uniformity and the Upholder of the Principle of Aristos—The Best—the Great Advocate of Infinite Deifference, diversity of physique, of intellect, of condition as man's birthright, Hadrian the Apostle of Simplicity. So it was that Corvo, for the purpose of his own life story, elected himself Pope and wrote *Hadrian VII*.'

Again a biographer set in motion a fanciful fact. Leo died

on 20 July 1903, but the final version of *Hadrian the Seventh* was begun four months before this event and was completed by the first week in July.

Rolfe set the story in the year 1910, although his dates in the novel are not always consistent. The date at the beginning of the opening chapter is 31 March 1903.

On page 2 Rose is poking 'the little fire burning in the corner of a fire-clayed grate. He was shivering: for ... March was going out like nine lions....' Taking up the newspaper, on page 3, he reads the news from Rome. 'Something was occurring in Rome: something mysterious was occurring in Rome.' And on page 57 he remembers 'how he had laughed at an Occ. Note in the *Pall Mall Gazette* some months before, to the effect that the old tradition of antipathy between the two peoples separated by the Channel was as dead as Georgian England and the era of Bien-Aimé, and suggesting that the two leading democracies of the world—(England a democracy indeed!)—ought to live on terms of good understanding and neighbourliness, or some such tomfoolery.'

On 31 March 1903 the weather for London was 'fair', with winds increasing in force and 'becoming rainy'. *The Pall Mall Gazette* carried two articles on the same day. An Occasional Note was entitled 'France and England' and, just below it, another was 'From Our Correspondent', telling of 'a certain alarm' being felt 'in interested quarters over the various postponements of the Consistory at the Vatican.' Although Leo was still alive when Rolfe started *Hadrian*, the pontiff was ninety-three years old and had been at the head of the Roman Church since 1878. Recognizing this, the newspapers of the day spoke about his 'conviction that he will live to be a hundred' no doubt being interrupted by death at any moment.

In the first chapter Rose is congratulated by Courtleigh (Cardinal Vaughan) for being 'an expert in the annals of the conclave.' As these words were being penned, Rolfe must have been completing his 'Notes on the Conclave', to appear in the August issue of *The Monthly Review*. Although Leo had died by this time, the article begins in the future tense: 'When Leo Pontifex Maximus XIII., Ruler of the World, Father of Princes and Kings,

Earthly Vicar of Jesus Christ, shall have reached the end of his life in this world....' Rolfe's new pope was created before the old one had died.

Not only are the majority of the personages in the novel real, certain scenes from his past life are faithfully depicted. After the primary interview, Courtleigh (Vaughan) and Talacryn (Mostyn) discuss the incident and the strange man they have just talked to. ' "For my part," [Talacryn-Mostyn] continued, "I'm going to try to make amends for the immense wrong I did him by neglecting him." ' The interview has taken place in the drawing room of the Broadhurst Gardens house. An interview, as unexpected as in the novel, occurred in the same place three years previously. Edward Slaughter had been told of the wrongs inflicted on Rolfe at Holywell. In April 1900 the young solicitor suggested a meeting between Rolfe and his cousin, Bishop Mostyn of Wales. The bishop visited Broadhurst Gardens and brought Rolfe back into the Church's fold.

On May 4th Rolfe wrote to Temple Scott in New York: 'Presently the Bishop of Menevia [Mostyn] was announced, and I went downstairs and found his lordship in the parlour, who said that he came to try to straighten out a tangle. He offered a hand, and I kissed his ring.... I really do not believe that he had had the slightest idea of the wrong which he has done me until now. All my letters of three years ago, do not seem to have made the very smallest impression on him. I really doubt that he read them. In any case he did not understand. When I made it plain to him, he was horrified. He assured me that he had pronounced no sentence of excommunication, and that I had never incurred the excommunication *latae sententiae*. He admitted that circumstances, and the absence of his benediction, completely justified me in thinking what I did think. He said that there was nothing else to think. Then, what could he do, to restore—did I want the Sacraments restored—I asked what he took me for, with indignation—the Sacraments? I said I didn't want any fuss, but considering the publicity of my degradation I thought that it would meet the case if his Lordship himself restored me, *and told the Cardinal*. So off he went to Archbishop's House for the faculties (being out of his diocese, he had to get special permis-

sion to officiate in this one) and next morning he heard my confession for three years, and put me straight again. Before leaving
town he begged me to look upon him as a friend, and said that
if I would let know in what way he could help me, he would
esteem it a favour.'

After the interview in *Hadrian*, Rose goes to Archbishop's
House for confession. He is heard by Talacryn-Mostyn, who has
said to Courtleigh, 'But I confess I'm strangely drawn to him.
It is such a treat to come across a man who's not above treating
a bishop as an equal.'

'The oddest and perhaps vividest *apologia* or autobiography
of present times' was written as such only accidentally. As 'your
black sheep,' he wrote to his 'shepherd,' Fr. Beauclerk, on 10
December 1898 about the newspaper attack. The Jesuit urged him
to defend himself against these 'false & malicious libels.' Rolfe
exclaimed that 'every man, who has ever known me, at any time
of my life, must have known these libels to be absurd, grotesque,
& maliciously untrue.' But he added: 'I am in no hurry [to
defend myself], because my conscience is quite clear—quite clear.
... Public damage has been done to me.... The lesion is too
serious for simple antiseptic treatment. It is a cancer; which a
lengthy operation alone can extirpate. I suggest nothing. I do
not say what I shall do. I only wait.' And four years of waiting,
four years of thinking, of bitter, misguided, paranoic thought
congealed itself into the single theme of *Hadrian the Seventh*:
an answer to the Aberdeen Attack.

The history of Rome's Conclaves, such as Rolfe set forth in
(Sir) Henry Newbolt's *Monthly Review*, did not exhaust his
knowledge of the Church. He was well versed in all of its
ceremonious lore. At a time when *Hadrian* was under construction, one of his letters revealed his deep concern about this and
one other subject. He was interested in public entertainment
and, whenever he could, as patron or guest, Rolfe attended the
theatre, opera or concert. He delighted in the musical airs of
Gilbert and Sullivan and admired Sir Henry Irving. Later in
the year, on October 20th, he heard a Promenade Concert at
Queen's Hall and wrote on the back of his ticket's counterfoil:
'This admitted me to search all parts.' Combining his love for

the religious and the theatrical, on May 8th he wrote a letter to Irving, whose *Dante* had opened the previous month:

> Will you allow me to say that the Archbishop of Pisa walks on as an *Abbot merely*, in that he carries his crozier with the *crook* INWARDS; that the Grand Inquisitor and inquisitors would be *Dominicans*, shaven, white habits and black cloaks, not bearded *Capuchins* (who were not invented till the fifth day of the Nones of July *1528*); and that nuns sing their offices in the quire-stalls, not huddled on the floor. Nevertheless, I for one am deeply grateful to you for your Dante.... Oh, and Cardinals were not 'Eminence' and 'Most Eminent' till 1630 (reign of Urban VIII). Prior to that date they were Most Illustrious Lord (Illustrissimo); or, in the case of the Cardinal-Dean and the Cardinal-Nephews, 'Most Respectability' or 'Most Worshipful' or 'His Worship' (Osservantissimo) (Colendissimo).

One of Rolfe's remarkable opinions regarding people was expressed at the theatre. The evening was Maundy Thursday of 1899 and he had written a letter to Cardinal Vaughan, informing him that he was going to cause a scandal by going to a theatre on Holy Thursday because the cardinal's interference had temporarily delayed his ordination. As they were settling down into their seats for the performance of *The Only Way* (adapted from Dickens' *Tale of Two Cities*), Rolfe's meagre but extraordinary costume attracted full attention. One lingering stare came from an opulent lady. Amused, Rolfe turned to his host and said in a loud stage whisper: 'It is a pity that so many rich men have the incredibly bad taste to use their wives as sandwich-boards to vulgarly display that they have superfluous wealth which they have locked up in diamonds. I wonder they don't realise that only jewellers can recognize that the stones are real diamonds and not glass. If I had the misfortune to be a millionaire and married to one of these females, instead of bedecking her with jewels I would plaster a banknote on her back. Then there could be no mistake about my wealth.'

'I think I will experiment with *The Saturday Review*,' Rolfe said to Frederic Chapman in a letter of May 1902. And again a word such as 'experiment,' prefaced an unknown adventure in friendship, with a person he was never to meet.

The Borgia book had been a disappointment. Grant Richards' 'command' for the book to be written in the form of 'picturesque gallimaufry,' in Rolfe's mind, completely tore the historian's mantle from his shoulders. He dissociated himself from any part of it. He caused to have 'printed, in America, a ferocious denunciation of his book and its London publisher; and gained the consolation of having an editorial article devoted to his case, emphasising all his points and gibetting [Richards] as the stealer of an author's trade-mark. It gave the death-stroke to the [Borgia book] which instantly became obtainable in second-hand book-shops at a third of its published price.' 'Curious Facts From Behind the Scenes, Showing How a Book Was Published Under an Author's Name Without Authority' appeared in *The Saturday Review of Books and Art, The New York Times*, 5 April 1902.

Towards the end of this year William Roscoe Thayer criticised the character of Alexander VI in *The Saturday Review*. The fifteenth-century pope was defended by Dr. James Walsh of New York. He maintained 'that a great change had come over the estimate of Alexander VI mainly because people now realized that he became pope when he was well past sixty and during the next eleven years signed nearly a million of documents ... and did an immense amount of work, some of it of the most enduring character.' Like Rolfe, he also thought 'that Lucretia Borgia was a saint and there has never been so much slandered a lady.' In a second letter to *The Saturday Review* Walsh mentioned Baron Corvo and his letter of repudiation over his book. This brought instant word from Rolfe.

He had 'read with great pleasure your letter in N.Y. Sat. Rev. (Jan 17) *in re* Alexander vi, wherein you note saliently that "it is historians outside the Church, who, from recent investigations, defend him." Will you allow me to say that I myself am a Roman Catholick not even on speaking terms with other Roman Catholicks ... and therefore am not inclined to approve of "those stupid craven Catholicks *who fatuously think to conciliate* by rabidly joining in the hue and cry against a Pope." You may recognize the last sentence as a citation from the (on the whole) contemptible "Chronicles of the House of Borgia" which I wrote in 1899 under my pseudonym "Frederick Baron Corvo" (now rejected by me), and repudiated 13 months before publication, as well as after, because the publisher, Grant Richards, announced an intention of garbling my m.s.'

To each new person he had to introduce himself by reciting part of his past. And to Rolfe each new person qualified for the same position—this unknown and unseen stranger, this New Yorker might be 'the man I've long been looking for,' the Divine Friend. As an American he also represented to the man in London a person of wealth or influence. For several years Rolfe had occupied himself in the building of his Borgiada, the genealogical tree of the Borgias, from their origin to the present day. This 'Genealogy of Borgia, 9 ft. × 6 ft., including 293 names as against 82 in previous genealogies, (e.g. Cittadella)' would bring him fortune and reputation, he hoped. Never losing an opportunity, he was quick to mention to Walsh that he was 'seeking the patronage of a private individual, an university, or a library, to enable me to put together a complete categorical and standard history of the Borgia.' Compiling a record of seven centuries, 'my work has been seen and praised at Oxford; and the Italian Embassador, being much interested, has offer'd me credentials to the Undersecretary of State (son of Minister of Publick Instruction Bacelli), with a view to bringing the matter before the Italian King and Government.'

Walsh was in no position to consider buying the Borgiada, but letters continued happily to be exchanged between the American and the Englishman. Notes of personality and history were compared. Walsh was a Catholic. Although a man of medicine now, he had once studied for the priesthood before he was told that he had no vocation. The American doctor sent Rolfe pieces of literature and the syllabus of his lectures, *The Thirteenth: Greatest of the Centuries*. In return Rolfe said that he was 'forced' into the fifteenth century but preferred it 'There's more in that. At least, more information is accessible. And WHAT a period is the Early Renascence! Aren't you drawn to the Byzantium. Well: history for me is there. It ends with 1530 or perhaps 1545. I really do know those years in Rome.'

Rolfe's personal life had to be shared. 'Frequently I don't leave the house for 20 or 30 consecutive days. Then I madly rush into the city to collect some of my earnings and submerge myself in work again. But I am well and vivid and vigorous, altogether wholesome and natural (except 2 artificial teeth) at 42. That's because I am being saved for the priesthood.'

This last letter, he thought, 'would choke you off.' When it was answered, he was 'glad that you have taken it urbanely: but Americans are exquisitely urbane.' Walsh had 'had 6 happy years and one vegetable,' Rolfe noted, which he deemed 'extraordinarily fortunate. Few have such luck. I take it that you always have had friends; and that you never have had year after year of terror that you will not be able to go on living simply because you never have an arm or a post to lean on when you are tired.' At present he was 'writing like a fool: for yesterday my doctor said that I must stop work at once and have a complete rest and freedom from worry for a year. If not, I shall have a serious nervous break-down within the month.... And, if I stop working for two days together, I shall be penniless and homeless, and the three books which I have completed and the one which I am completing now [*Hadrian the Seventh*] will all be wasted. So I am rather upset: but quite determined not to stop until I have the means to stop, or until I drop.'

The final words of another letter were: 'Pray that I may not be in a lunatick asylum when your response arrives. Do you know what it is to count the pulsations of your heart as you lie in bed at night—fourteen-am-I-going-to-say-fifteen—ninety-seven-shall-I-be-here-to-say-ninety-eight, and so on up to thousands? Thats how I've been for seven weeks. And I'm afraid.'

Walsh hoped that his 'blues' would disappear 'with the better weather.' At this Rolfe laughed. 'It makes them worse,' he said; 'for I curse to think that I'm pinned here in this 10 foot attic, instead of doing my work wholesomely in the open air and quiet of Oxford. So I try to take no notice of the weather. When it rains, well it rains and I work. When it's splendid, I also work and swear because I'm out of its splendour. If ever I do come to America (and I most earnestly desire to come—but can't) I'll count on you....'

'How glad I am that I never have seen you! I never could say this to a man whom I have seen. No. There is not the remotest chance of my having good news to send you,' another letter from London read. 'I am right down in the mire, the rocks are slippery and perpendicular and there are no ropes let down from above. I am swimming, and that's all. Presently I shan't be able to swim any longer: there will be a bubble and θ. I have just heard that the Monthly Review doesn't think it well for the Reviews of Unwritten Books to out-stay their welcome. So here I am with 15 returned m.s.s. on my hands; as well as my four complete books in m.s. which I cannot even get to the publishers.' Written on 6 July 1903, this is the first mention that *Hadrian the Seventh* had been completed. The letter continued: 'I simply daren't stop work. If I did some one would catch me idle; and then, when I die on a dunghill, they'll say I was a lazy devil. Well, I'll leave enough *manu*script behind me to give that the lie.'

Thanking the American for some books and magazines in one letter, he had to remark about one work: 'P. 707 an Italian vivisector is held up to odium for tormenting guinea-pigs and rabbits. What is the torture of beasts beside the torment of Catholicks by Catholicks?' But the letter went on with touches of personal history and unintentional humour: 'I never touch alcohol: I have not for years. Only once in my life was I drunk and that was an accident when I was six years old.' But the accident is not named. The old question of a patron followed. 'Nothing but a thousand pounds, I name a sum at random,— nothing but a sum, a lump sum will brush away these cobwebs, which are stifling, and give me *confidence*, sweet-reasonableness, strength to use myself well and aptly.... The secret lies in the lump. That is quite essential. Little bits are worse than useless. They irritate, they exasperate, they annoy, simply because they prolong my agony, but are quite useless to do me any real good. With the lump I could clear off my really paltry embarrassments; go to sleep for a month by some sunny sea and clear my soul of horrible dreams; and then go to work again with vigour, knowing that I had something behind me, that I need not be eternally worried about where the next meal was coming from, that I need not refrain from going for a long walk when the spirit moved me to it, just because of the necessity of saving boot-leather, of saving a clean shirt and collar for the time when I am obliged to go out to see a publisher or to comfort my mother and sister. This may give you a faint idea of the restrictions which make me writhe. The little bits which I get from my reviewing and my magazine articles only keep me alive. . . .'

This perversity of mind in the matter of support for his existence did not prevent his physical suffering. In his books and in his letters he could disclose his nakedness, but it was a nakedness to be hid from others in day-to-day life. Five months before this last letter to Walsh, Rolfe had written to Bainbridge. He had been invited to the other's family home. He desperately declined. 'During these years here [at Broadhurst Gardens] I have been wearing out my underclothes, shirts, socks, boots, handkerchieves, everything, all are in rags and tatters. I can just manage to present *outwardly* a decent appearance about once a week, not more. As long as I am here, that will do. But you see that I cannot possibly move from here, and expose my nakedness in any decent house.'

When Rolfe had written about his newly finished book on July 6th, it was unnamed. But on the 25th he described it as 'a very great book and a very bad book. I say "a very bad book" because I hate and abhor from the picture of modern Roman Catholicks which I have drawn. I am ashamed of such wretches. However, I have written and do write entirely against my will, and I only can write what I know. If Roman Catholicks don't like my work they must blame themselves for omitting to provide me with good models.' The book, he said, was 'the history of the one year's pontificate of an Englishman with the temperament of a cat and the predilection for American independence, who finds himself lifted to Peter's Throne about A.D. 1910.'

By nature and by habit Rolfe was never able to divorce himself from his work. During all of his adult life he made copies of his letters and retained various notes, words and phrases. Any form of writing for him was an act of creation and he never drew the line between the private letter and work for public publication. He may have headed his first letter to Walsh *'Private and Confidential'*, but one phrase in it had already been used and had become quite threadbare before the end of his life. Introducing himself to the doctor, he said that he was a Catholic not even on speaking terms with other Catholics, 'for I find the Faith comfortable and the Faithful intolerable.' On page 23 of *Hadrian*, Rose addresses his cardinal: 'As for the Faith, I found it comfortable. As for the Faithful, I found them intolerable.' The letters to Walsh, written at the same time *Hadrian* was being composed, illustrated how closely Rolfe's two lives—personal and literary—were interwoven.

A few examples of these paralleling natures are:

For I want most earnestly to love [Catholics] if they will give me a chance.... However 'it is not I who have lost the Athenians, it is the Athenians who have lost me.'

13 March 1903

'Eminency, "it is not I who have lost the Athenians: it is the Athenians who have lost me." I would say that in Greek if I thought you would understand me.'

Hadrian the Seventh, p. 33

I make no more approaches; and I almost have resolved to refrain from fulminating St. Matthew xxv. 41-43 at any one approaching me.

March 13th

'I really think I should have fulminated at them St. Matthew xxv. 41-43—'

p. 23

The exception [the Catholic who was not a Slanderer, an Oppressor of the Poor, a Liar] was an American who passed out of my life in 1888. He was the most exquisitely beautiful boy, body and soul, (with the most exquisitely horrible voice,) I ever met. I think of him now

'... yes, do you know that eighteen years ago he had the most exquisitely beautiful face and the most exquisitely horrible voice of any boy in [Oscott] college,—address the sixth [manuscript sheet] to Percy Van Kristen, 2023 Madison Avenue, New York.' p. 97

with ardent admiration. He was a great friend of Abp. Corrigan. His people lived somewhere on 5th Ave N.Y. His name was Percy O'Sullivan.

March 13th

I received a Divine Vocation to serve God as a secular priest when I was a protestant boy of fifteen. I was very fervent about it. I went to confession ... said the rosary, used the Garden of the Soul for a prayerbook. A few years later I was unfaithful to my Vocation, sowed wild oats (if you like) most precociously. But I never relinquished my divine gift. I just neglected it and said 'Domani' like a true Roman of Rome. Then at twenty-four I became intensely earnest.... Then came the verdict that I had no Vocation four years later. Well I said they were wrong. I swore and swear that I have a Vocation, to say mass for the dead in particular. I cannot for the life of me understand how anybody except myself can claim to know anything about it. I believe that someone carelessly lied, that someone clumsily blundered, and that all concerned were determined not to own themselves, or anyone else but me,

'My opinion concerning my Vocation, such as it was and is, had been formed when I was a boy of fifteen. I was very fervent about that time. I frankly admit that I played the fool from seventeen to twenty, sowed my wild oats if you like. But I never relinquished my Divine Gift. I just neglected it, and said "Domani" like any Roman. And at twenty-four I became extremely earnest about it.'

p. 28

'I followed the opinion that someone carelessly had lied: that someone clumsily had blundered; and that all concerned were determined not to own themselves, or anyone else but me, to be in the wrong. A mistake had been made; and, by quibbles, by evasions, by threats, by every hole-and-corner means conceivable, the mistake was going to be perpetuated. Had the case been one of the ordinary type of ecclesiastical student, (the hebete to be in the wrong. A mistake —a justifiable mistake seeing that I am an abnormal creature and my superiors were about as commonplace a gaggle of fatwitted geese as this hemisphere produces—was made; and, by quibbles, intimidations, every hole-and-corner means conceivable it has been perpetuated. Had I been of the ordinary type of ecclesiastical student, the hebete and half-licked Keltic class I mean, I furiously should have apostatized, or I mildly should have acquiesced and started in as a cheesemonger or a pork butcher. But the intellectually myopic authorities were unable to discriminate; and quite gaily wrecked a life.

June 4th

and half-licked Keltic class I mean,) either I furiously should have apostatized, or I mildly should have acquiesced, and should have started-in as a pork-butcher or a cheesemonger. But those intellectually myopic authorities were unable to discriminate; and they quite gaily wrecked a life. Oh yes: I formed an opinion; and I very freely stated it.'

p. 28

Well, as for me, I persist in maintaining that I have a Divine Vocation to the secular priesthood. I am not one of those flippertigibbets of the frothy flighty fervour, who can be blown hither and thither with a mediocrity's personally-biased opinion for a fan: but an Englishman, born under Cancer, tenacious. Naturally I persist.

June 4th

'My opinion, Eminency, [is] that I have a Divine Vocation to the Priesthood.... Eminency, I am not one of your low Erse or pseudo Gaels, flippertigibbets of frothy flighty fervour, whom you can blow hither and thither with a sixpence for a fan. Thank The Lord I'm English, born under Cancer, tenacious, slow and sure. Naturally I persist.'

p. 31

You sum up your doctrine 'I think we must simply do the next thing to hand and keep on bravely.' That is admirable. I am rather fond of mottoes and when I was a boy I painted a motto on my fireplace; and I have kept it before my eyes in every room or den which has been my own since. It is the same as yours only I use it in the Old English form in which I found it carved on a cupboard at Saffron Walden, Essex, twenty six years ago

De ye nexte thynge.
That's what I've always done. Turned out of one thing I've never stopped: but instantly have begun again at something else.

June 29th

'Now what shall I do? Advance one pace. "Do ye nexte thynge." '

p. 44

So [my doctor] applied blisters on the back of my ears. I am all raw and quite unpresentable: but I'm still here and still slaving; and when the booming in my head gets unbearable I just clap on another blister.

June 29th

Dr. Guido Cabelli ... found Him positively furious with the pain of physical and intellectual struggles. The physician exhibited Pot. Brom., Tinct. Valerian. Am., Tinct. Zinzil., Sp. Chlorof., Aq. Menth. Pip., once every three hours. It made the Pontiff conscious that He stank like a male cat in early summer; but He heard no more boom-booming in his ears.

p. 373

I rarely speak even to my kind.
March 13th

His little yellow cat Flavio lay asleep on the tilted board, nestling in the bend of his left elbow. That was the only living creature to whom he ever spoke with affection as well as with politeness.

p. 1

I hope that you will read [*Hadrian the Seventh*], mark, learn, & inwardly digest it. It should teach you a little more of ME.
3 November 1904

He chuckled at the thought that those same people would read, mark, learn, and inwardly digest, every word and every dotted *i* of His letters now—letters which were not going to be painfully voluminously conscientiously persuasive any more: but dictatorial.

p. 142

Rolfe's last letter to the New York doctor during 1903 was on August 17th and it was marked 'Strictly private and Confidential':

If I am to lose your friendship I shall do it now.... My affairs have come to a head. All my creditors are upon me. It is the dead season and publishers delay with my books. Even if they accepted tomorrow, I could not be published and paid till after Christmas. And when I have posted this I shall have just 3½d. in the world, no immediate prospect of more, not a friend to help. And at any moment I may be thrown out into the street, with nowhere to go. I must lean on you. Save me from going mad, losing all chance of success with my work. I do not know where I shall be from hour to hour so I beg you to wire your help to Henry Newbolt (Ed. Monthly Review).... I will keep in touch with him as long as I am alive. Whatever you do, *please burn this.*

There was no signature, but one more line was added: 'And you are taking your *Rest*.'

Walsh was five years younger than Rolfe. After his seminary days he had turned to medicine and was fortunate enough to study in Paris, Vienna and Berlin. In 1898 he began a practice in New York. As the new century progressed, he was to become a professor, to lecture and write on medicine, psychology and the Church, and to found the Fordham University Press. But in August 1903 he was not the wealthy American of Rolfe's mind. His new medical practice was his only source of income. Yet he could not disappoint a fellow human being. He sent all that he could spare in the form of ten dollars. For this act of kindness he was thanked—fifteen months later.

The contents of the August letter were all true. Rolfe's creditors were upon him. His rent was unpaid. In no way had 1903 been a profitable year. He emitted his loud pleas like the boy who cried 'Wolf!' Bainbridge had received the same frantic requests in similar phrases: 'I have just 8/- left, no prospect of more, and not a soul in the world to help me.' 'When the worst comes, it must be faced. That's all.' 'But all through this year I have been harassed with threats of expulsion and even now I may be homeless *at any moment*.'

The extremely personal attitude of his letters—between himself and the one person to which each letter was addressed—demonstrates the fine line between the various shades of reality within his mind. The actual and the imaginary overlapped into, not a confusing, but, for Rolfe, a clear definition of immediate events.

On the day before his letter was sent to America, Rolfe wrote to his literary agent, Leonard Moore.

> If you are going to pitch Constable a yarn about me as a writer who is bound to rise, and with whom it will be well to be connected, you might like to mention the favourable reception which my magazine work has had, and the article accepted by *The Westminster Review*.

On this day he seemed to know where he was going to be 'from hour to hour.' Yet in one day's time something had shifted his mood. As austere as he lived, financial demands upon him were greater than his income. In his adversity he had made a second plea for aid to the Royal Literary Fund. His application had just been returned when he answered the Fund on the 17th, the same day of the letter to Walsh:

> I can assure you that my life is hard enough, and the sacrifice of my self-respect (in coming before the R.L.F.) still harder, without these fresh degradations [of the Trustee's doubts of his bonafides]; and that I am the last man in the world to ask for help which I do not merit or need.

At Oban, Mme. Duhamel wrote to Lord Bute's wife about Rolfe's lies. At Scots College he was 'universally regarded as about the biggest liar we had ever met.' And Temple Scott also spoke about him as being 'a natural liar but he was a harmless one so long as he dealt with the things of his imagination. When it came to human relations this expression of himself, brought him many troubles.'

Subtle deviations from the truth were employed to accentuate his plight. In *Hadrian* his Broadhurst Gardens room is 'eleven feet square.' Twenty years later Bainbridge paced it and said in his *Twice Seven* that the measurement, compared with the one in *Hadrian*, was 'exact'. Yet in one letter to Walsh, Rolfe wrote that he was 'pinned here in this 10 foot attic.' Even the difference of one foot could be used cunningly, and hopefully, for advantage.

Between 1899 and 1903 he had made, and had alienated, a number of friends. But not all forsook him. Stressing his need for friendship and financial assistance in another letter to Walsh, he said that 'most men in my desperate position have friends or relations, on whom they can lean for a moment's respite when they are as tired as I am, or from whom they can derive help in need. But I have only one friend in the world, only one man with whom I am on intimate terms. He has known me for more than 20 years continually. But he is a poor Oxford Don, (E. G. Hardy, Vice Principal of Jesus) going blind (glaucoma) and likely to be in difficulties in the near future.'

232

E. G. Hardy first met Rolfe at Grantham Grammar School just before his conversion to the Roman Church. When the Aberdeen Attack appeared, 'only a single one out of all those scores came forward to assure me of friendship in that dreadful moment.... I was left to bear the brunt alone, except for that one; and he was not a Catholic. Except from him, I had no sympathy and no comfort whatsoever.' Hardy offered a solacing hand and the two were reunited when Rolfe walked from Holywell to Oxford in 1899. This 'splendid master' is Dr. Strong in *Hadrian*—'Strong of nature and Strong of name and station, Strong of body and Strong of mind, immensely my superior altogether, knowing all my weaknesses and all my imperfections: who, to me, is as much like [God] as any man can be!'

Hardy probably knew more about Rolfe's career from 1884 to 1907 than any other single person. He appreciated the young man's 'very attractive personality' and 'in spite of his little foibles I always found Rolfe a good and loyal friend, and he was distinctly *persona grata* in my family. I sometimes worked him pretty hard. In the two years I was Greats examiner he read papers to me for six or seven hours a day for more than two months on end.'

After their reunion in 1899, Rolfe acted as Hardy's secretary during examination periods at Jesus College, Oxford, until 1907. At such times he stayed at Oxford to read papers to his master and friend, whose eyesight was failing. For the first two years' work Rolfe earned £25. He received only three guineas for each period, but Hardy saw that he was well provided for as a friendly guest in his own house.

In letters to people during his Oxford stays, Rolfe would refer to them as periods of wasted time for him—time spent away from his writing, time during which he achieved nothing. Yet he greatly enjoyed this opportunity of helping others, and because of him, more students were passed. The part of his nature which yearned to do something for others was gratified at Jesus. He was given a role to enact in the struggle of the underdog versus an Establishment and, of course, his sympathies were allied with the students. Just one of his personal notes for 1901 exemplified his actions. To do his best for one student, he 'gave him 2½ hours extra translation as chance to amend—worse than ever—half hour viva dull, prayed much, unsatisfactory—placed D, the examiners "would not insult the Pass School" by giving him a pass degree—Fourth Class Honours less creditable than Pass—A perfect example of the Merciful justice of Greats Examiners.'

The kindness shown him by Hardy's family was repaid in *Hadrian*. Dr. and Mrs. Strong and their three children, 'typical of all that is best,' visit Rome and are guests of a gracious Hadrian. At their parting he presents them with 'five little crosses of gold and chrysoberyls set in diamonds,' saying: ' "You will accept a memorial of this happy day; and of course" (with that rare smile of His) "you will not expect the Pope to give you anything but popery. Good-bye, dear friends, good-bye." '

Hardy was never subjected to Rolfe's subtle dictatorial demands. Nor did he treat the younger man with any trace of charitable pity. With the absence of these two elements, a pleasant harmony existed between the two friends. Yet, when speaking of Hardy to others, it was always in the light of his own circumstances. To Walsh, Hardy was presented as a 'poor Oxford Don' soon 'to be in difficulties' himself. But at the time of the letter the vice-principal lived better than the average person. The house Rolfe knew at Oxford was not the only one belonging to Hardy. At the same time he and his family had houses at Shaldon, Poole and on the Isle of Wight.

The events of the 1890s had shaped Rolfe's mind into a twisted maze of persecution. Under the pressures of want, contempt and ostracism by the mediocre and in an earnest dedication to unmask Man's Insincerity to Man, untruths freely mingled with the truths of his isolated life. 'Lies' and 'ideals' may have become as synonymous to Rolfe as to Ibsen's Dr. Relling, who speaks of them as existing side by side 'about as closely as typhus and putrid fever.'

By the time *Hadrian* was finished the last of Rolfe's 'Reviews of Unwritten Books' for *The Monthly Review* had already appeared. At the time this same magazine printed his 'Notes on the Conclave', his Hampstead landlady was demanding her unpaid rent. Edward Slaughter introduced Rolfe to this house but he never knew what arrangement had been made between the penniless author of 1899 and Mrs. C. M. Griffiths. Nicholas Crabbe, at the beginning of the novel bearing his name, gives over '£140 cash down for four years' rent in advance.' Unlike his fictitious hero, Rolfe had no money in September 1899. And now, just four years after being received into the Broadhurst Gardens attic room, Rolfe owed his landlady £160. One guinea was the usual weekly charge by Mrs. Griffiths for room and board, but Rolfe's attic must have been less. Yet this was Mrs. Griffiths' only income and at this time she had only one other guest. Almost two years later she still had hopes about Rolfe's bill. On 11 June 1905 he wrote to Barnard & Taylor that Mrs. Griffiths was 'demanding money; and [I ask] you to reply, as she forced me to place my affair in legal hands & I cannot interfere.' But Rolfe's solicitors' records contained no reference of any payment to any landlady.

The magic wand of the fairy tale and the alchemist's mortar and pestle remained equally out of Rolfe's reach in his vain attempts to turn written words to gold—or even to copper.

Between 1902 and 1903 he would make triple copies of his work. To save postage, he carted them around by foot. They would be returned, 'thumbed or torn or crumpled or pencilled by rhypokonylose violent stultified editors,' to be recopied for another round. One editor suggested additions to his 'Reviews of Unwritten Books', 'to make a series of thirty.' Rolfe made the extra essays and 'sent in the series of thirty; and never saw or heard of them again.' Another editor admired the idea of these 'Reviews' but wanted something 'upterdight'. Rolfe feverishly composed sixteen new ones—among them, Maurice Hewlett's *Adventures of Sherlock Holmes*, Max Beerbohm's *Light That Failed* and J. M. Barrie's *Harry Richmond*. In eleven days he wrote 21,000 words, only to learn that the editor who asked for them could not find room for them now and then lost them before they could be returned.

Returned manuscripts, of books or shorter pieces, were instantly taken to other publishers and editors. The constant battle to write, to try to find an outlet for his work and somehow to survive while doing so told upon his weakened body. The sleepless nights became no worse than the days which anticipated the postman's call.

To the editor of *The Monthly Review* he wrote about his strained pecuniary position on August 13th. The rent from only one lodger was supplying the needs for this one Hampstead household, and Mrs. Griffiths was trying to wrest some of her unseen rent from her attic guest. In his letter Rolfe stressed the frayed relations between him and the landlady. How much longer he could remain here he did not know, but it was essential for him and his work that he should stay. But if he left he would have to be 'turned out of the house (I will not *go*) and that may be at any moment for Mrs Griffiths this morning is quite furious.'

On September 22nd he wrote to Bainbridge that he 'had just 6*d*. and no more.... The day was a day of horrible abuse. I began to feel like going mad. I hadn't a penny. I was expecting you every minute. In the evening I asked [my landlady] to let me wait till the last post. Then I would go and walk about till morning, and come again for my letters. She flung at me leave to stay for the night. I stayed and did not sleep a wink. This morning I got your letter. I told her you were likely to come. I have been walking up and down the room all day. Now at 5.30 I am writing to say that I feel sure she will turn me out to-night. Never mind. I will keep alive. On Wednesday morning I will come here again for my letters. Then I will continue to walk about near and call again at noon. And at night. I used to be able to go four days without food. I think I can do two now. I am placing all my confidence on you. When you get this, for goodness' sake *wire* me some money and leave to come to you. Four pounds will just do. Don't delay me a moment longer from my work. Here I am fast going frantic from forced inaction. The sooner I begin to work again the sooner I shall recover my lost ground.' He had already written to Bainbridge, 'All this is fatuous futile fatal rot. I ought to be writing continuously; and every day which is lost, in this brutally bestial hunt for a living, puts me a month further from the solid foundation which I already have laid. I ought to be building; and I am beating the air.' Rolfe's last letter to Bainbridge on the 28th ended: 'As you will not take in my belongings of course I must be content to lose my work and tools of trade. As you will not give me personally a chance—the last and only—there is nothing before me but the workhouse.'

Eight days later an account of Rolfe pictured him as 'a little weasel of a man.' The author Richard Whiteing spoke of Rolfe in this way in a letter addressed to Wilfrid Meynell, soliciting aid for the penniless Rolfe, not knowing their paths had unfavourably crossed ten years earlier. Whiteing had invited Rolfe to The Whitefriars Club for dinner one evening. Rolfe appeared 'almost tonsured with a close crop, and that indelible look of priest in every line of him which [Catholic] seminaries seem to give whether they call or reject.' To supplement his almost non-existent wages, Rolfe was offering to give Italian lessons. And, whatever his employment, he continued to live at Broadhurst Gardens throughout 1903. When Mrs. Griffiths moved to Cheniston Gardens, Kensington, early in 1904, he followed as a lodger. But the barren year between the completion of *Hadrian* and its publication left him destitute.

Urgency of the moment prompted temporary condescension. He was reconciled with a person from the past. Just before the appearance of *Hadrian the Seventh* in July 1904, Rolfe met his old friend Nicholson, who loaned him twenty pounds. Nicholson was one of the very few people who appreciated Rolfe's nature and predicaments. Speaking about Rolfe in a 1904 letter to Kains-Jackson, he wrote that 'we decided to accept him without prejudice and give him another chance. We obliterate the last twenty years; the world refuses to do so. Therefore F. and I are the only two people in the world he believes in or even can trust. We save him from himself by purposely ignoring anything amiss in him; and he responds to this attitude gallantly. The man I knew and loved twenty years ago was bound to do so. To us he is F. W. Rolfe, he assumes no other identity.... He is a jaundiced, bitter persecuted pariah: that is evident; he has done badly by the world he lives in and his fellow-men, and he naturally fears it and them. He has spoiled his life. And we want to bring a ray of hope and comfort into it, even if he doesn't deserve one.'

Favourable criticism heralded *Hadrian the Seventh*:
'The King .... A striking book.
The Queen .... Undeniably brilliant ... An able satire.
Court Journal .. The plot is a daring one, instinct with scholarly
                        forethought and audacious originality.'
These are three of twenty-five extracts from reviews printed by
Chatto & Windus, at Rolfe's instigation. He cannot be accused
—either here on earth or in limbo—of mere self-advertising. The
only purpose of these 'Notes on Hadrian the Seventh' was to
promote sales of the book. Of these, *The Court Journal* provided
the longest review of fifty-seven lines. Only five lines shorter,
The Queen, The Lady's Magazine, praised the author. Rolfe
then had to scrounge out the two-sentence review from *The King
and His Navy and Army*. The thirty-four words included the
name of the book, author and publisher, with the only three
quotable words being the ones used by Rolfe.

Neither advertising nor favourable reviews sold the book. Rolfe
was to realize nothing from it.

Shortly after *Hadrian* was published, Rolfe left Mrs. Griffiths,
still owing her unpaid rent which was 'placed in legal hands' a
year later. But he did not go to the workhouse.

With what little money they had, his mother and sister had
opened 'St. Alphage School and Kinder Garten' for small girls
at Broadstairs; and here he found a place to stay.

The two women could help him in no way beyond providing
him with a room and meals. With no money or clothes, little
more than the tools used in his writing, he offered payment by
aiding them in whatever way he could—mending things around
the house and cutting the grass.

The author of *Hadrian the Seventh* still wore the frayed
clothes of Baron Corvo. More than half a century later, Ethel
Hudson, one little girl from Miss Nellie Rolfe's school, recalled
the fact that her parents knew Freddy Rolfe at Broadstairs.
Knowing his circumstances and that his sister had no means to
help him, they were glad when they later heard that he had
gone abroad. They hoped he would be happier than he had been
in England. The little girl of 1904 remembered her mother

coming into the house one day. She told her husband that she had just seen Miss Rolfe's brother and wished she were able to buy a new coat for him.

11

'Whatever does not kill me, strengthens me.' In this framework of Camus' words Rolfe lived.

During the same year in which *Hadrian the Seventh* appeared, London lost its resident author. He had gone through money, credit, promises, friends. But there were always more to be found.

In November 1904 he thanked the New York doctor for his financial assistance a year earlier. 'I ought not to have asked,' he wrote. 'But the exigency was extreme. I was going down into the depths again, alone. I was terrified at the prospect; &, when I found myself slipping, I yelled. I ought to have gone down in dignified silence. But I didn't. I am not a hero. I writhed horribly; & continued to exist, even in the mire.'

His pontifical novel had just appeared and he told Dr. Walsh to 'read, mark, learn, & inwardly digest it. It should teach you a little more of ME.... I do hope that you will send me a long psychiatric prognosis of Hadrian. There is a distinct assertion of a secondary personality there, which greatly puzzles me, now that I read the book in print; & I feel that you could say something very illuminating. My new book contains more of Hadrian, *viz.* A series of imaginary papers written by George Arthur Rose, & a series of imaginary letters written to me after the publication of *Hadrian the Seventh* by various persons & personages named in the book.'

To another correspondent at the same time he also spoke of this sequel, *Rose's Records*. It would not be bitter, he said. 'Frightfully ferocious when poked at,' the hero is a Crab, but the Moon has made him soft inside. He had never lost his sense of the ridiculous. This again would apply to a second book, *Ivory,*

Apes and Peacocks, another successor to *Hadrian.* Rolfe merely would be the Barnum of each show, the daw pecking at other people. But neither of these—nor two others started at the same time, *The King of the Wood* and *Duchess Attendolo*—survive, if ever completed.

Three months after *Hadrian, Agricultural and Pastoral Prospects of South Africa* appeared.

In the November 1904 letter to Walsh, Rolfe said that 'a chance of salvation by menial disgraceful work' came just as he 'was going down into the depths again.' 'Notwithstanding that I am a dreamer,' he continued, he actually wrote the South Africa book 'for an expert of the Chartered Company & Rhodes Trustees to sign. He kept me alive while I was doing it: but afterwards, openly gibing at my powerless poverty, refused to make good the promises on which he had obtained my services. I found some lawyers who, on the security of all my own published & unpublished work, sent him a writ for £2000, & allow me enough to starve on till the case comes into court.'

Rolfe, the man of fancy, had once cast Walsh's horoscope, but added, 'And with regard to prognostic astrology, I frankly cannot reconcile it with my conscience as a Christian to practice it habitually. I have done it for myself [but] I am not at all clear where the line is which sharply divides white magick from black.' Yet, as the same year drew to a close, he did not hesitate to write to his solicitors, Barnard & Taylor, hoping they were 'pressing my case with all speed. Luna parallel Jupiter in my horoscope during this Nov. Dec. Dec. is supposed to give success in lawsuits & finance. It is not unwise to take advantage of such circumstances.'

In July 1903 the Rhodes Trustees paid Col. (later Brig.-Gen. and Sir) Owen Thomas £500 for a report on Rhodesian farming prospects. To complete the work Thomas advertised for literary assistance. Rolfe answered and was engaged by the 'obese magenta colonel of militia with a black-stubbed moustache and a Welsh-tongued proposition' to write the final report. The task of expanding the original 'twenty-page pamphlet' to the 366 printed pages of text began right after *Hadrian* and lasted eight months. He was paid £25 for the first month's work and another

£25 was spread over the remaining time. Considering the time spent on, and the prices received for, his earlier books, this price seemed fair. It was fair and prompt. Yet Rolfe thought otherwise. Here was another case of a monied organization cheating him. Here was a case similar to that of the Holywell banners. In Wales it was not merely Fr. Beauclerk who withheld the payment due, but the entire Society of Jesus. However wealthy or poor Thomas himself might be, he was backed in this endeavour by the Rhodes Trust, an association known to have money at its disposal. The pre-paid £50 was used up during the book's composition—as had been the money for the Grant Richards *Borgia*. Two negative and past experiences taught him a positive solution for the present. The painter of the St. Winefride banners and the Borgian historian rebelled. The finished South Africa book was worth much more than the initial verbal agreement.

J. B. Pinker, a literary agent, introduced Rolfe to a firm of solicitors and his case was quickly taken up. The poorly clothed author presented the details of the affair in person and Churton Taylor of Barnard & Taylor, a sedate and cautious lawyer, fell under Rolfe's most persuasive spell. The half of one afternoon was spent listening to the story of Rolfe's past life and future hopes, emphasized by the reviews of his books. The new client had no money. But this did not matter. Barnard & Taylor would consent to act for him from the proceeds on his future books. This time Rolfe would not lose out. For his share of work on the book for Thomas he asked four times the sum given to the colonel by the Rhodes Trustees. On 6 August 1904 a writ was issued against Col. Owen Thomas.

However congenial the association between the two might have been at first, by mid-summer Thomas had learned enough about the other to lose confidence in him. On July 20th he wrote to Rolfe about his impossible demands for payment. He also mentioned Sir David Hunter Blair. Rolfe was completely open with his lawyers about anything pertaining to the case. Thomas' letters were shown to them and on August 1st he defined the person of Hunter Blair. 'The Benedictine monk, Father Oswald, (Sir David Hunter Blair in the world,) is a person with much leisure on his hands, which he has employed for several years in libelling me. The reason is that I have been very severe with him on detecting him in the act of falsehood. You know that, among Roman Catholicks, the *Officious Lie* (which is told to excuse oneself or another,) is merely a Venial Sin. Hence, although I am myself a Roman Catholick, I am not on speaking terms with any Roman Catholicks. I make no secret of it; & consequently, I am much disliked. Father Oswald is one of several persons who have smarted under my pen; & he takes these illegitimate methods of salving his wounds. However, he actually knows little or nothing about me ...' Yet this 'little or nothing' was to be Rolfe's undoing when the case was finally heard.

On August 27th Rolfe sent his lawyers a literary opinion worth considering:

Lay before Counsel the following as an alternative suggestion concerning amount of claims:
Keep the category of particulars as it is.
Say that Thomas paid me £25 for a month's work.
Estimate the remaining eight months on the same scale, viz £200 *for literary services actually rendered.*
The modesty & sweet reasonableness of this perhaps will cause a proper value to be placed upon the claim for damages on a/c of the promises which induced me to neglect my own work, & on a/c of T's attack on my reputation, viz £1800.

This opinion was given 'for what it's worth.'

As 1905 began Rolfe added 'the ms. book now called *Don Tarquinio* to the list of my works which I have made over to you.' In the same letter to his solicitors he supposed that they 'will give me timely notice before my case comes up. Is it not possible & desirable to have it tried by a Judge only?' Barnard & Taylor could formally answer his letter but could indicate no date for the trial. They, as he, were at the mercy of a bureaucratic government.

Although the book brought him no money, *Hadrian* offered some odd prizes from time to time. The reading of the novel stirred two religists to contact its author. One was Robert Hugh

Benson. The other was Mar Jacobus, Bishop of Mercia and Middlesex, Administrator of the Metropolitan See of India, Ceylon, Milapur, etc., of the Syro-Chaldean Church, and of the Patriarchate of Babylon and the East, and Founder of the Evangelical Catholic Communion. The holder of these titles was Ulric Vernon Herford, who proposed Rolfe's accepting a bishopric over 25,000 Christians and twenty churches.

Born a Unitarian, Herford became a minister in 1892, six years before he built a red-brick chapel, 'The Church of Divine Love', with an adjacent house for young men living quasi-Franciscan lives. He dreamed of a united Christendom under one Evangelical Catholic Communion. In 1902 he went on a pilgrimage to India and was there ordained a deacon and priest in two days and given the name of Mar Jacobus, being granted the status of British Administrator of the Syro-Chaldean Metropolitan See in India. The 'Fr. Rolfe' on *Hadrian*'s title page attracted his attention. Although Rolfe's fondest dreams were directed within the Church, he desired nothing more than a humble role. Herford's offer to him of a neo-Nestorian bishopric was too grand to be eyed without suspicion. He made enquiries through his solicitors about the genuineness of the Evangelical Catholic. 'I particularly want to know the status ... from the Anglican point of view, ... from the R.C. ditto. For it appears that [Herford] introduced to me ... & (on the strength of *Hadrian*) he practically offers a bishoprick over the Christians of St Thomas on the Malabar Coast!!! I am inquiring: for the validity of Order is all-important.'

The offer by Herford was more genuine than the figures of Christians and churches to be served under the bishopric. In one of the wisest moves of his life, Rolfe declined the offer.

At the time *Hadrian* appeared, he had finished two more books, the South Africa one for Owen Thomas and *Nicholas Crabbe*. Perhaps the highest compliment he ever paid any one was given to Dr. Hardy in this book. George Arthur Rose, in a single published book, existed in the short interval between the two symbols Rolfe used as names for himself: the Raven and the Crab. To the Raven, or Corvo, he prefixed his own given name of Frederick. For Crabbe's first name he rechristened him-

244

self, taking that of his grandfather. In *The Weird of the Wanderer* he writes, 'For thou, Nicholas the Third, called the Crab, ... knowest no more of thine ancestors than the names of Nicholas the First who was the father of Robert who was the father of William who was the father of Nicholas the Second who was the father of thy gentle father James.' From his friend and master at Grantham and Oxford he had learned that, 'by Gk custom, children were named after their grandparents.' So Nicholas Crabbe began to exist in 1904, exactly one hundred years after Nicholas Rolfe had written a tragedy, his only adventure into the literary world.

Rolfe's unique character is indeed apparent in most of his work. Although, 'clothed in icy mail,' he introduces himself, his existence and his misadventures, real or imagined, he does not command the reader's full attention. Plot was a weak point with him, but one collaborator, Robert Hugh Benson, stated: 'What you can do (Good Lord, how you can!) is to build up a situation when you've got it. You are a vignette-, a portrait-, not a landscape-painter, a maker of chords, not of progressions.' Rolfe is a dramatist who allows his main actor a rest from the centre of the stage at the right moments. And he gives his other actors ample opportunity to convey his story to the audience. Sincerely interested in other people, if sometimes only clinically, he projects living hearts into the people he encounters in his books. How they look, live, talk, all is sketched into a series of individual personages. He never permits cardboard characters. And the real people who formed a part of his history in the London publishing world of 1899-1903 parade across the pages of *Nicholas Crabbe*.

Chatto & Windus had become his publisher with *Hadrian*, but Rolfe gave Lane one more chance. He sent him the *Crabbe* manuscript. Lane, Harland, Grant Richards and their dealings with him are all clearly pictured in the story, and the disguises are very thin. Lane heralded the return of the manuscript with a curt note. This was answered before the manuscript arrived.

I can only suppose that, when you indited the besottedly silly ill-spelt ungrammatical & purely spottily-punctuated letter just arrived, you must have been not yet sober or else suffering from the twinges of a blastemal conscience which naturally would afflict the liar of *The Ms. in the Red Box* & the swindler of Mrs Gertrude Atherton. For you seem to have missed my plain statement that *Nicholas Crabbe* is a Romance, & to have sniffed 'lampoons & libels' where none are. I was not aware that you had any friends; & I certainly do not know them. So I merely point out that, had my book been what you stupidly call it, it is hardly likely that I should have submitted it first to you. It is true that, when I write History, I take jolly good care to write from original documents: but I do not call *Nicholas Crabbe* historical. And it also is true that I myself have not read more than the title-page & the first chapter of the typescript, which went to you (in the presence of witnesses) straight from the typescribe's office. I shall examine it, when it comes back to me, with extremely careful endeavour to find out what can possibly have put you into such a maniacal & rhapsodical fury.

Although the story in *Nicholas Crabbe* is Rolfe's, the inspiration for the novel came from a book published in 1900. The locale of *Outsiders: An Outline* is New York City. 'About half past six' of the first morning in the book 'Oliver Lock started on a hunt that was to last as long as he did—the hunt that will never end while the human race survives,—the "Hunt for Happiness!"' Lock is a writer and the novel relates his attempts to be published. After a promising beginning, he is forced to leave his rooming house and pawn what little he possesses to meet his bills.

This general, and familiar, outline caught Rolfe's imagination, as well as certain sentences in the story. 'Stupidity is more than a Visitation of God: it is an exact science.' 'Mediocrity is a bacillus, whose culture begins and ends in over-culture.' 'The reward for sincerity is the plaudits or sneers of the mediocre, the bleatings of the fat-witted, the vacant stare of the self-satisfied, the squeal of the parasite and the sycophant.' 'He that careth not to please men, nor feareth to displease them, shall enjoy much peace.' 'Save me from my friends; and I can attend to my enemies.' 'It is wonderful how devoutly the devout can dwell together in discord.' Robert William Chambers was the book's author, who 'grows sillier and sillier,' once exclaimed H. L. Mencken, 'emptier and emptier, worse and worse. But was he ever more than a fifth-rater? I doubt it.' One of Rolfe's faculties was to translate the views of even a fifth-rater into his own first-rate work.

As Crabbe-Rolfe comes to the end of the story—a story of a promising author finally forced into financial and social poverty —'the loneliness of his life was worse than crucifixion. He was nailed to his room; and there was no one at all with whom he could exchange a single word. . . . People will give you anything, and will do anything for you, if you are in (and, shall I say, to keep you in) the gutter: but nothing—nothing to prevent you from sliding to that facile descent. . . . Not only was he troubled by all these things, and weakened by starvation . . . but all the time his creditors came and banged upon his door. He had not the solace of tobacco. That was paralysing.' And, when his only friend leaves him, 'that was all. He dropped to the table, hiding his features. He was alone and naked—all alone with The Alone.'

The friend Crabbe eventually loses in the novel is the second-ary character. This is 'Robert, famous in counsel: Fulgentius, the Radiant One: Kemp, the Champion,' primarily based on Sholto Douglas. The name Kemp, meaning 'the Champion', may have derived from H. H. Champion, especially in the manner of intimate conversations between the two. Kemp is befriended by Crabbe, an act Rolfe wished to perform but could only do in imagination at this time. Rolfe longed to help others; and he yearned to share his company with an appreciative few. Above all, he desired to be free of his own singularity, to be permitted inconspicuously to mingle with people and to exchange friend-ships and gifts. After the writing of *Hadrian*—in which Rose-Rolfe persists in his vocation against all odds—his stories allow of a different train of thought. Speaking to Kemp about George Arthur Rose, Nicholas Crabbe says:

'I'll tell you a joke about him. Last Leap Year, someone told him that he was a fool to waste his life for a fad; and advised him to settle down and get married. "Very good," says Rose, "now I'll make a bargain with my stars. If I get an offer of marriage during this year, from a good-looking charming girl under nineteen with fifty thousand a year, half of which she voluntarily will settle on me, I'll marry her and cultivate the art of husbandry ever after. If I don't get such an offer, I shall know that I am not meant to marry; and I will dismiss the subject for all time, and run for the Popedom".'

'Oh did he get an offer?'

'Yes: he certainly did—an enormous one: but he knew who made it.'

'Is he married?'

'No. He jumped at the loophole, which the anonymity of the offer gave him; and escaped.'

There are periods of Rolfe's life lacking factual documentation. During his own lifetime a mass of legend and fable was collected around him and increased after his death. Twice during his life strange rumours existed about an intention of marriage. At Aberdeen he was supposed to have proposed to Miss Georgiana Hay; and another person whose hand he solicited, rumour had it, was Cecily Gleeson-White of Christchurch.

During the month of February 1905, Rolfe wrote two letters. Together with the future profits from his books, he had entrusted his elaborate Borgiada to Barnard & Taylor. In a short note from Broadstairs he expressed concern about his case against Thomas. But the main purpose of the letter was to say that 'Mr Oscar Browning has written asking me to bring the Borgia Genealogy for his inspection, either to King's College Cambridge before xx Mar. or to Bexhill after that date.' Expressions of momentary interest were all that the genealogical chart ever produced. It was a by-product of his researches into the Borgia history. The publisher who commissioned Corvo to do this book in 1899 was now having his own reverses. The agonizing episode, associated with each step of writing and publishing the book were completely forgotten when Rolfe learned of Grant Richards' situation. In whatever way he could, Rolfe offered his aid, but in a way only he would have done. He wrote:

Li L fdg eh ri dqb dvvlvwdqfh wr brx, L vkdoo eh yhub kdssb li brx zloo irujhw wkh sdvw dqg zloo ph krz.

Rolfe did not hear from Richards, who, naturally, did not even know assistance was being offered.

A third letter during the same month came to Rolfe. An admirer of *Hadrian* wished to extend his sincere appreciation for the satisfaction derived from this book. 'I hope you will allow a priest to tell you how grateful he is for *Hadrian the Seventh*. It is quite impossible to say how much pleasure it has given me in a hundred ways, nor how very deeply I have been touched by it. I have read it three times, and each time the impression has grown stronger of the deep loyal faith of it, its essential cleanness, and its brilliance.' The letter from Herford, who also had read *Hadrian* and wrote to its author, had caused no mental or spiritual alarm. This letter did. It came from a priest, a Catholic like himself and a convert and author. The letter had been written by Fr. Robert Hugh Benson, the Roman son of the Archbishop of Canterbury and the brother to A. C. and E. F. Benson.

The years of misery and unrequited love from any person within the Church had created a barrier between Rolfe and the faithful. He had been wounded too many times by candidates for friendship not to be cautious of some new overture. Both weary and suspicious, he was in no hurry to answer Benson's first letter. On March 5th he wrote to Taylor about 'the serious state of things' at Broadstairs. His mother caused him 'great anxiety & I am tired out myself (mentally.) This means that I've had a bad week—work oozing out slowly & uneasily & having to be rewritten.' Fr. Beauclerk had written, 'asseverating his friendship,' which Rolfe did not 'believe in the last a bit.' As for Benson, he merely stated that the priest had written again, 'asking for a meeting.'

An exchange of letters between the two authors slowly broke

249

through Rolfe's 'icy mail'. A sincerity of affection, warmth and good humour filled the pages from Hugh Benson. They flowed daily, at a time when he said he was too busy to write more than once a month to close friends. To Rolfe he announced that he would 'put *Hadrian VII* among the three books from which I never wish to be separated.' To his threat of pasting together the 'sordid' pages speaking of Socialists, Rolfe replied, 'Do not paste down these pages, ... for the completely sordid Socialists will still exist under your paste, and paste is a notable nursery for microbes.'

Of the many bonds pulling them together, the strongest was the Church. The common bonds were also contrasting ones. Each had an interest in the arts, history and Church ceremony. One was an author struggling for his very existence. The other was a prolific writer of best-selling books. One of Rolfe's favourite historical personages was little St. Hugh. Associated with charities all through his life, Benson's favourite was the home for destitute boys established in 1885 at Southwark under the name of its and his patron saint, St. Hugh of Lincoln. Rolfe had been a Catholic for nineteen years, had sought for a place within the Church, had been rejected and abused. Benson had been a popular Anglican preacher, who, upon his conversion, was welcomed into the Roman fold with open arms. He chose the new faith in September 1903, when Rolfe had just finished *Hadrian,* and Dr. Mostyn confirmed him. Pius X himself shortened the length of time between his acceptance into the Church and his ordination; and his popularity only increased.

The letters from Benson were filled with personal news, questions and answers. He asked Rolfe's opinions on his own work and criticized the other's unpublished manuscripts. He was generous and earnestly tried to find publishers for his new friend, who shared with him an interest in the supernatural. Benson was thrilled by other-world phenomena: seances, Theosophy, Swedenborg, mesmerism, necromancy. At his request, Rolfe drew his horoscope—which Benson accepted with full confidence. Yet the two men of many talents, one in London and the other in Cambridge, did not meet until six months after the priest's first letter was written. In August a walking tour was proposed.

The two outwardly forceful personalities met as two shy people, each one almost reluctant to carry out the experiment of friendship. Yet, once begun, the walking tour was an immediate success. Each was equipped with 'a shirt or so, a tooth-brush, and a breviary.' Large towns were avoided and a 'mass-house' was sought each night. After 'much sitting under hedges and sleeping in small inns,' the tour ended as 'a notable experiment.'

Each of the two men was a lonely person, but Benson's loneliness was surrounded by things of this world. In contrast to Rolfe's brooding solitude, Benson's life was active. His energy was fed with a nervous fever. As a preacher he was busy. He was on good terms with his family and shared his life with his mother and brothers. These things crowded his mind and left him with little thought about himself. Reading *Hadrian* and meeting its author made him aware of only one small part of his inner being. In all of his dealings with people, he lacked one close friend; and in his own unconscious way he too was seeking a variation of the Divine Friend. Rolfe at this time filled all the qualifications.

Sensing Benson's genuine offer of friendship, Rolfe weighed all the arguments for and against this proposal. Here was a Catholic, and not an ordinary one, asking for his hand. To Rolfe the priest personified the entire Church. And if he ever were raised to such an office to do so, Benson promised, he would personally confer upon Rolfe the rite of ordination. Rolfe finally acquiesced.

What Benson did propose at the time was almost as satisfying. Why should not the two friends collaborate on a book? St. Thomas of Canterbury was chosen as a theme, to be worked into a romantic biography. This alone would restore Rolfe to the Catholic world. The damage caused by the Aberdeen Attack eventually could be erased, at least in part. To write a book with Benson meant two more things. Their names would appear together on the title page and, because of this, there would be a larger sale. By May 1906 Benson sketched the general outline for the story. By August it was begun. But, for a number of pressing reasons, Benson could not coordinate his leisure time with Rolfe's and the project had to be temporarily postponed.

At the time that Benson and Rolfe first met via letters, the priest knew a young man at Cambridge by the name of Eustace Virgo. While accepting every new devotee of his own new faith with all the uncompromising fanaticism of a recent convert, Benson did not approve of Virgo's entirely sincere and somewhat austere paganism. But he liked the young man and wrote to Rolfe at a time when Virgo's purse was nearly empty. He asked Rolfe if Virgo could visit him at Broadstairs. In reply, Rolfe said he would be delighted to welcome the young man. Virgo then ventured to the Isle of Thanet to meet Rolfe, his mother and sister.

Virgo found Rolfe 'to be a man about the middle height with a pair of curious and uneasy black eyes, in one of which he attempted in vain to wear a monocle. His fingers were covered with huge rings of tarnished silver, engraved with cabalistic signs, and when he bathed [Virgo] noticed that at least an equal number hung round his neck. He poured out the strangest stories to [Virgo] of his knowledge of the Cabbala, of his skill as an astrologer, and of his powers in necromancy.... His adventures had been many, according to [Rolfe]. *Stories which Toto told Me* had been written in a week in a workhouse, so he said, and sold to a London publisher outright for the sum of £10. But of these astonishing statements [Virgo] could not decide which were true or which were false. [Virgo], with all the goodwill in the world, did not like his host, who appeared to him to be both eccentric and egocentric. He enjoyed the society of [Rolfe] for two days, when he left him finally to his own devices.'

Rolfe wrote to him constantly, professing an unfaltering devotion to the young man and asking him to make some personal researches in Spain. For his labour, Rolfe said, Virgo would receive the noble sum of £1,000 a year—a promise easily made by a man with not even a thousand pence to his name. Virgo learned that Rolfe alone possessed 'the secret of the Borgias.' But he refused to say what this secret was, other than to hint that it would startle the historical and literary world and bring him much gold. If Rolfe were thinking of his Borgiada, 'the family tree in many colours he had drawn up,' he had made a sad error in the judgment of its value.

Rolfe had spent the first part of 1905 at Broadstairs and assisted Hardy at Oxford whenever he was called. In May his *Don Tarquinio* was published, dedicated to his brother Herbert. But his mind still rested on the pending lawsuit. 'It will be as well for me to see a complete Scheme of the manner in which you propose to present my case,' he wrote to Barnard & Taylor. 'I am fairly convinced of the possibility of presenting it in an unanswerable fashion that, with knowledge of the legal form & an opportunity of weighing the details, I feel sure that I could do much to remove any doubts which at present may possess you.' As for 'the immediate future,' he 'was sure that the most practical thing is to continue my output of literary work, without interruption. I suggest that with certainty of £150, i.e. £50 cash & £10 a month for 10 months I should have a fair chance to run clear. The two first reviews of *Don Tarquinio* ... are favourable —more favourable than those of *Hadrian the Seventh,* in that they proclaim the book as possessing interest for the general as distinguished from the particular reader. Messrs Chatto have appended a handsome recognition of my previous works to the end of the volume; & I am inclined to think that *Don Tarquinio* is a foundation on which one may build. It is too early to be duly sanguine. ... There is no chance of my coming to town in person because I simply have not the means to move. My Mother & Sister have risked removal to a better place here for their school; & I am camping out in their empty house, the lease of which falls in at Midsummer.'

Written in the Corvine style, similar to that of *Toto, Don Tarquinio* is brilliant in characterization, colour and description. The story follows young Tarquinio through twenty-four hours of adventure and love in Renaissance Italy. But it was far from the 'foundation' Rolfe expected. Of the 1,011 copies printed in

1905, Chatto & Windus bound only 650 for release. And these sold no better than *Hadrian*.

Yet a solution to Rolfe's future life had a beginning in 1905.

During this year two young men spent their Long Vacation on Iona, the island near Mull in the Hebrides and Oban on the mainland. Each of the two young men was already steeped in heraldic lore and the history of ancient Orders. In the midst of the primeval, windswept wasteland of Iona an idea was born. An Order, similar to the Order of St. John of Jerusalem, would be formed. Of the two young Harrys, Pirie-Gordon was the more eccentric and imaginative. He envisioned the Order to boast ten thousand members, with its headquarters on an island near Naples. When the summer holiday was over, the two returned to their schools at Oxford. The Order never had ten thousand members and its headquarters were never in Italy. Yet the Order, when created, was to become for a short time an integral part of Rolfe's life. During the autumn (later Col.) Harry Pirie-Gordon met Rolfe and the two eccentric natures banded together. Pirie-Gordon introduced him to (later Sir) Harry Luke and the first faint flame of the Order of Sanctissima Sophia (Wisdom) had been ignited.

Before the end of 1905 Rolfe assisted Hardy in putting together a book, *Studies in Roman History*. Expanding his former *Christianity and the Roman Government,* Hardy added various other published pieces. Rolfe 'has not only carefully gone through all the essays, preparing them for press, but has undertaken the entire work of correcting the proofs—a task of no small difficulty considering the intricate nature of the notes.'

At the same time that Hardy had written these words in his Preface, Rolfe 'had to go into a nursing home to have a cyst emptied.' In a letter to his solicitors he spoke about his own health, his hopes for the valuable Borgiada and possibly 'taking it to Rome,' and news about Hardy. 'The Viceprincipal's eye-sight has taken a very serious turn for the bad; & it seems to be almost certain that he will not be able to undertake next term's work without constant assistance. Nothing is definitely settled on this point at present: because a voyage to Jamaica & back during the vacation is being discussed.... I have worked with him now for six years; & know what is wanted; & there is not anyone else in that position.' As long as he remained in England, Rolfe continued to stand by Dr. Hardy.

In July 1905 a letter was sent from Oxford to Grant Richards. Rolfe's cryptic letter of February had gone unanswered and this one explained its contents. The cypher was Julius Caesar's, Rolfe said, and was used because it was a private letter and he had no idea into whose hands it may fall. 'If I can be of any assistance to you, I shall be happy if you will forget the past & tell me now,' the message had read. Richards was sincerely happy to hear from Rolfe. From the reviews of his books he noticed that others shared his admiration of Rolfe's work. He added that his failing business did not present as black a picture as Rolfe imagined. The business continued, but under Mrs. Richards' name, and her first book, Housman's *Juvenal*, had just been published. The expressed kindness in Rolfe's letters touched Richards deeply.

Until the beginning of 1906 the two exchanged letters and Rolfe submitted to his old publisher several of his manuscripts. *Reviews of Unwritten Books, An Ideal Content,* a revised version of *Nicholas Crabbe* and the Meleager were eagerly read. But they each had to be sent back. None suited Richards' present, and limited, plans. There was absolutely no outburst of emotion in any of Rolfe's letters at this period to the man who had published his Borgia book. The correspondence between the two merely dissolved into nothing after the beginning of 1906.

Nearly a quarter of a century later, Richards left a portrait of Rolfe in his *Memories of a Misspent Youth*. Speaking of himself at Oxford, he said that 'we little boys bathed and the under-graduates bathed and the dons and the clergymen all bathed at Parson's Pleasure without any sort of garment to cover our nakedness. So it was then [c. 1890] and so, I hope, it is now. I never heard that anybody came to any harm as a result of this pagan habit, although on the last occasion that I saw that erratic genius, Frederick Baron Corvo, he was sitting under the Parson's Pleasure willows on a decrepid chair, rolling cigarette after cigarette in his nicotine-stained fingers, and surveying the yellow flesh tints with unbecoming satisfaction. That was at the time he was active as secretary or assistant to E. G. Hardy, Principal of Jesus.'

The meeting with young Harry Pirie-Gordon came at an advantageous time. Rolfe had no security, no money or even place to live, beyond his association with Hardy. As a participating member of the Order of Sanctissima Sophia he had to see its headquarters, which was the home of the Pirie-Gordons in South Wales. 'He was invited down for a weekend and stayed two years.'

As a reward to himself for the years of unrecognized toil, he remained as a guest 'doing little, lavishly.' Not only was he a friend of their son, but Harry's parents had each read and admired Rolfe's books. They 'adopted' him and rechristened him 'Hadrian'. He accepted their genuine affection for him without any question, perhaps for the single fact that they were not Catholic.

The Order of Sanctissima Sophia was initiated on 7 October 1906, when Harry Luke became its first Grandmaster as Harricus I. His first 'Novelle' was written to Pirie-Gordon:

TO Our Most Trusty and Right-Entirely Well-Beloved Brother, the Eminent Lord Harricus Lord Herald of Our Order, Our Greeting and High Favour IT IS OUR WILL AND PLEASURE that you of your Science Heraldick and Knowledge Armorial do plot and devise a Shield or Coat of Arms meet and suitable that We may of Our Princely Grace grant the same to the Provost and Chapter of Canons of the Collegiate Church of Our Order.

Addressed to Pirie-Gordon, this official decree provided Rolfe ample opportunity to utilise his profound knowledge of Greek and obscure Renaissance history. Under the direction of Pirie-Gordon, he produced heraldic devices, coats-of-arms, letterhead and ornament designs for the Order. His inventive and artistic attributes combined with Harry's knowledge of heraldry to create the necessary requirements for Harricus I's decrees.

Rolfe once again had been expressing himself in art. *Hadrian the Seventh* was virtually his book from cover to cover. The type

256

was set according to his plan. His coat-of-arms, with the motto in Greek and Latin suggested by George Meredith, appeared on the title page. And he designed the front covers—Hadrian VII in the act of blessing, accompanied by his cat Flavio and the signs of Cancer and the Moon. The cover for *Don Tarquinio* was also done by him. This represents the young Tarquinio, standing in an upright rectangle, reminiscent of his 'Canzonata' door curtain of Christchurch in 1891. While at the Pirie-Gordons' Gwernvale house, Rolfe made a cover drawing for *An Ideal Content (Don Renato)* and created a series of medallion illustrations for his Meleager. Between the two Chatto & Windus books, Rolfe designed the cover for a magazine. At Broadstairs he persuaded his sister into publishing a school periodical. *The Fleurdelys: St. Alphage School Magazine* appeared in December 1904 in the only issue printed.

Working with the Order, drawing and writing, and trying to place his unpublished manuscripts still left Rolfe with time to help others. Harry had just unsuccessfully completed a book-length essay, *Innocent the Great*, for the Arnold Prize. Rolfe 'helped with the proofs,' suggested several words or expressions and adopted the transliteration of *kh* instead of *ch* for the Greek, which Pirie-Gordon later regretted. But Rolfe's full co-operation came in the form of collaboration. Harry had ideas for two stories, *Hubert's Arthur* and *The Weird of the Wanderer*; and Rolfe's Prospero endowed the purposes of Pirie-Gordon's Caliban 'with words that made them known.'

During the first week of 1907 Rolfe wrote to a kind correspondent to thank her for remembering him, his mother and sister at Christmas. 'My Mother and Sister are well,' he said; 'and they continue to struggle on: though of course, as you will well understand, they have a very difficult task in the absence of the support of influential friends. It will however be a satisfaction to know that, when success at length crowns their efforts, they will owe it to no one but themselves.' This was written on January 5th, eleven days before the Rolfe v. Thomas case finally was heard.

The long list of work done for Col. Thomas included, Rolfe said, numerous things other than the South Africa book. Writing letters, reports and articles, all based on an honest wage of 10s. 6d. an hour, including the book itself, totalled £1,049 9s. 6d. Subtracting the £50 Thomas had paid him, Rolfe claimed £999 9s. 6d.

In the two and a half years spent in waiting for the trial, Thomas was not idle in preparing his defence. Not only did he deny all of Rolfe's monetary charges, saying that each separate agreement was made verbally and paid for in cash, but he furnished evidence to weaken Rolfe's word. The information he had gathered from Hunter Blair and the Aberdeen Attack was enough to counteract any claim by Rolfe.

The hearing was not long, and during a cross examination Rolfe completely broke down. 'I feel exactly as though I had been beaten with beet-roots and mangold-wurzels all over, especially on my face, neck, and hands—quite sore and bruised by the court full of eyes which hanged on me all Wednesday,' he could write three days later.

The judge directed that judgment should be entered for the Defendant, with costs. Rolfe lost the case and was ordered to pay costs and damage fees, a total of £132 11s. 4d.

Rolfe was now deeply in debt to Barnard & Taylor. They had advanced him money to be recalled, they had hoped, at the end of the trial and from his books. Neither *Hadrian* nor *Tarquinio* had earned a penny, his manuscript novels had been bought by no publisher, and the lawyers had to pay for the case on his behalf. If on January 16th the Scottish and Catholic newspapers of 1898 were still effective in their damaging slander, Rolfe soon would learn of a new element of inquisition. Before the end of 1907 a second crucial blow would fall.

Convinced that the world had wronged him once again, Rolfe's suspicion towards his fellow creatures swelled to abnormal proportions. But the understanding Hardy family at Oxford and the Pirie-Gordons salved his feelings for the moment.

Sympathetic towards Rolfe in every way, Hugh Benson had sat through the hearing. He wished to do whatever he could to ease the pain of the defeated author. The projected St. Thomas book was far from finished. In February, Benson still said it was 'simply unthinkable for me at present.' So, as the months went by, the relationship strained. Rolfe had everything to offer in the way of friendship and expected the same in return. The crowded world around the priest caused him to drift away from the friend he had so hurriedly sought in a whirlwind of enthusiasm. By July he again talked of the book. It was 'taking shape and vigour in an outstanding manner.' With a feverish stride he listed wanted details and confessed that he believed 'the book can be Absolutely Exquisite—and yet as vivid and hot as you like.' Alternate chapters and notes went from one to the other in quick succession. And then the end came in October.

One day a letter came for Rolfe. Benson had been to London, he wrote, and was assured there that the book would make far greater profit if Rolfe consented to leaving his name off the title page.

The original agreement would still be enforced; Rolfe would receive a third of the profits. But, coming in the same year as the Thomas case, this seemed a final death blow. His hopes, his nerves, his very body was shattered. The financial salvation from the St. Thomas book was indeed an important factor for Rolfe. Greater, however, was the fact that the book, with his name coupled with Benson's would reinstate him in the Catholic world. But now nothing was left. And no one could come to his rescue. His wildest fears had proved to be indelibly accurate. Against his conscious wishes he had permitted Benson to become a friend, a friend who now was betraying him. This erstwhile collaborator had simply suggested that they continue on the book, but without both names appearing on it. He had said nothing more, but Rolfe could see 'the cloven hoof.'

In all innocence and sincerity, Benson wished to see their two names on the title page, but stronger forces willed differently.

On that January day in 1886 when he offered himself up to the Catholic Church, Rolfe had no idea of the sort of arena into which he was stepping. From the start his life was continually buffeted by forces and people within the Roman institution.

The decision to part Benson from Rolfe may well have been directly connected with a decree recently endorsed by the

Church. Ever since the time of Leo XIII's *Rerum Novarum,* another question was noted by Rome. The first admonitions against this new thought were directed towards Americans. Although Leo created letters concerning this new threat to Catholicism, 'Modernism,' as the head of the Church he made no official statement. A group of French cardinals were especially alarmed over this unchecked freedom. In February 1903, on the eve of *Hadrian the Seventh*'s composition, the Archbishop of Paris, seconded by Cardinal Perraud (Cardinal Perron in Rolfe's novel), saw Leo for the last time. His arguments to repress the encroaching doctrines of Modernism, especially within the Church, were in vain. But he refused to give up. With Guiseppe Sarto (Cardinal Sarda in *Hadrian*) now Pius X, the French prelate found success. Books by the French biblical scholar and religious historian, Loisy, were put on the Index early in 1904. This began Pius' campaign against Modernism.

The world of Socialism since 1891 generated new and conflicting problems for the Church. The opinions of Science were being advanced, in opposition to the traditional tenets of Catholicism. Pius, less qualified himself than his predecessor to deal with such matters, issued a decree, *Lamentabili,* on 3 July 1907. This contained a list of mistaken propositions taken from authors, Catholics among them, who, 'under the appearance of the highest intelligence and the name of historical research,' presumed to launch a 'progression of dogmas' that in reality constituted for the Church the corruption of dogma. Two months later, on September 16th, his encyclical, *Pascendi,* was published as a decisive attack upon the new wave of thought. 'The Pope then, reminding us rather of Sancho Panza than of Don Quixote, made war upon Modernism. Many of the Church's best scholars were expelled or silenced, papers were suppressed, a regiment of spies was enlisted; and in the end the Pope fatuously struck a gold medal which represented orthodoxy slaying the domestic dragon.' (Joseph McCabe, *A History of the Popes.*)

This official decree dealt with the writers of erroneous books, which should be prohibited and censored. Even priests were told to obtain permission before contributing anything to periodicals. A council of vigilance was to be set up in every diocese. A month after Pius' encyclical appeared, Cardinal Respighi, Vicar of Rome (Cardinal Respiro in *Hadrian*), excommunicated the anonymous authors of *Il Programma dei Modernisti*, Roman Modernists who protested against the encyclical and had their publication translated into several languages. On Christmas Eve, Cardinal Ferrari (Cardinal Ferraio in *Hadrian*) excommunicated all the publishers, editors, authors and collaborators of *Il Rinnovamento*, a review accused of Modernism.

Fr. Billot, Rector of the Georgian University in Rome, was said to have been part author of *Pascendi*. He was created a cardinal in 1911, but he resigned from the cardinalate in 1922 because of the pressure instigated by Pius XI against the attitude which Billot took to the condemnation of the *Action Française*. In 1907 reactions to the encyclical against Modernism were voiced throughout the Catholic areas of the world. The position of Rome in this clash between certain scholars and the Church was justified by Pius X in calling Modernists 'enemies of the Church' and adding: 'It is not from without, as We have already observed, but from within that they plot Her destruction; the danger today is in the most vital parts of the Church; their blows are the more sure because they know well where to strike Her.... Therefore, We may no longer keep silence, for it would henceforth be a crime! It is time to unmask these men, to show them to the whole Church in their true colours.' In the opposite camp, Loisy later exclaimed that the entire reign of Pius X was 'a vertiable orgy of fanaticism and senselessness.'

Having first opposed Agnosticism and Scientific Intellectualism, Pius' encyclical proceeded to cover all branches of literature. Although not mentioned in the decree itself, a separate act singled out one work of fiction as an example of this new doctrine. In Italy, Antonio Fogazzaro's *Il Santo (The Saint)*—since compared with *Hadrian the Seventh*—was read avidly, with seminarians and priests among its readers. It became the most discussed book of the year. But before this year was up it was placed on the Index by Pius X.

(While Patriarch of Venice, Sarto forbade priests and Catholics to attend the first Biennial Art Exhibition in Venice in April 1895 because it included a picture he considered offensive to religion. Fogazzaro openly dared to defend the picture by Giacomo Grosso. At the time nothing happened. When *Il Santo* appeared it was only another novel, neither expounding nor insinuating any theological or moral error. And even the highly cautious *Civilta Cattolica* reviewed it on publication, finding nothing in it of a reformist nature. Yet Guiseppe Sarto, now Pope Pius X, placed it on the Index of Forbidden Books.)

By the first decade of this century the Catholic Church had established itself in England. But not all Catholic literature was generally accepted by the reading public. Graham Greene pronounces *Hadrian the Seventh* 'a novel of genius' and says that it 'stands in relation to the other novels of its day, much as *The Hound of Heaven* stands in relation to the verse.' Yet, at the time, this meant little. 'The literary activities with which Thompson and the Meynells were associated were thus of scant interest to official Catholicism,' writes Paul van Kuykendall Thomson, one of the poet's biographers. 'Furthermore, many Catholics accepted the current feeling of other religious people that a devotion to the arts must somehow be immoral. Many shared the opinion set forth in Robert Buchanan's essay "The Fleshly School of Poetry" .... They associated the newer writers with the supposed sensuality of George Moore's *Confessions of a Young Man* (1888) or with the morbid search for exotic sensations exhibited in Oscar Wilde's *Dorian Gray* (1891) and the fictions of Frederick Rolfe. Judging by what they heard of the avowed decadent *fin-de-siècle* leaders of aestheticism, it appeared to many pious minds that modern literature and religious faith were destined to move far apart.'

Writers within the Church who were popular with the public, such as Benson, had to be preserved. He had everything in his favour. Rolfe, in the eyes of the Church, had nothing. Worse, he was living in the sin of poverty. Reading between the lines of Pius' encyclical and thoroughly digesting the mounting material published on Modernism, the Roman officials in London perhaps saw a parallel between *Hadrian the Seventh* and *Il Santo*. The English novel was known only in its native country. But there was the possibility of its exposure in Rome at any time. After all, its plot was a denunciation of the worldly tactics of both pope and Church. And, if such an exposure were to be made, what of the persons whose names might be attached to Rolfe's, especially in literature?

Francis Bourne, Bishop of Southwark, and Mgr. Arthur Barnes, assisted by A. C. Benson, descended upon Hugh and said that it would be fatal to his career if his name were linked with Rolfe's. Benson was now more concerned with the material aspects of this world and the vote of popularity. He had already been inoculated with the microbe of success, a success which made him hard and avaricious. Without hesitation he meekly accepted the opinions of others, letting the voices of greater authority prevail.

Mgr. Barnes had only a slight acquaintance with Rolfe, which he never wished to improve. Rolfe was 'a dangerous man,' he thought, 'always labouring under a sense of grievance, sometimes real, often imaginary; & not scrupulous in his efforts to get his own back.' Barnes 'expostulated strongly' when Benson told him of the projected collaboration. He 'told Hugh that it would be very unwise to let his name appear with Rolfe's on the same title page. Rolfe was ... not in very good odour with the authorities of the Catholic Church, & perhaps not without some reason.'

Benson suggested to Rolfe that the book should continue. To compensate for the loss of Rolfe's name on it, Benson offered him £100 for his share of the book on the day of publication, with royalties to follow. But there was an issue at stake here which Benson could not fathom. Human sympathy meant more to Rolfe than any amount of money. Benson's offer solved nothing.

The Holy Blissful Martyr Saint Thomas of Canterbury was published in 1908, but it was not the book of the collaboration. That had ended with Benson's decision. Benson could never understand Rolfe's unforgiving attitude; he even wrote 'how extremely foolish it is to behave like this, when there is nothing but friendliness on my side.' He never realized the enormity of his offence. The withdrawal of Benson's trust, which Rolfe so desperately sought and needed, nearly killed the latter. Benson's act, which parted him forever from Rolfe, did not prevent him from entertaining a fondness for the author of *Hadrian* until the end of his life. He even made a poetic confession:

> Almost a very god thou wert to me;
>> Haloed with brilliant virtues; every grace
>> Lived in thy look and shone about thy face:
> I bowed beneath thee, loved, feared, worshipped thee.
> Then in my folly and my jealousy
>> I let my critic thought prevail apace,
>> Which entered, swarming, tore thee from thy place,
> And dashed thee down in wrath and enmity.

Confiding to Mrs. Pirie-Gordon, Rolfe wrote to her on December 2nd, 'It seems to me to be quite impossible for me to go to Benson. He is making and saving money with hands and feet now; and the mere suggestion of spending 2d. turns him puce and magenta. You know I have agreed to retire my name from the *Thomas* book because he says that he will give me "£100 on the day of publication" and that the absence of my name will make a difference of "several hundred pounds" to me. Well: he refuses to promise to collaborate in a future book with my name on; and, what's more, he had laid *Thomas* aside for the present, and is engaged on quarrelling with me on a ridiculous matter of etiquette. My only consolation is that I do know how to keep cool when driven against the wall as I am now.'

In a single week during March 1907, Rolfe had two titles bestowed upon him. Harry made him Prior of St. George of the Order of Sanctissima Sophia and Mrs. Pirie-Gordon pronounced him to be the Protector of the Peacock and Puppy at Gwernvale. This 'last is simply Gorgeous and makes me Proud,' he had to tell her. Ten months later he was wishing her a happy New Year 'from the bottom of my heart.' In the same letter he had to thank her for a Christmas present, a silver ankh, 'the size, the medal, AND above all the adornment of it ... with my crab and my moon and my cross-potent-elongate, all of which make it my very very own. Such interest in ME, shewn by such an exactly intimate knowledge of my secret and not more than half-formed desire and taste, has never been shewn before. The effect is almost to strike me dumb. Thank you, I do: but thanks express but feebly what I feel.'

In this lengthy letter to his friend's mother, Rolfe, the realist, spoke of the present and the future when he no longer would be a guest at Gwernvale. The Christmas presents had made Rolfe 'notice the hundred thousand ways, little and large, in which you all watch my words for indications of my tastes and wants in order that you may gratify them.... And I can do nothing adequate in return. That makes these favours hard to bear. But what makes it harder still is the knowledge that you dear kind souls, *who have given me so long the hospitality which not a single Catholic would dream of giving*, are adding to my burdens all unconsciously. You are giving me lovely things which I like so much that it will be a most bitter wrench to me to part from them.... Pray then make it *easier* and not harder by not planting in me seeds which circumstances are going to tear me up by their tender roots. This is not ingratitude by any means, but the truest gratitude: for, now that I know how eager you are to please me, I can freely tell you how to please me better. So I say, do not give me any luxuries at all which it will hurt me to lose, and help me to live so that I have nothing which can be taken from me. I am sure you will understand.'

He had two ideas for the immediate future. He could either accept Benson's offer for the St. Thomas book or he could ask Barnard & Taylor for an advance while he finished *Hubert's Arthur* and other books while still living in the same town in South Wales. 'Now it is horrible to tell you what I think of Benson,' he added. 'So horrible that I am forcing myself not to come to any definite conclusion about him yet. I have only his actions before me; and I refuse to pronounce or even to form a final opinion about them.' Briefly outlining the history of the collaboration, he said that Benson finally and 'peremptorily required me to sign a bond agreeing that his name should stand alone as the author of the book. He said that his agent (whose name he refuses to give) told him that he could make more money this way.... The only ambition I have is to be independent. The original agreement was to help me to that. The new proposal kept me a sponger upon other people's charity. Which I detest with all my heart. Well: you know that, much against my instinct, I was absolutely loyal to him. On the ground that I had promised to let him have his way, I gave in. *And he instantly bought a house*, seven months before he can possibly use it, put the *Thomas* book on the shelf and has not said a single word about it, notwithstanding my frantic enquiries, from that day to this.—You know that Benson has continually consoled me in my troubles, saying that I never need worry myself with thinking that I must go back to the workhouse or sleep out of doors any more. He has always assured me that when all else has failed he would gladly take me in. I have impressed upon him that I yearn to be a help and not a hinderance: and I have shewn him heaps of ways in which I could be made not only self-supporting but profitable and only too willing to share my profits with him. And so now, finding myself without means and quite without means ever of continuing my work, I reluctantly fell back upon him. He tells me that to take me in when I am homeless and penniless will break his heart and cause him strong personal inconvenience; and in the roughest possible manner he offers me the situation of caretaker in his lonely house 2 miles from Buntingford at 8/- a week. There I am to be quite alone, to look after the place, do the gardening, and fowls, and be a 2 mile walk and a tram-journey from Mass for seven months. He emphasizes the fact that I am not to consider myself his guest but his paid servant; and asks for a bond binding me to repay him my journey-money out of my first earnings.'

Years of ill-treatment taught Rolfe to look beyond certain surfaces. 'Now all this has taken my breath away,' he continued in his letter to Mrs. Pirie-Gordon. 'It is totally unexpected. I have done nothing to deserve it. And I am quite unable to explain it excepting by an hypothesis which I am frantically refusing to entertain. Roman Catholic clergymen have behaved exactly like this several times before to me; and I believe the idea was to break me, heart and soul and body. That they have not done; and I will not let it happen again. Anything rather than that. But the effect of Benson's conduct is that I am inconceivably frightened of him; and all my old distrust of the clergy is rampant and paramount.... Years ago, when I could pay my way, I was not to be allowed to be a paying guest in priests' houses. The Bp of Aberdeen hunted me out of [Fr. Gerry's] house at Strichen where I was liked and where my money was serviceable. Remembering this I asked Benson to get, or to let me apply for, Abp Bourne's permission to live in B.'s house. He flatly refuses. . . . I feel that he has let me down badly, and that I must rule him out of my arrangements.'

The letter closed as it began, with Rolfe being most thankful 'for hospitality, generosity, forebearance, and the very truest of friendship.'

Rolfe was never a person to let matters rest unexplained. Their causes and effects had to be known. The people behind Benson's decision and their reasons were surmised. The opening sentence of *Hubert's Arthur* reads: 'It is not proposed to discuss either the authenticity of these documents, or the question as to senile delusion with its amazing circumstancial particularity: to attempt to do so would (perhaps) be poaching on the preserves of the professional critic; and, in any case, it is our most singular anxiety to avoid incurring any taint (however faint) of Modernism.'

Relieved from his job as secretary to Dr. Hardy, Rolfe welcomed the freedom to devote his time to literary work. The plans for the moment included two books to be written with Harry Pirie-Gordon. Advising him on *The Weird of the Wanderer*, Rolfe wrote: 'Please read *The Armed Hands*; and have it in your head when you place Nicholas Crabbe in your Egyptian book. I mean as a guide to the construction of the personality of N. C. As far as your existing MS. of the Egyptian book goes, I advise you—and mastering the *appearance* of N. C.—not to waste more than one hour in merely touching up here and there what you have already written of your hero.' Back at Gwernvale he saw the Egyptian book finished in its first version and started it off to publishers in London. He now looked to *Hubert's Arthur*, 'an awful piece of work. But it will be unlike any book ever written; and it will pay.'

Renewed activity was even favoured from the outside. Two of his manuscripts finally found a publisher. The Meleager and *Don Renato* were accepted by Francis Griffiths. And each book began the slow process towards publication during his last days at Gwernvale.

Although the author's signature is Fr. Rolfe, *Don Renato* exhibits the purest form of Corvine literature. Corvo was his own architect in constructing this polished maze of words. He manufactured the very thread which was used to weave this brilliantly picturesque and vividly colourful abstract tapestry of the Renaissance. For years he had added delicate phrases to the elaborate filigree of archaic language. Corvo's applied touches were those of a true artist, unlike Balzac's Master Frenhofer's canvas which showed nothing 'but confused masses of colour and a multitude of fantastical lines that go to make a dead wall of paint' after ten years' work. Neither were Rolfe's manuscript pages 'covered with illegible hopeless scribblings' as were those of Arthur Machen's Lucian, where 'only here and there it was possible to recognise a word.' Don Gheraldo's diurnal, basically recording the love between Don Renato and Madonnina Marcia, speaks of the day-to-day life in the Roman household: journeys, food, magic, medicine and men, noble and serving. Humorous, gossipy, factual, intimate, Corvo's portraits form an exacting masterpiece, if only for the connoisseur.

Everything at Gwernvale was shared with Rolfe, including the Pirie-Gordons' friends, and so it was that he met Professor R. M. Dawkins.

In August of 1907 the professor's cousin, John Doyle, died and left him a house in Breconshire. 'I came home from Athens to look after it and immediately met my neighbours, the Pirie-Gordons of Crickhowell, people whom I had met before on visits to John Doyle. They were extremely hospitable and I often went over to their house for dinner and so on, a distance of some two or three miles. One afternoon I met in the garden Rolfe, then being called Hadrian by the P-Gs. I was a good deal attracted to him; he interested and amused me. [Twenty-six years later] it is hard to remember how much I thought him a charlatan; I believe I thought him an amusing poseur. In his learning I never believed at all. I had previously read his book on the Borgias, I think when it came out, and thought it picturesque nonsense. I remember that I very nearly let out this fatal fact in my very first conversation with Rolfe at tea on the lawn at Gwernvale. In addition to the rudeness I should have been sorry to hinder further meetings with a man who so much interested me. He immediately showed me his genealogy of the Borgias.' Thus did Dawkins and Rolfe meet, exactly one year before the beginning of the final chapter in Rolfe's life.

Richard MacGillivray Dawkins was eleven years younger than Rolfe and the same age as Benson, whom he also knew. After he had spent a bitter period at two schools during the 1880s, his practical-thinking admiral father sent him to study engineering at King's College. Later apprenticed to electric light engineers and contractors, he found the work dull for his scholarly mind. In his leisure he turned to the Greek and Latin classics, adding Theosophy. Emmanuel College, Cambridge, provided him with his true vocation during its golden age of classical scholarship. In 1904-5 he directed excavations at the Minoan city of Palaikastro, Crete, and in 1906 he was appointed Director of the British School at Athens. The next four years were employed in the excavation of the shrine and temenos of Artemis Orthia at Sparta. Returning to England in 1919, he became the first Bywater and Sotheby Professor of Byzantine and Modern Greek Language and Literature in the University of Oxford. His interest in Greek literature and folklore coincided with Rolfe's, but he was too much the academic scholar to give any praise to Rolfe's self-taught knowledge.

On 24 November 1907 a correspondence between the two was begun by Rolfe. In a short letter the writer told the professor that his 'lawyers offered me £500 for 3 years if I could find a surety. I am looking for that person.' This initial statement of fact by Rolfe was not answered in any way, but the letters continued. They were long and were filled with gossip about common acquaintances, a quest for information about Greek and other, more obscure literatures, and general discussions of topics of the day. When Dawkins' younger brother John visited Gwernvale one day, Rolfe reported the event. He thought him 'charming' and liked his 'luminous innocence' and 'humour: (he said "So you know Father Hugh! Why we often go to SEE him preach!"

I shrieked with joy at such a lifelike portrait of Benson, who as you know is both contortruplicate and tolutiloquent in the pulpit).'

In the same letter he briefly touched on his history. He now had two books accepted by a publisher, 'but I shan't get any profit out of either of these books till March at the very earliest; and how in the world I am going to pig on after Edward Gordon has gone and this house is closed, the high gods only know. That, I'll have you know, is my damnable lot in life. I'm never able to stick on long enough in one place to bring any job to maturity. As soon as ever I have settled down, and got the gear to go, and the sausages to begin to ooze prolifically from the machine, I have to tear myself up by the roots and begin to sow my seeds all over again. I'm very sore about it: but I hope not sour.'

The Pirie-Gordons would be away from Wales, which meant that their guest eventually had to move. Whatever future plans may have been formulating in his mind, as early as July, Rolfe had written to a correspondent that he 'will never willingly come to [London] again.'

In November, Harry and his mother left Gwernvale for Rome, the first stop on a proposed trip. Edward Pirie-Gordon stayed behind for a few weeks and Rolfe was able to remain in the house through January. During this winter and the spring of 1908, the Pirie-Gordons and Harry Luke made an adventurous trip to the Near East. The two Harrys travelled through the mountains and monasteries of Greece and Mount Athos and the churches of Salonika, visited the Dodecanese and Cyprus and made a tour of Palestine and Syria and their Crusaders' castles.

In the first week of February, Rolfe went to Bristol to have 'my chin done.' At the Bristol Hydro his recurring cyst was attended and here he met 'a very large and handsome Jew of 15.' Rolfe preached to the boy and insisted that he rigorously practise his religion and 'drove him to synagogue.' One day, 'when an opportunity suddenly offered, I secretly baptized him with all the form and all unknown to himself—John Markoleone of the Tribe of Levi.'

After a fortnight at Bristol, he then journeyed some 130 miles into Cornwall, to Helscott Farm, Bude. A widow and her two

270

young sons worked the farm. They took in boarders and the primitive conditions of getting water from an outside pump, no bath and oil lamps appealed to him. The food was 'barbarous' but his board cost him only twenty-three shillings a week. He 'came here as the next best thing' to the insistence by his Bristol doctor 'of 6 months' absolute rest and sea-voyage.'

Just as Rolfe was leaving Gwernvale, Dawkins invited him along as a companion on a trip to Italy. At the close of a long letter in January, Rolfe exclaimed: 'Oh your Italian proposition is too lovely. But let's talk of it again when I'm through this impasse' of moving from the Pirie-Gordon house. In April he was thinking 'a bit about what I'm going to do next. For the Gordons don't come back till June and, after the end of Apr. I simply shan't have ½d. either to pig on here [at Bude] or to go elsewhere even if I had anywhere to go which I haven't.'

Barnard & Taylor had agreed to advance him £100 on the security of an insurance policy on his life. But he did not pass the medical examination because of his general health. They did send him £10 before the end of April and £20 in June: and before the end of July the Prudential Assurance Company insured his life. Apart from his daily worries, he kept his letters to Dawkins interesting with a variation of subject matter. He could write of 'a typical Old English May-day, blazing clean fresh sun, turquoise sky, and all the world like new-washed chrysoprase, emerald, beryl and green jasper.' And about a certain domestic scene:

Yesterday I found they had a No. 2 Brownie camera here: so today ... I have been photographing pigs and chicken. I suppose you know that 'chicken' is the proper plural of 'chick' as 'oxen' of 'ox'. But I do not allege that 'bricken' is the plural of 'brick': though I know no reason why it couldn't be. I don't know how they are going to be developed: but I ought to have got some absolutely comical ones of my game-cockerel in the act of crowing. That bird spoke yesterday. When ever he sees me, he comes sneaking up asking for a corn in a little curdling undertone, looking frightfully meek and apologetic. Well: he meandered round a corner at me last night, apologizing for his existence, begging a bit o' bread for Gawd's sake sir. Says I, 'You know I'm afraid you're a cadger by nature': and I gave him a corn. Says he, 'Thank-you-very-much' as plainly as possible! You can't think how ridiculous it was.

Of course, Rolfe also spoke of the Italian trip and made suggestions for camping, routes to follow and photography. By May 12th he announced to Dawkins: 'The Venice idea is lovely. I haven't seen Venice.'

Harry and his mother returned on June 29th and Rolfe met them at Abergavenny Station with a dog-cart. He was immediately 'in the thick of developing, clearing, reducing, intensifying, the negatives of H. P.-G.'s tour and making dodgy prints of them.' The Venice invitation was uppermost in his mind and he wrote to Dawkins about being 'deeply sensible of your goodness.' He was ready to start at any minute. 'The question is How much luggage to take?' he said in one letter. 'What I propose is this. If you will kindly tell me to go to Pendarren [Dawkins' house] on Saturday [August 1st], I will bring with me one of my hampers with what things I seem likely to want. Then, if you have any old bags in the lumber room there to lend me, I'll select the necessaries and send the rest back to G.V. The fact is I have only a hand-bag and the bulk of my things travel in dirty-linen hampers for want of more seemly arks. Which is indecorous, and would cause *"admiratio"* abroad. As for books I shall bring *Hubert's Arthur* to try to finish it, and a sweet little Pindar for you to read to me when you feel disposed.'

Dawkins later left an account of Rolfe's luggage. It 'was a laundry basket; this struck the customs people on the Italian frontier so much that they detained it and when ... the padlocked bar which fastened the basket had been withdrawn' nothing illegal was found inside and the contents had to be put back and the basket 'officially closed again. During the war I feel sure that the secret services of Europe would have quarrelled which of them should shoot Corvo as a spy; he looked always so extremely and so self-consciously odd.'

By the time the two left Wales for Venice, Dawkins had a set opinion of Rolfe. 'I had then ... a small collection of Cretan seal stones. It happened I was traveling to town and Rolfe chanced to be in the same train; he liked these stones, but merely from a sort of fantastic half-magical idea. With this sort of thing I have no kind of sympathy and this led me to regard Rolfe as a man of no learning, but a sort of amusing fool. A man of no real intellect but I perceived all along his personal power, and this was what attracted me. Myself of a scientific turn of mind and entirely devoid of any kind of mysticism or leanings that way, I cannot help having a kind of mixture of amusement, interest and contempt for people who differ from me; and Rolfe did differ from me entirely.... The particular kind of impressiveness he aimed at I doubt if he ever achieved. His scholarship would not have deceived any one. He used to say himself that all his goods were in the shop window. He was the artist; in no sense the scholar. This I know quite clearly because I am the second and in no sense the first.'

Rolfe had a mania for silver, Dawkins said, 'and for solid heaviness.... Wore always round his neck suspended by a fairly stout silver chain a crucifix designed by himself with the arms of the cross ending with T pieces.... The thing had a biggish foot and was heavily made; so much so that it made his skin sore and he wore underneath it a patch of I suppose gold-beaters skin.'

So, with his laundry-basket luggage, his silver rings and cruci-fix, the glasses fitted over his myopic eyes, the 'short and solid' Rolfe came to the city of his dreams. Here he would find some sort of realization of all of his former hopes. Here he would endure the bitterest privations of his life. Here he would write a love story of a man and a maid, of a man and a place which is Venice. Here he would eventually acquire a place of his own, a 'palace' on the Grand Canal. And here he would meet a friend to whom he could afford to offer respite and who remained loyal to him to the end of his days. The 'grandeur that was Rome' now was replaced by the splendour that is Venice.

12

What the Professor of Greek really wanted of me, I can only suspect. He belonged to that class of men which I (following Aristotle) call the Fusidowls, the Born Slaves, creatures absolutely incapable of performing a noble (*i.e.* a free) act themselves or conniving at such performance on the part of others. He was of the revolting flabby carroty freckled mug-nosed bristly blubber-mouthed species, toothed of Senigaglia cheesecolour, which has no chest whatever. His conversation was hectic gabble, produced in the voice of a strangulated Punch, punctuated with screams & stamps of rage in public piazzas when he found that he had given a hooker five centesimi instead of 'do schei,' or when any of his numerous poses (Erastianism, for example) were gently gibbetted. Poses, I say, for the fact is that he (like all Cambridge bachelors bubbling with a secret) was all pose where he was most savage. But he knew more Greek Archaeology than anyone else in the world. Habet haec res panem. And his brains were occasionally pickable.

In August 1908, Rolfe and Dawkins came to Venice for a six weeks' holiday. Since their first meeting they had seen each other and corresponded. But neither had imagined any sort of living with the other, not even for six weeks. Once in Venice, patience frayed and finally rent altogether. The holiday did not last the scheduled six weeks.

For a month we daily pervaded the lagoon north of Venice. So frequent were our progresses along all the main canals, as well as along the narrower ones which are not marked by piles, to Santerasmo & Treporti & Santamaria of the Mount & Sangiacomo in the Marsh & Mazorbo & Burano & Torcelo, that we became an object of interest to the military; & were warned not to photograph their forts. I indeed was making a frantic effort to finish writing Hubert's Arthur. But Baicolo, my second *gondogliere*, the hugest strongest fairest Venetian *toso* you can imagine, a tiger with a simper, had commended himself to the Professor, who swore that he was the very spit & image of the Agias of Delphi, & wished to have him anatomically photographed in the sun against a whited wall. If you know your lagoon, you will be aware that such a wall, suitably secluded for such a purpose, is hard to come by. Steam-boats & motor-launches swirl along all the main canals. The small ones are haunts of meditating fishermen. Such walls as you find—they are generally crimson—enclose vine-yards which swarm with barking brats & biting dogs. When-ever I stopped the *barcheta* & began to prepare the camera, at that very moment Baicolo would say with horror, 'Sior, people!' & shrink into concealment behind his cinture. I got in such a rage at last, that I roared, 'I will not go to work in this hole-&-corner way. Let us find a proper place, & speak politely to the *paron*, asking leave to have half-an-hour of privacy by his vineyard-wall.' 'Oh, God, no!' shrieked the Fusidowl. 'Then we must go further afield & find a ruin,' was my conclusion. And I stood up in the golden blaze of the sun to survey the vast lagoon.

We were in the main canal which runs from the marsh north of Torcelo by Burano to Treporti; &, very far away, I spied a blinding glittering stripe of white floating on its own reflection in the dancing blue, seemingly a walled island very much all alone. 'And there is your whited wall,' I pro-claimed. But it was four o clock in the afternoon; & we had a seven-mile row back to Venice: so we deferred approach till the following day.

On four several days thereafter we attempted to reach that wall. It was most elusive. Little canals (which seemed to be short cuts) were generally blind. The main canals led us round & round it. Once, when past high-water made one wide

shining mirror of the lagoon, we boldly left the depths &
tried to row straight across the shallows, with a dire result,
eight hours bogged on mud-banks till the return of the
tide, the Fusidowl a gibbering moist maniac, & my beloved
Waterman blubbering (despite the boasts of the advertisements) all over my beautiful ms. Needless to say that we
quarrelled violently till we were faint. My grievance is easily
explained. I wanted to do no more with those lovely late
Autumn days than to sit in my *barcheta* & be rowed & write
my book, until I felt inclined to row & bathe & eat & take
my forty winks, & so on again. The Fusidowl surely might
have been content to sit by my side, & revise his Greek
dialect-proofs, & otherwise do as I did. Nothing need have
prevented him from making as many photographs as he
pleased. He knew how to do it. Both the *gondoglieri* were
agreeable. Both might have sat for Giambellini—in fact I'll
swear that Baicolo did, in a previous incarnation, as you may
see any day at the Academia di Belle Arti if you do not
believe me. But no: the fatuous Fusidowl neither knew exactly
what he wanted, nor would let anybody tell him—neither
would do his job himself, nor would let anybody do it for
him. So, all of a sudden, my patience gave way here, with
a loud yell & embellishments of lurid notes & queries. Nemo
nostrum solide natus est.

We made it up again when we got home, after he had
sobbed & postured & gesticulated on my bedroom threshold
for some hours of the night; & I saw him peacefully off to
England by the eight o'clock train two mornings later. (Dear
me, how exhausted I was!) We two went down to the station
together, in a hired *poppe* because of his luggage, just to shew
that there was no malice. My *barcheta* was waiting outside the
station with Baicolo and Caicio beaming & ready for any
devilry. And, as soon as I had seen the last of the carroty
Professor, 'We will go, I pray, for pleasure,' I said to them
meaningly, 'by short way of the little canals to Rio Palazo
Reale, for I have a certain thing to do at the Ascension.'

By October 6th Rolfe could write to Dawkins, now back at

Emmanuel College, Cambridge, 'Beyond Torcelo, the desired "White Wall" turns out to be NOT a fort, but an abandoned island, *anticamente* the cemetery for *all the islands from Murano to Treporte*. And now it is a wilderness of the most lush vegetation, FULL of hundreds of human skeletons lying everywhere, skeletons of soldiers killed in the Italian wars from [18]48 to [18]66 carted (boated) there from various battlefields. Beside the photographs possible against wall and herbage, think of what one can do with the bones. I have already snapped G. and C. regarding a little heap and call it The Quick and The Dead. Consequently I am bleeding money like a pig to get a perfect mass of unique photographs.... So I'm risking being stranded under these circumstances. (Quite conscious of the liberty, and swear never to do it again. But Lord what a Chance!) N.B. This HAS been the time of my life.'

When the trip to Italy had first been mentioned to Rolfe, he had clearly outlined his financial position to the professor. The compliment that Rolfe paid the other in saying that Dawkins knew more Greek archaeology than anyone else in the world was not returned in any way. The professor looked upon Rolfe as 'a sort of amusing fool'. For the trip, he was to lend Rolfe 'his expenses which he would repay from money he made by writing and some kind of photography. I was glad enough to risk a little money for the pleasure and interest of his company and of course I never really expected to see it back again.' In his account of the Venetian holiday and of Rolfe, a quarter of a century later Dawkins recalled that 'it did not take me long to discover that Rolfe's idea of being helped along was to be allowed to spend as much as he pleased and this did not suit my book. He became extremely tiresome; tried a sort of worrying bullying, and in short I did not stay long in Venice but left him with enough money to get home to Gwernvale or indeed whatever he chose. But this he would not do. On various pretexts he stayed on at Venice, naturally running up bills. These I never paid but sent him some few pounds to clear himself; what I reckoned would be enough. By this time I was thoroughly sick of this sort of shiftiness and determined that he should no longer take advantage of me. So I entirely shut off supplies. He then started a series of letters describing his troubles, starvation and so on. But he had succeeded in making me thoroughly angry; he had fooled me by making excuses not to leave Venice and so get more money from me; I was determined to put a stop to it all and let him go on writing. I think I never left a letter unanswered, but my answers were brief.'

Rolfe's insistent demands—suggestions he called them—in time became monotonously irksome to those who attempted to aid him. His 'personal power' was always invigorating and original, at the beginning at least; and most of his desires were simple. Yet they were costly—if not in actual money, then in terms of time and effort. A Franciscan in physical discipline, his mind could nonetheless conceive a host of exotic trivialities. One reason why Dawkins tired of him, and did not take up the eventual quarrel seriously, was that 'I had a lot of other things to do; Rolfe had literally not another thing in the world to do but impress his so carefully cultivated personality on people and bully them into supporting him; his work was done only for the sake of his own self; the desire to make a figure in the world was always with him. I doubt whether he had any remotely disinterested feeling for any one else.'

Six years earlier a person with an extremely different nature than Dawkins' also realized Rolfe's uncommon life. But he accepted it in a different light. Sholto Douglas wrote to the man he was then collaborating with; 'Oh! but first, by the way, tell me about the tiara of Paul II: do not forget: you know everything useless. Tell me how he got the tiara. I must know that: I must know that. Do not cringe: expand your spectacles, and inscribe. Cover me with cold, and wrap me in wretchedness, but tell me how he got the tiara.'

In the early autumn of 1908 Rolfe was a complacent and free man. For the time being, he had a place to stay. He had money for food and photographic supplies. He was rid of his holiday companion, and he had made friends with the boys Dawkins had hired as gondoliers and whom he had commanded Rolfe to photograph. The two boys, Ermenegildo Vianello and Carlo Caenazzo, continued in their friendships with the Englishman and, in turn, were portrayed in his stories. In two published Venetian essays they become Baicolo and Caicio. Baicolo comes closer to his real name as Ermenegildo Vianel in a third published story. Rolfe was also to borrow his name for *The Desire and Pursuit of the Whole*, calling the girl Crabbe discovers Zilda (Ermenegilda) Falier. Almost twenty years earlier in Rome, Rolfe had elevated the lowly peasant boy Toto by granting him the added name of Maidalchini, a seventeenth-century cardinal. Gildo fared better. The name of three doges of Venice was bestowed upon him.

Rolfe's first letter to Dawkins from Venice was merely to ask for 'another tenner, by wire if possible.' A wire arrived, but without money. 'I suppose I had no right to expect it,' he replied, 'but I certainly did trust you to stand by me.' He had just finished 'a set of photographs now which will make you open your eyes when I send them to you. For I suppose you don't really mean to let me down. But the impasse is a beastly one. And at the moment I can't think of any other course to take but to sit still for another week here in the hope that you will do what I ask.'

In his next letter he thought that 'it would perhaps have been more satisfactory if you had stated at the beginning the "figure" which you were prepared to spend. Then I could have said whether a sufficiency of photographs could have been done by me to cover that figure. As it is, I have not spared myself, and have gotten a really large and unique collection of half-done work which is unmarketable in its present condition.' His own condition meant bills to be paid, including a 'ten days' hotel-bill.' '£10 a week ago would have cleared me and seen me back at Gwernvale. It won't now. In fact my position is serious, and I cannot believe that you will leave me in the lurch.'

Dawkins directed his London bank to forward £15 to Rolfe on October 15th. But a combination of Rolfe's pride and warped imagination prevented it from reaching him. On the following day he reported to Dawkins 'a very mysterious happening. A liveried person from Banca Commerciale Italiana has just called on me to offer me L.375 (Ital.) sent me from Turin. No message and no name. As I don't know a soul in Turin and am not expecting any money after your wire, and your letter, (even if you were in Turin, which you ain't), I have reluctantly declined to receive the said sum, all in proper form. I don't think any other course was open to me. A person in my position has to be damned careful about money matters.... Several dear good Christians would be delighted to catch me grabbing at gold fortuitously (most likely by some mistake) rained upon me.... The absence of sender's name or message strikes me as being extremely fishy. Yes: on the whole my suspicions are aroused.'

The professor had to reclaim the money and send it a second time. Rolfe acknowledged it on the 27th. 'This pays all up here: but will not take me home nor redeem from Mount of Piety [the municipal pawn office in Italy]. All the last proofs of *Don Renato* are waiting for me. I stay on here with renewed credit, perforce.' A week later he was writing to Pirie-Gordon that 'I fancy now that I see my way to come home about the middle of next week quite honorably and with a trophy or two.' He had been elected to 'the Bucintori of Venice', thereby becoming a 'most respectable Venetian, with the best Club.... Nothing could be more dignified. Remains only to have a house and gondola and to live here [and] it would be quite correct for a knight of the Order to keep a shop. Only, I firmly abhor from the notion that one might "begin small".... It is annoying to have to waste time and money in coming to England to get money: but, of course, I see that there is no other way.... Then I will finish *Hubert* ... and do what is necessary to return here in Feb. 1909.' Sixteen days later he thanked Harry for the 'annunciation of Ordinal Meeting and Dinner; and I beg you to indulge my absence on the ground that it is impossible for me to reach England in time.' He was 'much annoyed' by the fact 'that I shall within the next few days find myself without money or friends or future in this foreign country.' He ended the letter by 'kissing the Sceptre' and laying 'my predicament at the feet of Your Splendour, requesting advice and direction.'

One possible solution to his straitened affairs was Barnard & Taylor. On November 24th he sent them a letter, beginning with the 'misfortune' of falling into the canal, after his election to the Bucintoro. 'The result was a chill, a day of aches and a new outburst of my chin and skinned knuckles,' he said. 'Thanks to my robust health, the aches have gone, the knuckles are stiff but healing and the chin will ripen and empty in a day or two.' He then wondered 'whether the insurance on my life could be increased to a further loan or allowance made to me on it sufficient for a clear year of solid work. I am led to propose this idea because I am having great difficulty in raising the money to clear me of my ridiculous responsibilities here & to bring me back to Gwernvale. Further Gwernvale will be shut in February and the Gordons go globe trotting for two years, so that I shall be at a loose end then anyhow.' Namelessly speaking of Dawkins, he pledged never again 'to cultivate rich acquaintances. I have been a fool to try it. It only pleasantly interrupts progress. And I am convinced that my salvation lies in incessant work with literally nothing to do with other people.'

After Rolfe left England, Barnard & Taylor advanced him only £22. But they continued to pay the premiums on his life insurance.

In a short letter to Dawkins on November 26th Rolfe said he was sending a new batch of photographs and wondered if an earlier set had reached the professor. Having no word from England made Rolfe ask if Dawkins had let 'the sun go down on your wrath.' The letter ended by saying that he had just 'done the Excommunication of Harmsworth and the New Order for damning him in an Order of Chivalry.'

In August the two men on holiday had taken rooms in the Hotel Belle Vue et de Russie, next to the Clock Tower. Its upper windows gave a beautiful view of the Grand Canal, past the front of St. Mark's. Here Rolfe stayed on alone. During the pleasant weather of late summer he glided over the water, occupied with *Hubert's Arthur* and the beginning of some Venetian essays. When the autumn finally drove him from the lagoon, he continued his writing in the hotel. Although his bills were not steadily paid, Evaristo Barbieri, the proprietor, was impressed with this Englishman. The letters coming for Rolfe from England were encased within official and rich-looking envelopes, in some way assuring Barbieri of Rolfe's financial future. He had no immediate concern over the author. The winter season was beginning and one guest not fully paid could be endured.

For many years Rolfe had been wedged into the confinement of a small space, working hours, even days, without any recreational diversion. Conscious of the fact that his body was a temple of the Holy Spirit, Rolfe cared for it with almost rigid discipline. In Venice he now could indulge in the extremes of habit. Lady Layard had founded 'a small English Ospedale on Guidecca,' for the care of seamen. Rolfe freely offered his services, borrowing a sandolo from the Bucintoro to 'row convalescents about in the sun' and to do whatever other chores he could. When not working for the English Hospital, he wrote. On December 19th he was still awaiting notes to enable him to finish *Hubert's Arthur.* 'And SUCH a book!!!! A book to *revel* over,' he said to Pirie-Gordon just before wishing a 'Happy Xmas to you. I did hope to be home for Christmas.' And on the 26th he gave a full account of the Mass on Christmas Day, 'celebrated by the Patriarch in Saint Mark's at 4.30 p.m. on the vigil.' Two days later came the Messina earthquake.

The disaster left thousands of people homeless and without clothes or food. The citizens of Venice organized a relief programme and Rolfe begged for materials to comfort the victims and rowed his sandolo carrying cargoes of goods to the relief stations. For a fortnight his energy was added to the efforts directed towards those stranded by the earthquake. When the dust and rubble subsided, and he had rested from his exhausting mission, Rolfe discovered something. The Messina earthquake proved the beginning of a fascinating novel and his most original character, Zilda.

In Rolfe's numerous requests for aid he never 'insisted' upon any one remedy. He was always thoughtful enough merely to offer possible 'suggestions' for immediate relief. Yet even these were strongly underscored with a dramatic tone. In writing to Pirie-Gordon six days before Christmas 1908 he said that he was not 'asking for clothes for two reasons', One was that 'sending clothes six weeks by sea to a man who may be starved four weeks before they reached him and who anyhow hasn't got the money to pay carriage and customs never occurred' to Rolfe.

Although he could not 'afford to stay in Venice (or anywhere),' the other reason was that he 'would rather bear the cold and shabbiness and inconvenience for the week or two which may elapse before my death, than break up the nice little wardrobe which might (perhaps) be useful in the remote event of my getting home.' This was his way to thank Pirie-Gordon for sending some of his clothes. In the same letter he asked what 'B. & T. mean about my getting a job. I can't think of anything which I have said which could bear that construction. The only jobs which I will do at all now are Writing Books or Running a Photographic Business here in Venice.... I have been battered out of the Church and battered out of Art. If I am to be battered out of Letters too—Oh very well. I will make no more attempts.'

In March, Dawkins acknowledged a letter from Rolfe written in January. He congratulated him on his short story, 'Denion to Thely'—'that loveliest essay of its sort in English'—'though you probably will regard it as impertinence on my part'. Quickly answering, Rolfe thanked the professor for 'the impotence and disgrace to which you (who never hope to act as an enemy towards me) have reduced me'. Rolfe knew nothing about the published story 'excepting that I wrote a story by that name in 1904 and sent half-a-dozen copies to half-a-dozen magazines. There they are, and what has happened to them, is utterly unknown to me now, all my papers and property being lost to me through your accentedly inimical behaviour in preventing me from using my abilities to earn an honest living.' Here Dawkins was repaid in usual fashion for his share in Rolfe's history. He had invited the author to a holiday and had then given him money to return to Gwernvale. Instead, Rolfe had stayed on in Italy, to blame Dawkins and others for his plight. The distances of time and geography further breached the bonds of friendship between Rolfe and those back in England.

At Benson's suggestion Rolfe had sent six stories to Lord Alfred Douglas, then editing *The Academy*. In January 1909 'Denion to Thely' appeared. It was not until Rolfe read the letter from Dawkins that he knew it had been printed; and it was not until the end of the May that he received a copy of the magazine and payment of two guineas, '1/7 of my proper price'. He never again heard about the other five manuscripts. They were lost and this misadventure fed his grievances against the priest-who-had-sought-him-out. Through 'Benson's perjury I have lost about 3 months work and £16 sterling'.

As 1909 began Barnard & Taylor had sent Babieri something towards Rolfe's hotel bills. And on April 25th Pirie-Gordon sent a short letter to his literary partner, saying that 'I have been advised that your circumstances are less gloomy than when you last wrote [on February 9th]' and hoped that Rolfe would be able to go to Constantinople, 'where the [political] events are quite exciting enough to please even you'. This had been written eleven days after Rolfe finally was evicted from the Hotel Belle Vue and three days after his first disparaging note appears against Pirie-Gordon. He assailed Benson as a liar and a traitor and as Pirie-Gordon's ally. He had 'said four months ago that there was only one way for my deliverance. And I intend to reject and am rejecting all other ways.... *I am now simply engaged in dying as slowly and as publicly and as annoyingly to all you professing and non-professing friends of mine, as possible.*'

Mystery hovered over every move of Rolfe's in public. Aloofness was part of his character. But his sharp wits missed little. The guest at the Hotel Belle Vue during the autumn and winter of 1908-9 could be seen but not approached. Walking or sitting, his imposing and erect posture commanded attention. His attitude at dinner, reading a newspaper or engaged in his occupation of writing, could never be dismissed with a casual glance. The pose at this time was a genuine one, for he wished to keep separate from people. The lack of interference from others gave him more time to concentrate on his own affairs.

Just before 1908 ended, he wrote to Pirie-Gordon from the Belle Vue that 'now a pack of English are running after me. Canon Lonsdale Ragg the Protestant Chaplain here lives in this pub during the winter. He made the most comical attempts to know me. Now we nod.' But the unapproachable was the one who did the approaching.

The Anglican Chaplain of Venice, his wife and their small

284

child had an apartment in the city. For various reasons they came to the Belle Vue for the winter. The rooms were heated and sunny, facing the Piazza and, because of the season, quiet. Ragg was working on a book and did not want to be disturbed. When they learned that Rolfe was a guest, they at first thought he would become a nuisance. But it turned out that he had no friends and did no entertaining. He made polite gestures to them in the dining room, but in no way sought an alliance. The Raggs were greatly taken with his appearance. Yet he seemed reticent and shy. A few days before Christmas an envelope rested on Canon Ragg's breakfast tray. He had never before seen an example of Rolfe's beautiful script. With interest he read the message which asked for an interview that evening. Only the day before Barbieri had spoken to him about Rolfe's unpaid bills at the hotel. Ragg knew of *Hadrian the Seventh* and told the hotel proprietor that a future book should see Rolfe in funds again. He suggested that Barbieri be patient and even guaranteed the cost of meals for the other guest for a period of three weeks. The interview that evening between the two Englishmen was a long one. Rolfe exploded in a 'tirade' about his past. But, before Ragg had a chance to develop any immediate thoughts about a solution to these problems, the Messina earthquake intervened, employing Rolfe for several weeks.

At this particular time Ragg noticed a distinct and sudden change in Rolfe's manner. It came about when his work for the earthquake refugees ceased. His brisk good humour abruptly evaporated. Ever since his final days at Holywell, Rolfe's character had followed the words of Theodore Wratislaw:

> My soul is as a bird that flies
> Down unfrequented ways
> Of windy seas and cloudy skies
> Afar from human gaze,
> While in its heart through all its flight
> A poisoned arrow stays.

In most cases the 'poisoned arrow' resulted from good, if indifferent, intention of his friends. Dawkins recalled that at this period 'Pirie-Gordon sent around a hat for Rolfe and I gave I think nine pounds, thinking that the names of the donors would not be revealed. But they were and Rolfe wrote an abusive letter about daring to insult his poverty by alms and so on; but he spent the money.' Dawkins' word was written a quarter of a century after the event. At the time, on 28 January 1909, Rolfe's letter to him said:

I am not sure that I can explain myself properly. I have been having a most worrying time. Lucid thought never was my strongest point. Crab-like, I invariably sidle at my subject. And it has not amused me at all to have to explain my ghastly predicament here by confessing to other people that I am personally responsible for the imprudence of misunderstanding your intentions. And now, to-day, I hear from H. P.-G. that you have been contributing to a fund with him and Benson which my own lawyers propose to administer over my head. This annoys me. I decline to permit it.... I have asked H. P.-G. to return your money to you.

In November 1908 he had written to Pirie-Gordon about hoping to finish *Hubert's Arthur*. Then he would 'write that infernal Benson book' on St. Thomas. But this act of alms-giving charity severed him from the people he knew in England and their affairs.

Thinking perhaps that Rolfe's change towards bitterness stemmed from loneliness, Ragg engaged him in literary conversation. The chaplain was working on *The Church of the Apostles*, and Rolfe pressed him to accept a system of punctuation which he claimed to be derived from Addison. Ragg even invited him to the Monday evenings at Horatio Brown's. Although Rolfe had never visited John Addington Symonds' friend and biographer before, the name was not new to him. Brown's friends in England included Henry Tuke, Gleeson White, Kains-Jackson and Nicholson. His social evenings in Venice continued throughout the year. But they were reduced in the winter to log-fire talk, smoking and the drinking of coffee and liqueurs. Ragg's experiment in taking Rolfe to Brown's was not a success. Rolfe could never mix with a group of unknown people. The academicians and successful men of the world in their various fields offended his pride.

Ragg even spoke to Benson when the Catholic paid a short visit to Venice. The two had a chance to spend an evening in a gondola talking about Rolfe's problems. But nothing substantial came of it. Benson was reluctant to touch the case, saying, 'I am afraid the poor dog will always bite the hand which pets or feeds him.'

Rolfe was still at the hotel when the Raggs went back to their apartment at the end of February. On April 14th Barbieri's patience waned and the unpaying guest was evicted. His only home now was the Bucintoro. Here he wrote in the club's pavilion and slept in a sandolo. Remembering Horatio Brown's Monday nights, he returned twice 'in the frantic hope of finding a biscuit or a sandwich with your whisky and water, I being starving'.

Several members of the British Colony discussed plans for his assistance. He had told tales of thieving and mismanaging friends back in England. If given a chance to go back, no doubt he could straighten out these things, they thought. He was informed by letter that a first-class ticket to England in his name was ready for him at Cook's Travel Office. The offer was answered with scorn, derision, resentment and rejection.

About a fortnight after his eviction from the hotel, Rolfe and Ragg met. Rolfe had been sleeping in his boat 'in that rather fine "martial cloak" in which he fancied himself as looking like the Duke of Wellington. He was very proud & reserved, & correspondingly difficult to help. Very occasionally on some specious excuse I induced him to sup with me at a restaurant.' After four pleasing years in Venice, the chaplain had decided to accept the offer of a small parish in England. What belongings had not been sold were packed and awaited shipment. Ragg and his wife and child were staying in Palazzo Barbaro and their own apartment was empty. Ragg 'beguiled Rolfe to think he was doing us a service if he would use the flat (instead of the open air) as a dormitory'. Here Rolfe stayed until May 7th and 'here he came familiar with our future address ... & when I arrived on the scene I found insulting *postcards* awaiting me! So far as I know they failed in their object: & in any case I felt no real resentment. But it was distinctly embarrassing. I fancy my crowning offence was introducing him [while still at the Belle Vue] to a representative of Rothschild's in Paris, a man whom all my friends admired, & who, it was thought, could unravel his financial problems if they could be unravelled at all. They met & had their talk: & for some reason Rolfe's bitterness seemed to increase from that moment.'

As with the alms from England in January, Ragg never learned the full story behind Rolfe's outbreaks of bitterness. In his Venetian novel Rolfe records his first meeting with 'Rothschild's financier,' who 'was gaunt, bony, and extremely dressed. He had the vacancies and dusty dryness of canute old age (he at once proclaimed his age as seventy-seven) but he was jerkily active though rheumy-eyed with monocle and tinted nose; and he foamed at the mouth occasionally, champing a thin old van-dyked beard.' The Hardcastle of actual life is Sappytower in Rolfe's book. The conversation 'was entirely on one side, and mainly testimonial and reminiscent. The Sappytower ... went on to furnish the story of his life, his early perfection in the French tongue, his daily attendance (with intimate correspondence) in the old Baron Rothschild's bedroom, his adventures in that sanctum, his exploits in making coups to mar (or make) nations and men.'

Rolfe's case would be a simple one. Hardcastle, who had manipulated millions without ever seeing them, was amused by the way non-financial people disturbed themselves over a paltry thousand. A financial partner was all that was needed for Rolfe. And such partners were to be found fifty times a day. He scribbled a draft of a letter to a literary man in England, introducing Rolfe and signed it with his name, '(late of Rothschild's).' This act bucked up Rolfe and he was deeply grateful.

Leaving Hardcastle, Rolfe gave his news to Barbieri. All was going well, the proprietor thought, but he was pressed for funds himself. He asked Rolfe if he would mind taking care of his bill right away. He owed approximately L2,000. If Rolfe would sign a bill for L3,500, on which the Co-operative Bank would lend money immediately, Barbieri would keep him in the hotel. This would take care of his rent between November and April and assure him of another six months at the Belle Vue. Security for most of the year and freedom from agonizing worry made Rolfe cheerfully sign Barbieri's bill.

One night Rolfe was wakened to be told that 'a Signor Inglese' was downstairs. Hardcastle had come over at nearly midnight to talk with Rolfe's 'excellent landlord'. The hotel proprietor could understand just enough English to realize who Hardcastle was. He told the financier that everything between him and his guest had been settled and showed him the signed bill. Hardcastle read it and tore it up, saying that Rolfe should not have signed such a thing and that Barbieri should not have asked him to. Rolfe was furious and told Hardcastle that he had frightened Barbieri. But everything was to be left in Hardcastle's hands. Rolfe went back to bed and the man from Rothschild's stayed until 2.30, talking to a confused Barbieri in an effort to determine whether he was mad or drunk.

The following morning the hotel proprietor approached Rolfe after breakfast. From all Hardcastle had said the night before, he interpreted that he had no trust in Rolfe. To this he added that he wished Rolfe to pay his bill before noon or leave the hotel. Rolfe took his papers and belongings and went to the Bucintoro that afternoon.

Ragg's insistence that Hardcastle should help him and the way that this 'help' turned out was bad enough. But Rolfe made inquiries about the financier and discovered that he had not been employed by Rothschild's for the past forty years. 'Ragg grossly deceived me,' Rolfe wrote just a few months later. 'He did not try to help me.' 'Deceive' may be too strong a word, but Rolfe cannot be blamed entirely for thinking in the way he did. 'Ragg's intention was abominable,' he said. 'No one seems to have noticed that I was unconsciously Ragg's *Rival*.' By this Rolfe meant that Ragg himself owed a bill amounting to L500 at the Belle Vue, and he wanted to borrow £200, as well as find somebody to house him for the time. These were aims similar to Rolfe's. 'Naturally,' Rolfe said about Ragg, 'he was afraid to ask anyone to do these things for me, because *he* had to have them. And so he deceived me. I do not know which is worse—the evil which means well, or the good which hurts.'

Embittered by the final results of his association with Ragg, he now wrote to Brown, but only because of Nicholson. He said that his old friend told him 'that I ought to pocket pride & tell you the awful trouble in which I am'. The reasons for his penniless state in Venice were outlined. No one back home was doing anything for him. However, he added, a journey to England would be 'quite unnecessary' and even 'fatal'. In another letter he stated: 'Friends? I haven't any other than Nicholson. Charity? Please no. That's what everyone suggests.'

When he finally received a copy of *The Academy* containing his 'Denion to Thely' and the cheque for two guineas, he wrote to acknowledge them. He also said that his story 'contains (say) 3500 words' and that he 'shall be glad to have the balance of say £15.2.6 at your earliest convenience'—a request never answered. He sent the magazine to Brown as an example of his work. He wondered if Brown would 'now be inclined ... to guarantee my landlord £200 stg payable in a year's time or ... to lend me £100 at once on my giving you a lien on the serial rights & copyrights of my nineteen Venetian Toto Stories. If so I will get them, give them their final shape & send them out without any more delay.' Brown advanced him no money but he suggested editors in London for the Venetian essays.

Don Renato has the longest, most curious history of Rolfe's books, from its first mention to its appearance in printed and bound form. On 29 November 1897 Rolfe wrote to John Lane, suggesting 'a translation I have almost completed of ... a sort of diurnal of Dom Gheraldo Pinario, Chaplain of Prince Marcantonio Publicola of Santa Croce AD 1528-9-30'. This may have been the first mention of the book in any of Rolfe's letters. Writing to his brother Herbert on 26 August 1898 he said that he was working on two novels, without naming either. One may have been the prototype for *Hadrian*, begun at Holywell in collaboration with Holden, and the second may have been *Renato*. For several years he worked on it, adding to it, pruning bits from it and moulding it to perfection, like a doting parent. It was first known as *Don Ghiraldo* and was given to a small number of friends to read. By 16 March 1902 it had been completed and renamed. On this date Rolfe wrote to Maurice Hewlett, 'My romance, *An Ideal Content,* an attempt at historic fiction in an unworn formula, goes to-day to Heinemann.' Although many publishers saw it, it was not until October 1907 that Francis Griffiths agreed to take it. The contract called for a printing of 2,000 copies at six shillings each, the author receiving ten per cent of each copy sold.

In all the time Rolfe worked on the novel he had found no dedicatee for it. Almost every person who had seen it was a possible candidate, but each had failed to live up to Rolfe's expectations for such a title. In April 1908 he wrote to Dawkins, '*Don Renato* is dedicated *"Dino Amico, Desideratissimo, adnuc Latatenti"*. I wonder whether that is you.' Yet even without a name on the dedication page the book was set in hand for publication. The first proof sheets reached Rolfe just as he was readying himself for the six weeks' holiday in Venice. Through letters to Pirie-Gordon he remained in touch with Griffiths. Pirie-Gordon and the publisher agreed on the smaller points of the book. Then one day a letter came to him from Venice. Rolfe said that he possibly would be in prison for debt on the following Monday. Believing him not at liberty, Pirie-Gordon passed on the proofs to Griffiths with instructions to proceed with the book. There was an air of urgency connected with the book. Griffiths' printers were entering a state of bankruptcy and it had to be printed before their effects were sold. By 18 May 1909 Pirie-Gordon had become 'a feeble person' and 'a new enemy' and Rolfe asked him to 'please do nothing further about *Don Renato*'. In a letter to Dawkins eleven days later Rolfe listed this book as being 'printed, bound, and ready for immediate publication'. Yet something was to prevent it from appearing. Rolfe was proud of this book and extremely anxious to see it in print. But a combination of circumstances provoked his unpredictable character. Both Pirie-Gordon, in telling the publisher to go ahead with the book, and Griffiiths, for listening to him, acted without Rolfe's authority. Too, *Don Renato*'s author realized how much of the profits he would see. The gamble with Owen Thomas had an unfortunate finish for Rolfe.

He not only lost the case but all future income until Barnard & Taylor were paid. He knew that he was not the winner, but he never considered himself the loser. Now, if he were not allowed to reap reward from his own work, why should anyone else? Griffiths and the Publishers' Association in London were both told that he did not wish *Don Renato* to be published.

While he was still living at the Belle Vue on friendly terms with the Raggs, they did Rolfe a kindness for the future. Going to the opera one night with two friends, they invited Rolfe along. In this way he met Dr. and Mrs. Ernest van Someren. Finding himself in a desperate condition by June, Rolfe wrote to the doctor for the first time. The letter ended with a question, asking if the doctor knew of 'a situation at once as second gondolier ... so that I may go on living'. At the same time he first communicated with the British Consul at Venice, applying 'to the F. O. for the means for my repatriation in the terms of my passport'. To stress the urgency he added: 'Is it not a fact that Sigr Barbieri has no right by Italian law to sequester my necessary clothes, writing-materials & papers (i.e. tools of trade) as he has done, without legal process? As long as he sequesters my property, preventing me even from using it to earn money under his own supervision, can he also hold me responsible for my debt to him?' He closed his letter with a word of gratefulness for the 'courtesy & consideration which you are shewing to me in my paralyzing misfortune'. Before the end of the month he had their verdict. The circumstances of the case did not justify the Foreign Office in repatriating 'Mr F. Rolfe from Venice as a distressed person'. The only immediate solution would be a plea for work. His question to Dr. van Someren about a second gondolier's position was repeated to a number of other people. It even was advertised in the *Gazzetta di Venezia*. And Rolfe was given the job he sought.

As a gondolier he met an Englishman who was also a Catholic and a painter. As many times as he said he would no longer tolerate Catholics, Rolfe always eagerly greeted a new one, giving each in turn one more chance.

On this Catholic artist's behalf Rolfe was writing on July 5th to recommend George Demain-Cooke, 'who would gladly take

292

an Agency in Venice for such a machine & make it pay splendidly'. The 'Agency' had to do with boating and in another letter on the same day Rolfe thought that the proposed terms from one area were ridiculous. He wondered if it would 'be better to apply to Waterman Marine Motor Co of Detroit, U.S.A. for an Agency (not subagency) at Venice.... The Milan man wants to have sole agency for Italy. Why should he?' But in less than one month's time he discovered all that he wanted to know about the artist and withdrew from their agreement. At the beginning Demain-Cooke and Rolfe arranged to start a business with L500, half of which the painter was to pay him immediately. The proposed partnership for handling marine motors in Venice never materialized.

The slight sum due from *The Academy* prompted Rolfe to move to a small hotel at a fixed price of L5 per day. At the end of the second week he learned that he was paying L8.50. When a cheque arrived from one of the people he had met in Venice, Rolfe paid his bill and moved in with the artist, his wife and little girl. In return for his services as gondolier he was to receive a very modest sum. For the short while he stayed with the Demain-Cooks he paid them L97.50. He also loaned the painter L14 and spent other money on his affairs. This included paying back a sum of money Demain-Cooke obtained from Dr. van Someren in Rolfe's name without his knowledge.

In *The Desire and Pursuit of the Whole* this artist becomes Butler, who 'had moved to a little apartment in the Alley of the Angel.... It was a queer show: furniture (of incredible skimpiness and cheapness) hired from the landlord, mixed with the vaunted goods from Naples, which last consisted of a trunk of books worth perhaps ninepence and another of ramshackle paints with a score of amateurish dauby sketches. The funny thing about Butler, as I say, was that he shewed neither bumptiousness nor shame. He neither bragged of nor excused shortcomings. His sangfroid, or obtuseness, or insensibility was about the most densely stolid British thing that Crabbe had ever encountered. He stuck up his daubs with modest satisfaction, punctuated with "Lin-der gimme glass o' wine," and explained that little things satisfied him, adding the inevitable "Lin-der gimme cigarette."

His monumental wife tucked old photographs and picture post-cards and fans on walls, in the intervals of producing celestially-odoured soups from inconsiderable pans; and the baby of seven skipped among the medley, cackling and squinting.'

To the penniless Rolfe, the proposition of a job as a gondolier and a partner in a Venetian firm was indeed welcome. Each month Demain-Cooke was sent L800. Out of this dreams would be fulfilled. Rolfe was given 'an attic top' of their house, 'a plain garret under the roof [with] no outlook,' and 'grub'. In one short month he learned all about the painter that he wished. When the monthly cheque arrived it was used to pay debts, which did not include his own wages. Returning late one day, Rolfe was famished. He found his supper in the dark kitchen—'a plate of coagulate risotto undergoing the attentions of a cloud of blue-bottles and mosquitoes'. And the only place available to eat it, if he wanted to, was the water-closet of the house.

At the end of July he fled the Demain-Cookes and chastized the artist with the words of a long letter. 'It is such an amazing thing when one thinks one has found a decent chap to discover he is only a MOST PORTENTOUS FOOL.... All the facts about you are that you are a lazy loafer, never quite sober, always sodden with nippling & tippling, always cadging from anyone who will lend you money, & with no more ability for management even of the simplest affairs than the common puff-ball which you so closely resemble.... It's only dishonourable to take other people's money when you lounge about & get fat-bodied & fatter-headed & do nothing all day.... It is not particularly moral to go into partnership with a man on the principle of "halves"; & then go & borrow L22.50 from van Somersen for my bedroom, keep half of it for your own expenses & have the face to offer me L2 of that as my "share of the plunder". Nor is it particularly moral to take L250 of my L500, to have me to pay L6 for taking your wife's broach out of pawn (June 26th) to borrow L40.50 at various times for your own expenses, to send me out to buy your brandy, to help you dress yourself in the morning, let me pawn everything of my own even the cross & chain from my neck to help you going, to promise me faithfully that all would be beer & skittles when your cheque arrived—& then when it did to have the infernal impertinence to offer me a measly L10 out of it (less than half what I spent on your baby alone) to let me find out that you are insolvent & hounded by creditors, to expect me [to] eat my dinner 2 hours late in the water-closet after slaving for you all day, & to treat me to a week of sulks & filthy abuse of your wife & baby. Oh no, I don't think much of your morals.'

The reality of such treatment, at times, overtopped his imagination.

At the time Rolfe was beginning his artistic and literary career in England, a certain American settled in Venice. Curiously, this event followed a medical examination, similar to Rolfe's, for life insurance. The location of the examination in this case was San Francisco, where the subject had previously made his headquarters for thirty years, amassing one fortune from the manufacture of printers' inks and another from the export of Oriental goods. When the insurance company refused him a policy in 1895 because he was overweight, he immediately interested himself in the problem of health through nutrition. The work of Horace Fletcher soon became known and 'Fletcherism' was a household word. In Venice, Fletcher found a man who advocated similar ideas and took him into his employment. The two, Horace Fletcher and Dr. van Someren, carried out experiments in nutrition at Cambridge and Yale Universities and explored the many factors of their theories back in Venice. There was another common interest which cemented the bond between them: Horace Fletcher was the father of Ivy, the future Mrs. van Someren.

1909 was the year which saw the spanning of an almost twenty-year period. Rolfe's admired Duchess Sforza-Cesarini finally appeared in his writings for the last time during this year. She is 'the Old Princess' in 'Denion to Thely' and 'the Countess of Santa Cotogna' in *Don Renato*. In *The Desire and Pursuit of the Whole*, begun in this year, only the 'princely family' of 'Attendoli-Cesari' is mentioned. This book was started after Rolfe met another, much younger, woman of understanding in the person of the doctor's wife.

Following his first letter to the doctor, Rolfe called at his house. The charitable man listened to the distressing story his visitor unfolded and invited him to stay with the van Someren family. On June 26th Rolfe moved to Palazzo Mocenigo-Corner. A small room had been created on a landing with a large window. It had no fireplace, but it was just as warm as his Hotel Belle Vue room and certainly warmer than an open boat. He did small chores around the house, such as carrying wood and working a cream separator. The doctor gave him a small allowance and his laundry was done with the rest of the family's. In no way was he a nuisance. No friends ever visited him, and most of his time was spent in his room writing. If any guest arrived for a meal whom he personally did not know, his own food was taken to his room on a tray. At other times he dined with the family and with the very few people he did know. He did complain of 'the poor table'. This charge was never true as far as quantity was concerned, but the doctor's strict theories of nutrition did not always appeal even to Rolfe's austere appetite. The menu did not even include sweets for the children.

The security of a room, food and the price of paper, ink and postage enabled Rolfe's imagination to continue its charges against his real and supposed enemies. Post cards and letters were sent to local and foreign addresses. The stamps he used to settle his accounts with Demain-Cooke brought him nothing. Answers came from the painter, as well as from his brother and solicitors in England, but nothing of the money Rolfe had loaned him.

The recipients of his letters to England now included the Raggs. After the first few, they were returned or left unopened. The first ones contained an accusation against the canon, then a conditional offer of an olive branch or a suggested opportunity to share in some future financial scheme. As courteous as Rolfe had been to Mrs. Ragg in Venice, she never cared for him. She replied with curt answers to anything he said or did; and her Italian maid, Nina, was terrified by Rolfe's cold countenance, declaring that he had the *malocchio* or evil eye. Mrs. Ragg resented any hinted comparison between Rolfe and her husband. She opened one of his letters addressed to Canon Ragg

296

and answered: 'When my husband was a little boy, his mother was left a widow with seven children, an income of £150 a year, & only distant & by no means wealthy relations. The 5 boys worked hard, won scholarships, & made their way in the world winning kindness & respect on all sides. The girls did their part. The whole family practiced rigid economy & self denial & avoided debt. Canon Ragg has never had £100 in the bank at any one time; & it makes me smile to hear you talking airily of *borrowing* (?) twice that sum.'

Only a few days after coming to Mocenigo-Corner, Rolfe saw Ragg's published book. On July 31st he wrote to Benson and to Pirie-Gordon's father: 'Read preface to Canon Lonsdale Ragg's Church of the Apostles just published by Rivington's & be ashamed of having so readily snatched at an opportunity of suspecting evil.' In the book's Preface the author had acknowledged Rolfe's 'very careful and painstaking revision of the proofs'. On the same day that he wrote to Benson and the other Rolfe addressed Ragg himself: 'How dare you mention my name in your book (just published) after I explicitly prohibited you from doing so in the first letter I sent you in Mar? I am communicating with Messrs Rivingtons giving my reasons for not wishing to appear in such company as yours.' So another publisher had to conform to his whims. The Preface was removed and a cancel page was inserted with no mention of Rolfe.

During October, Benson was denounced to the Archbishop of Westminster, without any response. An acquaintance briefly met in Venice sent Rolfe five pounds. In reply he said that he 'will accept the note you offer most thankfully' if he 'may give 4/5 of it to Dr Van Someren. There is no doubt about it (though of course he won't admit it) that he is being made to suffer for supporting me. And I know that his affairs are in a very bad condition indeed.' The doctor's affairs were far from being bad and it was a subject never discussed between host and guest. They were not bad enough to prevent Rolfe from trying to sell Dr. van Someren a lien on the book he was writing.

Rolfe mixed amiably with the family. Of all the days he spent with them only one was sad. Christmas always held a special meaning for him, yet there were few for him of good cheer.

In 1909 he willingly helped in decorating a tree which was an annual treat for needy children. But for Rolfe the actual day was far from pleasant. Mrs. Fletcher invited her family to be with her, but her daughter's guest was not included. The spirit of the day, of family, of love, of giving, did not embrace him. He wandered alone into churches and ate a cold lunch. The doctor attended the Salvation Army in the evening and Rolfe was left to himself. Anticipating the events of the day, he had written a few letters on Christmas Eve. 'Mr Rolfe's Christmas greeting xxv Dec 1909' went to Benson, Pirie-Gordon and his two parents, Hunter Blair and Ragg. The basic greeting was the 'I was an hungered' message of Matthew xxv: 41-43. To Ragg's he added the words of Michelangelo:

> He who lends wings of hope, while secretly
>   he spreads a traitorous snare by the wayside,
>   hath dulled the flare of love & nullified
> friendship, whose friendship burns most fervently.

The most unusual woman Rolfe had met since 1890 was the young Mrs. van Someren. She viewed him with democratic understanding. Like the old duchess, the doctor's wife was an attracted and attentive listener. Her husband was frequently away in the evenings and she and Rolfe spent the time together after dinner. She played the piano for him, and in return he told her stories, about himself and about the Church. He knew everything about Roman Catholic ceremonies, their origins and their purposes. In stressing the ceremonial she wondered how sincere he was in his basic religious belief. A product of the New World, she did not comprehend the age of tradition in Europe and England. A modern woman with a spark of emancipation within her, and a non-Catholic, she believed in the freedom of the mind, that it should not be persuaded by the tenets of by-gone days. But, she maintained, in the now set habits of his ways Rolfe was 'too cantankerous' to admit freely the profound gratitude he felt for the doctor and his wife.

The highest compliment he could pay her was a silent one. During this period Rolfe quarrelled with all the people he knew in Venice, all save the doctor's wife.

Of course, there were skirmishes. Differences of opinions naturally occurred during their evening talks. But on only one night was there any indication of anger. Mrs. Ragg and 'the Resident Aliens' were subjects mentioned during one discussion. The canon's wife and Mrs. van Someren were friends and Mrs. van Someren now accused Rolfe of showing a frantic hatred for the absent woman. Rolfe's hostess passionately resented his attacks on the people she knew and admired and told him as much. The evening came to an abrupt conclusion. But for Rolfe her act did not terminate the conversation. To detail the justification of his charges he continued the matter in writing, listing 'Nineteen Sayings' to try to refute the accusations that he was childishly unjust and vituperative. These he slipped under her door:

1. As long as the Resident Aliens here persist in harrying & embarrassing my friends with detrimental gossip about me, it seems hardly le mot juste to call my simple precautions for defense 'vindictive'.

4. Disliking connection with a sectarian bigot of this character, I prohibited him from naming me in his book, then about to be printed. He was afraid to read my letter. (May 1909)

5. [Demain-]Cooke, intervening without my knowledge or consent, reported that Ragg accused me of not daring to return to England on account of being wanted there by the police. By means of a post-card I obtained Ragg's denial of this calumny. (June. 1909)

8. I made Ragg apologize for his wife's howls, & for the harm which he had done me. (Oct. 1909.) He begged that correspondence might cease. I consented. (I wrote on behalf of his former gondogliere Vincenzo when I found him in need. (Nov. 1909) Ragg did not reply to me: he knew the boy's address, & I did not.)

18. So, as people permit themselves to take liberties with me, I, in my turn will take the liberty of extracting diversion from them, by providing occasions & sets of circumstances for the purpose of observing the fashion of their

staggerings among them. If their antics happen to be ugly, awkward, agonized, or elephantic—that is their affair: not mine. No one compels them to gambol. I merely hang up caps: only the very clumsiest of duffers would clap them on.

19. It is necessary to demonstrate that I will not let myself be vilified by anyone, & that I know how to defend my rights at any cost.

Mrs. van Someren answered with her 'Replies to "Nineteen Sayings",' summing up her opinions in her last paragraph.

1. When have the Resident Aliens harried or embarrassed your friends with 'detrimental gossip' about you? I admit I was at a loss to defend you when I was told you were writing annoying letters to one of my friends and when I heard that you were slanging (you know what I mean) the Raggs who ... tried to help you I admitted that I believed that you had a vindictive and unforgiving disposition adding that you were quite sincere in thinking that the Raggs had injured you.

4. Can you not give him at least credit—if not gratitude— for the good intention? (5)

18. Is this worth while? (19)

~~Dear~~ Mr Rolfe, (I scratch out the 'dear' for fear it should offend you!), Don't you think your ideal of friendship is an impossible one? (20) You won't 'be friends' unless the other persons possess the unfailing wisdom to understand the peculiarities of your temperament—even to the divination to foresee what you would or wouldn't like under all circumstances. I think you expect too much and you should consider the motives and less the mistaken expression of your friends. These grievances you have explained to me are, *I* think, forgivable and forgetable. You would be happier if you forgot them. (21) You may not like my plain speaking, (22) but it is my way, and I must be I, as you are you. I said last night you didn't care for friendship sympathy affection whatever you call it, when it was 'pitched' at you and I being angered at your reply to my impulsive speech replied angrily, which I regret.

(24) I shall be less impulsive in future!

Rolfe could not let anyone have the last word. He numbered points on her "Replies" and commented on them:

5. No. Gratitude is paralysis (Victor Hugo.)
19. Yes: it is the one secular thing which helps me from going raving mad.
20. I deny it utterly. I claim nothing of which I am not prepared to give back double.
21. I agree. And the best way of forgetting a thing is to write it down. That is why I am slaving at The Desire & Pursuit of the Whole. It's all there.
22. I think it's the most friendly thing of you.
24. Don't laugh at me ... I should welcome an approach: but not as a favour, & not as a farce.
   Sorry.
   Pray ponder these things.

The indomitable spirit within Rolfe would accept neither total defeat nor any degree of detention. A galvanizing force perpetually propelled his day-to-day existence. In the face of all adversity Rolfe projected an enviable zest for life. Yet, the longer he lived, the more narrow the world became. His daily world extended hardly beyond the reach of his crab's claws, a world perhaps as imaginary as his secondary one of pen and paper. Only a line, the thickness of a single stroke of the pen, divided Frederick Rolfe from Nicholas Crabbe. His earthly being composed his letters. The artist of another age, a poet of form and colour, took over for the pages of his books. He was blessed by a personal muse with a talent for description and a genius for timelessness. Crabbe and Zilda and their boat glide over the waters of Venice for all time.

The Desire and Pursuit of the Whole is the last of his autobiographical trilogy. *Hadrian the Seventh* unfolds the story of his Roman Catholic career for 1886 to 1902. *Nicholas Crabbe* brings him to London for the start of his literary life at the turn of the century. His first year in Venice is depicted in *The Desire and Pursuit*. *Hadrian* is populated with the people in his former life, drawn with caustic characterization. *Nicholas Crabbe* is a novel of one man's disappointment. The people who deny themselves the opportunity even to consider him as another human being are drawn in a dim light. They include the professional and the friend. The Nicholas Crabbe of the Venetian book has humour and buoyancy, is hardened by his reverses and displays an understanding tenderness unlike his former selves in other stories. In a letter to Ragg, Rolfe nakedly expressed his own growth and his views of others:

Of course I must suffer hideously. That does not disturb my equanimity. Pleasure is always with the pain of winning it. To attain any sort of human knowledge (which means Power) it is necessary to pass through all kind of close-packed horrors, treacheries, battles, insults, in darkness & doubt, & without certainty as to whether the road leads upward or into some hopeless cul-de-sac through which one must dynamically force a way. I am well aware of this. I also think it quite worth while. Do you understand, dear chief object of my scrutiny? I tear my hands, I tear my heart & soul to catch & pin you on my cork that I may learn you. But I only want to dissect you, to differentiate your characteristics as specimens.

During the course of writing his Venetian novel, Rolfe naturally spoke of it to Mrs. van Someren, who was anxious to read it. In contrast to his behaviour in the days of the Borgia book and the Toto stories, Rolfe now was secretive about his story. But her persistent persuasions finally caused him reluctantly to part with the manuscript. The tale was not complete, but he permitted her to read what he had written so far—on one condition. He asked her not to tell her husband about it. Her anticipated delight soon turned to horror. Once the story had opened, she found it to be a satire on modern Venice, with her friends bitterly exposed. Breaking her vow, she showed the story to her husband. Together they confronted the author. Either he deleted or made changes in the characters in the novel they knew as real people, he was told, or he would have to leave their house. This ultimatum was delivered on the night of

4 March 1910. For Rolfe there was no alternative. He left Mocenigo-Corner the next morning.

The story of the novel covers the period of time between Rolfe's entry into Venice and his last escapade before moving into the van Someren house. Yet a portion of his life with the doctor and his family may have been injected into the atmosphere of the book, and Mrs. van Someren may have been translated into the form of Zilda. Nothing about the girl in the book compares with the woman Rolfe knew. Yet her kindness towards him may have been the tenderness transferred from Crabbe to Zilda in the story. It is true that Ermenegildo Vianello was named Falier in August 1908, but by Rolfe or by Dawkins? When Rolfe later used the Vianello-Falier name for the young girl in his book, he traced Zilda Falier's ancestry back to three Venetian doges. Whatever inspired this, of course, remains Rolfe's secret. Yet he was staying at Mocenigo-Corner, just one of the many places in Venice's history. Almost a hundred years before Byron had stayed at Palazzo Mocenigo, working on the Fourth Canto of his *Childe Harold*, his bohemian establishment presided over rather inefficiently by his English valet, 'the learned Fletcher', who hated foreign countries. When the Horace Fletchers first arrived in the 1890s, the host of Palazzo Mocenigo was the lineal descent of nine doges. And the Venetian essay, 'Daughter of a Doge'—the basis of Chapter IV of *The Desire and Pursuit*—was written in September 1909 at Mocenigo-Corner. Rolfe admired Dr. van Someren and deeply appreciated the gentleness of his wife. He was 'too cantankerous' to express himself openly, she once said. But he did ask the doctor to be the book's dedicatee. And the solacing nature of Ivy van Someren may have been carefully and tenderly preserved in the pages of Rolfe's book—in the person of Zilda, Daughter of the Doges.

13

When Rolfe had found a place of rest, a place to work, with the van Somerens, he began to write a novel and a series of letters. These went to an Englishman who had recently visited Venice, and their very existence and details of their subject matter later branded him a social outcast of the lowest order. A. E. Housman reported to his publisher, Grant Richards, after he had read them. He had 'been more amused with things written in urinals'. A. J. A. Symons comments that they are 'letters that Aretino might have written at Casanova's dictation'. Pamela Hansford Johnson, however, does not think 'the Venice letters can be written off as easily as some would think—neither for good nor ill. For there really is something splendid, almost mythological, about their ramping sexuality; it was so extremely wholehearted, as everything about him was. If one must read this kind of thing, Rolfe is incomparably better at it than Henry Miller. And there are a few passages of descriptive splendour as fine as anything in *The Desire and Pursuit of the Whole*, where the physical beauty of Venice is expressed as no one else ever did it, before Rolfe or after him.'

The letters first came to general attention with Symons' *Quest for Corvo*. At the outset of his quest, he first read *Hadrian* and, secondly, these letters. From the highest praise of the first, he sees in the second 'an unwitting account, step by step, of the destruction of a soul' and adds that 'they give an account, in language that omitted nothing, of the criminal delights that waited for the ignoble sensualist to whom they were addressed .... Only lack of money, it appeared, prevented the writer from enjoying an existence compared with which Nero's was innocent, praiseworthy and unexciting .... What shocked me about these letters was not the confession they made of perverse sexual indulgence: ... but that a man of education, ideas, something near genius, should have enjoyed without remorse the destruction of the innocence of youth ....'

For years the general public's only knowledge of the Venice Letters was from Symons' book. Critics and essayists deftly referred to them, in relation to the darker side of Rolfe's character, speaking to an audience who had never seen or read them. The letters themselves and the tale they told had to be accepted by those who were ignorant of their content. The critics spoke for the letters, whether they had read them or not, even adding at times bits of their own imagination. A few people heard of the letters in 1926, when Christopher Millard issued a book catalogue and offered them for sale. Devoting four pages to them, under the heading 'The Raven and the Fox', he quoted from or described each of the twenty-five letters, post cards or telegrams. Pirated typescripts of them were sold for some years, each with intentional errors to add to 'the amazing scenes of debauchery described in some of the letters'. It was not until 1964 that an edited version of sixteen of them appeared in *Art and Literature/5*.

The two letters which no doubt made Symons' hair rise were those of 28 November 1909 and 20-25-27 January 1910 (a letter 'done in bits'). The first of these began with 'another smack in the face'. On the day after his last letter to the English correspondent, Rolfe went round to the government pawn shop to pay the interest on and re-pawn his 'silver curiosities (antique rings, seals, chains and a massive cross)'. They had just been sold to a jeweller and Rolfe, discovering who this was, then pursued his goods.

After about an hour's quarrelling he let me pawn them privately with him at double rates [and] I was frightfully upset: but what could I do? From there I went off to the Quay of San Basegio on the Zattere to see the Knight of the Round Table. It was just getting dusk and I was just in time to see his lissome muscular figure come dancing down the long plank from the ship with his last sack of dried lily flowers silhouetted against the sunset. As I passed, I said, Do me the pleasure to come and drink a little beaker of wine. With the greatest possible respect to your valourous face, he answered passing on. When he had delivered his load in the warehouse, he came out and joined me. While he was working he had on a pair of thin flannel trousers tightly tucked into his socks, canvas slippers, and a thin sleeveless shirt open from neck to navel. Over this, his day's work done, he wore a voluminous cloak of some thick stuff and a broad brimmed hat. He flung one end of his cloak over his shoulder like a toga. I describe his attire thus particularly, for reasons which will appear later on. Take me, I said, to a quiet wine shop where we can have much private conversation. We went through a few back alleys to a little quay in a blind canal off the Rio Malcontent where there was a very decent wine shop kept by an apparent somnambulist. I called for a litre of New Red (very fresh and heady) at 6d. We sat at the back of the shop among the barrels, our two chairs being together on one side of the only table there. The counter with its sleepy proprietor was between us and the door; and no one was present. I asked him to tell me about the round table: and took care that he drank two glasses to my one. Of course I fed him with cigarettes. He said that there was formerly a house of round tables in the city in that house on the Fondamenta Osmarin: but, owing to the fear which struck all Italy last year, when Austria seized Herzegovina and suddenly placed 80,000 men on the frontier where Italy has only 6,000 ... then the Venetians took a hatred of all Germans and went and smashed the windows calling the boys and men there 'Eulenbergs'. Wherefore the committee (comitato) of the club, for it was a private club of Signiore of the very gravest respectibility, moved the club to a house which they purchased at Padova about an hour and a half by steamer and train. He said that the club used to be open day and night; and ten boys were there always ready for use. The fee was 7 fr. payment for the room and what you pleased to the boy but you had to pay the latter in the presence of the steward and never more than 5 fr. even though you stayed all day and all night, i.e. 5 fr. and 7 fr. for 12 hours.

Besides the staff, any boy could bring a Signiore. And many did, chiefly school-boys at some of the public or technical schools who liked to make a little pocket-money. But now, unfortunately these and other Venetian boys are out of employment; for at Padova there is a great university with about 1300 students of all ages besides many schools; and students were generally in want of money. However, some of the Venetian unemployed occasionally have the luck to find an employer; in which case they make a little journey to Padova together, generally from Saturday to Monday, and derive mutual satisfaction from a Sabbath's concubinage .... He himself started at 13 or thereabouts in this way. One of his cousins being left an orphan suddenly came to live in his house and sleep in his bed. The cousin was 14 and the bed being narrow there was a certain mixture which pleased both. And suddenly both spat together. (You'd have shrieked to see his great black eyes and his big white teeth and his rosy young lily-fragrant face simply burst out laughing). This being very diverting they hugged and hugged belly to belly and did it again. So for many nights. Then a whore ate 80 francs of his older brother aet. 20 and gave him a disease, very disgraceful and perturbing to the family. Whereat, he and his cousin congratulated themselves on knowing a safer pleasure, and vowed to touch no whores. In a little while his cousin (they both were occasional gondoliers as I had expected) heard of the Osmarin. A patron took him there. Amadeo Amadei, rather bucked, also went and asked for a job. They said 'Bring a Signiore.' So he went and prayed to the Black Madonna of Spain at San Francesco della Vigna and she sent him a Count. Then he began. Many Counts and Princes and illustrious Signiore had he served there having much strength and ingenuity in finding ways to give pleasure, all of which pleased him too as well as filling his pocket. He found his patrons in this way. His first, the Count, had spoken to him on the Giardinetto where he was by chance lounging one morning, being out of work, and his shirt being open as usual because he was appasionated for the air, the Count had stroked his breast while saying that he was a fine boy. To whom he said that he was as God made him and preferred to be naked. Upon which the Count took him to the Osmarine for the day. Thereafter, he always went with his breast bare, even in the Piazza, and soon Signiore walked after him, to whom he nodded in the first discreet corner and so he gained patrons. But, since the Club was moved to Padova, it was difficult for an honest lad—he is 16½—to find a way of employing his nights. During the day he works as a stevedore along Zattere or in the harbour of Marittima, earning 3.50 a day generally of which he has to give 3 fr. to his father, also a stevedore and earning the same .... Naturally he wants to earn money for himself. He assured me that he knew incredible tricks for amusing his patrons. First, Sior, see my person, he said. And the vivacious creature did all which follows in about 30 seconds of time. Not more. I have said that we were sitting side by side of the little table. Moving, every inch of him, as swiftly and smoothly as a cat, he stood up, casting a quick glance into the shop to make sure that no one noticed. Only the sleepy proprietor slept there. He rolled his coat into a pillow and put it on my end of the table, ripped down his trousers, stripped them down to his feet, and sat bare bottomed on the other end. He turned his shirt up right over his head holding it in one hand, opened his arms wide and lay back along the little table with his shoulders on the pillow (so that his breast and belly and thighs formed one slightly slanting lane broken by the arch of the ribs, as is the case with flat distention) and his beautiful throat and his rosy laughing face strained backward while his widely open arms were an invitation. He was just one brilliant rosy series of muscles, smooth as satin, breasts and belly and groin and closely folded thighs with (in the midst of the black blossom of exuberant robustitude) a yard like a rose-tipped lance. And—the fragrance of his healthy youth and of the lily flower's dust was intoxicating. He crossed his ankles, ground his thighs together with a gently rippling motion, writhed his groin and hips once or twice and stiffened into the most inviting mass of fresh meat conceivable, laughing in my face as he made his offering of living flesh. And the next instant he was up, his trousers buttoned, his shirt tucked in and his cloak folded around him. The litre of wine was gone. I called for another. Sior, he said, half a litre this time with permission. So we made it half. Would I not like to take him to Padova from Saturday till Monday? Indeed I would. Nothing better. But because I see that you, my Amadeo (i.e. Love God, quite a Puritan name) are a most discreet youth as well as a very capable one, I shall tell you a secret: for, in fact, you shall know that I am no longer a rich English but a poor, having been ruined by certain traitors and obliged to deny myself luxuries. To hear that gave him affliction and much dolour. But he wished to say that he was all and entirely at my disposal simply for affection; because, feeling sure that he had the ability to provide me with an infinity of diversions, each different and far more exciting than its predecessor, he asked me as a favour, as a very great favour, that I should afterwards recommend him to nobles who were my friends. And, without stopping, he went on to describe his little games .... Sior, I pray you to try me. Only for affection (pro affetto) let me make you know what I can do. I said I couldn't afford it. Would I not then let him come to my place. Any evening after five until six in the morning there; it was not convenient. Did he know of any place where we could go for an hour or so? It grieved him, but, No, not now. He had a patron, an artist, in Calle something on Zattere, also an English, who at 3.50 a day painted him naked on Wednesdays and used him for diversion then .... If I would go to Padova, he would pay his own fare. No. No. I was sorry. I was in despair. I would let him know when I could and then I most certainly would. Have some more wine. A thousand thanks. So we came away. He says that Peter and Zildo love each other and do everything to each other but to no one else, though he and Peter once had a whole summer night together on the lagoon in P.'s gondola. P. also is in much request among women but cannot spit more than twice a night. Whereas Amadeo has done it 8 times and vows that he could do 12 with a hot patron! Comments please.

'This letter is going to be done in bits,' Rolfe began on 20

January 1910. 'What amazes me is that, though you know so little of me,' he spoke to the man in England, *'you do believe what I say, instead of discounting it or pretending to* MAKE ALLOWANCES AS EVERYONE ELSE DOES. Of course this makes it possible and even delightful for me to treat you with perfect confidence and to give you absolute accuracy: whereas to all the rest I naturally answer fools according to their folly, and omit to cast my pearls before animals which prefer acorns.' The letter started with 'a budget of news':

(1) about Zozzi and Fausto: (2) about a Row between Piero and Zildo: (3) about a league against Piero by Carlo and Zildo: (4) and how the two last went to the play at your expense and wish to thank you for it. (1) Yesterday I had surprise visit from Zozzi and Fausto. Zozzi is 'Giorgio' the Greek. They came to present their respects to me at the beginning of the year (fairly late) and to ask whether I could do anything for poor Fausto. He has been sacked from the Bucintoro (where I don't dare to go till I pay my arrears) for the winter and wants a job.... Fausto looks haggard and miserable. His face is hideous though his figure is admirable. I'm not by any means keen on him, though I can't help feeling ragingly wretched at not being able to help him. Thanks to you I gave him a small tip and a cigarette and said I'd remember him if I heard of a job. *Oh for a little place only a little place of my own.* One could always squeeze in an extra, like this, at a pinch now and then. Impotence to help others, poor devils, is damnable. But Zozzi—Zozzi, my boy, is simply splendid. He grows on one.... He's a slight little fellow of 17, *steered the Bucintoro eight to victory at the Olympic Games at Athens two years ago,* and speaks English with the most delightful hesitation.... (2) Piero and Zildo have quarrelled and parted. For more than a year now they have been lovers, working all day in Zildo's father's firewood business. Now Piero has no end of a tale about Zildo's infidelity! I'm inclined to fancy that Zildo has got to know of Piero's very occasional lapses towards the Fondamento Osmarin, and has made the single experiment of going there too, on the sly. Zildo is very grave, so sweetly modest, that

he would be certain to make the first experiment all alone and try to keep it secret. But he is so huge, so bursting with young vigour, that I suppose he simply had to break out in a fresh place somewhere. He himself admits nothing.... Piero is almost incoherent with fury. Zildo, according to him, is a traitor and an infidel, black, and indeed almost Turkish! Beyond that, he gave me no details. And one only has the fact that he, Peter, is out of a job, pinched and wan with want of food, bunched up and shivering with cold, hanging miserably about on the Zattere in want of work. *Oh, my dear, my dear, if only I had a little place of my own*—what's enough for one is enough for two. If I had it, and Piero, I'd pick his brains and write such a book as never yet sold in Paris at 25 francs a copy, illustrated, oh yes, illustrated. *The part I don't quite like is that Zildo's father has given Piero's living to Carlo and that Carlo and Zildo are what Zildo and Piero were* till a fortnight ago.... I don't quite approve of it. C. always had a living, a poor bare one, it's true, at his father's traghetto.... But the unfortunate Piero is the eldest of about a dozen, and his father can't possibly help him ... and besides this I know that [Carlo] has in him the seeds of a born traitor who is congenitally incapable of being faithful to anyone for long.

(Here I go again XXV Jan....)

I had a word with Carlo that day XX Jan, when I met them on the Fondamenta. Zildo left us together while he carried a load of logs into a house up an alley leaving Carlo to mind the boat. 'How do you like sleeping with Zildo?' says I abruptly. 'Sior, a molto pesante—*Sir he is very weighty* and ravages me in his pleasure for an hour, suffocating me.' 'And you?' 'Twenty, thirty, forty thrusts through the sweet mountains and then goodnight in his arms.' Zildo came back and both their eyes glittered like blazes. The simple little devils that they are! And now I've got some real news for you. I had poor dear Piero all to myself yesterday morning on the Fondamenta Nuova. I was snatching a walk and met him on his daily hopeless tramp for work. (Lord how my heart does bleed for him.) I gave him five francs *from you* and took him to a trattoria and filled him with polenta and wine. Then I picked his brains for a good hour; and found out everything. It's frightfully funny—even delicious. His word for Zildo, Zildo's conduct, manners, thoughts, words and works is 'butto' —*ugly*. Nothing worse than that. But UGLY!! ...

XXVII Jan. Now I'm going to make you sit up. First of all I see that I've got this letter rather mixed, so I will finish it off as I began it, with number 4. I told you that I had tipped Zildo and Carlo in your name. Two days after they wrote hideous picture postcards saying that they had been to see Cavalleria and Pagliacci at the Rossini Theatre and thanked you for the pleasure of your gracious gentility. Very well. That ends that. Now about yesterday. It appeared to me that the time was come *to break out of all caution and prudence. So I did, as thoroughly as thoroughly as you please.* Peter met me as arranged on Fondamenta Nuova. I explained to him exactly how I stood as to money, and I offered to give him all I had left of yours for his needs or else to take him for a day's pleasure. If you could have seen how he beamed on me! He instantly chose the last. 'My pleasure is to be with my Paron' he said. Fancy a great big boy of seventeen being as sweet as that.... So we took the steamer to Burano where we lunched on beefsteak and cheese and wine not at the inn you went to but another up the street. Lord how we wolfed. It was a fiendish day—snow all night and the snow at Burano a good yard deep and still snowing.

[After lunch] Piero and I went upstairs. I never saw anyone strip out of his clothes as he did—like a white flash— he must have unlaced his boots and undone all his buttons on the way up. Then he turned to me. He was scarlet all over, blushing with delight, his eyes glittered and his fingers twitched over my clothes with eagerness. As for his rod—Lawks! As I came out of my guernsey he flung himself back on the bed, across the bed as he knows I like it, throat up, ankles crossed, thighs together and body expectant.

The clutch of us both was amazing. I never knew that I loved and was loved so passionately with so much of me by so much of another. We simply raced together. Not a speck of us did

312

not play its part. And the end came simultaneously. Long
abstinence had lost us self-control. He couldn't simply couldn't
wait his turn, and we clung together panting and gushing
torrents—torrents. Then we laughed and kissed, rolled over
and cleaned up and got into bed to sleep, embraced. His breath
was delicious. He pressed his beautiful breast and belly to
mine and our arms and legs entwined together. So we took a
nap.... We took the 5.30 steamer to return to Venice. On
the way he was most affecting. What a lover that boy is. He
said that Zildo was nothing in comparison to me, that of all
the pleasure he has taken, nothing has ever equalled this
afternoon. As for girls, let Zildo and Carlo take evils with
them. They were 'ugly' and never had he believed that it could
be so good as it was. Would I command him to come to my
place? No, that was impossible: when I was able to take a
little apartment of my own, he should come and live with me.
When? I did not know. Pray, Sior, let it be soon. I asked
whether he would serve you if you came here. He blushed. 'I
am the servant of the Paron and will be obedient always; but
Sior, I pray to sleep sometimes in your arms.' His word for
the action is 'un-lock'. He said that my key unlocked his
most easily; if I wished him to try your key he would do his
very best most willingly. But would I teach him to speak
English as that he might surpass that ugly Carlo.... When
we parted, I gave him the last 2 francs remaining to me and
promised to write to you at once.... God knows what is going
to happen to me.... I still stick on here. But I can't possibly
move for the better on my own account in any way, nor do
any new work, nor finish the old as things are. Don't think me
impatient. I know you're doing your very best and leaving no
stone unturned for me and I'm quite content to leave it at
that. Of course I'm always grateful, that you know. But you
just wait and see how grateful I can be, tangibly, when once
I'm free to make use of my powers. I think I shall surprise
even you.
N.B. *I really think I'd risk starting on my own with £50 if that
could be got in the meantime and the £200 and a weekly
allowance a little later.* I fancy it would be safe. Anyway,

though my only hesitation is on account of seeming too sanguine, *I do most earnestly yearn to finish off this damned book and float it* and get on with a new one.... Do write oftener.

Any reader of *The Quest for Corvo* was obliged to accept the events recorded in these letters as the indelible truth. Even Mrs. van Someren had to believe their damaging imputations about her guest of 1909-10. When she wrote about 'Baron Corvo's Quarrels' in 1947, it was in the light of what she had read in *The Quest for Corvo* that she said that 'some sides of [Rolfe's character] were carefully hidden from me.'

Vincent O'Sullivan read *The Quest for Corvo* and wrote that Symons 'offers at the outset a darkling version of a letter said to have been sent by his hero to a "sensualist of London" which seems to be a sort of "Guide to the Pleasures of Venice" (110th edition). But who knows what Rolfe had in mind? Perhaps he meant, when he offered to shew the town, to shame and reform the Sensualist of London, even as Carlyle, performing a similar office for Emerson, shouted at each emergence from a disorderly house: "Man, de ye believe in hell the noo?" What remains in the property-room for the make-up of Rolfe as a scoundrel has not even the value of "Chatter about Harriet". Nothing but variations on the entanglements about money which have beset the penniless since money appeared in the world.

  See now what woes the scholar's life assail,
  Pride, envy, want, the patron and the gaol.'

Between the two opposing views adopted by Mrs. van Someren and O'Sullivan can be placed the words of a person uninterested in the story of Rolfe. In some way they conjure up a picture of the Englishman in Venice nearing his fiftieth birthday. Lytton Strachey's pen portrays the Great Elizabeth, but the description also applies to the lesser subject of the Realm: 'Though, at the centre of her being, desire had turned to repulsion, it had not vanished altogether; on the contrary, the compensating forces of nature had redoubled its vigour elsewhere. Though the precious citadel itself was never to be violated, there were surrounding territories, there were outworks and bastions over which exciting battles might be fought, and which might even, at moments, be allowed to fall into the bold hands of an assailant. Inevitably, strange rumours flew.'

Rolfe's account of Amadeo Amadei's action in the one letter to Fox had already, years earlier, been used in a milder form. In *The Yellow Book*, October 1896, 'About One Way in Which Christians Love One Another' tells a Toto story. The Italian youth says of himself that ' "during the night, after my father had seen me go to bed, I rose, and I left my shirt in the porch ... and wandered about quite naked and happy and free"—(here he tossed his arms, and threw up his legs, and wriggled all over in an undescribable manner) ....'

When his book was published in 1934, Symons received a number of critical letters from his own friends and from people who had known Rolfe. On 11 February 1934 Lord Alfred Douglas wrote to Symons to call *The Quest for Corvo* 'a brilliant book,' but 'it makes rather painful reading though. One gravitates between sympathy for Rolfe and disgust for him.' Douglas then mentioned in his letter people whom he knew and who appear in the book: Lane ('a mean little brute'), Richards ('a decent fellow, but ... hopeless as a publisher'), Benson ('a great friend of mine [who] treated Rolfe *shamefully*'), Dr. van Someren ('a charming fellow'), 'that delightful chap Horatio Brown,' Millard ('a wholesale corrupter of youth'). He then proceeded, 'I think you should have produced some sort of concrete evidence of Rolfe's homosexuality. I mean it does not emerge in your book as a factor of his life. We just have your word for it, and that is all.'

But every legend is based on facts and what were those behind the Venice Letters?

In September 1909 John Nicholson wrote to Rolfe. A friend of his was planning a short Venetian holiday, stopping to see Horatio Brown. The Scotsman received a letter from Rolfe, saying that 'Nicholson tells me that Mr Masson Fox is about to visit Venice, & expresses a hope that I will be kind to him.' Apprehension was stirred within Rolfe. He was not certain how he stood in Brown's favour and, therefore, in what light he would be described. To Nicholson he wrote that 'if your Masson Fox approaches me with a proper introduction, prepared to trust me as an equal (at least) & not to look at me with that awful expression of face which means "Now, I do hope, to God, that you're not going to ask me to do anything for you," I will do the best for him which my circumstances permit. Or, if he cares to employ me as his barcariol, I know my place & my job thoroughly & can & will serve him faithfully & well. ... But I must regret to tell you that you presume too much in suggesting to me that you "cannot exploit" Mr M. F. "for gain". ... My own position is just this: Having no friends, I should welcome the opportunity of making one. But I refuse to lay myself open to suspicion of interested motives, *now that you have mentioned them*. Hence, I hold aloof, having made the foregoing statement, which you can shew to Mr M. F.; & you & he can act precisely as you please.'

In 1909 Masson Fox was a person new to Rolfe. He had never heard his name before, although Fox had a circle of friends including Nicholson, Brown, Tuke, Kains-Jackson and the late Gleeson White. Born into a Quaker family at Falmouth, Fox lived there all of his life, serving on the board of a firm of shipping agents and in the family timber firm. For several years he was the Russian and Swedish Vice-Consul in Falmouth. Community affairs, gardening and chess filled out his outward activity. Leading a quiet, business-like life left little to be remembered about him. But, unknown to Falmouth society, he managed to lead a very private life. With close, and respected, friends he could exchange verbal thoughts. To what extent he may have participated in the actual enjoyment of his perverse desires is a question no longer answerable. He possessed a strong character. At one time he permitted himself to be involved in a law suit resulting from attempted blackmail. A woman claimed that Fox had seduced her son. The outcome of the case was in his favour, but the publicity damaged him in society.

Who were the people Fox knew, names familiar to Rolfe?

Henry Tuke. Noted for his paintings of nude boys, he also spent a great deal of his time at Falmouth. When not painting, he was busy with his yacht, sailing or preparing for races. As an artist, he and his work were admired. He had known the late John Addington Symonds. One of the letters from Venice to

Fox was almost entirely about Tuke. 'One thing this world wants is some Tuke pictures of the Venetian lagoon and some Tuke pictures of mediaeval *gondolieri* poised on *poppe* in Venetian canals,' said Rolfe. 'But "Tuke has all he wants at Falmouth." Hum! Arnold of Rugby held that no man ought to be a schoolmaster longer than 15 years at a stretch. And I fancy that the principle of that doctrine may apply to painters.... Tuke has made himself an immortal name with the flesh and sun and sea of Falmouth. He cannot better it; and by persistence he may very likely worsen it.... I suggest Venice.'

Nicholson. Throughout his life he had homosexual tendencies, but he enjoyed a proper and respected career as a schoolmaster. He was devoted to his boys. He had personal favourites, all strappingly healthy specimens, and he kept a photographic record of their growth. He was liked by all of his pupils and was welcome by their parents into their homes at any time. The only escape from his frustated emotions was in writing. The titles of his collected verse and novels included *A Chaplet of Southernwood*, *A Garland of Ladslove* and *The Romance of a Choir-boy*, surprising titles to come out of the Victorian era and to be associated with a schoolmaster. The poems were all too obvious about his feelings towards the boys. Yet his Wesleyan upbringing caused him to be shocked when these same baser facts of life in other people were made apparent to him.

Brown. As a sympathetic friend of John Addington Symonds, he lived in Venice with his mother. Among the books he authored, only one contained any homosexual thoughts. A volume of verse called *Drift*, it was printed by Grant Richards in 1900.

Kains-Jackson. He approached the subject of the beauty to be found in the form of a boy in an artistic and intellectual vein. He believed in the freedom to worship the boy, as found in the literature, art and history of Greece and Rome. But he disapproved of any physical extension beyond the aesthetic. Using the name Philip Castle, he wrote an essay, 'The New Chivalry', expressing his opinions as to the proper understanding of worship-love for youth, an essay written in the guarded language of 1894.

Three years before Rolfe first heard of Fox, Nicholson had written a poem about him, a poem called 'Sour Grapes':

Look how this sunlit tract of sandy shore,— ...
What unseen realms this journey holds in store!
    From yon hill-top what new discovery! ...
    And all behind an envious fence, ah me,
That frowning says, *Thus far, and then no more!*

Fit setting such for unripe Boyhood's pose!
    In this fair picture of Love's fortunate hour
    Youth calls on Passion with a wondrous power;
But ere you come where laughing lips unclose,
Mark the symbolic rod and shun its blows,—
    Poor fox, methinks again the grapes are sour!

Even earlier, by some ten years, Kains-Jackson voiced an opinion of Fox in poetry:

See Mass. On Fox. Your name should bid you go
The road to Rome, make ending orthodox
And certainly like Peter you show
Yourself an authority on cocks.
    See Masson Fox?

Rolfe possessed neither a reformer's nor a criminal's mind. O'Sullivan's suggestion that Rolfe may have wished 'to shame and reform the Sensualist of London' was not part of any plan. Neither did he see any case of blackmail. O'Sullivan was nearer the truth when he spoke about the letters and Rolfe's 'variations on the entanglements about money.' The only 'blackmailing' Rolfe did was to hint, as gravely as he dared, about his need for money. Disregarding Nicholson's warning about not being able to exploit Fox 'for gain', Rolfe showered him with begging letters. And, as always, they were most personally directed.

Of all the Venice Letters, only one spoke of a homosexual act in the first person. There is no other surviving evidence to confirm Rolfe's participation in any of the vices in 'the dark byways' of Venice. In no other letter to any person or in no part of a story or book is there anything to parallel the action on his part described in this one letter to Masson Fox. With no other concrete proof, therefore, this one Venice Letter can only be examined in the light of negative evidence.

The letter, then, is a confession. But how many confessions to the police each day are discarded as unreliable?

The Venice Letters should be read, firstly, in the light of their origin. They were written in a warm clime. Rolfe was no ordinary man or writer. He acclimatized himself to the periods, situations and environments around him, time and time again. In Venice he absorbed the Venetian nature, speaking and writing its dialect. One of the first accomplishments there was to learn to row a gondola. And he saw, and understood, the morals of the southern peasantry. In *Hubert's Arthur*, completed in Venice, he says: ' ... I nourish an extremely grave doubt to whether the Venetians are christians or some sort of sib to the filthy fanatics of the Albigeois. For the names of the Trinity which they exclusively adore are not those to which we christians are accustomed, being as follows, namely, first, Pajancha or Money, second, Pojenta which signifies Eating and Drinking Enormously, third, Amor which signifies Lechery, as anyone (unafflicted by deafness) may know who has walked for a single half-hour among articulate Venetians.'

The exchange of physical affection between youths has been an accepted and natural phenomenon since the days of Greek and Roman supremacy. The love of youth for youth was only a preamble to a later normal life of marriage and family. No doubt, to some this practice is a novelty, but one which dissipates itself in time. Rolfe was only relating to Fox the facts he heard around him in Venice. He thought nothing of their possible misinterpretation by Fox and he did not think that anyone else would see and read the letters. The persons who did read them in the 1920s and were shocked came from an entirely foreign background. Brought up in the staid England of Victorian or Edwardian times, they were the exact opposite of the boys in the letters. The behaviour of the peasant youths was distorted, not only by a northern climate, but by a northern puritanism based on a contrived notion of existence. The letters spoke of a natural reality. But they were read, in the 1920s, with the sense of a criminal reality in them. The members of London clubs and society who saw them still existed under the dread shadow of Oscar Wilde and Sir Roger Casement.

When first spoken about to the public, they were presented in strong language. Rolfe, even without money, was pictured as descending 'to depths from which he could hardly hope to rise'. He made a shocking portrait because he was 'willing for a price to traffic in his knowledge of the dark byways of that Italian city; that he could have pursued the paths of lust with such frenzied tenacity'. A belated pity was offered 'for behind the ugliness of their boasts and offers, these letters told a harrowing story of a man sliding desperately downhill, unable to pay for clothes, light or food; living like a rat in the bottom of an empty boat.'

During the composition of the letters Rolfe gave no evidence, not even in the letters themselves, that he enjoyed 'an existence compared with which Nero's was innocent, praiseworthy, and unexciting'. Not the letters themselves, but the interpretation of them have daubed the blackest blot on the Corvine legend. Rolfe's five years in Venice has been summed up too many times by essayists because of this single phase. Pamela Hansford Johnson even based a character in a novel on this episode of Rolfe's life. Shifting the scene from Venice to Bruges, she has Daniel Skipton procure the delights of perverse entertainment for visiting Englishmen in *The Unspeakable Skipton*.

When Rolfe did speak to Fox about 'the dark byways of that Italian city', he did so, in the letter of 28 November 1909, not with his knowledge but with Amadeo's knowledge told to him. This was merely repeated to Fox by Rolfe. As for the letters telling 'a harrowing story of a man sliding desperately downhill,' the author of this statement does not say whether he means it in a physical, moral or financial sense. If the latter, Rolfe had been sliding downhill ever since he left Christchurch in 1891. No matter how hard he tried in all these years, he hardly ever was able to pay for clothes and other necessities. Moreover, the author of the Venice Letters did not live 'like a rat in the bottom of an empty boat' while they were being composed. More than half of them were written from the van Somerens' Palazzo Mocenigo-Corner. With the exception of one post card, the remaining letters were written from the Belle Vue. Between the two, Rolfe spent a few nights walking the Lido, having no other place to stay.

In chronicling the letters, it is said that Rolfe, 'as despair deepened in the heart of the lost Englishman, [it] subdued all his persuasiveness to plead for five pounds. "For God's sake send me five pounds," concluded the concluding letter.' The last letter, of 21 August 1910, is a long, chatty one. Rolfe mentioned his personal relations with Benson, Pirie-Gordon, Barnard & Taylor, the British Consul in Venice and Barbieri. His position elsewhere would be just as hopeless. *'And besides,'* he added, *'I'm just as powerless in England, without friends or money, as I am here. More so, in fact.* So you see that, strategically speaking, my obvious duty is to say [to them all], "I feel it my duty to warn you that I am at the end of my endurance and quite tired out." And having said that, I stop writing and calmly go out to live in the open air—somewhere like that lonely part between the Excelsior and Malamocco.' The last paragraph read: 'So I say lend me five pounds. With that in my pocket, I fancy I can do the trick. ... If you can manage more, so much the better. The more I have the better and the sooner I can reach a successful conclusion. Do answer me at *once.* This is the "psychological moment".'

The surviving Venice Letters comprise a series of eighteen letters, five post cards, a manifesto and two telegrams. Although not dated, other than 'Tuesday', the first letter was written from the Palazzo Mocenigo-Corner probably in October, soon after Fox's return to England. Not knowing him before, Rolfe may have learned about his inclinations towards boys through a chance remark or even a discreet conversation on the part of the gentleman from Falmouth. In his letter to Nicholson, Rolfe made it plain that he would see Fox only because he was called upon to do so. After the meeting Rolfe no doubt saw the Englishman as a man of money and one to be cultivated. As in any small community, the word-of-mouth news spread around the canals that Fox was in Venice. But his stay was cut short. In the first letter, Rolfe told of a 'Corfiote Greek Jew' who came to offer his services, only to learn Fox had already left. The letter also contained the fact that the gondoliers Fox had been introduced to, in a perfectly polite and official way, had been given clothes with his money and what was left was divided between them to console them when 'you had been suddenly called to England'. Rolfe concluded: 'Do write often, and freely. I'll always answer and burn your letters. Do this with mine please.'

Now assuming that the timber merchant was safely back in Falmouth, unlikely to return to Venice for a long time, Rolfe felt free to associate with him through correspondence. In speaking of Piero, Ermenegildo and Carlo and 'what was wanted in the way of service', Rolfe revealed his position at the beginning of this episode. The three boys, he said, knew what was expected. 'So I suppose they understood the indications which you and [your American friend] Cockerton must have given,' he wrote, 'though I'm to say that I was quite unaware of anything definite.' This indicated that Rolfe had not been made a partner in Fox's schemes when he first arrived in Venice.

The next letter began with a question about doing 'something for me. The state of my wardrobe is appalling.... So I think a couple of dark blue woollen jerseys would be a boon,' to be sent and marked 'SAMPLES'. He continued with the stories told him by Piero and Carlo before he talked about a 'smack in the face'. His London literary agent had just failed in placing '£180 sterling's worth of Venetian essays and stories' and had returned them. He complained about his host being a pious crank and 'eating cranky food sauced with the most unctuous of rancid piety'. Dr. van Someren was 'in a bad way', he said, having 'no patients and ... living on God'. As for Fox's interests, he asked the man in England to 'remember that I will look out for places here, as often as I can shew myself decently in public. At present I can't.'

The letter of November 8th was almost entirely about his own affairs with solicitors, hoping a new firm would serve him better. He had written to Barnard & Taylor and to Pirie-Gordon about this on the previous day. A sweater from Fox had arrived, not marked 'SAMPLES'. Rolfe had to pay L2.65 'for the parcel which means no tobacco after Friday'. A fortnight before Rolfe had written to another correspondent about the poor financial status of Dr. van Someren and saying that the doctor was suffering 'for supporting me'. Yet on November 7th he gave the doctor 'a first charge or lien to the amount of One Hundred Guineas (£105)' on his new book, a proposition later turned down for other than financial reasons.

About this time Nicholson received from Rolfe 'a series he wrote me from Venice in 1909 ... so Rabelaisian and sexual-psychological' that the schoolmaster in England destroyed the manuscript. This piece of written perversity was serious on Rolfe's part, but not in the way Nicholson understood it. In a November letter to Fox, Rolfe answered affirmatively to the question whether or not he would like being sent a 'confession'. 'I want to see it particularly. I'll tell you why; and that will enable me also to explain my meaning about Nicholson. You must know that I know by heart all the books (ancient and modern) on the subject; and I always maintain that the modern ones are vulgar, cloying, inartistic, because they are written by amateurs. And I also said that I could write two books (certainly two) which would have a *rattling good story* in them, *told artistically with a vividness and a plain-spokeness hitherto unheard of.* Such books, privately published in Paris or Antwerp at £1 would sell like blazes. Well, talking like this to Nich, I wrote a specimen 10,000 words or so, giving it as my personal experiences; and sent the MS. to him for discussion. I thought that he ... would be able to give some unique criticisms.... Well: the result was startling. I'll give it in the order it occurred. (1) Nich wrote voluminously, shrieks of joy, and descriptions of his own experiences (written however in a style precisely like that of the storiettes pencilled up in the jakes at the Marble Arch) vulgar and commonplace beyond words, and shewing a total absence of the faculties of observing detail, of perceiving fine shades of difference, and so.... (5) N. said he couldn't keep my writing and even *was going to expunge it from his mind* because it made him feel more wicked than he had believed it possible for anyone to be—, and at the same time, the thing was so beautiful that he didn't dare to destroy it. ... (6) Naturally I sat still, roaring with laughter .... (11) ... I asked [ten weeks later] what had happened to my literary work, which he couldn't keep even in his mind, and daren't destroy, and yet hadn't the decency to return to me. (12) He had told Edward Carpenter about it—and—then—burned it!!! Well: so I say, in the absence of further explanations, a man who could behave with such duplicity and cant, and who could take such a damned liberty with a writer's MSS, is not only a hypocrite but a dangerous person. The unscrupulous way in which he stole my sonnet and printed it in his book years ago, was bad enough. I thought he had grown out of that dirty habit. But this theft of my MS. beats all. Comments please.'

In this one long letter to Fox, Rolfe claimed to know 'by heart all the books (ancient and modern) on the subject' of pornography. Discussing perverse literature in letters to Dawkins, Rolfe cited several authors. 'Poliziano's tommerotica about Giovanni and Giulio de' Medici his pupils (Leo X and Clement VII) ... are simply more meleagrose than Meleagros; and several other screaming specimens of abnormal Havelock Ellisism.' 'Well: the moment I have time I think I can see the way to do something quite as yellowed as [Jean Lombard's] *L'Agonie*, nothing like as nasty, (why do Frenchmen always describe croups and erections in minute detail?) and on the note really high tragedy. Did it ever strike you that the Common Scarecrow is the lineal descendant of the Garden God?' 'Somehow I don't like Petronius.... I find the Latin so exotic, the story so incoherent, the stuff so really dreadfully dirty. There is such a lot about corpulent matrons. I can't call it a book to pick up and read a bit of at odd moments. I have to whirl straight through it, always omitting the poetry of course .... The English [by Addison] is simply divine.'

At the same time Rolfe answered the destroyer of his manuscript. He wrote to the neurotic Nicholson, a victim of sexual frustration and now follower of spiritualism: 'That you trust in "Guides" & "Inner Lights", who do not teach you to detect the difference between literary sketches (which so move you that

324

you ask for their instant suspension) & a true confession of real actions, is somewhat singularly misplaced. . . . I am only amazed at my stupidity in imagining that my actual way of life was properly appreciated.'

One of the confessions made by Rolfe is true. His life was one long pose. But he was a poor actor. If he would have thought of doing so, he would have been an even poorer confidence man. Nearly all of his dealings with people was through correspondence. To obtain money, he first worked for it. By an unfortunate choice, his work never brought him enough. He then had to crudely ask for money, employing, at times, the medium of the begging letter. Rolfe's guise was 'as transparent and guileless as a child', and his letters, with their unceasing requests for aid, grew wearisome.

The prose Rolfe wrote for publication met with little attention from publishers or public in his day; and the prose of his letters, on the theme of needed money, added little more to his pocket. The scanty return from his work was supplemented only with stray alms from correspondents. 'Why is it that I have had so many friends in the past,' he asked Fox in one letter, 'and now have lost them all? The reason is simple. They got tired. They liked me; and they pitied my penury; and they gave me little teaspoonsful of help. But friendship is only possible among equals. There must not be any money mixed up with it. And, by and bye, you also will get tired and bored and annoyed by the continual groans which I'm forced to emit, howling for a strong hand once for all to come along and haul me out of this damned bog and set me on my feet.' This prophecy, reflected from the past, was again true. Even during the correspondence, Fox was not liberal with his money. And, in time, even his letters came to an end.

The Venice Letters, filled with literary descriptions, lack his usual humour. They are hardly more than begging letters. Through the merits of his writing talent, he offered his imagination for a fee. At first his requests received little answer. By November 28th he might have thought that a good impression might earn him something substantial. And so he wrote down Amadeo's account of the Round Tables. Amadeo and his tale were no doubt quite real. There is an encounter between Crabbe-Rolfe and a young gondolier of fifteen in *The Desire and Pursuit of the Whole*. Coming at this time in his life when he was working on the novel, the young Ghezzo tells Crabbe about his trips to a bordello and one of his friends who 'went when he was thirteen'. Nor was Fox the only person Rolfe wrote to on the 28th. A letter also went to Canon Ragg. Rolfe had 'met your late gondolier today in Campo Santangelo & he tells me that he has just finished his 3 months' military service (the portion of an only son) & is badly in want of a job. I said that I would let you know' and he asked Ragg to use his influence to help the boy.

The Amadeo letter to Fox resulted in a postal order, which Rolfe changed *'without signing it* and got 6.25 for it, i.e. 2½d. more than its face-value'—or about 5/- or $1.20 altogether—little reward for his efforts. In thanking Fox for this meagre showing of friendship, Rolfe offered him *'a first charge on my new book* ready in Feb., for two hundred sterling down and two pounds a week for six months'. He spoke of a recent cold and being treated by the doctor on 'pure barley water .... coffee and bread twice a day'. And he asked the letter's recipient to 'come to my rescue instantly. Here's Christmas close at hand. Is it to be my second in this miserable and hopeless impotence or the first of a new era?'

Fox did respond to this last appeal, but only because of the season. He sent a letter and several postal orders, which Rolfe shared with three boys. Explaining the source of the money to Piero, Rolfe wrote back to England: '"Ah," says P., "it goes well. That lord has a heart like his moustaches, of pure gold. May his soul sit on Mary Virgin's lap!"' His own Christmas, however, was not a happy event. He had never spent 'such an unchristian Christmas in my life. Never! Neither beef nor turkey nor plum-pudding nor mince-pie have passed my lips, and I ADORE them all.... That abominable Nicholson sent me a picture of a gondola (coals to Newcastle) and a verse out of Isaiah about affliction being for one's good. He has a talent for the inopportune which amounts to positive genius....'

For more than two months he had been sending letters to

Falmouth, but the timber merchant's wallet did not open in the direction of Venice. On January 6th Rolfe sent a post card saying 'Immediate need. Wire!' The reply was not the desired one and Rolfe answered with a tart note on Fox's niggardly generosity. 'You amuse me, you know, by the way you chuck it about.'

From his own drastic affairs, he quickly changed to the subject of 'the Confessions' offered by the Englishman. Fox possessed written 'confessions' by schoolboys and photographs of them. Rolfe did not care if these were 'poor. Of course they will be poor, because they are not written by a trained writer. But let me see them all the same. It's the FACTS which I want. Give me the facts, and the personal emotions, feelings and experiences, and I'll guarantee to put them in a readable shape.'

In another week's time he was beginning the letter to Fox which told of his own personal experience. He continuously spoke of picking people's brains, especially those of the young boys on the canals. The November letter with Amadeo's tale had been worthless in the terms of any monetary return. Fox reacted to the pleas from Venice in lire and not pounds. By January, Rolfe was in a desperate state. There was a possibility that the van Somerens would move. If so, this would mean another trek into the Venetian winter. With a forlorn sense of hopelessness Rolfe may have written the long January letter for two reasons. In his own 'confession', he may have wanted to show what he, as a writer, could produce; and it may have been written as a last effort silently to make a further application for financial aid.

What expectations had gone into this singular letter came to nothing. Rolfe had no answer from Falmouth and he himself did not write again until the first week in March. He then said that he had left the van Somerens.

In his correspondence with each person he knew, Rolfe drew on each man's personality to fill his letters. The subject matter of some of the Venice Letters was, of course, chosen to suit Fox's personal desires. And perhaps the lack of Rolfe's humour in the series reflects, not Rolfe, but the doleful nature of the Sensualist. As these letters were penned, Rolfe's novel of modern Venice was also being composed. In contrast, the work is filled with the wit that was natural to him.

Rolfe never fully ended his friendship with Pirie-Gordon. His letters to Wales became aggressive in tone because they lacked immediate and desired replies. But no abusive letter was ever sent out to Harry Luke. In trying to discover an answer to the Pirie-Gordon silence, he wrote to Luke in a friendly mood: 'Will you kindly supply me (or cause me to be supplied) with the proper Form Of Exciting (Or Of Nerving) a Knight Of the Most Splendid Order Of Sanctissima Sophia To Defend His Knightly Honour. The fact is that I am quite at a loss to know what to do next with C. H. C. Pirie Gordon. I have searched Roget's *Thesaurus* through & through for obloquious & exasperating epithets. I have mocked him, & made a song of him, & written a complete novel for publication in America. I have taunted him with treachery. I have given him of Fool, of Knave, of Liar, of Thief, of Peacock, & of Niddering, in due progression, to keep my hand in, privately & also publicly. I have even gone so far as to call him "Scotch," & "Judas". And he takes it all like the meekest of possums, like the most timid of Brer Rabbits. I can only conceive that the fault lies with me—in that I have not provided myself with the Regular Formula For Spurring A Knight (of the fore-named Order) To Do His Devoir. But for the moment, I can't think of anything else to do to make so large (but so loathly) a worm as C. H. C. Pirie Gordon turn correctly. Do help or at least instruct me.'

In any area, Rolfe was 'always seeking to find out my faults and weaknesses' in writing 'so that I may improve them.' In this letter to Luke, he wittily implored to be shown a proper, or better, method to assail Pirie-Gordon. How was he at fault? he asked himself and Luke in this letter written on 25 January 1910 —the same day he wrote to Fox a third of his long 'confession'.

Late in acquiring the mastership of his own ideas and convictions fully, Rolfe was nearly thirty before he conducted himself as an independent adult. And from that moment he was possessed by an attraction to beauty in art, in nature and in the human body. The Renaissance, clear air and the sea, and the boy were the simple requirements of his aesthetic life. His

328

approach to the human form was an innocent one. He admired paintings and sculptures of boys, from the viewpoint of an artist—from the viewpoint of a religious person seeing a picture of his near-naked Lord. In the innocent simplicity of his reasoning, Rolfe admonished the hypocritical moral attitudes of his day. Answering one of Professor Dawkins' letters, he had to admit that he 'never heard anything like what you tell me about the [present-day] Greek horror of nakedness. It's inconceivable. How in the name of—well—Hermes (on their stamps) do they dress in their blooming Olympic games. Aren't they open to conviction? It would be a fine thing to escort a caravan of beefy handsome animalian English fifth and sixth form boys through windy Lakedaimon some summer, in shorts and zephyrs, and let them bathe *in puris* and generally display themselves. How would your modern Spartans like that I wonder?' This he wrote to the professor who had ordered him to make anatomical photographs of the same boys named in his letters to Fox—the boys introduced to Rolfe by Dawkins.

In December he was glad that Fox liked 'my descriptions. Tell me, do they make you see, feel, and give you pleasure really? I particularly want to know: because writing is my trade, and I am always seeking to find my faults and weaknesses so that I may improve them. Writing's a poor sort of job: but I want to get mine as perfect as I can. And it's only perfect when I succeed in exciting my reader, carrying him out of himself and his world, into my world and the things which I am describing. ... I want [my reader to] see and smell and hear and taste and feel what I describe.' The beginning of this letter spoke of the L6.25 Fox had sent him. On another page he commented: 'I'm afraid I made rather a failure of the Amadeo incident.'

The letters end in August. After the long one in January, Rolfe asked for any possible financial consideration which could come from Falmouth. But he added nothing more about the boys. The letters, some at length, tell of his plight and his dreams. Living in a dark room at the Belle Vue, he worked on his books—past the day when he last heard from Masson Fox. The letters with their personally intended descriptions and the single 'confession' earned him no more than mere 'tips'.

In *The Desire and Pursuit of the Whole,* Crabbe proposes that Zilda dress and act the part of a boy. But this does not add necessarily to the detriment done to Rolfe's character by the Venice Letters. Zilda does act the boy in the story, but the reader is constantly reminded of the fact that 'he' is a girl. Again Rolfe has been taken out of context because of this literary invention. But it is not a new invention. The girl-boy character is not unique with Rolfe and no other author who used the theme has been accused of suspicious motives. In the novel Zilda 'was simply a splendid strapping boy—excepting for the single fact that she was not a boy, but a girl'. Her name derives from Ermenegildo Vianello, but she is not the young gondolier Rolfe first met in August 1908. The lithe young creature in the book is not the Zildo who was 'so huge'.

It is interesting to note a parallel in Rolfe's writing. In January he said to Fox, 'I never knew that I loved and was loved so passionately with so much of me by so much of another.' At the same time he was writing an episode in his novel, about the time when Zilda and Crabbe first recognize each other for what she and he are to the other:

So far, Nicholas had known himself for Nicholas. He was himself; and his body was his own habitation—his own. Other people's were theirs .... [Zildo] says that he made a certain discovery, on the topo, at the moment when Nicholas told him that he was absolutely alone in the world. For the rest, he was called Zildo; and that was all about it. And then, all of a sudden, on this iridescent morning of opals in January, when the lips of Zildo touched the hand of Nicholas, owner of lips and owner of hand experienced a single definite shock: an electric shiver tingled through their veins: hot blood went surging and romping through their hearts: a blast, as of rams' horns, sang in their ears and rang in their beings, and down went all sorts of separations. They were bewitched. They were startled beyond measure. Of course we others are well aware that this was merely the commonplace casting of the commonplace spell by their millions of dead ancestors recognizing (in these two) the possessors by inheritance of the multitudinous charm of all other own dead loves—that it was nothing more than the quickening in these separated entities of the dormant prenatal knowledge of homogeneity. At the moment of recognition, Zildo says that he felt only satisfaction. to him, something liable to appal him unless he was careful, ... But Nicholas only knew that something had happened something absolutely antecedent to any previous experiment of his.... He had nothing to hold on by. He was naked and unarmed to all the world. His citadel was open. Crab-like, he instantly shut himself up in his shell, throwing up ramparts and earthworks to conceal and protect his individuality .... He would not even permit himself to think of (much less to analyse) this latest phenomenon.

The most tender scene in any of Rolfe's stories appears in his Venetian novel. As Crabbe comes on to the pupparin at one point, 'Zildo puts away a very clean-looking roll of cleaning rag.' When he later decides to clean the balustrade he looks under the poop.

He pulled open the panel ... and put in his hand. The most suitable thing for wiping up the mess would be that roll half-wrapped in blue linen. The wrapper was loose, and fell off, leaving a roll of old blanket. How nice and dry, and how extremely clean, it was. As he was about to dip it in the water, something in its appearance arrested him : and he examined it more closely. It was a close roll, about ten inches long and three in diameter, curiously tied with thread at three inches from the top and again in the middle. In the top part were stuck two little black tacks—resembling eyes. Why, it was not unlike a rag-doll. Host! And the dainty bit of blue linen which had enshrouded it? He quickly went back to the cupboard. The other roll, there, was the one used for the bark .... the doll, had lain in a place by itself. He folded it in its shawl again; and put it reverently back, closing the panel.... And he must not pry again under the poop of his pupparin, where his servant kept private and sacred affairs Zildo's baby was cradled there.

Man may not meddle with Nature's law; she laughs and defies him. Motherhood cannot be kept from the mind of a maid.

The Venice Letters have a curious history. The London book dealer, Christopher Millard, had them as early as 1920. During the next few years he tried to sell them. They were read by a number of people before A. J. A. Symons finally bought them, selling them later to J. Maundy Gregory. *The Quest for Corvo* appeared one year before Masson Fox died.

By an odd twist of fate, (Sir) Shane Leslie saw the letters for the first time on the day his article, 'Frederick Baron Corvo', was published in 1923 '— a nice anticlimax! The invocation to Tuke to paint Venice was the only literary letter,' he noted in a letter to Millard. 'The rest seem the cries of a lost soul and lost he was unless the divine *misericord* is exceeding indulgent. The spasm of an attack on Benson is amusing.... The misery of the letters made me unhappy.... Poor Nicholson! really too hard on him—but Rolfe was the Holianated Englishman called diabolical in mediaeval proverbry.'

'Only lack of money, it appeared, prevented the writer from enjoying' the wares himself that he was supposed to exhibit in 'the dark byways' of Venice. Lack of money did not prevent him from certain goals at other times. And, in the letters to Fox, he said he was offered pleasures. Each offer he declined, he said. There was the excuse of no money or no place, but always an excuse. Insistence on the part of the boy did not change his mind.

The boys had a true respect for Rolfe and he treated them to whatever small kindnesses he could afford. Regardless of his decaying habitation and wardrobe at times, or even his sarcastic writing, he remained religious. He persevered in his priestly ambition until the age of fifty, the last year of acceptance. As for himself, he thought of the spiritual welfare of other, and mostly younger, persons. In Bristol in 1908 he met a fifteen-year-old Jew, whose brains he picked and then insisted 'on his rigorously practicing his religion [and] *drove* him to the synagogue. And, one day, ... I secretly baptized him ....' As 1910 began he was concerned over the fact that Benson had not sent him his 'usual New Year's Benediction'. He attended Mass regularly. 'He rose at 6 o'clock, after a frightfully restless night, and hurried with Zildo into Sanmarco to find a mass,' he says in his Venetian novel. 'One thing which had been worrying him was the health of the boy's immortal soul.'

One seemingly insignificant little piece of paper may add to this side of Rolfe's character. While he was with the van Somerens, he lunched one day with Miss Violet Milman. She worked at the English Hospital and was a mutual friend of his and the doctor's family. During the course of a conversation, he wrote down a list and gave it to her. In purple ink, he had written the Greek words opposite the English ones for 'Jesus / Christ / of God / Son / Saviour / Fish (Ichthys).'

Under this Greek title for 'Fish' he wrote a poem which was sent to *The Tablet* on 31 January 1910, but not accepted:

'Or, if he ask a fish,' (he—the son) 'will he give
        him a serpent?'
  Yea: to the least of Thy sons, that is just
        what they give.
Christ, in response to Thy Call, I ardently
        asked to be number'd,
  lustrums five ago, on the roll of Thy priests:
proof of that Call there is none, save this—my
        unfailing assertion
  vowing a bare bed, still persevering alone.
Also, I asked for the love of a friend which beareth,
        believeth,
  hopeth, endureth, all things, nor ever shall fail.
Those were the fish I asked. These are the
        serpents they gave me—
  (why do I strive to slip clean from the taint
        of their coils?)—
'Clerk that thou art,' so they said, 'thou shalt live
        in the world as a laic,
  lonely, slander'd, a butt for the babble of fools:

bricks thou shalt make without straw, & be spoiled
            of the fruit of thy labour:
nor will we spare thee the fire & ordeal of shame.'
King, I appeal from this gang of tormentors, malignant
            or stupid:
not unto man any more do I cry, but to Thee—
Fish, Who swimmeth, serene, in the crystal ether of heaven
    Fish, Who swimmeth, clean, in an ocean of peace
oh, let me swim, serene & clean, pressing breast against
            current
nerved & nourish'd & graced with the gift of Thyself.

The most significant thing that Rolfe wrote about himself is in the opening of the fifth chapter of *The Desire and Pursuit of the Whole*: 'To furnish some small proof of [Crabbe's-Rolfe's] vocation, he vowed twenty years' celibacy [when he was dismissed from Scots College, 1890]; and, for twenty years, he proclaimed the barbaric absurdity of which he was a victim.'

'Barbaric absurdity' or not, on 5 January 1910—twenty-two days before he sent his 'confession' to Masson Fox—he wrote to 'My Lord Archbishop' of Westminster: 'I beg leave again to remind Your Grace that I am an ecclesiastic subject of Your archdiocese, expelled from the Scots College of Rome in 1890 as having no Vocation, but still a Tonsured Clerk & persisting in my Divine Vocation to the priesthood. I should say also, that my vow of twenty years celibacy (which I offered in proof of my Vocation) expires this year, & that I am not at all moved to avail myself of liberty, but propose to renew my vow for life at the year's end. Will not Your Grace ever deign me one single word? Kissing the Sacred Pall, I remain my Ld Abp Your obedient servant in Xt.

                                                    Fr. Rolfe.'

14

In March 1177 Pope Alexander III arrived at Venice after his stately wanderings throughout Europe. Doge Ziani was absent, commanding the fleet against Emperor Frederic Barbarossa. When he returned victoriously in May, Alexander stood on the Lido beach to welcome him. He was the first to congratulate the doge. He blessed the brave seamen; and he placed his own signet ring on Ziani's thumb.

In March 1910 the Lido beach rather ingloriously was the scene of the self-created Hadrian VII's only refuge. In February, Rolfe had written to Dr. Walsh of New York that 'I have been fixed here since Aug 1908 & am about 25 years old simply because this is the city of my dreams.' The exuberance of this message was only momentary. Twelve days later he left the van Someren house, with no prospect of food or shelter. The Lido was his only home, and he walked it on the icy cold nights of winter. Two days after his confrontation with the doctor and his wife, Rolfe wrote to Masson Fox: 'Row with pious doctor, and left house on Saturday. Ate last on Friday evening. Walking all night on Lido beach beyond Excelsior. Often questioned by Police who are on watch to see that no one evaporates salt from the sea. Say that one is writer studying the dawns. So far satisfactory. But the cold is piercing and two nights have made me stiff as a post.... Something must be done. But spirits and determination undimmed.'

Fortunately, after a few days in the open air he was able to persuade Barbieri to receive him once again into the Hotel Belle Vue.

Rolfe's last full day at Palazzo Mocenigo-Corner was March 4th, a day when the eyes of all Europe and Russia were focused

335

on the small assize court in Venice. The entire city turned out for the procession of the four prisoners from their respective prisons to the courtroom. Troops were posted to prevent the mob from lynching 'The Enchantress', who arrived at 9.00 o'clock, escorted by two officers amid the cries of 'Death! Death!' About a hundred persons broke through the cordon of police and charged up the stairs, trying to force their way into the court before they were beaten back.

The prisoners entered their cages in an atmosphere of dead silence, broken only by the clicking of thirty newspaper cameras and 'a cinematograph apparatus'. The face of the chief prisoner 'is one that once seen is never forgotten'. Dressed all in black, except for a dazzling white cravat, she wore a large black hat with a flowing veil over a mass of brown hair. She was the centre of attraction for the whole world. 'She would make an ideal heroine for one of my tragedies,' said Gabriele d'Annunzio, the Italian man of letters admired by Rolfe and one of the few privileged occupants of reserved seats at the trial. 'What a Basiliola and what a Mila she would make!'

And so the Countess Tarnowska Trial began.

Born in Russia, she was the daughter of the Irish Count Nikolay Vladimirovich O'Rourke and his Russian wife. At an early age she displayed all the qualities of a *femme fatale*. At eighteen she had eloped with an officer, Count Tarnowski. Their tale of Russian society, high living, wild parties and unfaithfulness was but one of many which led to the country's downfall in the coming Revolution. Their unhappy married life began at Kiev. The lovers she attracted all came to abrupt ends, either by suicide or by Tarnowski's pistol. One lover shot by the count lingered on for a year. It was during this time that she employed an old friend of her husband's to sue for divorce, which was decreed in 1903. The lawyer she had chosen fell desperately in love with her. He left his wife and family, embezzled money from his clients and travelled throughout Europe with her for two years. At Paris she met Count Kamarowski, a widower who already knew her. Prilukoff, the lawyer, had gone through his money and, for the moment, was no longer wanted. The countess went back to Russia with Kamarowski. At Orel,

Kamarowski introduced her to a young student, Dr. Nicola Naumoff, who immediately fell under her hypnotising spell. Kamarowski and the countess then visited Berlin, where he implored her to marry him.

At the German city she again met Prilukoff and the two plotted the riddance of both lovers. For the security of money, the count first would have to be persuaded to take out a life insurance policy, naming Countess Tarnowska as the beneficiary. Then Naumoff would enter the scheme unsuspectingly. He would shoot the count and be tried and convicted for the murder. With the count's money, she and Prilukoff could enjoy a pleasant life together.

Because of the way it had to be worded, the insurance policy was not easy to obtain. Finally a Vienna company insured the life of Count Kamarowski for £20,000, 'even in the case of a violent death'. She then showed Naumoff a faked telegram. The count was supposed to have sent it, saying 'I know all. Naumoff is a rascal.' In a night of frenzied love, she worked upon the jealousy of the student and implored him to follow the count to revenge her. Kamarowski had gone to Venice at the end of August 1907, and Naumoff now left Russia on his murderous errand. Welcomed by the count almost as a son, he entered his apartment and shot at him. At first the shooting looked like suicide and Naumoff was free to leave and escape from Venice. Kamarowski was not fatally wounded, but a clumsily conducted operation—during which the chief doctor went insane—brought an end to his life. He lived long enough, however, to implicate the young man, the countess and her lawyer. Naumoff was apprehended at Verona. On their way to Italy, Tarnowska and Prilukoff had stopped at Vienna, where the police arrested them and took them to Venice. The three prisoners, faced with each other, made mutual accusations and were placed in prison in September 1907 to await their trial.

The small first-floor court certainly could not accommodate all the curious and the seats were judicially meted out. On March 15th Rolfe sent a jubilant post card to Masson Fox: 'Have got Press Ticket for the Tarnowsky Trial here. Amazing!!!!' The colourful and lurid aspects of the case appealed to him as a student of all the ways of humanity; and there was enough interest in it for him to leave two records of the trial. In his sketchbook he covered three pages with drawings of the courtroom with several of the leading players, all in red ink. Towards the end of *The Desire and Pursuit* he writes of Lady Layard-Lady Pash: 'Invitation, wheedling, command, force, bribe—she, a sanctimonious Tarnowska of Erastianism, could attract and suggestionize minions to work her will—and to wreak her revenge. Terrible is the Female.'

The Tarnowska Trial was to last until May 20th. The countess' maid had been arrested and held with the rest, but she was absolved of any responsibility in the crime. Each of the other three was pronounced guilty and given a sentence, from which was subtracted the time already spent in prison. Young Naumoff was sentenced to three years and one month. The countess was to serve eight years and four months. Prilukoff was given ten years in solitary confinement. Friends and the Russian government managed to secure a pardon for the countess. This was granted on 30 August 1912, but she was expelled from Italy.

A near-fatal illness prevented Rolfe from seeing more of the trial than he had.

On the day after the 'Tarnowsky Trial' post card to Fox, Rolfe wrote a 'Private & Personal' letter to Horace Fletcher, Mrs. van Someren's father. 'I have left Pal Moc Cor under circumstances of some incandescence. It was originally agreed that I shd contribute my share of the expenses. This I did by means of a first charge of my work, by cash instalments on a/c occasionally, & by serving as facchino. But, lately, Dr van Someren's religious mania burst out in a fresh & more fantastic direction than ever; &, while retaining the cash, he passionately destroyed the charge (which he had accepted six months before,) declaring that Christ had recently forbidden him not to muzzle the ox that treadeth out the corn. As this puts me in the beastly & intolerable position of a recipient of Christian Charity & levelled me with the mob of "Recommended Christians" who spunge upon & rob Dr van Someren—& as, at the moment, I happened to be stoney [broke]—I went & walked the Lido shore, nights, telling amiable carabinieri that I was studying colours of darkness & dawn, till I could make a respectable arrangement elsewhere.... I therefore thank you kindly indeed for your promised introduction to your publishers; & I will not ask you for it. In fact, I have already sent half my book to Messrs Stokes ON MY OWN ACCOUNT; & the remainder is following immediately.'

(The Frederick A. Stokes Company of New York had published Fletcher's *A B-Z of Our Own Nutrition*, 1903, and *The New Glutton of Epicure*, 1905. The latter was published in London in 1903 by Grant Richards. C. D. Cazeove & Son of London had published his *Menticulture, of the A-B-C of True Living* in 1895. And in September 1909 Rolfe had sent several of his Venetian essays to a literary agent in London, C. F. Cazenove.)

The most colourful part of Rolfe's life in Venice was the period set down in his *Desire and Pursuit*. The people and episodes of his own life are faithfully depicted here. The financial situation in which Crabbe finds himself can be traced to 'the Welshman' (Owen Thomas) and his lawyers, Messieurs Morlaix & Sartor. The Professor of Greek, Macpawkins, brings Crabbe to Venice. The story then begins with Crabbe as a guest in the Albergo Bellavista, whose proprietor is Parrucchiero. His services as a gondolier are engaged by the British Infirmary, 'the Universal Infirmary as it dubs itself,' managed by the Directress (Miss Edith Chaffey) and Lady Pash. At the hotel Crabbe meets 'this thiasarkh,' Exeter Warden and his wife and child. In turn, Warden introduces him to the ex-Rothschild financier and to Nelson Mactavish's Monday evenings. Crabbe's correspondents include C. Harricus Peary-Buthlaw of Uskvale, Wales, 'a rude Scot ... and Lord Mostotherthings of the Splendid Order of Sanctissima Sophia, and Goodnessknowswhatbeside.' Of course, the other person with whom he exchanges letters is the Reverend Bobugo Bonsen, 'a stuttering little Chrysostom of a priest, with the Cambridge manners of a Vaughan's Dove, the face of the Mad Hatter out of *Alice in Wonderland*, and the figure of an

Etonian who insanely neglects to take any pains at all with his temple of the Holy Ghost, but wears paper collars and a black straw alpine hat. As for his mind, it was vastly occupied with efforts to evade what theologians call "admiratio". By sensational novel-writing (his formula was to begin so that you must read on till there is nothing left for you to do but to end with a Bang [for choice of the slammed door of a Carthusian convent] behind the hero) and by perfervid preaching, he made enough money to buy a country-place, where he had the ambition to found a private establishment (not a religious order) for the smashing of individualities, the pieces of which he intended to put together again as per his own pattern. He did not exactly aspire to actual creation, but he certainly nourished the notion that several serious mistakes had resulted from his absence during the events described in the first chapter of Genesis.'

The core of the novel is woven around the words of Plato: 'The Desire and Pursuit of the Whole is called Love.' In the wake of the Messina earthquake Crabbe sees the wreckage and desolation and momentarily forgotten dead. In the silent ruins he discovers one live soul still united with its body; and this begins the story of the meeting of two hearts. The unconscious body of a young girl is brought to his boat and to Venice. Already orphaned, he learns, she had been cared for by an aunt and uncle, now victims of the earthquake and leaving her without home or relations. She is Ermenegilda Falier and Crabbe 'had scratched out of the rubbish heap nothing less than the daughter of a Doge—of three Doges, to be exact, namely Vital Falier and Ordelaf Falier and Marin Falier of the eleventh, twelfth, and fourteenth centuries respectively.' Pondering the problem of her future he decides to 'dispose of her as a boy' and employs her as a 'boy' working for him on his boat.

The original Toto of twenty years before had never been far away from Rolfe's spirit. In the two decades he had only advanced two years to become the boy-girl Zilda. The sun and soil and history of Italy had burned within him for a long time; and now Venice was to provide the climax to his dreams. The abstract expectations of his life are now passed on to Nicholas Crabbe, whom Rolfe knew well. In an accidental way Crabbe meets Zilda, the ultimate personification for the solution to all the loneliness Rolfe knew in life. The intensity of his search throughout a weary life conjured up one creature, if not a reality for Rolfe himself, at least one to crown and reward Nicholas Crabbe.

The bitter paranoiac, the seeming ego-maniac who arrived in Venice with no money of his own, who lived by his wits and other people's 'alms', housed by occasional friends or in the open air, now alternately scorched the pages of his letters to 'enemies' and wrote a love story of tender sincerity. Of all of the books concerning himself, *The Desire and Pursuit of the Whole* alone has a happy conclusion.

On one occasion years later Mrs. van Someren was to say that she was 'the first person to read six chapters of the MSS and congratulate the author. After which hatred and spite took charge and poisoned his story.' She had forgotten her initial surprise at finding uncomplimentary and libellous portraits of her friends in it. Neither hatred nor spite 'poisoned his story' afterwards. Before Rolfe consented to show her the manuscript she already had his word, in writing, that 'it is necessary to demonstrate that I will not let myself be vilified by anyone, & that I know how to defend my rights at any costs'—by writing everything down in *The Desire and Pursuit of the Whole*. 'It's all there.'

Neither hatred nor spite filled out the book. In his study on James Joyce's *Ulysses*, Stuart Gilbert praises this work and its author. 'Typical, too, of the [eighteen-ninetyish] period was a near-great Catholic writer whose first work appeared in the *Yellow Book*: Fr. Rolfe ("Baron Corvo"),' he writes. 'Indeed, had the Fates been kinder, that unhappy genius might have moved parallel, if on a somewhat lower plane, to Joyce's. Nicholas Crabbe, the hero of Rolfe's ... *The Desire and Pursuit of the Whole*, had a good deal in common with Stephen Dedalus. ... Some of Rolfe's cadences and word-patterns are in a Joycean vein [and] Rolfe shared Joyce's fondness for out-of-the-way words, such as "contortuplicate" and "tolutiloquence" (a new coinage derived, through Sir Thomas Browne, from the Latin *tolutim*).'

In 1906 Rolfe had written to Grant Richards: 'Each chapter of *Don Tarquinio* ended with an hexameter & a pentameter. Each chapter of *Nicholas Crabbe* ends with an hexameter or hexameters. This dodge finishes each division with a clang. But no critics have spotted it so far.' Had he remained alive, Rolfe would have waited a long time for the first critic to spot this 'dodge'. Not until spring 1970 did 'A Classical Metrical Pattern in Rolfe' make itself known. In an article on this subject John Glucker speaks of the strange, poetic style in the last few lines of each chapter, discovering it independently. 'If, as I believe, this metrical pattern is there,' he says, 'it is a very interesting fact. Apart from [Robert] Bridge's *Ibant Obscuri* (which is a little different, being an attempt to translate a poetry originally written in hexameters), this is one of the few examples in modern English literature—indeed, in English literature of any period —to write in dactyls and hexameters. It should also make one think twice about Rolfe's acquaintance with Greek and Latin: the dactylic type of metre is not very frequent in any modern literature. On other grounds, too, it looks as though Rolfe's real acquaintance with the Classical languages, their literatures, and the more technical sides of these literatures has never been seriously examined.'

The fullness of Rolfe's creative powers are witnessed in this novel. While working on it, he had complete faith in himself, in his writing, in life and in religion. The portion of the story dealing with love is not the age-old tale to be found in countless romantic novels. It is a much more complicated, and integral, part of the whole. With different coloured strands of thread, it is woven into the entire fabric of the book. *The Desire and Pursuit of the Whole* is a love story of a man and a maid, and of a man and a place, which is Venice; it is also the story of a man and his faith. Nicholas Crabbe's agony in Venice can be identified with Christ's Passion. Between the mechanically metred cadences at the ends of its chapters, Rolfe illuminated the story with the outcries of his profoundly personal faith.

'Work was his panacea.' Slaughter, one of Rolfe's two fellow-lodgers at Broadhurst Gardens, said that he 'put in most of his time writing'. The other fellow-lodger, Bainbridge, stated that Rolfe 'was a cannibal for work'. In his first nineteen months in the Italian city he had completed twenty Venetian essays, had worked on *Hubert's Arthur* and finished the Prologue to *Nicholas Crabbe*. He had written his novel of modern Venice— saying to Masson Fox on 6 June 1910, 'By the bye, in connection with the idea that I am idle—please consider that I have invented and written every word of *The Desire and Pursuit of the Whole* FIVE TIMES since last July—148,900 words x 5 = 744,500 words!!!' Added to this were his voluminous letters to people and the altering of certain portions of *The Weird of the Wanderer*.

Before the end of March he had been approached by a London publisher over this novel. A personal letter from Rider & Son *'Asking me to name my own terms* FOR *The Weird* AND ASKING ALSO TO HAVE A SECOND BOOK FROM ME' was the jubilant message he had to convey to Fox on August 1st. *'I've done all the work,'* he added, *'and I want some of the proceeds.'* He asked Fox not 'to look upon me as an impracticle dreamer. I don't claim any particular commercial smartness. But I think I've got ordinary common sense. Facts are facts, and the fact is that I am the only person in the world who has ever sold my books. I sold *Toto, Rubaiyat, Borgia, Hadrian, Tarquinio* all by myself. First wrote 'em: then hawked 'em. No agent ever did a thing. And now the same thing's happened again.' In a sense this statement was true. No agent handled the first three books. Nor did Rolfe hawk them. These had been commissioned. *Hadrian* and *Tarquinio* were given to agents, but it was Rolfe who sold them to Chatto & Windus, to his financial detriment.

The consistent and engrossing habit of his life in relation to work, coupled with years of physical want, finally had its toll.

On the morning of March 5th he left the van Somerens. He took his belongings to the Bucintoro. He rested here during the day and walked the Lido at night. By the end of the month he was back at the Belle Vue. The proprietor of the hotel had acquired the Clock Tower for rooms and here he gave Rolfe 'an empty attic to sleep in'. His cold at the end of 1909 and the nights spent on the Lido combined to damage his body. On April 21st the Consul at Venice wired the Foreign Office in London: 'please wire Masson Fox Falmouth fr Rolfe dangerously ill penniless hotel Belle Vue here.' Within a few days Rolfe was placed in Lady Layard's hospital, 'dangerously ill,' and given the Last Rites.

His stubborn determination to live rallied him through the near-fatal illness. While still at the hospital, he wrote a note in pencil in a shaky hand to Mrs. van Someren at the end of April. 'I beg you dear lady to let me ease my mind,' he started; 'I don't know how many minutes not delirious I can count up. But I can see that an enormously stupid thing has been done, in causing me to write a book. Then in forming a judgment & sentencing the criminal, on *far less than half evidence*. Then the complication of the Consul compelling me to let those who wounded me feed me—processes like going through a cream separator emerging in vistas of turquetwill lampshades—cannot prevent whats done, nor would it be honourable to either of us ii. But I don't know anything. No one speaks to me & things are carefully kept from me & I think & think & think till I *know* that I'm thinking askew.'

Released from the hospital on May 11th, he was admitted into one of Barbieri's Clock Tower rooms on the first floor. Six days later he was busily writing letters, short notes to tell of his illness of 'bronchitis, pneumonia, heart ... due to exposure and privations of past year'. 'For which I have to thank you' was a phrase he tacked on to the message going to Pirie-Gordon and Dawkins. On the 13th he wrote a much longer letter to Dr. Walsh:

I am just out of hospital after bronchitis, pneumonia, heart, last Sacraments—result of exposure & privations of precisely one year—weaker than I could have believed it possible for anyone to be, & with a fluttering thing under my ribs which annoys me immensely. I'm told to make a slow & gentle convalescence, which is out of the question. Mortified as I am at the breakdown of my endurance, I'm bound to say that everyone has treated me most kindly: but—excited Venetians have been capering among my affairs, & I've a good month's hard work before me to reduce these to order, picking up dropped threads & disentangling the rest. This is my excuse for neglect of your letter & cheque of 13th ult.

The letter had asked a question and the cheque was in payment for the answer. After the opening of his letter, Rolfe gave Walsh an account of thirteenth-century Venetian glass, to be incorporated into the doctor's book on this century. Rolfe's letter continued:

You are lucky never to have been 'in sight of lack of money' in your life. I have never been anything else. Had I ever been 'unius lacertae dominus,' master of a bare but regular competence so that I could work *uninterruptedly*, I should have attained comfortable circumstances long ago. As it is, I dance on a slack wire all the time. And just now when I'm so tottery, it's rather difficult.... I want to know whether you'll let me send you the ms. of my new novel, with some essays & things, for transmission to [an American literary agent] with an introduction from you advising & urging him to run me for all he's worth. Notwithstanding my present ridiculous physical weakness, I am keener & more resolute than ever; & I feel that my life has been handed back to me to have another try in.

For the moment Rolfe had a place of shelter. He had given Babieri the lien on his novel. 'Everything is at a standstill,' he wrote to Fox in June. 'I am stronger: but have had no rest or convalescence at all. Cough persists and top of lung isn't clear yet.... Your last two letters have been disappointing. So reserved [and] I have no one to look to but you, even for the means to grub on.'

Nearly a month later he was beseeching the British Consul to provide means for him to carry on his work in Venice. 'Owing to the malfeasance of my agents Messrs Barnard & Taylor ... & the treachery of two friends C. H. C. Pirie-Gordon ... & Rev. R. H. Benson ... I was robbed in June 1909 of my mss., books, notes, life-work, & stranded here homeless & penniless & prevented from pursuing my literary career.... I possess a Foreign Office Passport ... requiring all whom it may concern to afford me every assistance & protection of which I may stand in need.

345

But no one here ... will afford me anything of the kind, & I of course refuse "Charity".... I have therefore to ask reluctantly for your official intervention. All that is necessary is to appoint & instruct a competent person in England to take over my obligations & assets & to let me have a chance to resume my work.'

The answer to this was a regretful one, saying that no one was able 'to take action in this matter'. A comment was added to Rolfe's letter: 'What an extraordinary request.'

Continuing his pleas to the Consul, he begged 'to acknowledge the receipt of your letter of the 9th instant' and wrote that 'my life being in danger, I appeal to you to take order that I shall have every assistance & protection of which I stand in need, as the terms of my passport ... require'. Ten days later two comments to this letter were exchanged between the Consuls at Florence and Venice: 'I am afraid Mr Rolfe understands the terms of his passport too literally' and 'But it is a queer case.' Consideration was given him for his repatriation to England 'at the cheapest possible rate ... & that no expenditure is incurred on his behalf in respect to luggage'.

On July 11th Role had written to the British Consul. On the same day a letter went to Masson Fox: 'No one speaks a word to me here, nor can I get anyone in England to write to me, excepting on business.... I'm *quite deprived of air, water and exercise* of any kind unless I go and walk about the island of Santelena at 4 o'clock in the morning. I do that, as often as I can pluck up the energy: but I'm so hideously shabby that I daren't shew myself in the street by day.... Not once this summer have I been able to swim, merely because I have no means of getting out on the lagoon. I'm just pinned down to my room, a back room on the first floor of that narrow alley which leads from Piazza to Calle Larga, so close to the ground that I can touch the hats of the whores and drunks who roar there all night long, where never a ray of the sun has ever come, so dark that I can't see to write there on these brilliant days without the light on, and a playground *of rats* of which I have trapped and drowned in the slop-pail the *thirty-sixth since July 1st*!!! And the effect on me is that my hands shake like a palsy, my whole body tingles inside and has fits of giddiness, I can't lie on my left side because it stops my heart, and I cough with a chest filling up again. Heavens only knows what's going to happen. I don't.'

The bizarre turn of Rolfe's mind spoke of nothing to be done 'unless I make up my mind to have a jolly good row'. Pirie-Gordon had 'stolen my life-work and my goods' and with Barnard & Taylor, was simply sitting tight to 'let me die'. If Rolfe could find 'that financial partner ... I would recover all these things within a fortnight just by demanding them. It is merely my helpless condition which prevents that. And P-G and B. and T. have made up their minds to take the fullest advantage of that condition. It isn't necessary for them to commit murder. *All they have to do is just keep quite still while I die* .... Now mark me well,' Rolfe commented to Fox, 'I won't die, till I've had a good kick all round. So this is what I've done.' He reported that he had denounced his lawyers to the Prudential Assurance Company and to the Law Society and had denounced them and Pirie-Gordon to the Publishers' Association and to the Foreign Office. He told Pirie-Gordon the same thing in a letter two days later and further said that he had now refused all offers for *The Weird of the Wanderer*. Rider & Son had agreed to publish the book as a six-shilling novel and to pay Rolfe eight pence 'per copy royalty from the commencement'. Answering a letter of his of July 21st, they returned the manuscript, but asked the author to reconsider the offer.

At this junction in Rolfe's life some unknown thing happened to alter his formerly characteristic personality. Between the time of his near-fatal illness and his fiftieth birthday, he began a comparatively new life. Half of his life had been primarily devoted to some, no matter how minor, official function within the Catholic Church. But the Church never would recognize his vocation. He persisted in this endeavour until 22 July 1910, until he was of an age no longer acceptable; and the most complete testament of his unalterable faith flows across the pages of his *Desire and Pursuit of the Whole*.

347

His relationship with the people he had known suddenly changed in most cases. His letters to Fox dwindled to nothing in another month's time. A long letter to his lawyers was dated 1 August 1910. Pirie-Gordon was a person with whom Rolfe never intended to quarrel and did so only in letters from Venice. Yet after July 13th, the very few which he wrote to Wales were friendly. On September 6th he wished to introduce to Pirie-Gordon the Rev. Justus Stephen Serjeant of Christ's College, Cambridge, the Rector of Warboys. And his last post card, 7 March 1913, read: 'Read four pages of praise of *The Weird of the Wanderer* in current *Rivista di Roma* and howl.'

On his fiftieth birthday, 22 July 1910, he wrote to Dawkins: 'If you could first contrive to read the formula of the Last Sacraments, and would try to conceive his feelings in whose interest it has been used, you may be able to understand something— this. I am trying to make the next fifty years of this life clearer than those completed now; and I have been examining the shocked bitter violent letters which I have written to you since Feb. 1909. Why am I so infuriated against you? And am I justified? To-day I fancy that I have discovered the reason of my rages. I am leaving the question of justification till I know what you say to this. I think that I have been inflamed all along by your failure to answer a letter which I wrote Jan.-Feb. 1909. Why did you not answer it?'

The 1909 letter was written to say that Rolfe had not dropped their friendship, although Dawkins had expressed anger towards him. Money matters was another subject mentioned. But the chief complaint of Rolfe's was the unsolicited appeal by Pirie-Gordon and Benson to help him, the appeal to which Dawkins contributed. 'So now I write to ask exactly how we stand. If you have changed your mind about wanting my friendship, please have the frankness to say so. If you are still lonely and friendless, you know that I am likewise and not unwilling to be your friend. But let me know how we stand, please,' Rolfe ended his letter, 'as friends or enemies.'

Dawkins' abrupt reply came a month later. 'Returning from a journey I found your letter. The *return* which you have made me for helping you has been to write me *violent* letters, and the last time when *Pirie-Gordon asked me to help you* and I sent him money, you accused me of *conspiring* with him against you. I do not desire servility, but this *return* is not what one expects, and the answer to your question as to whether I have acted in cold blood, is that I *have acted in anger.* I have I believe received all your letters and the camera for the return of which I thought I had acknowledged with thanks. I thought this last letter of yours a shade less *hostile*; if it was at all an *olive branch*, I take it very gladly as such.'

'I am glad to know that you have acted in anger,' Rolfe replied, further explaining the points of the January 1909 letter which Dawkins had omitted to answer. As for his last letter being an olive branch, he added, 'No. If I offer olive-branches, I label myself a sucker-up, a toad-eater, the potential sponger, you think me. So I wait for olive-branches to be offered to me. It's no good writing any more. I shall never make you understand. You had a chance of making an equal and a friend. And you threw it away. We were both losers. But I'm the one who suffered. *L'amor xe fato par chi lo sa fare.*'

Dawkins could never be consoled.

For twenty years Rolfe was a regular correspondent, asking questions, trying to sell his wares, pleading his cause, gently and tenderly speaking to some, or answering back such persons who warranted his caustic replies. Through this period his history can be traced with the letters. But all of sudden, beginning with his fiftieth birthday, an uncanny silence all but engulfed him. Instead of the main actor, he now only can be seen in glimpses. But he had become a part of Venice, 'the city of my dreams'. 'Things belong to people who want them most,' Dashiell Hammett once said, a comment easily to be used for Rolfe and the results of his life.

In May, two months before the close of his forty-ninth year, he had written to Dr. Walsh, 'I feel that my life has been handed back to me to have another try in.' And this other 'try in' was to last three years.

The Weird of the Wanderer offer indeed was tempting, but

Rolfe's financial obligations to Barnard & Taylor forced him to hesitate in accepting it. He would not 'make money for other people for nothing, any longer'. In his next letter to Fox he drew an imagined plan to throw all of his 'conspirators' into a frantic turmoil. If he 'suddenly stopped ... and calmly [went] out to live in the open air,' his disappearance would disrupt all their smoothly devised intentions. His scheme to vanish, to force attention upon his situation, may never have meant to materialize. But he outlined this supposed solution to his problem to Fox in his last letter to the man of Falmouth. 'So I say lend me five pounds. With that in my pocket, I fancy I can do the trick. It will take about a month: for that I must be prepared to shift from Malamocco to Pellestrina perhaps. *I must be in a position to defy*—if you understand. If you can manage more, so much the better. The more I have the better and the sooner I can reach a successful conclusion. Do answer *at once*. This is the "psychological moment".' Thus ended his letter of August 21st, a letter which brought nothing in reply.

Six days earlier the British Consul at Venice had noted that 'Mr Rolfe does not wish to return to England.'

Although Rolfe's personality had begun to be less critical, one person was to discover his explosive nature only now. The cause of the eruption was due to immediate circumstances. Since the beginning of 1903 Rolfe and Dr. Walsh had exchanged letters across the Atlantic; but it was only now that Walsh received the first letters that enabled him to formulate his final opinion of his correspondent. 'That was the impression produced on me by not only my own experiences with him,' he declared, 'but also some heart to heart talks with Monsignor Benson ... a dear friend of mine.'

Earlier in the year Rolfe had asked if he could send some manuscripts to Walsh. On August 16th the New York doctor wrote to Venice and on the 28th Rolfe answered with aggressive outbursts. Writing his reply on Walsh's own letter, he started, without salutation: 'I answer on this, not out of disrespect or lack of love, but just because you will get my points more easily this way. June 6th I sent you *The Desire* in 2 vols ms. June 8th 9th I sent 2 vols typescript *Nicholas Crabbe & The One & the*

Many. June 10th-June 20th I sent 8 *Reviews of Unwritten Books,* 2 short stories, 2 Venetian essays, all serial manuscript & all registered. Your letter only speaks of *The Desire* & fills me with the awful thought that the rest of my work is lost.'

Walsh had written: 'I left for the West shortly after the arrival of your manuscript and that delayed my finding a Literary agent.'

Rolfe replied: 'The delay is terrible. I have been quite alone, powerless, living on hope.'

Walsh (after a delay in finding the literary agent): 'Then I took the liberty of reading the manuscript myself as to be able to tell the Literary Agent something about it and had two friends read it.'

Rolfe: 'I did not think of your reading it: but I am glad that you have read it—because now you know perhaps half.'

Walsh: 'I fear that it will be difficult to find a publisher for it here in America, for while it contains an excellent bit of love story quite unusual in its way and with the absolutely essential quality of a happy ending there is so much besides that publishers hesitate.'

Rolfe: 'A book with guts in it can be made as much a commercial success as a patent pill, by enterprizing commercial advertizement.'

Walsh: 'Here we are then with nothing done formally and only discouragement with regard to the outlook.'

Rolfe: 'Yes: I see. And it has taken my breath away.'

Walsh: 'May I add that personally I have been a little hesitant about pressing the matter in any way because the book contains so many personalities. These are quite obviously hidden beneath masks that make them easily recognizable. I should feel that if the manuscript went through my hands to an agent I should have to tell him that, though it is probable that the disguise is so thin that he would recognize that real persons are involved.'

Rolfe: 'So did *Hadrian the Seventh.* So do all big books— Benson's *Sentimentalists* & *Conventionalists* for example. So much the better from a commercial point of view. I know no risk: but I take all responsibility. Am I to be killed without defending myself? Or gagged?'

Walsh: 'You see what a case of conscience I have. Do tell me what I shall do.'

Rolfe: 'Is it fair to ask *me* that?'

Walsh: 'I am just going up to read a paper at the Eucharistic Congress at Montreal and I shall not be back for twenty days and I should like very much to have your letter solving my case of conscience when I come back.'

Rolfe: 'I am living in a filthy hole where I have caught *sixty-one rats* since June. The sun never comes here. Whores howl day & night under my window. I have not bathed since last November, nor changed my clothes since August 1908. Ought you to put it to me to solve your case of conscience?'

Walsh: 'I am very sorry indeed to seem to have been neglectful of you. It has not been neglect but the feeling that a little waiting might mean much as regards your state of mind towards some of your quondam English friends.'

Rolfe: 'I know that. And it wounds me hideously to come into your life. But what else can I do? You don't understand that nothing happens to change my state of mind. No one restores my stolen property or reputation. They are strong. They sit tight, silent, & see me die. That's all.'

Walsh: 'Now tell me if friends of yours of whom you thought much were thus fallen out what would you do if some public expression of their animosity were passing through your hands? I know that you will not misunderstand me.'

Rolfe: 'My own practice in such a case is rigidly simple. Without delaying a single second on any account whatever, I instantly take off my shirt & waltz in whole-heartedly on behalf of the weak & oppressed. If he happens to be wrong, that puts him right. But I instinctively prefer the One to the Many. He has always been my Master.'

Walsh: 'Do command me still.'

Rolfe: 'How can I "command" you? I only implore you not to give the work of my miserable sufferings to my enemies. If your conscience will not let you help me to live, or to defend me, at least don't do anything else. Your letter has knocked me flat & gasping. If it had contained one word of encouragement it would have extended my credit, on which alone I have kept alive so long. But now that is gone. I do not know how much more endurance I shall be able to scratch together when I have posted this letter. But I see that I must go adrift again at once. Luckily the weather is not inclement. But the city & the Lido swarm with summer visitors; & it will be a frightful task to hide my misery. If you answer me at all, only a cable c/o English Consul is likely to find me. But I have no hope that I actually can last out twenty days. Of course I shall try: but I wish I could be with you for a bit to make you understand.'

Ending with a similarity of words to the earlier letter of 17 August 1903, this letter again was not signed.

A week later he was writing to Pirie-Gordon that he had just met the Rev. Justus Serjeant.

In a letter to Walsh in 1903, Rolfe had stated that 'the literary "patron" no longer exists'.

When Serjeant appeared in Venice, Rolfe made no overture, and it was this new Englishman who took the first step. Rolfe was courteous; but no one who talked with Rolfe could escape from the story of his life. This story—of his past, of the immediate present and of the future, involving some likely person to invest a sum of money in his literary endeavours—had become second nature to him. Serjeant listened to these tales of the friends and lawyers in England who had let him down. Rider & Son had offered to publish *The Weird of the Wanderer*, but any profits from the book would be swallowed up by his obligations in London. These words convinced Serjeant. He suggested a possible partnership. Some money would be coming to him in the near future, he said, and, fascinated by Rolfe and his work, he planned an alliance. Rolfe would be paid while he worked on his future books, with no intermittent worries.

In the two years he had been in Venice, Rolfe had undergone a most trying existence. Nightmarish hunger, illness and loneliness were not alone in plaguing him. Disappointments had also followed each other in rapid succession. No matter what he attempted, his work received no response, not until he finally heard from Rider. Now he realized a deeper disappointment. Even if his work were accepted, others would reap the profits. So he intensified his search for a person with enough money to settle his account with Barnard & Taylor and to leave his mind at peace. When his wild dream of such a patron suddenly came to life before him, he must have suffered a shock. Yet his dream was not to be realized quickly. The money Serjeant spoke of was not available at the moment. When Serjeant returned to England he did see Rolfe's solicitors and made arrangements for the release of their claim to his books. The problem of the money, the most acute problem to Rolfe, was now a problem of time. As sincere as Serjeant was, he could do nothing until his inheritance came to him. In the interim Rolfe had to wait.

'Half-recovered from 2nd bronchitis this winter have been turned adrift and am walking on Lido. There is a thick white frost. Congratulations,' he wrote to Dawkins on 28 January 1911.

Rolfe's second winter in Venice ended in the hospital. His third caused another severe illness. While he had lain in his weakened condition in the English Hospital in 1910, Queen Alexandra, on a visit to Venice, had come to see Lady Layard's patients. Knowing that she had spoken soothingly to the apparently dying man, a year later Barbieri's secretary wrote to her. Her Majesty was asked 'to give Her interest to the English writer, Mr Fred. W. Rolfe, who after being unable to satisfy his living expenses since last spring is now wandering homeless on the Lido island in this piercing cold. ... He will not ask anyone for help and my position of hotel secretary does not allow me to give him any assistance, especially because I am employed by his creditor.'

The queen sent to the British Consul at Venice 'Ten Pounds Sterling to be laid out for Mr Rolfe's benefit.' The Consul, Edward de Zuccato, duly acknowledged it on February 11th. 'The proprietor of the Hotel de Russie, to whom [Rolfe] owes more than 300 francs, refused, a few days ago, to give him credit any more,' he explained. 'As he told me he was in want of clothes, I have given him the Ten Pound Note and I herein enclose his receipt,' he added, saying that he would not mention the source of the gift to him, whose 'case is a most difficult and delicate one'.

Rolfe's desire to communicate with others by letter, so insatiable for twenty years, now suddenly ceased. The people he once addressed heard little from him after the middle of 1910. During most of 1911 his return address was 'Consolato Inglese'. And during this time he lived and wrote in an open boat.

On March 16th he sent a letter to America, saying that Dr. Walsh's 'letter of 1 Mar shews me that you were unworthy of my confidence & admiration; & you have forfeited both. I suppose that what makes me such a terror is my astonishing adherence to truth.... Naturally it upsets the careless & inexact, & causes the excandescence with which you sputter. I have a few remarks to make about your letter. (1) ... I told you (xviiij May 1910) "You are lucky never to have been 'in sight of lack of money' in your life. I have never been anything else...." That is exactly true; & I have nothing to add to it. And, that you should skulk behind an anonymous calumny, without remembering, or believing, what I told you, disqualifies you for my kindness. (2) I DID ask your permission to send you my mss (xviiij May 1910); & you gave it with every sign of gladness. (3) The carriage on the parcels was fully paid at this end.... (4) As far as I am concerned, the mss. which you say you dispatched Dec. 1910 are lost to me, simply because you mucked my careful & explicit directions. There was about five years bitter work there: so you & your precious Benson can congratulate yourselves.... (7) It seems to suit you to denounce the Express Co as guilty of "an Italian trick": but the fact remains that I owe the loss of my work to your American trick, & decline to clear up the mess which you have made. (8) I have never sent you any request, direct, or indirect, for what you mean by "help". (9) I repudiate, with contempt, your expressions of sympathy & your invitation to tell you what you can do for me. They are the feeblest hypocrisy, when you know that I am quite alone, & have been homeless & often starving since Jan 27th, robbed of years of work by you & Benson & Pirie-Gordon, robbed even of my clothes & tools of trade, & fighting my third bronchitis since Christmas caused by awful nights on the open shore of the Lido only keeping alive for fear of crabs and rats,—when you know that you have never tried to get me suitable work, & have helped to spoil me of the work which I have done by force. Your letter is among the most disgusting & disgraceful & most typical catholic which I have ever read. Chivalry? Knighthood? Christianity? O Heavens!' Above the signature were the words: 'Yours no longer.' And it ended: 'N.B. This is all without prejudice; & I reserve all rights in this & in all previous letters.'

Walsh knew Pirie-Gordon through the Order of Sanctissima Sophia. He and Benson had corresponded and had met in New York. The two 'had three precious hours of converse on all sorts of subjects in The Borderland Between Spirit and Matter,' as well as on the subject of Rolfe. In the eight years they had known each other through letters, Walsh's position in Rolfe's mind had diminished from a possible Ideal Friend to another detested enemy. All the manuscripts sent to Walsh in 1910 had been shipped back to Venice. The short stories could find no market and the novels spoke too freely about living people. The Venetian novel, thought Walsh, 'was almost libelous and hit very hard some of my friends, the Jesuits, in England and particularly Monsignor Benson.' Rolfe's fury was two-fold. That his work should be unsaleable in America was a bitter disappointment once again. Time had been wasted. Though the doctor paid the necessary charges to the American Express Company in New York to handle the novels, extra charges were added for customs inspection when they reached Venice. This infuriated Rolfe. He had no money to pay these charges. His work was 'lost' to him when he wrote to Walsh and remained 'lost' until he finally paid the required fees.

His final word to the New York doctor was a post card, dated 14 May 1911. Walsh had had ample time to answer Rolfe's last letter. Rolfe reminded him of a few points which 'deserved your earnest attention: but, what with your allegiance to the freemasonic Grandmaster of the Order of Sanctissima Sophia & your infatuation for the banausic fire-insurance agent R. H.

Benson, I can quite understand that you prefer esconcement in a sulky silence.'

Between 1910 and 1911 two pieces of literature were published in London. In October of the latter year Nicholson's volume of verse, *A Garland of Ladslove*, was privately printed. It contained one sonnet, 'A Mistake. *(From the Italian of Baron Corvo).*' Corvo was a name long forgotten by Rolfe. With Rolfe away in Venice where he could never see or hear about it, Nicholson was not reluctant about its appearance. Unlike the much earlier poem which he fashioned from Rolfe's original, this one was only a parody, 'A pure fiction!'

During the previous year a short story had appeared in a collection by Saki. In 'The Reticence of Lady Anne' there is a cat by the name of Don Tarquinio—christened by a 'page boy, who had Renaisance tendencies.'

During this same two-year period Rolfe's only printed piece was the small 128-word contribution to Walsh's *Thirteenth: Greatest of the Centuries*. His most earnest concern at this time was over the Venetian novel and *Hubert's Arthur*. For the first he had the good fortune to stay with the van Somerens. Illness, recovery, loss of home and makeshift accommodation in a boat on the lagoons delayed the latter. His letters to Serjeant were answered. But the man in England was in no position to grant his pressing, and real, appeals for financial help. And at this one time in Rolfe's life he had no one close by.

No matter how he had sought assistance in Venice, nothing but the alms of charity were given to him, the one thing which made his very soul cringe. For twenty years he had lived in the shadow of privation. And he had always survived. 'The meek shall inherit the earth,' or, at least, he proclaimed to himself, that portion of it due to him as a fitting reward for his work. No longer welcome at the Belle Vue, no longer seeking aid from the few persons remaining in Venice whom he knew, he depended solely on hope. He no longer could sit in a room and write endlessly. Living in an open boat on the lagoons, he was at the mercy of the elements. Only between the sea and physical adversity did he have a chance to write. *Hubert's Arthur* was written in no empty garret; it was finally composed amidst the lashing spray of the lagoons, under the glaring sun, and with a hand shaking from the labours of working as a boatman and from starvation. Would the reality of Serjeant's promises ever take place?

In October 1911 Rolfe wrote to this future benefactor:

I'm in an awful state; and I firmly believe that I'm finished if I don't get relief *instanter*.

The last fortnight has been a chapter of misfortunes. I've been literally fighting for life through a series of storms. Do you realize what that means in a little boat, leaky and so coated with weed and barnacles by a summer's use, that it is almost too heavy to move with the oar, and behaves like an inebriate in winds or weather? I assure you it's no joke. And storms get up on this lagoon in ten minutes, leaving no time to make a port. I'm frequently struggling for 50-60 hours on end. Results: I've lost about 300 pages of my new MS. of *Hubert's Arthur*. Parts were oiled by a lamp blown over them: winds and waves carried away the rest. At every possible minute I am rewriting them: but, horrible to say, grey mists float about my eye-corners just through sheer exhaustion. The last few days I have been anchored near an empty island, Sacca Fisola, not too far away from civilization to be out of reach of fresh water, but lonely enough for dying alone in the boat if need be. Well, to shew you how worn out I am, I frankly say that I have funked it. This is my dilemma. I'll be quite plain about it. If I stay out on the lagoon, the boat will sink, I shall swim perhaps for a few hours, and then I shall be eaten alive by crabs. At low water every mudbank swarms with them. If I stay anchored near an island, I must keep continually awake: for, the moment I cease moving, I am invaded by swarms of swimming rats, who in the winter are so voracious that they attack even man who is motionless. I have tried it. And have been bitten. Oh my dear man you can't think how artful fearless ferocious they are. I rigged up two bits of chain, lying loose on my prow and poop with a string by which I could shake them when attacked. For two nights the dodge acted. The swarms came up (up the anchor rope) and nuzzled me: I shook the chains: the beasts plopped overboard. Then they got used to the noise and sneered. Then they bit the strings. Then they bit my toes and woke me shrieking and shaking with fear.

Now this is what I have done. I am perfectly prepared to persevere to the end. So I have taken the boat to a 'squero' to be repaired. This will take a fortnight. When she is seaworthy again I'll go out and face my fate in her. Meanwhile I'm running a tick at the Cavalletto, simply that I may eat and sleep to write hard at restoring the 300 odd pages of *Hubert's Arthur*. When that is done, the boat will be ready. I will assign that MS. to you and send it.

My dear man, I am so awfully lonely. And tired. Is there no chance of setting me right?

Hubert's Arthur was completed on 1 November 1911. But the winter had to pass and it was not until March 1912 that Serjeant was in a position to set Rolfe right.

Legal litigation can be time-consuming, as Rolfe found out over the Owen Thomas lawsuit. After an eternity of hopeful waiting, Serjeant came into his money and sent Rolfe the first cheque. In London he paid Barnard & Taylor £53 10s. od. for the relinquishing of any further claim on Rolfe's literary efforts. The partnership between the man in England and the man in Venice, between a source of security and the writing of books, had begun. And one of the first things Rolfe did was to pay debts and reclaim certain goods. On April 2nd he was able to tell Dawkins that 'I have paid the Venice debts and have recovered your changing-box which I am instructing [Thomas] Cook [& Son] to send you.' His return address was still the English Consulate. But within a month's time he moved into the Albergo Cavalletto.

The poor, shabby and forlorn person who had been merely the Rolfe who lived off of other people's alms now became the prosperous Rolfe. The days of hiding in shadows and walking the Lido at nights because of a total lack of decent clothes were over. The shy man who sought the bare and simple means to support himself now did not care if his mannerisms attracted attention. Before the summer appeared he had his own boat and painted the sails for it himself. The years of the austere Franciscan taught him certain simple ways to live. Yet he was never the miser. Money had only one purpose: to be spent.

Accused in *Hadrian*, through the pages of the Aberdeen Attack, of being idle, Rose-Rolfe answers back: 'I never was idle.... It's comical to say it: but my indefatiguability was nothing but a purely selfish pose, put-on solely to make philanthropists look unspeakably silly, to give the lie direct to all their idiotic iniquitous shibboleths. It wasn't that I *couldn't* stop working: but that I *wouldn't*. The fact is that I long, I burn, I yearn, I thirst, I most earnestly desire, to do absolutely nothing. I am so tired. I have such a genius for elaborate repose.'

Now, with Serjeant's money, he could do more than merely dream About Doing Little, Lavishly. He now could realize the words of his own Toto story: 'For three weeks, I have been busier than any seven and thirty bees; thoroughly enjoying toil. Allowed to consume latent energy, I taste relief.' After fifty-one struggling years, Rolfe achieved his reward.

At last freed from the legal ties binding him to Barnard & Taylor, Rolfe accepted Rider's offer for *The Weird and the Wanderer*, now entirely rewritten by him. In the negotiations for the book and reading the proofs, Rolfe corresponded with Ralph Shirley. As a favour to himself, this man from Rider's asked Rolfe to look up his 'nephews' while they were in Venice. These were Llewelyn and John Cowper Powys. In May and June 1912 they and Louis Wilkinson and his wife Frances visited Italy. When they came to the City of the Lagoons, they found that Rolfe 'was living well: he had his private gondola, beautifully manned.'

Rolfe was too assiduous. We [Wilkinson reports] would all have enjoyed seeing something of him, but we did not enjoy seeing too much. John, especially, found him a waste of time. 'He'll be wanting to introduce us to some of those sham Italian countesses he talks of.'—'Why not?' said Llewelyn. 'I'd rather like to meet a few sham Italian countesses.' But we didn't meet them, and after a little while the pressure of 'Corvo' grew too severe. John has described how the end came, but his account does not show the occasion quite as I remember it. It was at the bottom of the Campanile that we parted for good from Corvo. He had asked when our next meeting was to be. 'To-morrow?'—'We're engaged, I'm afraid, for to-morrow.' John, as the eldest was our spokesman. —'The day after?'—'I'm afraid we're engaged then too.'— 'Well, perhaps Thursday?' At that point John lost his nerve. 'We're *engaged!*' he shouted. 'All the time! Up to the hilt! Engaged! *Up to the hilt!*' Corvo turned on his heel with one of the swiftest movements I have ever seen and shot away from us across the Piazza.

The starvation through the years of body and heart made Rolfe also greedy for companionship. His unlimited generosity could no doubt overwhelm some people. After a puppy has been fondly patted, in its appreciation it can then dog the foot-steps of the donor of affection and hamper his natural gait. So some interpreted the overly kind deeds administered by a gracious Rolfe. In sharing goods or time, perhaps he did so in an abundance irritable to the other person. Yet, given a fair opportunity, there was no more pleasant a person. An American, Mrs. Morgan Akin Jones, on holiday in Italy during the same June with her husband, has given an attractive sketch of Rolfe.

Our first meeting was in a dining car, when we shared a table at dinner on our way from Florence to Venice, and he (we learned later) was returning from a few weeks in Florence where he was collecting material for a life of Botticelli.

I noticed he was reading an abstruse French book dealing with higher mathematics and dismissed him, with his thick lenses which made his eyes appear to be looking at you from a vast distance, as a dull college professor. Dinner over we asked for some cigarettes and ... our neighbour across the table leaned over and in a most cultured English voice said, 'Won't you have one of mine? They are from Montenegro....' The night of our arrival in Venice was memorable. The first glimpse of that fantastic city must always be an experience, but when it happens to be the full of a June moon it is almost too much beauty to be borne. We were leaning out of our window ... when there was a knock at the door—and a boy brought in a box, with a note from our recently acquired friend saying: 'These are my own brand of cigarettes, made for me in Montenegro. I hope you will like them. Also I have a gondola of my own with painted sails—which I shall send you tomorrow morning.'

That was the beginning. There were long talks about life—mostly his life—for he seemed eager to unburden to an understanding ear. 'Simpatica' was the word he used, and he seemed grateful for our friendly interest.... With his mellow old Piazza, his books, and his writings, which he did mostly while gliding in his gondola, he seemed content. His gondola, with sails he painted himself, was garishly beautiful and a striking picture among the less decorated ones of the Grand Canal.

Mr Rolfe was a very absent-minded man. I remember his frantic search for his glasses which usually he was wearing; and ... a dreamy way of reaching up his sleeve and pulling out of his cuffs a handkerchief, that was reminiscent of legerdemain. One expected to see at least a rabbit pulled out by the ears!

On our walks and rides through the small canals he made Venice live again for us. Each stone and building, each statue had its story.

The legend of the Baker's Boy is lost in the mists of time, but I have always been grateful he gave it back to me one day when we were walking across the Piazza....

His handwriting was most unusual—almost like the illuminations seen in old manuscripts—each phrase a beautifully wrought and complete bit of craftsmanship. After our return I had many amusing letters from him. Perhaps it would just be the message: 'Remember what the doves in the Square say—"Look at the fool! Look at the fool! Look at the fool!"' Or, 'You promised to come back next June when the moon is full, and Pietro will sing to you again!' Or,

'Don't forget the Baker's Boy!' Just some short terse phrases but so characteristic of the man.

The money now at his disposal was used in various ways. He visited Florence to gather material for a novel on Botticelli and another one on the Sforza family. But Venice was truly his city. The zeal with which his books and letters once consumed him was now replaced by sailing the Venetian water. His excursions over the lagoons, across the canals and into the Adriatic occupied most of his time. Pinned down in dark, airless rooms for half of his life, Rolfe now lived in the open air on the water. His literary projects were now no longer as prolific as during the days of necessity. But what was now prolific, up to a point, was the money which came from England. During 1912 Serjeant had supplied Rolfe with £1,000.

Although Rolfe did not complete as much work as before, he was keener than ever about publishing his earlier novels. And the profit from these would be justly divided between him and his patron in England. To date, however, Serjeant had realized nothing and the source of his money to Rolfe had exhausted itself. As 1912 closed, he sent a last cheque to Rolfe and informed the author living in Venice that there was no more money. But for once in his life Rolfe was not disappointed. His credit was excellent. And in November, Rider had published *The Weird of the Wanderer*, with royalties going to Rolfe as sole author.

For more than half of his life Rolfe had been a wanderer upon this planet, feverishly searching for some little niche for himself and his talent. The Church afforded none. A small crevice which he found in the world of literature did not easily yield to his writings. As a singular individual he fitted into no society. His life was his own and he lived it alone. Now, finally free from any worry and the fear of tomorrow's doom, he lived in relieved comfort. The sky and water of Venice were absorbed into his soul.

Signor A. Arban, the proprietor of the Cavalletto, found an apartment for Rolfe early in 1913. 'At last he had a place of his own,' Rolfe said about Nicholas Crabbe when he (and Rolfe) found a small single room in London in 1899. Now Rolfe, creator of Crabbe, could recite the same words for himself with all the exuberance his heart could exclaim. His new Palazzo Marcello apartment consisted of at least two furnished rooms overlooking the Grand Canal, next to Wagner's Palazzo Ver-dramin-Calergi.

The rejected clerk for holy orders had elected himself pope in 1903, if only on paper. Perhaps now he wished to be in sur-roundings worthy of that state. A trip to Rome provided the necessary material. One day Rolfe met Nina, the Raggs' former maid, 'and asked her if she would do some sewing for him. He conducted her to his apartment and showed her his bedroom. It was hung with scarlet cloth, and had damask curtains and bed-coverings to match. Thrusting some material of the same vivid hue into her arms he asked if she would make cushion covers from it. Her old aversion to him revived: she would not stay in the room, and saying that she had a sewing machine at home she took the material away. Determined not to go near Rolfe again, she asked a neighbour to convey the finished work to his apartment. The man delivered the parcel but waited in vain for payment.' So Mrs. Ragg described this event.

In the spring of 1913 the Raggs spent a week in Venice. No secret was ever kept from Rolfe. And his encounter with Nina may have been his way of letting them know of his present situation. For the Raggs little remained of their old friends. Horatio Brown was a sick man, his mother had died and the death of Lady Layard 'had greatly changed the structure of Venetian society.... Only Rolfe—as we learnt from our former gondolier—was flourishing like a green bay tree. He had an apartment and a gondola and was reputed to be a rich man.'

Enough material had been bought by Rolfe to provide a huge scarlet bow for a little black dog which he kept for a short while. The bow complemented the colour of his own hair, which was now dyed red. In his flourishing appearance in February 1913 he sat to Gaele Covelli for his portrait. The scarlet cloth from Rome, the Rome which was the Seat of St. Peter, satisfied his inward connection with the Church. Unlike the portrait of him-self which he drew ten years earlier in the pages of *Hadrian the*

Seventh, the Covelli painting had no ecclesiastical pretensions. He posed not as any officer within the Church, and the oil painting simply depicted the every-day Rolfe in his street clothes —stiff collar, tie with silver guard and dark suit.

From his Palazzo Marcello he would appear as a guest each night in Arban's Cavalletto restaurant. In this way he met another Englishman. Arban noticed that this person who had just arrived at the Cavalletto had no friends and that his funds were near an end. In a polite and humanitarian gesture, he introduced the two to each other one evening over dinner. This was the opportunity for which Rolfe had been waiting: to be able to help somebody in need. In *Nicholas Crabbe* he (as Crabbe) befriends an unfortunate person by offering him a room in his flat. His 'flat' at the time was only a single room at 69 Broadhurst Gardens. In no way had he ever been able really to help some other person, with money or shelter. But now he could. He took this new friend under his charge. He installed him in a room in his apartment, adjoining his own room. The two were inseparable. Whenever Arban saw one, the other was also present, and so they remained until the night the Cavalletto proprietor saw them together for the last time—the night of Rolfe's death.

Although Rolfe's new friend was a derelict in Venice in 1913, his background was in sharp contrast to his benefactor's.

A man by the name of Wade Browne came from Ludlow to Regent Street, London, and in 1831 married Anne Pennefather, daughter of the Lord Chief Justice of Ireland. They soon moved to Monkton Farleigh, Wiltshire. On his estate he built a tower, 'Browne's Folly', which overlooked Bath and another 'folly', Beckford's Lansdown Tower. Soon after their first child, Edward Pennefather Wade-Brown, was born, Anne died. Browne married again to become the father of other children and died in 1851. Edward married Evelyn Powys in 1869 at Aberford, York. Moving to London, their first child, Thomas Pennefather Wade-Browne, was born at 35 Charles Street, Berkeley Square, on 31 August 1870.

Edward had been in the Army during the Crimean War as a lieutenant in the 71st Foot Soldiers of the First Battalion of the

Highland Light Infantry. In 1866 he retired as a captain. His son, the eldest of three children and the only boy, was destined for the Army. He was sent to Wellington. During the two years he was there, 1882-4, he had an accident which crippled one foot. This prevented his entry into the Army, to the grave disappointment of his father. The accident compelled Thomas to wear a surgical boot for the rest of his life.

The Pennefather and Wade-Brown families had a number of illustrious members. One of these was Richard Theodore Pennefather, Auditor-General of Ceylon in the late 1800s. Edward Wade-Browne's family moved to Kensington at the turn of the century; and at this time Thomas left England for Ceylon to work in a tea plantation. The father died in 1904, leaving a sizeable legacy. Thomas' annual visits back to England stopped in 1905. When his mother and unmarried sisters later died, each left a large part of their legacy. In 1913 Thomas had next to nothing when he appeared in Venice, though a year previously he had been appointed a tea plantation superintendent in Ceylon.

During the last year of his life Rolfe was employing Leonard Moore in London to act as his literary agent. Just after moving into his Palazzo Marcello, he wrote Moore in April. He was 'just beginning the year's cruising on the lagoon. My new house is convenient as I have my boat moored at my front door in the Grand Canal. Benedetto Marcello [composer, 1686-1739] was born and worked and died in this palace.' In May he asked Moore, 'If you were a wet-bob, and can eat in a fourteenth-century pub [the Cavalletto] when ashore, and think of coming here for a holiday, you just let me know in time, and come to me, and I'll give you The Time Of Your Life.' He and his friend had just returned from sea at the beginning of September when Rolfe wrote, saying that he had 'told Blackwood to send you my last and so far greatest work, which in my opinion should confirm Maurice Hewlett's prediction: "will float you out among the greatest galleons very soon". It is called tentatively, *The Desire and Pursuit of the Whole....*' During 1913 *Blackwood's Magazine* published three of Rolfe's Venetian essays in their June, July and September issues.

In August a letter to his London agent read:

Yes. The interest in my works is legally vested in the Rev. Justus Stephen Serjeant, Rector of Warboys, Huntingdon, for my protection and convenience. But I have an absolutely free hand in conducting all negotiations for my work.... It's an awful pity you haven't been here. Apart from the splendid summer on the lagoon, which is still in full force, they've been commemorating Verdi with a series of performances of his opera *Aida* in the huge old Roman Arena at his native Verona near by, to 60,000 persons nightly, with an effect positively stupendous. We can't do that sort of thing, you know.

Rolfe's works were legally vested in Serjeant's name. Yet, although assigned to the English rector, Rolfe sent *Hubert's Arthur* to Morgan Akin Jones in America.

In his last letter to Moore, October 3rd, Rolfe wrote at length about his unpublished books and sent along a 'few blue prints,' or photographs, 'which may interest you and two hideous libels of me [taken by Wade-Browne] to make you laugh.'

Whatever his reasons, Rolfe did not care for the British Consul at Venice, Edward de Zuccato, and was probably relieved when he heard that he was to be replaced early in 1913. The newly appointed Consul was (later Sir) Gerald Campbell. Rolfe had to call at the Consulate to inspect him. This was the first of only two times Campbell saw Rolfe and the only time he did so when the English author was alive.

On May 1st Campbell employed a Clerk, Harold Couch Swan, who was to act as Pro-Consul when he was away. Swan had seen Rolfe's boat on the Grand Canal with its painted sails and Union Jack, but he was to speak with the eccentric Englishman only once. While Campbell was on holiday in June, Rolfe came into the Consulate to ask advice. He said that he was in trouble with the Venetian police. They had accused him, he said, of making overt advances to young conscripts on the Lido. What should he do? Swan advised him to take the next train out of Venice.

Was Rolfe's story true? Or was he only testing the young clerk? Seventeen years earlier he had told young Holden at

Holywell of his 'chance romances of the street' at Rhyl or Manchester. But no one, until the very few who read *The Desire and Pursuit* in 1910, knew of Rolfe's vow of celibacy for twenty years made in 1890. Although he was only a boy at the time he knew Rolfe, Leo Schwarz never believed this tale told to Holden. Venice is indeed different in every respect to Holywell and Rolfe could use a more lurid, and plausible, story. Seeing the young Swan alone, perhaps Rolfe wished to impress him in some way, if only with a shocking statement. As at the Belle Vue and with the van Somerens, Arban knew of no visitors for Rolfe at the Cavalletto. Nor did he do any entertaining. When not on the water, he was writing in his room. And neither Arban nor the British Consul was ever visited in relation to Rolfe by the Venetian police, who have a thorough knowledge of people's conduct within the city. Whether his report to Swan was true or not, in a manner of speaking Rolfe followed the young Pro-Consul's advice and left Venice. But not by train. From June until the first of October he was away, sailing into the Adriatic with Wade-Browne. For a day or two each month he returned for fresh provisions before the two sailed off again.

On July 22nd Rolfe celebrated his fifty-third, and last, birthday 'at sea'. If he had known one thing about Campbell, this would have been truly a mirth-filled holiday. When the new British Consul came to Venice, he cited his forthcoming expenses at '£100 a year,' plus '£15 a year for a second gondolier and £50 for the purchase of a gondola'. His excuse for being provided with one because of the movement of the Italian warships in 1913 seemed rather thin to his superiors in Florence. The Foreign Office, he was reminded, provided no carriages, or gondolas, for the Consular officers. The expense was not sanctioned. And he also was instructed immediately to 'furnish a detailed statement as to the manner in which the Official Allowance of £200 a year is spent'. Curtailing him from the beginning in any grandiose plans while he remained at Venice, this reprimand arrived on July 22nd .

Rolfe wrote to Moore in June that he had received the agent's last letter and 'three others, two from English publishers and one from an American, asking me to submit books to them.

God knows why this astounding spurt. I don't. However I have made up in packages four MSS. and I have sent them off, of which yours is one. And I am going to make bets with myself as to which of the four of you sends me the first gold. If it is any comfort to you personally, I'll make you this sporting offer —if you dispose of *Nicholas Crabbe* for me before the other three do anything, I'll put the disposal of those three MSS. in your hands, i.e. I'll tell those publishers that you are acting as my agent if they want to treat.' If Moore really wanted to be Rolfe's agent, the author in Venice wanted 'heaps of little things' done in London. He asked for a copy each of four of his published books and various things for his boat. And he ended his letter by saying that 'to-morrow I'm going to get up at dawn 3 a.m. to paint a new set of sails for my ship in a diaper of black ravens on white'. These were to be used on his new boat and in contrast to his other set, the main sail of which depicted a nude Perseus-St. George in front of a sun-burst, above his motto in Greek.

On July 12th he had been cruising for twenty days and asked to be excused in delaying an answer to Moore. He thanked the man in London for sending the flags for his boat. He and Wade-Browne were 'only back for provisions and blankets, the weather having turned cold'. And they were off again until August 5th, when the weather was 'blazingly lovely. There's a serenade on Saturday night on the Grand Canal, which passes under my window.' The first of September he had 'returned from sea' for the last time.

Moore's letter of September 30th found Rolfe 'towed back shipwrecked from a lovely cruise' along the coast north of Venice. In his reply, Rolfe spoke about his books and their possible publication. 'And why ever not issue *Don Renato* for the Christmas Sales, it being ready, and the *Meleager* in the Spring (early).... I howl to you across the Narrow Sea, saying, "GET ME PUBLISHED AND TALKED ABOUT, INSTANTLY AND CONTINUOUSLY." ... *The Desire and Pursuit of the Whole* ought by rights to MAKE me if published now.... Remember, *The Desire and Pursuit of the Whole* is far away the most urgent and profitable thing you're ever likely to handle, all the other things being merely side-dishes.' In a P.S. he asked for another flag and copies of two of his books. If ever received, Rolfe never had the opportunity to say.

One of the books Rolfe wished Moore to send him was *In His Own Image*. Under the title, 'Miscellanea I: Pious Jests', N. K. (C. C. Martindale, S.J.) wrote about this book in the September 1913 issue of *The Month*:

For there is, finally, a certain mysteriously quaint or humorous envisagement of august realities which is indubitably the spontaneous product of an absolutely vital faith. Thus jest (and thus, alas! blaspheme) those triple-dyed Catholics, the Neapolitans. To see them at work with San Gennaro is, in a sense, a liberal education. This mood is expressed in a story towards the end of Mr. Belloc's *Path to Rome*, and finds its perfect literal enshrinement in Baron Corvo's *In His [Own] Image*. (And since with this author the tears often enough so nearly underlie the laughter, we shall mention the brave merriment of those who feel that thus alone may the world's tragedy be faced.) That is a book which had caused some to pull long faces. Yet we have known of one who gave it regularly to all intending converts of his acquaintance. So might the temper of their faith be tested: if they rightly appreciated the stories, it was sound.

Therefore, how may one laugh at pious things? Aristotle would always have us smile at the Harmless Ugly. And by ugly, he means the disproportionate or incongruous. And when this strikes us suddenly, it shakes laughter from an untired mind. Now in all religious statement or action, there is a strong human coefficient, and thus an incongruity and a disproportion. Anything on the Merely intellectual or practical plane is bound to be indefinitely disproportionate to the Divine: and some notions, some actions, what we call 'ludicrously' inadequate.... How shall we smile in Heaven?

Robert Hugh Benson was referred to here by Martindale as the person who gave Rolfe's book 'to all intending converts'. And in a footnote to his article Martindale spoke about a Toto story pertaining to the Jesuits: 'And should perchance this page reach the Baron's eye, may the writer earnestly assure him that the poisoned figs, chopped though they were never so fine, yet were not enough—not half enough—to go round? And then, that was so long ago. And then another Angel administered an antidote and turned quite a number of the pebbles back into what they were before, and better.'

But, perchance, this page did not reach the Baron's eye.

By October 1st the summer of 1913 was over. The lagoons of Venice and the Adriatic were abandoned; and Rolfe and Wade-Browne had come back to Palazzo Marcello.

Referring to the Saturday night of October 25th, Gerald Campbell sent a letter to Herbert Rolfe of London:

Your brother had been in good health and spirits of late and dined at his usual restaurant, Hotel Cavalletto; on Saturday night, leaving there at about 9 p.m. with a friend Mr. Wade-Browne, who occupied rooms in his apartment. On Sunday the latter called out to him but receiving no answer thought that he was still asleep. Towards three o'clock in the afternoon he went into the bedroom and found your brother lying dead upon the bed. He was fully dressed and it would seem that he had died in the act of undoing his boots and fallen on the bed knocking down the candle which, fortunately, went out....

15

*The Corvine legend is held by some to be purely
a myth and by others a tale of reality too contemptible to be raised out of the mire whether it was
trampled by so many feet both annointed and
profane.*

Sir Shane Leslie

..... The English doctor was called in but could do nothing
beyond helping Mr. Wade-Browne to notify the authorities
and summon your brother's usual medical attendant. The
police came in the evening and removed the body to the
Hospital Mortuary and locked up the apartment. The following morning the hospital doctor certified that the cause was
in all probability heart failure. This diagnosis was subsequently confirmed.

Thus, recorded by the English Consul, the ending for the
caustic Raven and the tenacious Crab was uneventful and un-
dramatic.

The *Gazzetta di Venezia* merely reported that 'a certain
Frederick Rolfe, aged 53, died unexpectedly from paralysis of the
heart' and that his body 'was taken by a boat of the Blue Cross to
the mortuary at the Hospital'. The *Gazzettino*—'that charming
little journal of Venice,' Rolfe had stated, 'which gives, not only
a decent summary of the world's and the country and city's news,
but a really liberal education in Venetian manners, customs, and
delicious dialect, all for the sum of three schei, less than three-
fifths of a halfpenny'—said the same thing, with only a few addi-

tional 'facts'. 'It was a chambermaid who on entering the room made the sorrowful discovery,' it noted and named Rolfe 'a rich Englishman who had been living in our city for some time.' The longest account of Rolfe's death was given in the *Adriatico*:

Frederick Rolfe, the son of Augustin, born in London fifty-three years ago, a historian and writer, was a characteristic and strange person. An assiduous visitor to the Marciana, he led a somewhat bizarre life in Venice. At times he would spend whole days, alone, on the lagoon, in a boat which he had built for himself; at times he would disappear unexpectedly from the town without his friends knowing where he went and would then reappear unexpectedly. Recently he lived in an attractive apartment in the Palazzo Marcello at S. Marcuola 2137, and lived with a fellow countryman, Thomas Pekfoller. On Saturday evening the two friends had talked until eleven o'clock, when they retired to their respective rooms. Yesterday [Sunday] morning round about mid-day Pekfoller, who did not see his friend come out of his room, went to waken him and found him dead on his bed, still dressed; the bed was still untouched.... When the police officer of the Cannaregio was informed, his deputy Scialdone was called. On the deceased were found a revolver, 'cheques' and other private documents....

The origin of the gun and the reason Rolfe had it are unknown. But he did use it, if only for target-practice—shooting at pigeons. And his astonishingly colourful sails may have injected the thought that the boats themselves were hand-made.

In London, Rolfe's brother had to excuse himself from his War Office job and as church organist to travel to Venice. Herbert and Freddy had exchanged a mutual admiration for each other. Freddy had adopted the name of Nicholas to recount his own deeds, frustrations and dreams on paper. Nicholas the artist, Nicholas the music-writer, Nicholas the grandfather was Nicholas of the Past. Next to Rolfe himself Herbert was the only creative member of the present family. He also wrote music, music accepted as part of the service in the Church, even if the Church were Anglican. But for him Venice was not the same as the city of Freddy's dreams. For Herbert it afforded only the sad duty of attending to his brother's burial, before he quickly returned to home and family.

Whatever reward he expected from his earthly life, Rolfe continually lived with a desire towards a spiritual one. He never for a moment lost hope in the fact that he would be called into the Church's inner fold. When he finally lived beyond the age of candidacy, he wrote in his *Desire and Pursuit*:

No fruit came from his sowing. Nothing was left in him, or of him, but un unconquerable capacity for endurance till sweet white Death should have leave to touch him, with an insuperable determination to keep his crisis from the hideous eyes of all men....

He went, every evening, to the sermon and benediction at the church of the Gesuati on the Zattere: first, to pay the prodigious debt of the present to the past—the duty of love and piety to the dead; and, second, for the sake of an hour in quiet sheltered obscurity. The grand palladian temple, prepared for the Month of the Dead, draped in silver and black, with its forest of slim soaring tapers crowned with primrose stars in mid-air half-way up the vault, and the huge glittering constellation aloft in the apse where God in His Sacrament was enthroned, replenished his beauty-worshipping soul with peace and bliss. The patter of the preacher passed him unheard. His wordless prayer, for eternal rest in the meanest crevice of purgatory, poured forth unceasingly....

Whatever the eternal judgment of purgatory, Rolfe was now at rest.

Born an individual human being, Rolfe, unlike many others, never permitted himself to be absorbed into the daily pattern of mass civilization. He imagined that he alone could fight the entire world and be victorious. With Don Quixote, he attacked the giants, who turned out to be mediocre windmills. Firm as they were during the onslaught, they have now all perished into the dust of time. Only their attacker remains. For by the end of his life Rolfe had achieved much.

In the eyes of some, he appeared to be an unfortunate and even an undesirable person. Half-ashamed of his natural position in life, he invented tales about his background, tales which antago–nized rather than impressed. With his profound dislike of alms, he developed an incapacity to express gratitude. Yet he was never selfish. The man which alone was Rolfe runs through his stories. He is always self-concerned but never self-centred.

Rolfe was unfortunate in one sense. He was never at the right place at the right time to have his work exploited to the fullest. Speaking of his wall-hangings of 1891, Kains-Jackson had written that 'we are glad to notice that a really respectable piece of work has found a place in a Roman Catholic place of worship. The pity is that in a secluded village like Christchurch a design of this character should be hidden from the notice of the Roman Catholic world.'

He was also unfortunate in choosing the wrong books to be 'a foundation on which one may build'. *Hadrian the Seventh* was never a favourite of his as a possible best-seller. Some quirk with-in him envisioned prosperity coming from archaically written literature. For his first book he rebelled against Grant Richards' publication of the Borgia history because he commanded Rolfe 'to write vividly and picturesquely to suit the Library Public'. The author preferred to be his own master, even in dictating to himself the subject and style of his own writings. The two books dearest to him were *Don Renato* and *Hubert's Arthur*. He laboured the longest on these, writing and rewriting until the finished projects emerged.

Don Renato and *Hubert's Arthur* could never have been the popular books of Rolfe's dreams, much though he cherished them. At first he merely reworked Pirie-Gordon's original story, before entirely rewriting it as his own. When *Hubert's Arthur* was finally published in 1935, Rolfe's collaborator said, 'It amuses me a lot—but either [Rolfe] must have altered it a good deal or I have sadly forgotten what it was like. I think he must have touched up the heraldry now and then as there are several coats which would not have passed even my ignorance as it was a ¼ century ago. In places it produces hearty laughter:—as being both anti-clerical and anti-Jew—a translation might sell well in

Germany! I may have trouble in persuading my Jewish friends that Caliban had no share in Prospero's imaginings about their predecessors.'

No matter how much sympathy Rolfe's predicament evoked from others, he had the eternal resilience to remain above the surface of the mire. However masterful *Nicholas Crabbe* and *The Desire and Pursuit* are, *Hadrian* remains the one work to illustrate Rolfe's complete true nature. What it portrays better than the other autobiographical novels is a mind with the capacity to contain so many overlapping emotions. Perhaps the most startling paragraph in the whole book, one which conveys so many facets of his knowledge and nature, is:

> Hadrian threw His cigarette-end at a lizard on the gravel, and laughed shortly. ' "Pippety-pew, me mammy me slew, me daddy me ate, me sister Kate gathered a' me baines—"' He quoted with deliciously feline inconsequence. 'How you theological people do split straws, to be sure! Go on, though. You're intensely interesting.'

E. G. Hardy had known Rolfe for more than twenty years. He testified to 'the unfaltering devotion with which [Rolfe] has given himself up to his work. He has been ... at every disadvantage throughout. He has had no influential friends ... and has been almost hopelessly weighed down by want of means.... [His work] represents an amount of self-denying labour, almost wholly unrewarded, which in almost every other profession could hardly have failed to win success.' And, to Hardy, Rolfe was always 'a refined and honourable gentleman'.

Dawkins' account of Rolfe ended with the words: 'I think perhaps that I may have been unkind to Rolfe; but he contrived matters so that any assistance given to him would have been at the price of my own self respect...'

Canon Ragg summed up his opinion of the penniless author in Venice by saying, 'There was something definitely attractive about him as well as something repellent. And the attraction was dominant when he would allow it to be so. Certainly he can only have been partially responsible either for his actions or for his words. R.I.P.'

His wife saw only the repellent in Rolfe. Referring to his work, she said that she and her husband read *Hadrian* only after their meeting with its author. This 'had destroyed our capacity for a dispassionate estimate of its merits. We compared it too with *Il Santo* (*The Saint*) with which it had some points of resemblance; and besides the work of that sincere novelist and great gentleman Antonio Foggazaro (whom we knew and revered) the language and phantasies of Frederick Rolfe seemed thin, malevolent and tawdry. Corvo had neither patrician birth nor breeding nor the sentiments of one of "nature's gentlemen". His outlook on life and literature was that of a cad, with an intermittent streak of genius. Even his belauded picture of a Conclave became to me insignificant when I remembered and re-read that painted by Shorthouse in *John Inglesant*. Today I should compare it un-favourably with a chapter in the American novel, *The Cardinal'* —which, unknown to Mrs. Ragg, was inspired by *Hadrian*.

Sir Harry Luke remained on friendly terms with Rolfe. This was probably due, he said, to the fact that he never tried to help him materially. Although Rolfe became a partner with Pirie-Gordon in several books, this subject was never approached between him and the other Harry. Yet he caused a spark of inspiration to enter Luke's mind. This young Harry, Rolfe and Pirie-Gordon's father 'were basking in the heather on the sunny brow of a Welsh mountain engaged in the game of composing theoretical savouries' one day. A suggestion by Rolfe—'The mushroom must be isomegethic with the disc and five drops of lemon-juice should be squeezed upon the grouse just before serving'—did not agree with Luke's epicurean theories. But it was the foundation for the germinating thought which finally produced a most delightful cook book, *The Tenth Muse*.

Throughout his long life Harry Pirie-Gordon continually felt the kindest regard for his collaborator. 'Mr. Rolfe's later letters to me (and also to Professor Dawkins) led me to think that his mind was affected during the last months of his life,' he later said, 'but during the earlier part of our friendship I found him a most interesting companion and much enjoyed the display of his unusual gifts.' For Rolfe he always had 'a tender spot in my heart'.

377

At one time the editor of an American magazine asked Temple Scott for 'my reminiscences of [Rolfe], but I refrained from giving them because I felt I ought to let the afflicted fellow sleep undisturbed after the fitful fever he had passed through during his life.... For remember he suffered much. Be to his virtues very kind and to his faults a little blind. This may be hard to do, I know, but it is the best I think.'

Although Rolfe had not contacted his former friends in Venice during his last days, there were some he had not forgotten. During the 1912-13 winter an epidemic of influenza broke out in the Italian city. Treating the cases, Dr. van Someren accompanied one of his patients out of the city back to his home. There, in February 1913, he suddenly died. Hearing this, Rolfe sent his calling card to the young widow. On the back he had written: 'Sincere sympathy. If the services of a man will be of any use, please command me *in all ways*.'

The unexpected death of her husband, the illness of her family and the caring for growing children made Mrs. van Someren move to England. In the confusion of things, the calling card was misplaced when it was delivered. It remained the one item of his which she kept throughout her own life. She saw and read it for the first time only after she had learned that Rolfe himself was dead.

Barnard & Taylor could now close their books on Rolfe's case. Serjeant had purchased the rights to Rolfe's novels from them for £53 10s. od. But they still held a life insurance policy on his life. Advances to Rolfe from 1904 until 1909 totalled £222. The court case came to £258 15s. 6d. and £118 2s. 2d. was paid on the insurance premiums. In January 1914 the Prudential Assurance Company paid Barnard & Taylor £543. Their dealings with Rolfe over the years had cost them £2 7s. 8d.

The letters found behind at Palazzo Marcello were from relatives, friends and business associates, the greater part being from Herbert. The more recent ones were from Wade-Browne's mother and Pirie-Gordon. When he heard of Rolfe's death, the latter was willing to 'prepare the whole' of *Hubert's Arthur* 'for publication and make over half of the profits to Rolfe's heirs'. But this project never took place, because the manuscript was missing. It had not been sent to Serjeant and no one had any knowledge that Rolfe had shipped it to America. The finished and unfinished books Rolfe had left behind him and had assigned to Serjeant were *Nicholas Crabbe, The One and the Many, Don Renato: An Ideal Content, The Songs of Meleagros of Gadara, The King of the Wood, Amico di Sandra, The Burrowers, The Desire and Pursuit of the Whole*, an unfinished manuscript about the Sforza family in Latin and Italian, and the Genealogical Chart of the Borgia Family.

(Delivering his talk on Frederick Baron Corvo in 1926, A. J. A. Symons said that 'Rolfe was working on a counterblast to Edward Carpenter, entitled *Toward Aristocracy* ... when he died of heart failure'. This since has been repeated by other essayists writing on Rolfe, including Cecil Woolf, who further has stated that 'one of Rolfe's lost writings is a novel entitled *Sebastian Archer* [and] this manuscript may still survive in Venice'. Working on *The Desire and Pursuit of the Whole* between 1909 and 1910, Rolfe writes: 'Years ago, [Crabbe-Rolfe] had read, with pleasure and admiration mingled with disgust and detestation, Edward Carpenter's *Towards Democracy*.... And Crabbe had written, on the tablets of his mind, as something to be done on a fitting occasion ... a counterblast, magnificent hexameters, bright iambics, melodious hendecasyllabics—a new whole duty of man, from the gardener's boy and the scullery-maid ... to the King and the Pope, in their progress *Toward Aristocracy* on the road which leads to The Best.' Rolfe's Prologue to *Nicholas Crabbe* was also written in Venice during this same period. Speaking of Crabbe, Rolfe says that he 'determined to go in peace and live in peace and touch up his lovely *Toward Aristocracy* in peace on board a cargo-liner,' from which he left at some port, probably Larnaka, and never returned.

The story of *Sebastian Archer* is described in Chapter XV of *The Desire and Pursuit*. Its locale is Australia, the land to which Rolfe's Anglican brother emigrated. But the general description of Archer is mindful of Rolfe himself and, in a vague way, Hadrian. *Sebastian Archer*, an integral part of *The Desire and*

379

Pursuit, finally proves to be Crabbe's financial salvation (much the same as *The Weird of the Wanderer* actually was Rolfe's). Placement of this title in *The Desire and Pursuit* dates it shortly after Crabbe-Rolfe 'returned a batch of revised proof-sheets' of Ragg's *Church of the Apostles,* published in July 1909. On May 8th Rolfe wrote to Pirie-Gordon in relation to *Hubert's Arthur:* the manuscript, he suggested, should first go to Smith, Elder & Company. The *Archer* book goes to Ferrer (meaning 'Smith') Senior and Company. In a letter to Dawkins on May 28th Rolfe sought a sponsor for a 'financial undertaking', to enable him to continue his literary work. He listed his published and unpublished books, as well as 'four more books half-done', books already started before he left England. The list included neither *Toward Aristocracy* nor *Sebastian Archer.* At this same time Rider was interested in *The Weird of the Wanderer* and offered Rolfe terms to publish it, offers similar to those proposed for the *Archer* book in *The Desire and Pursuit. Sebastian Archer* and *Toward Aristocracy* no doubt were written only 'on the tablets of his mind'. As such, they do not appear on the list of books Rolfe left behind, a list compiled by the British Consul at Venice in 1913.)

Rolfe's will had been made out in favour of the Rev. Alfred J. Rolfe, the brother in Australia. But the distant brother took 'no steps to execute it'. At the time of his death, the English author had accumulated debts in Venice amounting to several thousand francs. His assets only came to one thousand.

For a quarter of his life Rolfe had placed the highest hopes for fame and fortune in his Borgiada. At the end of the British Consul's statement of Rolfe's effects, it was said that the curator 'states that in the opinion of the director of the Venice Library the Genealogical Tree of the Borgia family was of little value'.

The story of Rolfe, now dead, took on a new dimension. His eternal existence had hardly begun before witnesses appeared to testify about his temporal days. As an artist he was almost unaccepted during his life; as a person he was shunned and ignored by the many, tolerated by the few, and lived in spite and defiance. Release from mortal life brought no relief from casually formed opinions about his personality. To these was quickly added the taint of notoriety.

'During the Autumn of 1913' Llewelyn Powys wrote a letter, quoted in Louis Wilkinson's *Welsh Ambassadors*. It included the sentence: 'Did you see in the paper that the Corvo had died in Venice in bed with a boy?'

The previous year, as related already, Llewelyn and his brother were in Venice with Wilkinson and had met 'the Corvo'. Wilkinson also knew Masson Fox and, no doubt, either in person or by letter, Rolfe's name was mentioned in relation to Fox's interests. Such stories must have been passed on to Llewelyn to warrant this remark. The newspaper is unnamed; but what newspaper in 1913 would have printed a story about a man dying 'in bed with a boy'?

Thus began the malicious tales about Rolfe, who was now dead and unable to defend himself.

In *The Quest for Corvo* the searching through the dead man's papers for an address of his relatives by Gerald Campbell is told by Symons. 'The horrified Consul found letters, drawings and notebooks sufficient to cause a hundred scandals, which showed plainly enough what Fr. Rolfe's life had been.'

What had his life been?

When Campbell came to Venice in the spring of 1913 his predecessor, who shared no love for Rolfe, told him nothing adverse about the man's character. There were no reports or complaints at the Consulate against him or of any conduct attributed to him. No Venetian, no member of the English Colony or of the police registered any word against him. The government of Venice would have had little toleration for any undesirable person. And at the time of his death the newspaper reporters—who thrive on gossip from any quarter, especially from the police, if there be any—had no indictment to pronounce against him.

Campbell called Rolfe 'a curious type, cynical & critical, & not popular with the British & American residents who particularly resented his behaviour on the occasion of the burial of one of the most esteemed lady members of their community [Lady Layard]. They had all assembled in the English Church (corner of Rio San Vio & the Grand Canal), &, after the [Venetians], formed a procession of gondolas to the burial island. But lo & behold there was Rolfe in his gondola, dressed as a Cardinal, & as the procession passed him he shouted out all sorts of epithets, blasphemous & obscene, which damned him forever in their eyes. This was before my arrival there, but when I heard the story I realized why I was warned to keep clear of him. I do not remember hearing anything about his personal morals or lack thereof.'

The rich and colourful story of Rolfe 'dressed as a Cardinal' appears only in Campbell's memoirs. It bears the stamp of truth on the Consul's part, since he makes it clear that the tale was only told to him. But by whom? There is no account of such an incident in any of the contemporary Venetian newspapers. Mrs. van Someren, who lived in Venice after Lady Lavard's death in November 1912, makes no reference to such an event. And Mrs. Ragg, who particularly did not care for Rolfe and who knew all the members of the English Colony, was visiting Venice early in 1913. Lady Layard's death, she said, 'had greatly changed the structure of Venetian society'. But she gave no hint of Rolfe's misbehaviour at the funeral. The Venetians referred to him as 'l'inglese matto' ('the mad Englishman') and the English Colony simply ignored him.

Campbell was called to the morgue 'by the police to identify him on his death from heart failure. Then followed a search in his room for a will or the address of some relative, and I have been described in a book written around his life and works as a shocked Vice-Consul, when I discovered, as I did, not his will but a large collection of incriminating letters and photographs which more than confirmed the suspicions of scandalmongers as to his unnatural proclivities. I tried to push some of these and other *objets d'art* out of the window into the Grand Canal, but I was being closely watched by two police officers. In the end I got safely rid of most of it, but what a haul it would have been for a blackmailer!'

In a letter to a correspondent, Campbell said that he found Herbert Rolfe's London address, wrote to him and the brother 'came out. He was a most unromantic person, but I left him to fix things up. As a token of gratitude for what I had done he gave me leave to choose some of his brother's books for myself. I was glad to have them until I began to look at one or two, & then found that any reference to male or female anatomy had inspired him to write copious notes in the margin which, in turn, inspired me to take all the books & throw them into the Canal ... outside our door.'

Without being able to see the books with their marginal notes and the 'incriminating letters and photographs', it is impossible to form any verdict. The London brother certainly was not the open-minded individual Freddy was. Yet he knew his brother. They had corresponded frequently and Herbert certainly must have learned something about his brother's personal and artistic tastes. Herbert was a staid Englishman, but some amount of curiosity must have compelled him to look through Freddy's things, including the books he felt free to give to Campbell. The Consul, on the other hand, may have been one of those people all too easily 'horrified' in seeing anything 'inartistic'. If he were under the surveillance of two Venetian police officers when he searched Rolfe's apartment, the amount of time spent in seeing the letters and photographs must have been short. A cursory glance at one or two letters may have led him to think that all the letters in a certain group were of the same nature. He had no time to examine them. He knew nothing of Rolfe's affairs. He could only assume that the letters and photographs were personally linked with the dead man.

Rolfe was an assiduous maker-of-notes, 'always the student'. He 'was a real artist with a style, poignant and nude and athletic, shrewdly humorous and trenchant', as he describes Crabbe or himself in *The Desire and Pursuit of the Whole*. For years he collected notes, books and pictures. The male, the celebrated and youthful male of sculpture and painting, decorated his Broadhurst Gardens room. In the 1880s and 1890s he exchanged pictures, photographs and verses with others and pasted into scrapbooks those items interesting him most. In their 1902 correspondence Sholto Douglas and Rolfe exchanged personal thoughts on literature and art. Douglas acknowledged one of Rolfe's letters 'with the photograph' and spoke of some he was sending. 'There is one nude standing figure of which I am very fond, with the arms clasped behind the head. After all, the whole value of photographs is this power of recalling the original: therefore to you these have not the same interest which they have for me.'

Ever the student, Rolfe used every opportunity afforded him to pick someone's brains. In a letter to Dawkins in May 1908 he sent a long list of anatomical terms in English and in Greek. He had made 'a fairly complete list of Greek names for every part of the body. It certainly shows that they were extremely discriminative and knew and named quite as many details as the ordinary South Kensington student of anatomy knows now.' He wanted the professor to check the accuracy of his Greek in this list from 'Belly (from navel, Abdomen)' to 'seman genital'.

At the time he was writing to Masson Fox, Rolfe had a wonderful idea for a type of revenge on his friends in England. He would write a pornographic book in French, Italian and English, to be published in Paris at fifty francs. On the title page the initials R.H.B. would appear, with the Pirie-Gordon coat-of-arms on the cover and a note attesting to the book's authorization by the Order of Sanctissima Sophia.

The photographs found by Campbell may not have been ones taken by Rolfe. When he and Dawkins first arrived in Venice, the camera accompanying them belonged to the professor. He told Rolfe to take photographs—anatomical studies, he called them—of their gondoliers. The only two known sets of photographs from Rolfe's Venice days are these and the ones taken in 1913 by Wade-Browne with Rolfe's camera. After Rolfe had completed the professor's assignment and sent on the negatives and prints, he left the camera with the English Hospital. He later shipped it back to Dawkins. During the time he was without money, clothes and even shelter, he had no camera. With Serjeant's money he bought one again, but the only surviving photographs from this camera were taken by Wade-Browne.

At the time Rolfe was photographing the young Venetians for Dawkins, he also made drawings of them in his sketchbook. The ten sketches are no more than mere life-class poses.

'I'll always answer and burn your letters. Do this with mine,' he wrote to Masson Fox at the beginning. Rolfe's letters were certainly meant to lure some of the timber merchant's money into Rolfe's pockets in Venice, and Rolfe employed all his talents as a writer to produce this result. Any sport involving two contestants has only one winner. Rolfe's plans concerning Fox's money were never realized, even though he persisted, for a time. In his eagerness to please, ever bearing in mind a possible reward, he said that he was in agreement with Fox on all points. At the end of November he thanked the man of Falmouth for sending some photographs. 'I'll give photos to P. and C. when I see them, two to each. I'll keep the boat one if you don't mind in memory of a decent day.'

Because of the mention of the boat, these photographs sent by Fox may have been taken by Tuke. The painter was in the habit of taking nude pictures of his male models, some of which were employed by him on his boats. Rolfe 'found these photographs of Carlo and Zildo' by January and sent them to England. 'The clothed ones you might like to give to Tuke. I think the ones of Carlo rowing are very sweet. Pity he has but one ball.' These easily could have been prints from the lot ordered by Dawkins. In return Rolfe was asking Fox, 'Have you forgotten the photographs of the two entwined which you talked of sending me'. 'Oh Lord yes, by all means send me as many photographs as you can spare,' another letter said. If Rolfe had sent almost all of the early photographs to Dawkins and had only Wade-Browne's 1913 'landscape' photographs, then the horrifying ones found in his apartment could have been those sent to him by Fox.

To Dawkins he had once written from Gwernvale, 'You know I like having a locked glass bookcase, with the two top shelves labelled respectively "Purgatory" and "Hell", the books on which are only accessible to me.... Since [Mrs. Pirie-Gordon found one of these books], I've been giving away all my hellish and purgatorial books, books which I shouldn't care to be found on my corpse ...' He was then living in someone else's home. In his own palace he was not so discreet. In letters to Fox, he implored to be sent 'the FACTS' contained in the schoolboy 'confessions' the Falmouth man possessed. With these, Rolfe said, he could delve into 'research and revelation of very secret matters indeed'. Such letters, to Fox and not to Rolfe, no doubt were the ones found by the Consul. But nowhere did Campbell mention 'drawings, notebooks sufficient to cause a hundred scandals', as Symons eagerly maintains.

At the time of his death Rolfe was engaged on another historical novel, beginning with the assassination of Duke Galeazzo Maria Sforza in 1475. The finished portions of this work were written in Italian and Latin, with the notes at the beginning of each chapter mostly in English. Whether he intended to use the words in the actual text or not, the phrases describing one or two characters are interesting to note at this period.

Dec. 1475 & *Jan.* 1476 Intense cold....
Conspiracies begin....
    26 *Dec* Galeazzomaria murdered—....
Dec.Jan 1476-7 Intense cold
Messer Agnolo Politiano in love with Alessandra Scala, extraordinarily beautiful and singularly learned, daughter of Bartolommeo Scala—I came naked, devoid of all possessions, of very humble parents, with much faith, with no wealth at all or settlements, no patrons, no connections—servant to Cosimo, industry, erudition, noble, senator, secretary to Republic—Allessandro loved Michele Marullo—messer Agnolo versified at him—M said messer A had a crooked neck—messer A said 'sodomite', 'with a large penis', heir abandoned by a squalid father—that lewd fellow, drunken, gamester—illegitimate, filthy, lousy, dirty, foul—ragged, greasy, shaggy, country-bumpkin—greedy, stupid, insolent Marullo—squandered his inheritence in one day—with ever-open gullet and eyes of a cuntlicker—with ravenous arsehole and fucked-out penis—Marullo shut him up with two urbane epigrams to the address on Angelus Pulcianus (flea).

In his latter days the sworn celibate had evidently begun to use freer modes of expression to illustrate desired images.

In one of Rolfe's Toto stories, 'About the Penance of Paisalettrio', San Gabriele Arcangiolo assists Signora Pafia in the making of an arras. Pieces of coloured cloth are cut out and sewn together to form an image of the 'arcangiolo'. When Robert Hugh Benson bought and moved into the historic Hare Street House, Buntingford, he had an idea for a tapestry to decorate a private chapel. Referring to *In His Own Image* as 'the fifth gospel', the priest had read Rolfe's tales enough times almost to know them by heart. The Paisalettrio story inspired him to create a large arras on the subject of the Holy Grail in the manner described in the Toto story.

Although Rolfe was a domineering force behind Benson's personal and artistic life ever since they had first corresponded, the priest was much too occupied in other enterprises seriously to consider just this one relationship. In October 1905 he had written to Rolfe: 'I am slowly tasting *Hadrian* again, with renewed joy. My dear man ! ! !' This letter was sent at the time when he was beginning work on *The Sentimentalists*. This book's chief character, Chris Dell, was primarily based on two people, Eustace Virgo and Rolfe. In December of the same year Rolfe suggested the plot of Benson's *Lord of the World*, the story of 'a dechristianised civilization sprung from the wrecking of the old regime', a book of Antichrist.

Benson's novels were called 'psychological' in his day. But now they reveal very little depth of true character. In a way, they were stamped with a brand of propaganda. The people in them are Catholics, endowed with a certain taint of favouritism. Benson was not a man of any prolonged emotional concentration concerning individual problems. He was deeply sincere in all of his work, but he expressed an impetuous willingness to embrace the whole world instead of single questions one at a time.

The break with Rolfe was never understood. In his own mind Benson had acted justly and could not comprehend the other man's interpretation of his deeds. Cut off from Rolfe but bombarded with letters written in the heated acid of a friend betrayed, the priest never wavered from his first impression of the author of Toto and *Hadrian*. Only a few days before Rolfe's death, Benson claimed that he was a genius whom he loved. If he only would have apologized, Benson would have asked him to live with him and offered him everything he had. Yet the compassionate friendship had never taken root. Rolfe died in Venice and a year later, almost to the day, Benson followed.

The person who had written of Rolfe's Toto stories and Benson in *The Month*, September 1913, had something further to say on this matter. In a later letter he spoke of a certain lady who at one time had loaned him 'The Toto Stories to see if I thought them irreverent. I thought the stories charming but also pervaded with homo-sexuality and I thought Rolfe was ego-centric and arrogant and could be cruel. When I read *Hadrian*—still knowing nothing of his history—my guesswork became conviction'. So wrote C. C. Martindale, S.J., the person chosen by A. C. and E. F. Benson to write their brother's life. During the year before his life of Benson appeared, a collection of Martindale's short stories came out. One story, 'Unchanging Lakedaimon', caused a certain stir. The Jesuit's biographer, Philip Caraman, says that Martindale 'insisted that "Lakedaimon" was not in the least degree a study of homosexuality as some people took it to be' and that he 'was keenly interested in Spartan education and was now interesting himself in Jesuit education'.

Arthur Christopher Benson did not seem content with the Jesuit's monumental work on his brother and brought out his own book. Present when Hugh had brought Rolfe to their mother's house for the first time, his instant dislike for the stranger grew in intensity over the years. In the book about his brother he speaks of Rolfe without ever naming him. Hugh, he writes, 'made friends once with a man of morbid, irritable, and resentful tendencies, who continued, all his life, to make friends by his brilliance and to lose them by his sharp, fierce, and contemptuous animosities'. E. F. Benson was not as callous. In his own memoirs he speaks of Rolfe and his relation with Hugh in a quite matter-of-fact way. He tells of Hugh's last days and his wish 'to be buried in his garden in a brick vault ... accessible by a small flight of steps. This vault was to be closed with an iron door which could be unlocked from within ... so that in the event of [his] being buried alive, [Hugh] could escape, and that a key (of the vault) should be placed in the coffin.' E. F. Benson 'wondered whether a story of Rolfe's in that remarkable magazine *The Wide World* had induced this obsession?'

The Martindale book was hampered in its preparation by A. C. Benson's constant interferences. When it finally was finished the Rolfe-Benson papers and letters were returned to Arthur, who destroyed them. The ever-widening split between Rolfe and Benson now seemed complete. Yet something was overlooked. Hugh's poems were published posthumously, and these included the one titled 'Hero Worship'. Benson had also written one more novel in the last year of his life, *Initiation*. He had not read of the Reverend Bobugo Bonsen in *The Desire and Pursuit of the Whole*. *Initiation* was published the year after Rolfe's death, so Rolfe, in turn, had no chance to read a work in which he figured.

The two major characters of the Benson story are Sir Nevill Fanning and Enid, and the barest outlines of their association are subtly familiar. Sir Nevill and the girl meet in Rome and have deep discussions in the hills above Frascati. They fall in love and are engaged and return to London. In this new environment he discovers that any innocent action on his part is interpreted to his disadvantage by the girl he is to marry.

Dr. Walsh of New York had met Benson and knew of the association between him and Rolfe. Speaking about their estrangement, he thought that 'Rolfe seemed very bitter in the matter and it always struck me that he was really jealous of the success which Monsignor Benson had achieved after his conversion to the Church. His attitude was very much that of a jealous woman'.

A commentator in *The Month* spoke of Benson's novels and the people in them. Coming to *Initiation*, he said, 'Then there is Enid. One is almost afraid she is drawn from life. No one can possibly imagine her. "In the latter days there shall be ... men without affection." One always suspects some hidden and forgotten evil at the back of such a nature. There is really no light and shade—it is all dark there.'

In the novel itself Sir Nevill sees Enid as she is for the first time: 'But what held him ... in something like terror, was the shocking change in her whole character from that which he had previously believed it to be: it was as if a mask had been torn suddenly away, and a frightful face disclosed. He had thought her very nearly sublime—unlike others, spiritual, aloof, unique.... He had loved this presentment that he had seen—loved it as he had never loved any living being before, to his knowledge: he had thought that she understood him perfectly; he had hoped humbly and simply that he was beginning to understand her. Yet now, in an instant, a terrifying kind of coarseness disclosed itself; she snarled at him; she framed, as well as she could, sentences and phrases with the object of giving as much pain as possible; she tortured things and words into sinister intentions that had never even crossed his mind. ... He had had no conception ... but that human nature itself was capable of it.'

The person of Frederick Rolfe had been reflected in both Benson's 'Hero Worship' poem and in the bitter Enid.

Thomas Pennefather Wade-Browne and 'Thomas Pekfoller' of the *Adriatico* were the same person. The excitement and confusion caused by Rolfe's death resulted in the inaccurate translation of his uncommon English name by an Italian-thinking newspaperman. The fact that his last name was not used and that his three-syllable middle name had been corrupted did not bother him. There was no reason why it should have been printed in the first place. So, to him, no harm was done. The twisted name was the last of his worries.

On the Sunday afternoon of October 26th he was horrified. The finding of Rolfe's dead body meant only one thing to him. He now would be without friend or shelter. At the time he had a mother and two sisters back in England, but he made no attempt to contact them. The family of Campbell's assistant took him into their home. Harold Swan's father was the manager of the Seamen's Institute in Venice and he, his wife and Harold lived in the city. They housed Wade-Browne until he was able to move on his own. He stayed with them for a year and left Venice in August 1914. He went to Paris at the start of World War I to join the Foreign Legion. On October 6th he entered their services, at the age of forty-four and with a game leg. But he was invalided out and struck off their rolls on 5 March 1915. Yet, once in Paris, he decided to stay.

In his *Looking Back*, Norman Douglas writes of Wade-Browne under the name of Edmund Barton. The two met in Paris during the early part of the war and used 'to meet at dinner in a cheap restaurant ... when both of us were on our beam ends. I was living on Montmartre [and] he had a room in the dim regions behind the Gare St. Lazare—I never learnt the exact location. Barton was a broken man of about forty-five, lean and even cadaverous in appearance. He had been a schoolmaster, I think; among other things he had gone out as a tea-planter to Ceylon. He possessed a rich store of memories and a crapulous turn of mind; he was obscene to the marrow. He was obscene from a kind of ancestral necessity—obscene in a heart-sick and unmirthful fashion. He left Paris before I did, about October 1918, and continued to write me from London, where he had discovered some kind of coaching job in Bloomsbury. His letters were spiced with indecencies, and so profusely embellished with coloured nudes in ambiguous poses and in the style of Etruscan wall paintings, that I used to wonder what the Censor thought of them. One of them was worse than the rest—quite atrocious. and not in the least funny; it also gave bad news of Barton's health and ended with the words "Morituri te saluant". After that I begged him not to write me any more unless he could bridle his pornographic instincts.... He took no notice of this admonition but continued to bombard me with epistles containing his favourite dancers and warriors.... He had been friendly at Venice with that phenomenon, that unlovable but not despicable creature, F. W. Rolfe, *alias* Baron Corvo. They were both poor, and during that final period, he told me, he was Rolfe's only friend; everybody else had dropped him on account of his tattered clothes and insufferable manners. The wicked fairy! Here was a man possessed with a most rare gift, who might be alive and prosperous at this moment [in 1933], and whose venomous nature cost him his life. I have just glanced into *Hadrian the Seventh* again. How correctly he describes his own character! ... Barton told me that he, and he alone, was with Rolfe when he died of exposure in that open boat in which he passed his last days, for lack of money to live on shore.... I asked him about Baron Corvo's literary doings, but he knew nothing; he thought it likely that poverty and other hardships had extinguished his interests in such matters. "But I'll show you exactly what he looked like", said Barton, and proceeded to draw a side-face sketch of Rolfe. Of those deplorable Etruscans not one specimen survives, but here is Rolfe's portrait, pasted into a copy of *In His Own Image* (a smirky book, not much to my taste). It represents him as younger-looking than I should have expected, clean-shaven, with prominent chin; a hooked nose is the most remarkable feature of his face, and there is a slender pipe in his mouth and a yachting cap on his head.'

How much truth and how much fiction is there in Douglas' story about Wade-Browne? Some of Douglas' facts conform to those known and some do not. Rolfe's friend in Venice did live where Douglas says. Although the author 'never learnt the exact location', Wade-Browne lived in the Rue de Constantinople, running from the Place d' Europe, directly behind the Gare St. Lazare, to the Boulevard de Courcelles. He was a 'broken man', mentally as well as physically, and he was forty-five in 1915. Signor Arban of Venice thought that he was much older than Rolfe, although the reverse was true. From a small image on a 1913 photograph, showing him and Rolfe in a boat wearing yachting caps, he does not look 'cadaverous'. He never was a schoolmaster and he worked on a tea plantation in Ceylon continually from 1900 until the beginning of 1913.

Douglas says that Wade-Browne left Paris 'about October 1918' to go to London, 'where he had discovered some kind of coaching job in Bloomsbury'. From the time he arrived in Paris at the end of 1914, Wade-Browne never left the French city. He certainly was Rolfe's closest friend during 1913, but neither lived in any style which can be termed poor. During his earlier period in Venice, Rolfe's clothes were tattered and he gained no new friends because of this outward appearance; but his clothes in 1913 were far from being tattered. At the time the two Englishmen met in Venice, Rolfe was sitting for his portrait, wearing a new suit.

Rolfe and Wade-Browne had indeed lived in an open boat

during the summer, cruising the Adriatic and coming back to Venice by the first of October. But 'poverty and other hardships' had never 'extinguished' Rolfe's interest in literary matters. During his last year he was writing, though admittedly not as prolifically as before, and he was extremely interested in the publication of his novels.

In the year that Wade-Browne lived with the Swans, young Harold had ample opportunity to talk with him every day. The guest spoke of a number of things, but he never mentioned his family or very much about his background. He had been in Ceylon, but he never gave the Swans his reason for leaving and coming to Venice. As described by Arban at the Cavalletto, he was an extremely quiet and reserved man. There was no suspicion about his character; and in his talks with Harold the subject of morals was never approached. He wrote not one letter during this year and he received none. Most of the time was spent in his room, reading and just vegetating. Occasionally he would indulge in his keen interest in photography, using the camera once belonging to Rolfe. He had travelled to Venice with little luggage and he left the same way. Camera and books remained behind with the Swans.

The obscenities in Barton's letters must have been particularly note-worthy to solicit comment by the author of *Some Limericks*. In fairness to Douglas, the letters could have been real. There can be little doubt that Wade-Browne and Rolfe must have talked about, or at least mentioned in passing, the 'incriminating letters and photographs' found by Campbell. During the year he was vegetating at the Swans', something may have been incubating within him. There is no great mystery connected with the Foreign Legion accepting a man forty-four years old with a game leg. But it was unlikely for them to invalid out a person who had just joined their ranks. Could it have been a mental reason? In *Looking Back* Douglas speaks of a desire on Barton's part to flirt with death during the nightly air raids and the daily Big Bertha bombardments. Being invalided out of the Foreign Legion, the only form of military service to take him, and the uncertainty and weariness of the war may have released certain pent-up emotions within him

393

which could only have been expressed through the form of obscene letters—if Wade-Browne were the person to write them.

Looking Back was published in 1933 and the period from 1915 may be a distant one from which to recall exactly one single person and his habits, especially if the acquaintance were a war-time one. Douglas' memory may not have fitted the pieces of Barton's stories together in the right order. In the same year in which his book appeared Douglas was asked a direct question about Edmund Barton. A. J. A. Symons had written to him at Florence about the man who was with 'Rolfe when he died of exposure in that open boat'. 'As to revealing the name of "Barton",' he replied, 'this is the difficulty, which you will of course understand, that he would not be flattered with my description of him in *Looking Back*. Perhaps, if you should succeed in tracing him, you will bear this in mind, and not refer to the book? But I fear it will be a hopeless search, as his name was E. (? Edward) Browne, and I have not heard from him since 1918. I have no idea where he is, or whether he is still alive; and not a single letter from him to me has survived.'

After twelve years of steady service, working his way into a good position, Wade-Browne suddenly left the tea plantation in Ceylon. He swiftly abandoned security, his personal goods and money. This rather rash act may have caused him to think reluctantly about his relations in England and not to contact them. The choice of Venice may have been accidental. In his hurry to leave Ceylon, he may have merely boarded the first departing ship. Under normal circumstances, Wade-Browne's actions were much the same as anyone else's. But under stress, he could not endure any uncertainties of life, sudden or not. For years he had suffered from mental depression. But this was only evident under tension; and from sudden, horrifying tension he fled Ceylon.

As far away as Toronto, Ontario, seismological reports were received of an eathquake in Ceylon on 19 January 1913. The experience was unusual for Ceylon. The greatest tremors occurred over the central and southern parts of the island and several nearby ships felt the shocks. Such an event certainly caused grave concern in a 'broken' mind; and, as soon as he could, Wade-Browne fled Ceylon, leaving almost everything he owned behind him.

Venice proved a satisfactory and solacing haven. During 1913 he lived as Rolfe's friend and then as the Swans' guest through most of 1914. Discharged from the Foreign Legion, he was now uncertain of any future. The flirtations with death during the bombardment of Paris left him unscathed. But his mental depression had not vanished. During a black moment he jumped into the Seine. He was taken from the water during the cold, wintry weather, still alive, and placed in a hospital. A visiting priest learned his identity and wrote to his sisters in London. The elder one came to Paris to see him just before he died.

The story of Rolfe's life and works was first told to the general reading public in a short article by (Sir) Shane Leslie. With 'Frederick Baron Corvo', printed in the September 1923 issue of *The London Mercury*, the mechanism was started in the unravelling of Rolfe's story. Although it dealt more with books than with his career, this article was enough to fascinate those who, in their turn, fell under the hypnotic spell of 'Corvo the enigma'.

One month after Leslie's article appeared, John Nicholson wrote to Christopher Millard, 'Shane Leslie wrote to me on Sept. 11th from Rye: "I tried to write the Corvo article in charity as well as in clarity. A good fifth of the article was cut out." ' (All the elements of the uncut article appeared as Leslie's Introduction to the 1924 *In His Own Image*.) 'Herbert Rolfe (aet. 65 perhaps) was expecting me to visit him at Purley on Sept. 29th,' Nicholson's letter to Millard continued, 'and had Mrs. Rolfe senr (aged 86) staying with him that week-end. I was not well enough to go. Since then H. R. writes: "I have read the article several times; of course I wish it had not been written, but, having said that, I can make no further objections to it." Horatio Brown writes to me from Venice: "I have missed Shane Leslie's article on Rolfe. I may get sight of it later on. I could have supplied a queer lot of stuff. If it was necessary to modify concerning Rolfe—a free-lance with no ties—imagine

what I was forced to do in my J[ohn]. A[ddington]. S[ymonds].
books, with his daughters and their husbands insisting on seeing
the MS. before it was printed!"'

During 1925 Herbert read *The Desire and Pursuit of the
Whole* and commented on it in a letter. 'It contains so much
that is painful, offensive, and highly undesirable for publication.
... Further, as regards the story proper, it reveals the great
disparity between the ages of Crabbe and the girl, and in my
opinion, to render the story itself palatable, this feature would
have to be toned down. How this could be done without destroy-
ing Crabbe's identity as a man hardly used by the world and
altogether "down on his luck" I do not quite see.... A younger
brother of mine [Percy], who happens to be home from China,
has also read the MS. and he says in effect, "burn it".'

In answering Symons' appeal for information about his late
brother, Herbert wrote to him on 28 September 1926, 'I am certainly anxious that whatever may be written about him may be
correct.' But he did not live to read *The Quest for Corvo*.

After Herbert's death, Percy Rolfe wrote to Symons in 1933,
'As regards ... the late Mr F. W. Rolfe's works, let me make
it plain to you that neither I, nor any of the members of my
family in England, have any interest in the same'. On July 29th
he wrote again to say that he could add 'no information'. On
the same day, Alfred sent a letter from Australia to Symons:
'Judging by your article "Frederick Baron Corvo" in Life &
Letters Vol 1. No 2. July 1928, I imagine that you know as much
about [my brother] as I do. In any case I do not propose to supply
further details which a clever and cruel pen might twist to a
dead man's discredit.' Neither brother shared Herbert's admiration for Freddy. Left to the will of the family alone, Frederick
Rolfe never would have emerged from the shadows.

If Leslie publicly 'discovered' Rolfe, credit is also due to him
for Rolfe's actual preservation. According to the official custom
of Venice, after a specified period of time a body, unless re-
claimed, is placed in the common ossuary. When Rolfe died
in 1913 he was buried in the ground on the cemetery island of
San Michele. In December 1923 Theodore Anderson, the British
Vice-Consul at Venice, wrote to Leslie, naming two alternatives

for Rolfe's body. For a 'payment of Lire 250, an extension of term can be obtained for ten years in respect of the present grave' or 'by payment of the larger sum of Lire 500, his remains can be transferred to an urn which will be placed in a permanent vault'.

Leslie immediately wrote to his lawyer friend in New York, John Quinn: 'Would you and your friends care to save poor Rolfe's bones—at 250 or 500 lire! It cannot be many dollars. You alone of all his readers dreamed of subscribing to such a cause. It was typical of your generosity and imaginative sympathy with all the fine arts. To you then I commend Rolfe's ashes'.

Herbert Rolfe had been in correspondence with Edward de Zuccato 'with a view to the transfer of the remains [of his brother] to a niche in the permanent Mortuary'. Herbert was 'not well off and could ill afford even the cost which had been forseen for the transfer of the remains to an urn in a small niche'. When Rolfe's grave was opened, on 12 January 1924, 'it was found that the body was not yet decomposed. This is due to its having been enclosed in a zinc case. It will now have to be decided, either to pay for ten years extension,' the Vice-Consul wrote to Leslie, 'or to purchase a large niche in the Mortuary, big enough to hold the coffin.'

Quinn paid for the reburial; and so, in January 1924, Rolfe's remains were 'transferred to a perpetuity niche. The ceremony took place in the presence of a capuchin friar, of the Representative of the Municipality and of Mr. De Zuccato himself'. Although Herbert had intended to repay the New York lawyer, he never had the opportunity. Six months later, in July, John Quinn himself died.

(Added to the aloof mysteries surrounding Rolfe is one concerning his death and burial. In January 1924 his body was removed from the cemetery ground, where every inch is impatiently needed and constantly used over and over again. Yet, since the date of the removal, Rolfe's grave from 1913 to 1924 has never been re-used.)

*　　*　　*

Perhaps the final testimonial to Rolfe's character is in his own words. One record survives to show another person's views about Rolfe's words, if only in a silent way. The Mr. Wade-Browne who had dined with him on the eve of his death had lived with him for most of 1913. Staying in Venice for another year he read *Hadrian the Seventh*. As he did so, he marked or underscored sixty-three words, phrases or facts in the book. In letters Rolfe had the habit of repeating himself unceasingly. These same words and phrases may have become a part of his daily vocabulary and were heard by Wade-Browne even before he read them. Finding an understanding friend in Wade-Browne, Rolfe no doubt unburdened the story of his life to listening ears—a story interlaced with fact and fantasy.

The first mark in the book is on the dedication page, opposite 'To Mother'. The first mark in the actual story is on the first page, for the expression, 'some one will have to be made miserable for this'. The marks in Wade-Browne's copy of *Hadrian* reflect Rolfe's singular personality. Either in word or deed, this personality was made aware to Rolfe's companion, who recalled the strange author's life through the words of his novel. 'All my life is a pose ... of *strange recondite haughty genius, very subtile, very learned, inaccessible ...*' '... *his smile was an alluring illumination.*' 'He ... tucked His handkerchief into His left sleeve ...' 'Contact with senile humanity made His juvenile soul shudder.' 'On the one hand, with His principle of giving He could not even grasp a problem which involved taking: while, on the other hand, He utterly failed to realize that most people are averse from giving.' 'His external serenity was unflinchingly feline.' 'Hadrian winced: and marked the man.' 'The Pope went to a writing table and produced a couple of lines in His wonderful fifteenth-century script'. 'Most human ills were caused by the lack of scope for energy.'

Rolfe's great aversion towards reptiles was noted by Wade-Browne in the pages of his book. 'The Pope preferred to sit here where the pavement was of marble: because lizards avoided it, and their creepy-crawly jerks on grass or gravel shocked his nerves. He was sure that reptiles were diabolical and unclean; and His taste was for the angelic and clean.' The cross Rolfe designed for himself and carried around his neck was pawned in 1909 during the short month he was staying with the English artist, between the Raggs and the van Somerens. He must have retrieved it by 1912 so that Wade-Browne knew of it. Another person in *Hadrian* speaks to the pontiff about Macleod-Mc-Varish, 'Look what a fine chap he is to look at—just like that lovely Figure on Your cross.' Wade-Browne was not devoid of humour in remembering his benefactor. The part of one sentence marked reads: '... His Holiness was a most difficult man to get rid of, if one wanted to get rid of Him, whatever.'

From the marks, Rolfe must have told him the full story of his life, at least, paralleling the facts found in *Hadrian*. 'Had He been trained in boyhood at a public-school, *in adolescence at an university*, had His lines been cast in service, He would not have had to put so severe restraint upon Himself.' Rolfe had told Wade-Browne about 'the defalcations of a Catholic [that] ruined me' and the attacking articles in the 'dirty Keltic woodpulp'. He had carefully outlined the newspaper accusations and covered the events by saying exactly how he had acted and lived. Wade-Browne had noted where Rolfe had spoken of people in his book, people such as 'the cotton-waste merchant', Meynell and the Mr. Thomson of Aberdeen, Mrs. Crowe-Mrs. Gleeson White and Macleod-McVarish.

The account of Rolfe's being sent to Scots College was marked. 'The priest who recommended me, and Canon Dugdale, assured me that, *in return for my services, my expenses* would be borne by the Archbishop.' In the margin opposite these underscored words Wade-Browne had drawn a question mark. Another section of the book marked was that dealing with the money available within the Church, the money Rolfe always thought was at his disposal. At the time the two met in 1913 Rolfe could fully enjoy himself as he had expressed himself in *Hadrian*: 'I long, I burn, I yearn, I thirst, I most earnestly desire, to do absolutely nothing.... I have such a genius for elaborate repose.'

The one continuing physical comfort to Rolfe had always been tobacco. With money or without, he smoked. When in funds he sought his own mixture, in London, in Oxford and in Venice. On one page of *Hadrian* Rolfe speaks of 'the *Crab*

Mixture which George Arthur Rose had invented'. More than mere words, this was something actually shared by the two men. In the margin opposite these words Wade-Browne had written: 'see coat'.

Not only at the time *Hadrian* was composed, but during most of his life, Rolfe posed in various ways. As much as possible he concealed his miserable poverty. '[The dead body] lay upon his back staring at the sky. He was dressed in an awkward suit of yellowish brown. ... the soles of his shoes had been worn to the thinness of writing paper, and from a great rent in one the dead foot projected piteously. And it was as if fate had betrayed [him]. In death it exposed to his enemies that poverty which in life he had probably concealed from his friends.' These words were not written by Rolfe but are from Stephen Crane's *Red Badge of Courage*.

The most succinct passage marked by Wade-Browne in his companion's novel deals with the parting of the two friends. Rolfe writes of Hadrian, and himself: 'He became inspired with an appalling consciousness of the absolute necessity for instant active continuous exertion,—if He were to continue alive upon this earth. He felt that, if He were to permit Himself to relax for one instant, if for one instant He were to abdicate command of His physical forces, to let Himself go,—that instant would be His last. With this in His mind, He prepared for momentary unconscious lapses from violent activity. He posed with care, so that, if Death should seize Him unawares, He might not present a disedifying or untidy spectacle to the finders of His corpse. He carefully avoided postures from which, when He should be reft from the body, His form would fall indecorously.'

The one passage—written by one man and marked by the other—united and separated them. The finder of Hadrian's-Rolfe's corpse later died himself and dissolved into the silent and clouding nothingness that always had been his life.

No less a personage than Hadrian VII, in the words of his creator, sums up Rolfe's entire life in a moment of humbleness: 'God, I am very worldly. I have enjoyed the triumph.'

BIBLIOGRAPHIES

BIBLIOGRAPHY I

Before a list of books in which Rolfe has been mentioned is given, it may be interesting to note a few examples of his name, Corvo or Rolfe, which have appeared in history.

Perhaps the oldest form of the name Corvo is the northwest island in the Azores group.

In 1824 the Prince Alliata, Duca di Salaparuta, planted the first vineyards on the slopes of Mount Corvo in northwestern Sicily. Corvo grapes still produce ordinary, white, red and sherry wines, and their bottles carry the Corvo label with the original duke's arms and signature. This is 'the golden wine of Nido di Corvo' in 'About These Tales, the Key and Purgatory' (*In His Own Image*, p.213) and the wine Rolfe was proud to order in the presence of an amiable host in some Soho restaurant.

A 346-ton schooner was built at Boston in 1827, which was given the name *Corvo*. For disciplinary reasons, his father apprenticed the young Samuel Colt to Capt. Spaulding on this ship for a trip to India and back. She left Boston on 2 August 1830 and, by the time the *Corvo* sighted the New England city again, young Colt had completed a working model of his six-shooter, a device to make his name synonymous with revolvers.

Today there is a Corvina Press in Hungary. The publisher's title-page imprint is a *C*, in which is standing a raven, looking as though it is holding a ring in its beak, reminiscent of Thomas Ingoldsby's *Jackdaw of Rheims*.

And the word 'corvine' has crept into journalistic literature, referring to a personality or life similar to Rolfe's.

The most notable Rolfe in history is John (1585-1622). Born in Norfolk, he and his wife left for Virginia in 1609. His first child was born in the new colony. The infant died, soon followed by the death of the mother. In 1614 John Rolfe married Pocahontas and returned to England. Before sailing back to her home, Rolfe's Indian wife died at Gravesend, leaving their son in his care. John Rolfe returned to Virginia and made his fortune as the first person to grow tobacco in the New World, cultivating it to European taste. No documented relationship exists between John and Frederick and the latter never referred to him. The only intangible relationship is that of tobacco itself. A ceaseless smoker, Frederick Rolfe mentioned cigarettes in his writings. In *Don Tarquinio*, the son of the narrator, 'born xiii Sept. 1513,' introduced tobacco into Italy. In 'Herodotus' "History of England"' ('Reviews of Unwritten Books', *The Monthly Review*, June 1903) Raleigh brings back to England 'the wonderful new herb nikotiana'. There follows a 'discursion on the use of tobacco among the ancient Greeks,' one of whom is Sokrates, who 'smoked a home-made mixture of blackberry leaves and tea-leaves, when he was unable to come by ship-tobacco honestly'. This repeats Rolfe's actual experience at Holywell during his days of extreme poverty. What would he have said to a news item of 21 September 1970: 'British scientists today claimed that they had developed a synthetic tobacco pleasant to smoke and less hazardous to the health than natural tobacco. They plan to market it but don't know when. A spokesman ... said: "We have a number of research staff who have been smoking NSM (New Smoking Material).... I understand that it tastes not at all unpleasant."'

The following is a list of books and articles in which Rolfe is mentioned or are first appearances of some aspect of his work.

c. 1545 *Here after foloweth the boke of Phyllyp Sparowe* by *John Skelton* (c. 1640-1529), Poet Laureate, Rychard Kele, London, p. 19.
In this poem appears the line:
'The rauyn called rolfe.'
Edward Hutton (*Catholicism and English Literature*, 1942, p. 217): 'This is surely the origin of the pseudonym of that strange and unhappy figure, Baron Corvo.' There is no evidence that Rolfe ever saw this line. The name Skelton gives to 'raven' may have

been no more than heraldic nomenclature. This Rolfe easily deciphered for himself independently.

1796-c. 1890   *Grove's Dictionary of Music and Musicians*, edited by Eric Blom, Macmillan, London; St. Martin's Press, New York; fifth edition, 1954; Vol. VII, p. 211.
There is an entry for Wm. Rolfe & Co.

Nicholas Rolfe composed and had printed seventeen pieces of music for the pianoforte, one *Preceptor* and one set of *Observations*, c. 1810-1820. Only two of these works are in the British Museum.

1877   *The School Magazine*, August, pp. 502-4, 507-8.
In this number there are presumably Rolfe's first two appearances in print. One is a poem, 'Seeking and Finding: A Sequel to "The Lost Chord".' The other is a piece of music composed for the poem, 'The Fishwife's Lament'. This perhaps is Rolfe's only published piece of music, thus linking him with his grandfather Nicholas and with his brother Herbert. (The title of the poem is reminiscent of a cheap print of the day, 'The Fisherman's Widow'. This was the only wall decoration in the shabby room of Mary Jeannette Kelly, No. 13 Miller's Court, Dorset Street, Spitalfields, less than a mile away from Rolfe's birthplace. She was Jack the Ripper's last victim, on the morning of 9 November 1888, the date of the Lord Mayor's Show and the Prince of Wales' birthday and two nights after H. H. Champion's dismissal from the S.D.F.)

1880-1881 *Tarcissus*
This poem is Rolfe's first separate publication. It was no doubt paid for by him and printed at Saffron Walden while he was an undermaster at the local grammar school. Although the dedication page is dated 29 September 1880, it may not have been printed until December or very early in January 1881. Anxious as he always was over the publication of his books, the young twenty-year-old Rolfe must have awaited the appearance of this first work with eager anticipation, to give away copies to the twenty-two dedicatees as soon as possible. John Nicholson received his on 6 January 1881. *The Church Times* reviewed it, ever so slightly, on 1 April 1881.
In a letter of 11 March 1924, Nicholson wrote to a friend: 'Corvo admitted years later that it should be "Tarcisius".' The name of this boy saint is one which can be spelled a number of ways.

1881 'Public Baths for Saffron Walden,' *The Herts & Essex Observer*, June 25, p. 3.
This may be Rolfe's first published letter-to-the-editor.

1888 *The Oscotian: A Literary Gazette of St. Mary's College, Oscott*, July, p. 100.
This lists Rolfe's entry at Oscott.

'Sestina yn Honvr of Lytel Seynt Hew,' *The Universal Review*, December 15, pp. 585-91.
This poem of seven stanzas—printed one stanza to a page, each decorated with a large initial. These water-colours are the first published art work executed by him.
'A wall painting [which should read: "wall-hanging"], situation unrecorded,' but apparently of the Christchurch period, appears in *The Quest for Corvo*, 1934, p. 78. His 1891 oil painting of 'St. George and the Dragon' is reproduced in 'A Baron Corvo Exhibit', *Books at Iowa*, October 1964.
A water-colour of 'a mysterious group of divers in the clear of the moon' (*Hadrian*, p. 8) appears in *The Observer Magazine*, 3 November 1968, p. 64. This may have been done to accompany his poem, 'Ballade of Boys Bathing', but was not used when the poem appeared in *The Art Review* for April 1890.
For his books, Rolfe designed the title-page coat-of-arms for *In His Own Image* (1901), *Hadrian the Seventh* (1904), *Don Tarquinio* (1905) and *Don Renato* (1909, 1963). For the last three books he also designed the front covers, as well as the front cover of *The Fleurdelys Magazine* (1904). For *Don Tarquinio* he also designed a tailpiece and he did the cameo illustrations for *The Songs of Meleager*, not published until 1937.
(Between 1830 and 1881 there were six Rolfes listed as London artists in *A Dictionary of Artists* (1884). None was related to Frederick. Three were known for their paintings of fish. The home of the Pirie-Gordons in Crickhowell, Wales, was situated near the Usk River, and is called Uskville in Rolfe's *Desire and Pursuit of the Whole*. In 1854 Henry Leonides Rolfe, one of the artists noted for his fish paintings, composed 'A Morning's Sport on the Usk'.)
('Ten Sonnets on Coleridge's "Ancient Mariner"' by Nicholson appear in *The Universal Review*, 15 November 1890, pp. 387-91 (pp. 169-78, *Love in Earnest*, 1892). Rolfe either may have suggested the magazine to Nicholson or told Harry Quilter, its editor, about the poet.)

1893 *The Studio*, June 15, pp. 104, 106, and July 15, p. 157.

The article 'The Nude in Photography' is illustrated with two of Rolfe's photographs. These are the first by him to be reproduced. One photograph, taken in Rome, is reproduced in W. I. Lincoln Adams' *In Nature's Image* (New York, 1898, p. 64). The second photograph may be of Cecil Castle, taken at Christchurch. (These two photographs are reproduced on the seventy-fifth anniversary of the magazine, April 1968, p. 176.) The July 15th photograph, 'taken with a flash light', is of Gleeson White's son Eric.

The only other published photographs by Rolfe, taken in Rome 1890, appear in *The Observer Magazine*, 3 November 1968, p. 63, and in Brian Reade's *Sexual Heretics* (Routledge & Kegan Paul, 1970), opp. p. 276.

The four photographs appearing in Leonard Moore's 'More About Corvo' (*The Bookman*, April 1934, pp. 9-10) are by Wade-Browne and are not by Rolfe, although the photographs were taken with Rolfe's camera. Eleven photographs which Rolfe sent to Moore in 1913 survive with the correspondence. The footnote on p. 66 of *Letters to Leonard Moore* (1960) is in error when calling these 'Rolfe's photographs'. (Thirty-three additional Wade-Browne photographs and negatives survive.)

1894 *To-Day: A Weekly Magazine-Journal*, April 21, pp. 324-6. 'An Unforgettable Experience' is Rolfe's first serious effort at a short story, an experience based on an actual incident when he was staying at Fr. Lockhart's Ely Place at the beginning of 1892.

The magazine's editor in 1894 was Jerome K. Jerome. In *Nicholas Crabbe*, Rolfe speaks of an editor who accepted manuscripts from unknown authors by 'the sense of Touch'. 'When MSS. come to me,' he once told Crabbe-Rolfe, 'I open the packet, shut my eyes, and finger the first page or so. If I like the feel of the paper ... well. If I don't like the feel of the paper, I scribble N[o]. G[o]. on the back and chuck it.' When he opened Crabbe-Rolfe's manuscript, he 'shrieked in a moment "This is going to be damn good!" A man who would dare to send a tiny tiny packet containing a story typewritten in blue italics on Japanese silk copying paper, should be worth reading.' The only known letter written by Rolfe in 1894 is typewritten in blue on Japanese copying paper, dated March 24th, the same period he would have been sending an article to Jerome, who is also mentioned in the letter.

In Symons' copy of *Hadrian* he had written 'Jerome K. Jerome' in the margin opposite 'Bertram Blighter' on p. 380 ('More Light on "Hadrian the Seventh",' *The Antigonish* (Nova Scotia) *Review*, Spring 1970, p. 56). The reference in the book is to 'the novel-man'

407

telling Rose-Rolfe that the editor of the *Daily Anagraph* is putting him on the newspaper black list. In *Hadrian*, Rolfe dates this about the end of 1899. This was at least five years after his story appeared in *To-Day* and when Jerome was no longer connected with the magazine. In almost the exact words, the same story about the editor of the *Daily Anagraph* is told in *Nicholas Crabbe* (p. 63). This time Sidney Thorah, or Henry Harland, is 'the novel-man', the same person as Bertram Blighter.

1896-1897   *The Holywell Record.*
This periodical was an integral part of Rolfe's personal and literary life. Therefore, certain of his contributions to it should be listed. Rolfe no doubt persuaded Hochheimer of Blackburn to start this monthly periodical. There is much in the first issue's Introduction (May 1896, pp. 26-7) to indicate that Rolfe himself wrote it. In the fifth and sixth numbers (September and October) 'a large new banner' and 'Mr. Austin's beautiful banners' may have been his own writing. And he may have contributed two pieces, 'Purgatory' and 'Christmas Customs', to the November (p. 15) and December 1896 (pp. 23-30) issues. His first recognized piece is the three-part story, 'The Man From Texas', beginning in the March 1897 number and no doubt written in collaboration with John Holden.

His Beardsley-influenced art appears in the 31 May (p. i), 22 June (p. i) and October 1897 (inside back cover) numbers, each as an advertisement for The Record Publishing Company. Each had been also used as a letterhead and the St. Winefride design is reproduced in *The Quest for Corvo*, 1952, p. 267. Photographs of street processions showing five or six of his banners appear in the June (p. 24) and July 1896 (p. 24) issues. (One banner has been reproduced in detail in The Mermaid Theatre Programme for *Hadrian the Seventh*, April 1968, p. 18; in Her Majesty's Theatre (Melbourne) Programme, April 1969, p. 23; and in the Tivoli Theatre (Sydney) Programme, May 1969, p. 19.) With the beginning of his steady contributions in the March 1897 issue, his new layout for the magazine made it more visibly pleasant to read. With the 22 June 1897 issue, in a larger format, his typographically designed advertisements started to appear.

The banners and the reproduced art in *The Holywell Record* revealed his signature as a raven for the first time.

1898   *The Wide World Magazine*, November, pp. 139-46.
The first photograph of Rolfe appears at the head of his 'How I Was Buried Alive'. This was soon to be reproduced, as a line-cut, in at least two newspapers printing the Aberdeen Attack. It is a

favourite photograph of Rolfe and has been used several times since. Other photographs of Rolfe appear in *The Quest for Corvo*, 1934 and 1952, Timothy d'Arch Smith's *Love in Earnest*, 1970, opp. p. 24, and as part of Leonard Moore's article in *The Bookman*, April 1934, p. 9. (One photograph which Rolfe sent to Moore in 1913 shows him in the nude.)

At the head of 'The Cardinal Prefect of Propaganda' (*The Candid Friend*, 22 June 1901, pp. 303-4) a small oval portrait of Rolfe appears showing the back of his head. The Corvine profile is shown and he is wearing glasses and a biretta. The picture is captioned: 'Frederick Baron Corvo. (Photo by Wort.)' A different photograph of Rolfe has also been a favourite over the years, showing his face in repose, without glasses and with his eyes almost closed, wearing a biretta and against a woven damask background. It was first used by A. T. Bartholomew in 1926 for a small four-page commemorative folder on Rolfe and the photograph was dated '*Circa* 1890'. The photograph appears in the 1934 (opp. p. 1 and dated 'at the Scots College') and 1952 (opp. p. 11 and dated 'About 1890') editions of *The Quest for Corvo*. It is again used and dated during Rolfe's period of training at Scots College in Woolf's *Bibliography of Frederick Rolfe*. In fact, this picture was taken by William Wort, the Sutton Coldfield photographer employed by Rolfe during his student days at Oscott. The priestly dress of biretta and soutane was a favourite with Rolfe during the period elapsing between Oscott and Scots College.

'How I Was Buried Alive' is illustrated by Alan Wright, 'under' Rolfe's 'supervision'. Wright's line work appeared in periodicals during the 1890s. He lived near Kains-Jackson and Gleeson White in London and was also a designer of bookplates. He created one for John Lane, one for Kains-Jackson and several for White. His style for drawing a naked foot was to draw a big toe and merely outline the other four. It is interesting to note that Rolfe's method of drawing feet included each separate toe, until he saw Wright's work. After 1898, Rolfe's feet were drawn in the same manner in which Wright drew them.

The (Aberdeen) *Daily Free Press* and *Evening Gazette*, November 8, p. 5; November 12, p. 5; November 26, p. 4.

This Aberdeen Attack was repeated in several British newspapers, including *The Catholic Times and Opinion* (December 16, p. 9). These articles exposing 'Baron Corvo' constitute Rolfe's first biography.

In *The Quest for Corvo*, Symons writes how he first heard of this attack. When he met Kains-Jackson, the latter 'produced two long newspaper cuttings,' Symons says, 'dated 1898, taken from the *Aberdeen Free Press*'. In fact, they were taken from *The Catholic Times*.

1901   'Begging Letters' by Frank Holmfield, *The Harmsworth London Magazine*, August, pp. 67-72.

This is the curious article which some believe to be written and even illustrated by Rolfe with a self-portrait. Nothing in the text or in the portrait can be attributed to him.

1902-1903   *The Outlook in Life, Politics, Finance, Letters and the Arts.*

Throughout his work, published or in private letters, Rolfe proved himself a shrewd critic. Yet, these are the only known book reviews done by him. By his own statements, he had been paid for only six or seven for the 1902-3 period. From something he had said or from internal evidence, six can be attributed to him: 'Tennyson in Mist' and 'A Knave of Hearts' (for Sir Alfred Lyall's *Tennyson* and *The Memoirs of Jacques Casanova de Sein-galt*, 18 October 1902, pp. 321-3), 'A Scented Garden' and 'Flipperty Gibberty France' (for Prof. E. G. Browne's *Literary History of Persia From the Earliest Times Until Firdawsi* and Georg Brandes' *Main Currents in Nineteenth Century Literature*, Vol. III, 21 February 1903, pp. 71-3), 'Miscrocosmic Macedonia' (for G. F. Abbott's *Macedonian Folklore*, 5 September 1903, p. 134), and 'Galilaee Vicisti!' (for J. J. Fahie's *Galileo: His Life and Work*, 24 October 1903, pp. 334-5).

(Rolfe had started his review for *A Literary History of Persia*: 'Professor Browne's Prolegomena to Persian Literature (for this is the apter title for his latest book). ...' This may be a case where an author read a review of his book and approved of a suggestion which he found in it. In his second volume, ... *From Firdawsi to Sa'di* (1906), Prof. Browne writes: 'For the sole of brevity I shall henceforth refer to [my first volume] simply as the *Prolegomena*; a title which best indicates its scope, aim, and character.')

(Browne's *Literary History of Persia* was reviewed by M. M. in *The Author*, 1 December 1902, pp. 78-9. The review immediately preceding was by St. John Lucas on John G. Robertson's *History of German Literature*. During Rolfe's Venetian period, he knew Lucas, then staying in Florence. This probably means that the two met first in 1912. They were no doubt introduced to each other, directly or indirectly, by Prof. Dawkins. No more is known at present of the Lucas-Rolfe association and very little about Lucas himself has come to light.)

1903 *Charlotte Mary Yonge: Her Life and Letters* by Christa-
bel Coleridge, Macmillan, London, p. 321.

1906 *Records of the Scots Colleges at Douai, Rome, Madrid,
    Valladolid and Ratisbon: Volume I, Registers of Students,*
    New Spalding Club, Aberdeen, p. 189:
  'Fredericus Gulielmus Rolfe, diocesia Westmonasteriensis, Jacobo
  et Helena Elizabeth Pilcher Acatholicis legitime natus
  Londini. ...'
  On pp. 33-4 of *The Desire and Pursuit of the Whole*, Crabbe-
  Rolfe speaks of this entry, 'inaccurately stated (as one might
  expect, seeing that the new rector of the college himself supplied
  the copy from which the Spalding Club printed)—and then follow
  three plain dots such as are ordinarily used to signify incompletion. It is charitably supposed that the notorious details of the
  case being too shameful for publication while the rector who
  expelled Crabbe still infested this world ....'
  The rector of Scots College in 1890, Mgr. Campbell, began this
  record, but all the papers pertaining to it were lost when he retired
  in 1897. A new record had to be compiled by the new rector, Mgr.
  Fraser. Campbell died in 1902.

1910 *Converts to Rome: A Biographical List of the More
    Notable Converts to the Catholic Church in the United
    Kingdom During the Last Sixty Years,* compiled and edited
    by W. Gordon Gorman, Sands & Co., London, p. 236.
  Rolfe was not entirely forsaken by Catholics. This 'record of a
  spiritual change among *the intellectual classes of these Islands'*
  included his name, listing him as a 'sometime Master at Grantham
  Grammar School' and 'journalist'.

  [On p. 45 of *The Desire and Pursuit* Crabbe debates the problem
  of presenting a young girl (Zilda) as a boy (Zildo). This novel,
  written in the early months of 1910, is basically about a man, a
  girl-posing-as-a-boy, a boat and water. At the very same time
  another incident was taking place in actual fact employing these
  same elements. In London on the night of 10 February 1910, the
  Michigan-born Hawley Harvey Crippen murdered his over-
  domineering wife Cora. He fled to Canada on the S.S. *Montrose*
  with his young secretary, Ethel Le Neve, disguised as his son
  John. There were two notable firsts for crime history in the
  Crippen Case. Wireless telegraphy was used for the first time in
  preventing a criminal's escape. Crippen and Miss Le Neve were
  arrested at Quebec and brought back to London for trial.

Although forensic medicine had had a small beginning in the mid-1800s, a gross error in 1859 deterred the progress of the new science; but by this means the dismembered body found beneath Crippen's cellar floor was identified as his wife's. The trial began on 18 October 1910 and Crippen was hanged on November 23rd.]

1915 *Hugh: Memories of a Brother* by A. C. Benson, John Murray, London, pp. 235-6.

Although unnamed, Rolfe appears as 'a man of morbid, irritable, and resentful tendencies'.

Robert Hugh Benson: An Appreciation by Olive Katharine Parr, Hutchinson, London, pp. 143-50.

Although Rolfe again is not named, Miss Parr had sensed that Enid's character in Benson's *Initiation* was based on a real person and asked about this. Benson only admitted to her that Enid had been a friend who was a man, 'one whom he rescued from exceedingly trying circumstances'.

1916 *The Life of Monsignor Robert Hugh Benson* by C. C. Martindale, S.J., Longmans, Green, London, Vol. II.

The letters and papers quoted here pertaining to the Rolfe-Benson association were destroyed, probably by A. C. Benson or according to his directions.

Philip Caraman (*C. C. Martindale: A Biography*, Longmans, London, 1967, p. 123): '[Martindale] did not really like Benson and did not dare to explain how Benson constantly recast his memories and dramatised himself, but he did hint at the extent to which Benson became thoroughly hysterical towards the end of his life and believed that no form of literary composition was beyond his talents.' (Curiously, death in 1914 did not stop Benson's flow of literature. Four books have been written 'by' him since 1914, and they are all in the form of spirit communications. Written 'through' Anthony Borgia, whose name appears on the title pages, Benson 'speaks' from the other world. Borgia says that the communicator of these books 'was known on earth as Monsignor Robert Hugh Benson. ... We are old friends, and his passing hence has not severed an early friendship.' These books are *Beyond This Life* (Feature Books, London, 1942), *The World Unseen* (Feature Books, 1944), *Life in the World Unseen* (Odhams, London, 1954), and *More Life in the World Unseen* (Odhams, 1956). One statement 'made' by Benson is to the erroneous comments he had written on spirit communication in his *Necromancers*, 1909.)

1918 *Robert Hugh Benson: Captain in God's Army* by Reginald
J. J. Watt, Burns & Oates, London, pp. 30-1.

1923 'Frederick Baron Corvo' by Shane Leslie, *The London
Mercury*, September, pp. 507-18.
This had been edited for inclusion in the magazine. The original
essay appears as the Introduction to *In His Own Image*, John
Lane, London, 1924; Alfred A. Knopf, New York, 1925. The same
Introduction also appears in *A History of the Borgias*, Modern
Library, New York, 1931, and *Hadrian the Seventh*, Dover, New
York, 1969. A short checklist accompanies the original article.

1925 'Purple Blood' by Alfonso de Zulueta, *The Oxford Outlook*, May, pp. 143-50.

'Baron Corvo' by D. H. Lawrence, *The Adelphi*, December,
pp. 502-6.

1926 *A Catalogue of Modern Books Belles Lettres and First
Editions*, Christopher Millard, London.
Millard was the first book dealer to appreciate Rolfe as a collected
author. Although several of Millard's catalogues include scarce
and unique Rolfe material, his Catalogue No. 14 is the most
interesting. On pp. 9-12, under the heading 'The Raven and the
Fox', he lists and quotes from the Venice Letters, which he
possessed before 1920. He eventually sold them to Symons, who,
in turn, sold them to J. Maundy Gregory. (The letters were
offered again, for the last time to private collectors, in Elkin
Mathews' Catalogue No. 93, 1943.)
Books from the Library of John Lane are listed in Catalogue
No. 165, Dulau & Co., London, May 1929. Item 932 includes a
letter from Baron Corvo relating to his *Yellow Book* stories. Item
1159 includes a letter from Shane Leslie at the time he did his
Introduction for *In His Own Image*, in which he wrote: 'The
great John Quinn has apparently changed devotion for Conrad
to Rolfe.' (In 1923 Quinn sold his Conrad collection of books and
manuscripts which realized $120,461. The typed manuscript of
Victory sold for $850 and went to Jerome Kern. At the Kern sale
in 1929, this same item was sold for $4,000. Kern had one of the
largest private libraries in America at the time. More than anyone else, the one person responsible for its growth and what it
contained was Temple Scott, who had by now become a gentleman

book dealer, working from his New York apartment in West 72nd Street.)

Elkin Mathews' Catalogue No. 42, 1932, *Books of the 'Nineties'*, with an Introduction by Holbrook Jackson, includes Rolfe material. The items in the catalogue came from Symons' library.

In J. I .Davis & G. M. Orioli Catalogue 57, item 58 is *Don Renato*, 1909, and is priced £31.10.0: 'Six copies *only* known to exist. One of the rarest of all modern books.' (In Percy Muir's 1934 *Points: Second Series*, Symons says 'five are known to survive'. In his *Bibliography* Cecil Woolf has 'examined all four that survive'.) The Davis & Orioli catalogue says that an inscription is in *Don Renato*: 'To *my* friend A. J. [A. Symons]. From *his* friend A. J. [Maundy Gregory]. As from one Corvine to another Corvine. (No. 2 of the 1st Edition of only oo [*sic*] copies.) 13.1.30.' The date of the Davis & Orioli catalogue is June 1932, just two years after the *Renato* had been presented to Symons.

1927 *The Golden Book*, New York, August.
This included Rolfe's first story in an American periodical, 'About Doing Little, Lavishly', pp. 170-6. The editor, Henry Wysham Lanier, praised this work (pp. 4, 6) and wondered why he had not heard of the author before.

Frederick Baron Corvo by A. J. A. Symons, The Curwen Press, London, March.
Published as No. 81 of Ye Sette of Odd Volumes, according to the title page this paper was read on 23 October 1926. In fact, it was on 23 November 1926. Thus read the announcement and programme for the 418th meeting of the society at Ye Royal Adelaide Gallery (Gatti's), 13 King William St. (On November 24th Kains-Jackson wrote to Symons: 'Congrats. You are indeed the sleuth of sleuths. One might have set oneself Corvo as a task like those of Hercules or the Knights Errant. Even now I fancy he was a were-wolf and took another form for some years. You deserve a very hearty reception from the Odde Volumes who will I fear be deploring the loss of Clement Shorter [who died on November 19th] since their last dinner.')

199 copies were printed. Seventeen of these were 'specials', with a sheet of Rolfe manuscript acting as a frontispiece in each. (Symons possessed perhaps Rolfe's last manuscript of at least twenty-three sheets, written mostly in Italian and Latin either in 1912 or 1913. He cut nine of these in half for the seventeen frontispieces.)

Receiving his copy, Shane Leslie immediately remitted his thanks on 30 March 1927, concluding his letter:

We receive you in sign of our favour into the most rare and secret Society the Corvine of which there are no rules neither printed statements—only the sacred talismans which are repeated by one to another—
V. Cor ad cor loquitur
R. Et corvus ad corvum. Amen.
The names of the Corvine society are kept secret as yours in the breast—in pelto—of the Grand Master

Shane Leslie.

1928 'Frederick Baron Corvo' by A. J. A. Symons, *Life and Letters*, July, pp. 81-101.

This includes a reproduction of Rolfe's handwriting for the first time, p. 88. The page of manuscript is from his *Bull Against the Enemy of the Anglican Race*.

1929 *Ambrose Bierce: A Biography* by Carey McWilliams, A. & C. Boni, New York, p. 286:

'[Bierce] was immediately enthusiastic about Baron Corvo's "In His own Image" when it was first published ....'

Only a few books from Bierce's library are preserved in the Bierce Collection of the University of California, Berkeley. Most of his books had been given away by Bierce, including a copy of Rolfe's *Rubaiyat of Umar Khaiyam*, which went to a friend in Washington, D. C., but survives.

(Hardly more than a month after Rolfe's death, the seventy-one-year-old Bierce disappeared on the U.S.-Mexican border after writing his last letter. In the ensuing years a broad category of myths have been created about his fate.) This McWilliams book on Bierce is dedicated to Vincent O'Sullivan.

c. 1920-1940

During the 1920s, the early 1930s and 1940s there had been three proposed biographies or memoirs on Rolfe. Philip Sainsbury, of The Cayme Press and a young kinsman of Henry Tuke, planned to write about Rolfe. He knew Grant Richards, who collaborated with him as publisher on at least one book in 1928. But his life of Rolfe was committed more to talk than to paper and nothing was ever written. At the same time A. T. Bartholomew, Under-Librarian at Cambridge, was interested in Rolfe and his work. But his study of Rolfe was also never fulfilled. Grant Richards himself tried to interest some publisher in a book based on his experiences with Rolfe, but in vain.

1932 *Memories of a Misspent Youth: 1872-1896* by Grant Richards, with an Introduction by Max Beerbohm, Heinemann, London, p. 26.

1933 *Henry Scott Tuke, R.A., R.W.S.: A Memoir* by Maria Tuke Sainsbury, Martin Secker, London, pp. 90-1.
The author speaks of Rolfe, 'whose unexpectedly realistic fresco still adorns the little Catholic church' in Christchurch.

Looking Back: An Autobiographical Excursion by Norman Douglas, Chatto & Windus, London, Vol. II, pp. 309-12.
Under the name 'Mr. Edmund Barton', Douglas discusses Thomas Wade-Browne, mentioning Rolfe's last days in Venice as poverty-stricken ones. Douglas says that Wade-Browne told him that Rolfe had died in an open boat. This statement is corrected by Douglas in one line in *Late Harvest* (1946, p. 66), but nothing further is said about Wade-Browne.

Twice Seven: The Autobiography of H. C. Bainbridge, Routledge, London, pp. 76-139; Dutton, New York, 1934.
The most remarkable part of his chapter, 'Corvo the Enigma', is the series of letters written to him by Rolfe, which are printed here. Bainbridge may have been the first person to create a certain Corvine myth. He writes: 'On July 20th, 1903, Pope Leo XIII died. Now was Corvo's opportunity. Now, instead of simply making his "brother Catholics especially clerks smart and wince and squirm", he would scorch and wither them up. ... So it was that Corvo, for the purpose of his own life story, elected himself Pope and wrote *Hadrian VII*.'
In a letter to his literary agent, Leonard Moore, written on 6 September 1903, less than seven weeks after Leo's death, Rolfe wrote that Constable already had the manuscript of *Hadrian*. The book had been completed early in July, before Leo's death, and had been composed during the previous three months. Neither Leslie nor Symons adopts this theory, yet a number of later biographers have.

E. Nesbitt: A Biography by Doris Langley Moore, Benn, London, pp. 187-90. Revised 1967.
In his Introduction to *Nicholas Crabbe* (1958) Cecil Woolf speaks of the persons from real life who were used by Rolfe in the novel. 'Mrs Arkush Annaly,' he says on p. 7, 'is Mrs Hubert Bland, better known as E. Nesbit. ...' In a footnote on p. 61 he again refers to

416

Arkush and Alys Annaly: 'E. Nesbit, the prolific author of children's books, and her husband Hubert Bland entertained lavishly at Well Hall, Eltham. In his *Experiment in Autobiography* [1934], H. G. Wells says ... that Rolfe was among the many people present at the Blands' Parties.' Rolfe must have written *Crabbe* soon after *Hadrian* was finished in mid-1903, for he offered it to John Lane exactly one year later. *Crabbe* covers Rolfe's life during 1899-1902, or pre-*Hadrian* period. H. G. Wells does not date Rolfe's appearances at Well Hall, but he links Rolfe's name with Benson's, who may have taken his fellow Catholic along to Eltham. There is nothing about the Blands in Benson's biography by Martindale. In *E. Nesbit* a letter by Rolfe to the Fabian Society, dated 15 February 1906, is quoted. E. Nesbit's biographer then says that 'two or three months later he wrote to Hubert Bland, with whom he was still unacquainted'. In this letter to Bland, Rolfe wrote that 'R. H. Benson of Cambridge read your *With the Eyes of a Man* [1905] with me during the vacation'. This dates Rolfe's first meeting with the Blands about 1906.

In a letter to Symons quoted in *The Quest for Corvo*, John Bland spoke of Rolfe as an occasional visitor to Well Hall 'when I was a little boy of 6 or 7'. This would have been about 1906. When he left England, E. Nesbit's biographer says, Rolfe even managed 'writing very agreeable letters—he who had written some of the most disagreeable letters ever conveyed by the post!— to John Bland, then a child'. In 1899-1900 John was still a baby and Rolfe, if he had visited the Blands then, would not have noticed him.

In *Without Prejudice* (1963) part of Letter 49, p. 56, from Rolfe to John Lane, dated 1 April 1901, reads: 'After Harland's libellous statements [mentioned on p. 119 of *Crabbe*] to the Hannays; and his threat about the Newspaper Black List; I think it a pity to neglect any chance of procuring a favourable notice [for *In His Own Image*].' In a footnote to this letter (p. 110), Woolf identifies the Hannays: 'James Hannay, the editor of the *Daily Telegraph*, and his wife Margaret, were friends of the Harlands. According to *Nicholas Crabbe* ... the Hannays appear under the name of "Arkush and Alys Annaly" ...'

A. Bridget Appleyard, *The Daily Telegraph*, 27 November 1969: 'James Hannay was never Editor of the Daily Telegraph.' R. F. Farmer, General Secretary, The Institute of Journalists: 'I am sorry but I cannot find any reference to James Hannay in the Institute records.' Lord E. F. L. Burnham (*Peterborough Court: The Story of* The Daily Telegraph, Cassell, London, 1955, p. 161): 'In its hundred years the *Daily Telegraph* has had six Editors—

Thornton Hunt, Edwin Arnold, Sir John Le Sage, Fred Miller, Arthur Watson, and Colin Coote.'

Rarely did Rolfe make a pseudo-anagram of an existing name for one of his characters. His usual method was to link the character with something related to the actual person, be it a name, a place or a definition. 'Annaly' ('analie') means 'to alienate or abalienate' (*The Oxford Dictionary*). (In *Nicholas Crabbe*, 'Annaly had been tapping his store of knowledge of precious stones, especially that very rare and precious gem called alexandrite, alexandrolith—the stone which is Man's Defender'—the opposite of the title of one who alienated Rolfe by threatening to place his name on the newspaper black list.) In *Crabbe*, Alys Annaly is 'a lovely Frenchwoman ... the wife of the editor of the *Daily Anagraph* and useful'. At this time in Rolfe's life *The Author*—a periodical read by him, which printed three of his letters and which is mentioned in *Hadrian*—had a series of 'Paris Notes' by Alys Hallard. This may have been the origin of Alys Annaly's first name or, at least, the spelling of it, as well as, perhaps, her nationality in Rolfe's story.

One wonders what Rolfe thought when visiting the Blands at Eltham, the home of Robert and William Rolfe. The sixteenth-century house, surrounded by a moat, was less than half a mile from the churchyard in which the Rolfes were buried. Margaret Taylor: 'The Blands' house was demolished in 1922 or 3, only the bell survives. E. Nesbit was hospitable, but since the front door opened directly into the lounge hung a notice on it saying "The front door is at the back".'

1934 *Autobiography* by John Cowper Powys, John Lane: The Bodley Head, London, p. 411

The 1912 incident in Venice between Rolfe and the Powyses and Louis Wilkinson is mentioned here. It is repeated in *Welsh Ambassadors* (Chapman & Hall, London, 1936, pp. 240-2) and *Seven Friends* (The Richards Press, London, 1953, pp. 70-1), both by Louis Marlow (Wilkinson).

'Frederick William Serafino Austin Lewis Mary Rolfe, Baron Corvo' by A. J. A. Symons, *Points: Second Series, 1866-1934* by Percy H. Muir, Constable, London; R. R. Bowker, New York, pp. 99-103.

This checklist of Rolfe's books was the most complete in 1934, listing nineteen items. (He had only eleven items listed in his proposed but never published *Bibliography ... of the Eighteen Nineties*.) Facing p. 100 is a reproduction of the first page of the suppressed Appendix III for Rolfe's Borgia book, 'A Suggested Criterion of the Credibility of Historians'. (This Appendix, pp. 368-84, was printed on proof paper and suppressed before publication. This has never been published, although Rolfe slightly modified it for *The Westminster Review*, October 1903, pp. 402-14.)

Item 10 in this list is *The Bull Against the Enemy of the Anglican Race*. 'This is a bull of Hadrian VII,' Symons says, 'which was omitted from that book owing to its libellous content.' In fact, it was written in Venice in 1908, four years after *Hadrian* had been published.

The Quest for Corvo by A. J. A. Symons, Cassell, London; Macmillan, New York.

Further editions, some with Introductions and additional material, have been published by Penguin (1940 and 1966), Folio Society (1952), Cassell (1953) and Michigan State University Press (1955). It has been translated into French (1962) and Italian (1969).

Symons was also responsible for the publishing of Rolfe's *Bull Against the Enemy of the Anglican Race* (1929), *The Desire and Pursuit of the Whole* (1934), *Hubert's Arthur* (1935), and *The Songs of Meleager* (1937).

'More About Corvo' by Leonard Moore, *The Bookman*, April, pp. 8-11.

This includes four photographs: two of his 1913 boats, his 'palace on the Grand Canal,' and Rolfe at the oar. (This latter was translated into art for the paperback cover of *New Quests for Corvo*, 1965.)

'Baron Corvo' by Mary Butts, *The London Mercury*, May, pp. 619-24.

'More Light on Baron Corvo' by Sir David Hunter Blair, *The London Mercury*, May, pp. 625-9.

1935 'The Gall of Human Kindness' by Vincent O'Sullivan, *The Dublin Magazine: A Quarterly Review of Literature, Science and Art*, January-March, pp. 9-25.

With slight revisions, this is printed as 'Frederick Rolfe' in *Opinions* by O'Sullivan, with an Introduction by Alan Anderson, The Unicorn Press, London, 1959, pp. 150-73. This is the most sympathetic essay on Rolfe written by any of his contemporaries, a gesture not repaid by Rolfe. (*Nicholas Crabbe* was not published during his life, so he did not see Rolfe's remark about 'that silly O'Sullivan'. Nor did he see 'Walt Whitman's Grandee Spain Succumbing' (*The Monthly Review*, May 1903) with its beginning words: 'Certainly Walt Whitman is the triumphant fact which justifies the enterprise of Christopher Columbus. We could have done without the ... Vincent O'Sullivans ... and Henry Harlands ... for they may be met on the street any day.')

O'Sullivan's life was just the reverse of Rolfe's. Born into an American millionaire's family, he did not pursue the priesthood after Oscott. He turned to literature, living in London and France. He was generous, as in the case when he gladly gave Wilde money to travel to Naples in the autumn of the year he came out of prison. But O'Sullivan's money dwindled away before the end of his life. At such a time he wrote from Biarritz, France: 'If one must be beggared it is certainly better that it should happen very early in life. In middle life when a man has formed habits and no profession it is demoralizing.' Five years after his death, his bones were placed in a common ossuary.

1936 *John Lane and the Nineties* by J. Lewis May, John Lane: The Bodley Head, London, p. 82:

'Corvo, I have heard it said, was not infrequently verminous, and after his departure [from Lane's office] it was found necessary to treat with abundant doses of insecticide the armchair on which he had reposed.'

Rolfe's totally shabby appearance may have led some to think of him as 'verminous', but he was almost fanatic about his bodily cleanliness. Immediately before visiting Lane in London, Rolfe had spent a month in the Holywell Workhouse, walked to Oxford and spent several weeks with the Hardy family. If he had become verminous on the road from Wales to Oxford, this condition would have been remedied in the Hardy household. During Rolfe's four years at 69 Broadhurst Gardens, during which time he was in Lane's office, his landlady's only complaint against him was not for being verminous, but for being a non-paying guest.

1943 *The Letters of Llewelyn Powys*, selected and edited by Louis Wilkinson, John Lane: The Bodley Head, London, p. 87.

1945 'The Battle of Holywell: A Story of Baron Corvo' by Julian Symons, *The Saturday Book: Fifth Year*, Hutchinson, London, pp. 215-34.

This includes several of Rolfe's letters written at Holywell. Letter No. 8 is misdated. Rolfe had dated it 'Jan. 15th, 1898,' although it should have been one year earlier. Written to the Reverend Mother Superior of St. Winefride's Convent, the letter spoke of a possible fashion to be formed among young ladies to seek some retreat 'for writing their stories'. This idea was based on an announcement 'that Mrs Isabella Craigie ["John Oliver Hobbes"] has entered the Convent of the Assumption in Kensington Square ... "to have peace and quietness for writing her new story."' In his *Life of John Oliver Hobbes* (1911) John Morgan Richards quotes one letter from her to Charles Lewis Hind, written on 30 January 1897: 'I am called at six a.m. Mass at seven. The day is well filled, and I shall feel weary when the Retreat is ended.' (At the end of this book there is an essay, 'The Religion of Mrs. Craigie', by Fr. Gavin, S.J., one of Rolfe's 'friends' of 1887.)

(On p. 22 of *The Saturday Book* and on the back cover of the dust jacket are pictures of Keir Hardie.)

1947   *Of True Experience* by Sir Gerald Campbell, Dodd, Mead, New York; Hutchinson, London, 1949; pp. 33-4.

'Baron Corvo's Quarrels' by Ivy van Someren, *Life and Letters and The London Mercury*, February, pp. 104-9.

c. 1950
Book dealer George Sims issued three catalogues of Rolfe material in 1949 and published several works of Rolfe in limited editions. One is *Three Tales of Venice* (1950), reprinted from the 1913 *Blackwood's*. Another is *Amico di Sandro: A Fragment of a Novel* (1951). This much was written by Rolfe, possibly in 1912. When Mrs. Morgan Akin Jones met Rolfe in 1912, he 'was returning from a few weeks in Florence where he was collecting material for a life of Botticelli'. Rolfe gave no name to the unfinished story. 'Amico di Sandro' was the title of an article on the Italian painter by Bernard Berenson, *Gazette des Beaux Arts*, 1899. Sims' third book is *Letters to Grant Richards* (1952), including only the letters in the David Roth collection. Cecil Woolf soon followed Sims in causing the publication of Rolfe's work.

1950   *A. J. A. Symons: His Life and Speculations* by Julian Symons, Eyre & Spottiswoode, London.

1951   'Frederick Rolfe', *The Lost Childhood and Other Essays* by Graham Greene, Eyre & Spottiswoode, London, pp. 92-7.

Henry Irving: The Actor and His World by Laurence Irving, Faber & Faber, London, p. 651.

Dated 3 May 1903, Rolfe sent a letter to Irving dealing with his production of *Dante*.

Admiring Irving and Ellen Terry, Rolfe saw at least one other of their plays. When he was in London in early 1892, he saw *Henry VIII*. Part of the scenery was designed by Joseph Harker, the programme stated, and the Acting Manager was Bram Stoker, who remained with Irving for a long time. In Harker's *Studio and Stage* (1924) he writes: 'My friend Bram Stoker ... one day announced that he had appropriated my surname for one of his characters [Jonathan Harker] in "Dracula". ...'

'The Quest for Corvo: A New Judgment' by Sir Norman Birkett, *Go: The Travel & Leisure Magazine*, December 1951-January 1952, pp. 66-7, 78.

1952   *James Joyce's* Ulysses: *A Study* by Stuart Gilbert, Faber & Faber, London, pp. 95-6.

Francis Thompson and Wilfrid Meynell: A Memoir by Viola Meynell, Hollis & Carter, London, pp. 132-5; Dutton, New York, 1953.

A letter by Rolfe from Aberdeen to Wilfrid Meynell, 21 February 1893, is quoted here. The author adds: 'Meynell introduced Rolfe to the owner of the *Aberdeen Free Press*, and he was offered a post as "reader", which however was not to his mind.'

1955   'Encounter With Corvo' by Mrs. Morgan Akin Jones, *Desiderata*, August 5, p. 12. *Letters to Leonard Moore*, 1960, pp. 18-20.

1953   *Cities and Men: An Autobiography* by Sir Harry Luke, Geoffrey Bles, London, Vol. I, pp. 115-9.

This volume also tells of the 1908 trip with Harry Pirie-Gordon.

1957   *A Bibliography of Frederick Rolfe Baron Corvo* by Cecil Woolf, Hart-Davis, London.

Woolf previously contributed checklists of Rolfe's work to *The* (London) *Book Collector* (Spring 1955, pp. 63-8) and to the American *Amateur Book Collector* (May 1955, pp. 1-5). He also compiled Bertram Korn's *Corvo Library* (1963).

Other collections appearing in print have been 'A Corvo Collection' by David Roth (*Desiderata*, 4 February 1955, pp. 1-4), 'The

Anatomy of a Corvomaniac' (*Private Libraries Association Quarterly*, July 1957, pp. 30-4), 'A Corvo Collection' (*Corvo, 1860-1960*, pp. 108-14; *New Quests for Corvo*, pp. 93-7), 'Copies of "Chronicles of the House of Borgia"' (*Notes & Queries*, July 1969, pp. 238-9), and 'More Light on "Hadrian the Seventh"' (*The Antigonish Review*, Spring 1970, pp. 54-69), the latter four being by Donald Weeks. Printed accounts of exhibitions of Rolfe material include *Baron Corvo Centenary Exhibition* (Marylebone Road District Library, London, 19 October-12 November), 1960, and 'A Corvo Exhibit' (at the University of Iowa) by Clarence A. Andrews, *Books at Iowa*, October 1964, pp. 18-27. (Andrews introduced the work of Rolfe to Dwight Macdonald, who included two 'Reviews of Unwritten Books'—'Machiavelli's Despatches from the South African Campaign' and 'Tacitus's "Scripturae de Populis Consociatis Americae Septentrionalis"'—in his *Parodies: An Anthology from Chaucer to Beerbohm—and After* (Random House, New York, 1960; Faber & Faber, London, 1961, pp. 330-8.) (An exhibition of Rolfe material at Wayne State University, Detroit, July 1960, had no printed catalogue.)

Woolf since has been responsible for the publication of the following, with his Introductions and footnotes:

The Cardinal Prefect of Propaganda (1957), *Nicholas Crabbe* (1958), *Letters to C. H. C. Pirie-Gordon* (1959), *Letters to Leonard Moore* (1960), *Corvo, 1860-1960* (1961; *New Quests for Corvo*, 1965), *Letters to R. M. Dawkins* (1962), *'Without Prejudice': One Hundred Letters ... to John Lane* (1963), *Don Renato* (1963), and 'The Venice Letters' (*Art and Literature/5*, 18 June 1965).

Letter 1 in the Leonard Moore series is misplaced. Rolfe wrongly dated this letter. Instead of 6 January 1903, it should read 1904, and be placed between Letters XI and XII.

The Introduction to the Dawkins letters (pp. 63-4) says that the letters, with one exception, were preserved after Dawkins' death with 'two books—a Petronius given by Rolfe to Dawkins and a Meleager lent him by Rolfe'. The Meleager was lent to Rolfe by Dawkins and neither of these books was preserved with the letters. Dawkins' library was sold to a bookshop in Oxford and was catalogued in a miscellaneous group of books. On p. 104, footnote 3 says that the Petronius given to Dawkins 'has remained with the correspondence and is now in Mr Donald Weeks's Collection'. The Petronius and the Meleager are now with the correspondence, but only after a period of searching had been expended. Both books were sold independently by the Oxford shop before they were realized to be from Dawkins' library. Eventually, the Meleager was procured from an English collector. The Petronius was finally acquired from Prof. Gilbert Bagnani of the University

423

of Toronto, an expert on this early Roman writer and author of *Rome and the Papacy*, 1929. Any transaction would be made, he said, only by a replacement of this particular edition, translated by Mr. Addison and published in London, 1736. Another copy was duly found and the Dawkins-Rolfe copy joined the letters. The travels of this one copy of a book once belonging to Rolfe passed through several interesting hands, including Bagnani's, for he remembered Rolfe. He met Rolfe one afternoon in Rome in either 1912 or 1913. Rolfe was paying a social visit and may have been in the city to purchase the scarlet cardinal's material for his Palazzo Marcello apartment in Venice.

Footnote 25 to 'The Venice Letters' (p. 62) identifies a person in one letter written in 1909 (p. 29) as: 'Frank Victor Reardon (born *c.* 1890) ... was a member of Caius College, Cambridge, where, in 1909, he took the Wesleyan Lay Preachers' Examination. He went out to India the following year and is believed to have died there shortly afterwards.' This person (whose name is withheld here because of the wishes of his family) was born in 1888. After achieving First Class Honours in Mathematics at Cambridge in 1910, he did go to India. There he married in 1915 and formed a family. He returned to England and died in 1945. Reardon was the surname of the drowned boy to whose memory *Tarcissus* was written in 1880.

1959   *Brief Voices: A Writer's Story* by Ethel Mannin, Hutchinson, London, pp. 239-41.

Mentioning Rolfe's books, she praises his *Desire and Pursuit*, saying: 'I have never in my life been so excited over a book. ...' In *Loneliness: A Study of the Human Condition* (1966, pp. 89-102, 105) she tries to define Rolfe's loneliness, saying that his 'trouble stemmed directly from his homosexuality'. She again speaks of *The Desire and Pursuit* as that 'profoundly moving—and profound—novel' in *Practitioners of Love: Some Aspects of the Human Phenomenon* (1969, pp. 11-3).

Kenneth Grahame, 1859-1932: A Study of His Life, Work and Times by Peter Green, John Murray, London; The World Publishing Co., New York; pp. 224-5.

1960   *A Study in Yellow: The Yellow Book and Its Contributors* by Katherine Lyon Mix, University of Kansas Press, Lawrence; Constable, London; pp. 232-3.

This author repeats the John Lane-'verminous' story, only

placing it here in Harland's house. She also relates that 'Miss [Ella] D'Arcy said [Rolfe] had confessed that "Corvo" meant "unforgivable sin".'

1961 *George: An Early Autobiography* by Emlyn Williams, Hamish Hamilton, London, p. 107.

1962 *The Tenth Muse* ... by Sir Harry Luke, with the collaboration of Elizabeth Godfrey, Putnam, London, second edition, p. 11 (quoting from the review of the first edition, 'Culinary Spells', *The Times Literary Supplement*, 24 December 1954, p. 839).

1963 'The Fascination of the Paranoid Personality: Baron Corvo' by Pamela Hansford Johnson, *Essays and Studies: 1963* ..., John Murray, London, pp. 12-5.

This is the same essay as the Introduction to *Corvo, 1860-1960 (New Quests for Corvo).*

1964 *Bishops at Large* by Peter F. Anson, Faber & Faber, London, pp. 139-40.

This falls within the chapter on 'Ulric Vernon Herford ....'
Speaking of Rolfe's use of the Baron Corvo title (p. 161), Anson says: 'In Britain it is no offense to assume a bogus title.'

'The "Tin" Cathedral at Oban: 1886-1934' by the Rev. Roderick Macdonald, *The Innes Review*, Spring, p. 53.

1968 Programme, The Mermaid Theatre, *Hadrian VII*, Notes by Iolanthe Latimer.

In the Credits, The House of Vanheems is listed for supplying the costumes for the various members of the Catholic Church in the play. In the novel, when Rose is being accepted for priesthood, he refers to this same firm: '... he said to himself, "Go into [47] Berners Street, and buy a gun-metal stock and two dozen Roman collars (with a seam down the middle if you can get them). ..."'

'The Many Lives of Frederick Rolfe, Alias Baron Corvo' by Cecil Woolf, *The Observer Magazine*, November 3, pp. 60-6.

1969 'A Second Edition of Rolfe's "Tarcissus"' by Donald Weeks, *The Times Literary Supplement*, July 17, p. 784.

'"Hadrian VII"' by Donald Weeks, *The Times Literary Supplement*, August 28, p. 955.

This is a note pertaining to the Penguin 1963 edition of *Hadrian*. In setting the type for this edition, some of the words have been modernized. 'Keltic' becomes 'Celtic', etc. In Rolfe's story (1904, p. 50) he speaks of Edward III's words to his wife in reference to the six burgesses of Calais: 'Dame, I can deny you nothing, but I wish you had been otherwhere.' Rolfe uses the archaic spelling of 'Dam' here. In the Chatto & Windus and all American editions this spelling has been kept. In the Penguin edition (p. 51) it appears as 'Damn'.

The *TLS* note ends: 'Colonel Harry Pirie-Gordon ... comments: "It is interesting to think that the Penguin version of King Edward's remark is likely to supersede the archial word—so is History made."'

Frederick Rolfe 'Baron Corvo' by Carla Marengo Vaglio, Mursia, Milan.

In Italian, this is the first full literary criticism of Rolfe's work.

1970 *Love in Earnest: Some Notes on the Lives and Writings of English 'Uranian' Poets from 1889 to 1930* by Timothy d'Arch Smith, Routledge & Kegan Paul, London.

Opp. p. 72 is a photograph of Masson Fox with the Falmouth Boys' Club football team, 1909, the year Rolfe met him and began his series of Venice Letters to Fox.

'The Metrical Pattern in Rolfe' by John Glucker, *The Antigonish* (Nova Scotia) *Review*, Spring, pp. 46-51.

The author has discovered an odd pattern at the end of chapters in Rolfe's work, a pattern dating to the Greeks' use of hexameters, dactyls and spondees.

(Edward Alexander Crowley changed his name early in life to Aleister Crowley, because 'that to become famous it is necessary to bear a name with the metrical value of a dactyl followed by a spondee'.)

'Fr. Rolfe and the Scots College, Rome' by the Very Rev. Alexander MacWilliam, *The Innes Review*, Autumn, pp. 124-39.

BIBLIOGRAPHY II

In his 1923 article on Frederick Baron Corvo, Shane Leslie says that Rolfe 'failed to be mentioned in any contemporary save in Fr. Martindale's *Life of Mgr. Benson*.' 'At least he existed,' Leslie continues, 'and Benson embalmed him in parodic form in *The Sentimentalists*. Perhaps his truest literary memorial occurs in Henry Harland's novels, for both the *Cardinal's Snuffbox* and *My Friend Prosper* owe an immense amount of their Italian colour and detail to Rolfe.... Harland was a good friend to one with whom friendship was a minor experiment in demonology.'

Biographically, Rolfe had been named only once during his life, in the Aberdeen newspaper attack. But before his death his name or personality or something about his work had crept into several pieces of fiction—more than the three named by Leslie. This act by some other author calling upon Rolfe himself or some aspect of his person or talent did not stop in 1913. Surprisingly, this has continued to the present day. Although Rolfe's work has been overlooked by the literary historian and serious critic, it is encouraging to note that many literary people have known of him and have made mention of the fact, no matter how slightly. The list of pieces of fiction, including poetry, over the years is a long one, considering the minor position of Rolfe in the field of English literature. All the works below speak of Rolfe in some way, of him, his work or character. Some do it in only a few words. This list, presented here chronologically, can be regarded as by no means definitive.

1891 'Ballade: of the Serpentine (Suggested by some lines of the Rev. F. W. Rolfe)' by Charles Kains-Jackson, June 8, unpublished.

427

The 'lines' by Rolfe are his 'Ballade of Boys Bathing', *The Art Review*, April 1890.

1892   'St. William of Norwich (Painted by F. W. Rolfe)', *Love In Earnest* by John Gambril Nicholson, Elliot Stock, London, p. 164.

In the first issue this originally is Rolfe's sonnet which Nicholson reworked for his volume of verse. A threatened lawsuit by Rolfe made Nicholson and the publisher remove the poem and substitute a new one on the same theme, 'St. William of Norwich'. (This latter version is included in Brian Reade's anthology, *Sexual Heretics*, London, 1970, pp. 302-3.)

(Of all the sets of boys' initials used as dedications of the individual poems in this volume, one (p. 67) is the same as a set used by Rolfe for the dedicatees of *Tarcissus*: C[harles]. J. R.[oope].—a fellow-student of Nicholson's at Saffron Walden.)

c. 1895   *The Story of Venus and Tannhauser....* by Aubrey Beardsley, Leonard Smithers, London, 1907, p. 86.

Brian Reade, Victoria & Albert Museum: 'The book was in gestation during 1894. It was advertised as *The Story of Venus and Tannhauser* in *The Yellow Book*, Vol. III, October, 1894. Beardsley was at work on the manuscript through 1895, and it was intended to be published by John Lane in that year. However, the Wilde scandal and Beardsley's dismissal from *The Yellow Book* put a stop to that. During the same year too Beardsley made a double design for a frontispiece and title page to the book, dated 1895. These designs were not used when Smithers published the bowdlerised version of the story in *The Savoy*, Nos. 1 and 2, January and March 1896. About the middle of 1896 Beardsley seems to have abandoned all work on it. *Under the Hill* was acquired by Lane and published by The Bodley Head in 1904. Smithers kept the original manuscript and published it unillustrated in 250 copies in 1907. I suspect more copies were actually in issue.'

1900   *The Cardinal's Snuff-Box* by Henry Harland; John Lane: London, New York.

1904   *My Friend Prospero* by Henry Harland; John Lane; London, New York.

1906   *The Sentimentalists* by Robert Hugh Benson, Pitman & Sons, London.

The character of Christopher Dell is actually based on two people: Rolfe and Eustace Virgo.

1907 *Lord of the World* by Robert Hugh Benson, Pitman & Sons, London.

In this novel laid in the future, Rome's arch-enemy, Freemasonry, is the supreme power of the world. From Benson's notebooks, it seems that he drew upon Rolfe's personality for both Julian and Fr. Percy Franklin. In Martindale's biography of Benson he says that in the political view of the world 'everyone traces the influence of Mr. H. G. Wells. That is there; but the guiding hand was rather, at this point, Mr. Rolfe's. His *Hadrian VII* is responsible for a very great deal of *The Lord of the World*, not least the introduction.'

This was written shortly after the two first met. After their break, Rolfe wrote of his some-time friend in a light objectionable to those who revered Benson. Rolfe did not speak of Benson only as a mere co-religionist, but rather placed him on a much higher plane. In *The Desire and Pursuit of the Whole* (pp. 36-7) the author says of Benson: 'He did not exactly aspire to actual creation, but he certainly nourished the notion that several serious mistakes had resulted from his absence during the events described in the first chapter of Genesis.' To a mutual acquaintance Rolfe spoke of Benson in 1911 as 'that banausic fire-insurance agent'. Rolfe possessed a most remarkable memory, retentive and devious at times, correlating the most unusual combinations of facts. Rolfe had read Wells' *War of the Worlds* (1898), in which (p. 114) Wells has his hero try to comfort the scared-out-of-his-wits curate, ending with these words about God: 'He is not an insurance agent, man.'

1908 *The Holy Blissful Martyr Saint Thomas of Canterbury* by Robert Hugh Benson, Macdonald & Evans, London.

This is not the Rolfe-Benson collaboration, which was to be more of a historical romance. After its appearance, Rolfe referred to it as 'a slipshod tract', although Martindale says that the illustrations are based 'wholly upon Mr. Rolfe's contributions'.

1909 *Septimus* by William J. Locke, John Murray, London.

'The Literary Man from London' in this novel bears a striking resemblance to Rolfe. If he never actually met Rolfe, Locke certainly heard of him during visits to Harland's Saturday evenings, from which Rolfe absented himself.

Although this novel was put out by Murray, John Lane published more than thirty of Locke's books since 1897.

1910   'The Reticence of Lady Anne', *Reginald in Russia and Other Sketches* by Saki (H. H. Munro), Methuen, London, p. 8.

During his lifetime Saki had one book published by Grant Richards and several by John Lane.

1911   'A Mistake (From the Italian of Baron Corvo)', *A Garland of Ladslove* by John Gambril Nicholson, Francis Murray, London, p. 83.

In the copy of this book of verse which Nicholson sent to its dedicatee on 21 October 1911, he wrote beneath this one poem: 'A pure fiction!'

Rolfe was in Venice at the time this book appeared and Nicholson refrained from sending a copy of it to Horatio Brown; fearing that Rolfe might see it and object to his name being used. The storms between Nicholson and Rolfe were many and even included one anti-inscribed book. Nicholson belatedly had sent a copy of his *Chaplet of Southernwood* (1896) to Rolfe in November 1903, inscribed: 'To F. W. R. From J. G. N. ... intervening.' The book was returned to Nicholson and Rolfe had written in it: 'Things being as they are, F. W. R. refuses consent to intervention.' It may have been given back to the poet on November 15th, an evening when the two met. (The letter Nicholson wrote to Kains-Jackson about this meeting appears in *The Quest for Corvo* with slight variations, p. 161.) Yet the incident of the returned book did not alienate him from either Nicholson or the 'intervening' person. For to the latter Rolfe sent a newspaper article which appeared nearly a year later on September 11th. This was the 235-line review of *Hadrian* by Henry Murray in *The Sunday Sun*.

J. M. Stuart-Young wrote a poem closely resembling 'A Mistake'. His last line reads, 'Upon our lintel, one word, Ichabod!' —where Nicholson's says: 'And written o'er the portal, *Ichabod*.' This imitation appears as one of 'Five Nature Sonnets' in *Who Buys My Dreams?*, Cecil Palmer, London, 1923, p. 120.

[1912

'Der Tog in Venedig' by Thomas Mann, *Die Neue Rundschau*, Berlin, October (pp. 1386-98)-November (pp. 1499-1526). S. Fisher, Berlin, 1913. 'Death in Venice', *The Dial*, New York, March (pp. 213-35), April (pp. 311-33), May (pp. 423-44) 1924. Alfred A. Knopf, New York, 1925.

This story forms a coincidence between art and real life. Written at the time Rolfe was beginning to prosper and living at the Hotel Cavalletto, Thomas Mann's hero parallels the Englishman in a number of ways. Gustave von Aschenbach has been 'the poet-spokesman of all those who labour at the edge of exhaustion; of the overburdened, of those who are always worn out but still hold themselves upright'. To him 'the figure of [St.] Sebastian is the most beautiful symbol' in art. He visits Venice and stays at a hotel. He remains because his affections have been touched by the sight of 'a long-haired boy of about fourteen,' whose 'face recalled the noblest moment of Greek sculpture'; and his life ends with his death in Venice.]

1914 *Initiation* by Robert Hugh Benson, Hutchinson, London.

'Hero Worship', *Poems* by Robert Hugh Benson, Burns & Oates, London, p. 60.

1916 *The Coaster at Home: Being the Autobiography of Jack O'Dazi, Palm Oil Ruffian and Trader Man, of the River Niger* by J. M. Stuart-Young, Arthur H. Stockwell, London, pp. 168-9:

'Once I came across a wonderful photograph by Baron Corvo. It had been taken somewhere in Cairo, and it showed a nude boy sitting astride an earthenware jar. This picture (it appeared in the *Sketch*) aroused in my spirit the first ardent impulse to make a home of the tropics.'

The photograph in question appeared in *The Studio,* just after the article, 'The Nude in Photography' (15 June 1893, pp. 104-8), and was by Baron Wilhelm von Gloeden, probably taken in Taromina, Sicily. (As early as the turn of the century, post cards with reproductions of von Gloeden photographs had been printed. Several were sent (c. 1904) to John Gambril Nicholson from Berlin by Bernard Esmarch, who translated some of Nicholson's poetry into German.)

Stuart-Young knew both Nicholson and Charles Kains-Jackson, who selected and edited his verse in *Candles in Sunshine* (Arthur H. Stockwell, London, 1919).

1917 *The Iniquitous Coaster....* by J. M. Stuart-Young, Arthur H. Stockwell, London, pp. 140-163, 269-77, 344-6, 370-1.

Chapter XXX is the first version of 'Nigerian Supernaturalism', with a boy called Worsu telling his tales to the author.

Chapters LV and LXII are 'A Story Worsu Told Me' and 'Two Other Stories Worsu Told Me'.

Stuart-Young asks: 'I wonder if you ever met Baron Corvo's *Toto* stories? ... Dear Toto! To have known him would have been

431

to know the folklore of all Italy, Sicily, Greece and the East,—but then ... Fr. Rolfe—to give Corvo his other pseudonym—is a man of infinite learning, and his creations reflect their creator's mental cunning.'

1920 'Nigerian Supernaturalism' by John M. Stuart-Young, *The Occult Review* (edited by Ralph Shirley and published by Rider & Son), Part I, February, pp. 72-80; Part II, March, pp. 131-7.
The second version of this essay has the boy's name changed to Bosa.

1926 *The Cantab* by Shane Leslie, Chatto & Windus, London.
Rolfe in this novel becomes Baron Falco, who says: 'I myself have been recently pilloried by Father Robert Rolle in a novel, called, I think, *The Sensationalists*, for a crime of bourgeois vulgarity which I could never have contemplated.'
In 1924 Leslie had dedicated his *Masquerades: Studies in the Morbid* to Baron Corvo.

1929 *Life at a Venture* by Eustace Virgo de Fontmell, Eric Partridge, London.
In this autobiographical novel, Dominic Vesta is Virgo. Rolfe or Corvo retains his name in the book, whereas Benson becomes Fr. George Mason.

c. 1930 *Don Tarquinio, an Operetta* (Conceived only.)
Mary Butts and her husband, Gabriel Atkin, spoke about working on an operetta based on *Tarquinio*. Nothing was actually composed for this intended project.

Don Brianelli: An Epileptic Automatic Romance, unpublished.
Mary Butts and Atkin probably learned about Rolfe from A. T. Bartholomew, whose friends visited him during weekends at Cambridge. Knowing of his enthusiastic interest in Rolfe, some would leave behind 'momentoes' of their visits, in the form of parody on Rolfe's work. Atkin, an artist, did several water-colour sketches of Corvine cardinals, Bartholomew being one. Of all the written work, perhaps only this piece, *Don Brianelli* by Brian Hill, survives today. It was written in March 1930.

[The W. C. Fields films form another coincidence with one work by Rolfe, if only an obscure one. Fields' first English booking was for four weeks at the London Palace Theatre, beginning 18

February 1901. His 'capital' juggling act was part of a special matinee at the Palace arranged to let people see the American Biograph newsreels of Queen Victoria's funeral procession. (See *Nicholas Crabbe*, pp. 144-50, for a copy of Rolfe's letter to Temple Scott, then in New York, about the funeral of his Divine Victoria.) When Fields moved to Hollywood, he waged a continuous and relentless battle to have things done his way. In his biography by Robert Lewis Taylor (*W. C. Fields: His Follies and Fortunes*) it is said that he 'could voice tea-party pleasantries and make them sound profane ... so that "Godfrey Daniel" always came out "Goddamn", not only to the Hays office but to the general public'. The origin of this exclamation with Fields is unknown. Perhaps he picked it up during his first trip to London, the date of Rolfe's *Nicholas Crabbe*, in which Rolfe has Neddy Carnage (Edward Slaughter) say (p. 75): 'God—frey—Dan—iel—Simp—son!']

1936   *The Mirtle Tree* by Robert Godfrey Goodyear, Boriswood, London, pp. 135-7.

Lucy picks up *The Quest for Corvo* by 'A. J. A. Symonds' [*sic*], opens it to page 158 and reads:

'I am struck aghast every now and then ... by the strange thing people call love. One would be silly to deny it—because every now and then examples crop up of a sensible man or woman having their life tangled up with the life of another in blind mystery. They actually support each the continual presence of the other. Oh, there must be something in it.

But it seems excessively funny to me. Carnal pleasure I thoroughly appreciate, but I like a change sometimes. Even partridges get tiresome after many days. Only besotted ignorance or hypocrisy demurs to carnal lust, but I meet people who call that holy which is purely natural, and I am stupefied. I suppose we all deceive ourselves. To blow one's nose ... is a natural relief. So is coition. Yet the last is called holy, and the first passes without epithets. Why should one attach more importance to the one than the other ...'

With minor changes, this is the letter, quoted by Symons, from Rolfe to Temple Scott in New York, c. 1900.

In Bertram Rota's Book Catalogue, Spring 1970, item 198 is a group of three letters from Symons to Goodyear. One asked the novel's author to correct '*The Quest for Coito* by A. J. A. Symonds. The misprint ... coupled with the extract concerning carnal love, may put some readers on the wrong track!'

1942   *To Be a Pilgrim* by Joyce Cary, Michael Joseph, London, p. 208.

1945 *Not Expected to Live* by Marten Cumberland, Hurst & Blackett, London, p. 165.

That Hideous Strength: A Modern Fairy-tale for Grownups by C. S. Lewis, John Lane, London.
In this book there is a jackdaw by the name of Baron Corvo.

1947 *Hearsed in Death* by Marten Cumberland, Hurst & Blackett, London, p. 148.

Treadmill by Michael Harrison, John Langdon, London, p. 195.
The priest's room (p. 199) has an air similar to Rose's at the beginning of *Hadrian*.

In the same year Harrison's *They Would Be King* (Somers, London) was published. It is a history of four men, one of whom is Jean Baptiste Bernadotte. Born the son of the town bailiff in France in 1768, Bernadotte lived to ascend the combined Norway-Sweden throne as King Charles John XIV, after Napoleon had made him Sovereign Prince of Pontecorvo.

1950 *The Decline and Fall of Practically Everybody* by Will Cuppy, illustrated by William Steig, Holt, New York; Dobson, London, 1951, p. 98.
Although this is essentially a non-fiction work, it is classified by librarians under Wit & Humour.

The Cardinal by Henry Morton Robinson, Simon & Schuster, New York; Macdonald, London, 1951.
Mrs. Ragg ('Epilogue', *Letters to R. M. Dawkins*, 1962, p. 179) assails *Hadrian the Seventh*. Its language and phantasies seem 'thin, malevolent and tawdry' in the light of *Il Santo*, a work, she says, by a 'sincere novelist and a great gentleman'. 'Today,' she adds, 'I should compare [his picture of a Conclave] unfavourably with a chapter in the American, *The Cardinal*.'
She did not know the association between Rolfe's and the American novel. One of Robinson's friends in New York was a book dealer and the two would spend hours in each other's company, drinking and talking. One night Robinson was in a depressed mood over the unpopularity of his work. The dealer could think of only one way to answer this mood and loaned Robinson a book to read. When the book was read and returned, the dealer asked what he thought of it. Robinson did not think much of it

and said that he could write a better one himself. The dealer had loaned him *Hadrian the Seventh* and Robinson's next book was to be *The Cardinal*, a long-running best-seller, later to be adapted into a film.

1954 *Unto Death Utterly* by Marten Cumberland, Hurst & Blackett, London, p. 57.

1956 *Homage to Mistress Bradstreet* by John Berryman, illustrated by Ben Shahn; Farrar, Strause & Cudahy; New York; stanza 33.1 and footnote. *Homage to Mistress Bradstreet and Other Poems*, Faber & Faber, London, pp. 21, 30-1.

1959 *Broken Boy* by John Blackburn, Secker & Warburg, London, p. 73.

Murmurs in the Rue Morgue by Marten Cumberland, Hutchinson, London, p. 75.

The Unspeakable Skipton by Pamela Hansford Johnson, Macmillan, London; Harcourt, New York.
Daniel Skipton is a study 'of an artist's paranoia', and the author uses the life of Rolfe as a source for her characterization.

Brother Cain by Simon Raven, Anthony Blond, London, p. 203.

Hadrian The Seventh, adapted by Rayner Heppenstall, BBC Third Programme, December 4.
Max Adrian played Rose-Hadrian.

1960 *The Quest for Corbett* by Harold Lang and Kenneth Tynan, Gaberbocchus, London.
Only the title of this radio play (BBC Third Programme, 15 July 1956) is linked with Rolfe and is taken from the Symons biography.

1961 *An Intrusion Upon Eternity* by Donald Weeks, Adagio Press, Grosse Pointe, Michigan.
A Christmas card, the story is supposed to be a hitherto untold Toto tale.

1964 *The Terrible Door* by George Sims, Bodley Head, London.

This mystery story is based on the Venice Letters.

Did any of the mystery writers who utilized Rolfe's name or work in their stories ever suspect that he wrote a murder mystery himself? One of the Toto stories is 'About Our Lady of Dreams'. Published in *In His Own Image* in 1901, it was written either in Holywell in 1898 or in London during the following year. After a long preamble, Toto tells the tale of Diodato, Coronata and Aristide. Eighteen-year-old Diodato is fond of young Coronata. So is Aristide, the village butcher. Coronata favours Diodato and one day the two youths fight over her, Aristide wounding the other with his knife. One wintry night soon after, the butcher 'went creeping, creeping, towards the lonely hut of Coronata ... high up, on the lower bordure of the forest'. A black frost covers the ground and the frozen bushes tear at his face as he climbs the rocky path along the summit of a cliff. In the bright sunny morning he is found dead, fallen from the cliff, with a wound in his throat. No weapon is found. Diodato is taken prisoner as the murderer. Frat' Innocente-of-the-Nine-Quires (forerunner of Fr. Brown?) believes the boy to be innocent and is told how the crime was committed by a dream-angel. He takes the authorities to the scene and restages Aristide's death, using a pig as a substitute victim. On the cold night, the butcher had looked up as he climbed. At that instance, a long sharp icicle had fallen, fatally struck him in the throat and melted in the morning sun.

Was Rolfe the first to use the melted icicle—the no-weapon plot —in a mystery story?

Julian Symons: 'It is possible that Rolfe was actually the first writer to use the icicle as a weapon in fiction. The first book I know of to use the trick is Anna Katharine Green's *Initials Only*, which was published in 1911. The *actual* use of an icicle has been attributed to the Medici.'

1965   *The British Museum Is Falling Down* by David Lodge, Macgibbon & Kee, London, pp. 79-82, 159.

1968   *Hadrian VII* by Peter Luke, *Plays of the Year*, Vol. 33, edited by J. C. Trewin, Elek Books, London, pp. 15-114.
This superb adaption of Rolfe's novel first appears in *Plays and Players*, May 1968, pp. 27-42 and then separately by Andre Deutsch and Samuel French, London (1968); Alfred A. Knopf and Vintage Books, New York, and Penguin, Harmondsworth (1969). It has been translated and published in Argentine and France.

Its première was at The Birmingham (England) Repertory Theatre, 9 May 1967. Its first London performance was at The Mermaid Theatre, 18 April 1968, and the first New York production was on 26 December 1968 at the Helen Hayes Theater. Alec McCowen played Rolfe-Hadrian at each of these three theatres. The play has since been produced in most major cities of the world.

During the week of 22-28 June 1968, the BBC 2-Light Programme, *The Dales,* mentioned The Mermaid Theatre production of *Hadrian.* On 5 December 1968, the BBC 1-TV *Omnibus* went to The Mermaid for its first visit to a live theatre. It presented the first half of *Hadrian,* then starring the Canadian actor, Douglas Rain, as Rolfe-Hadrian.

(Once again the unfortunate Rolfe chose the wrong thing. He thought that *Don Tarquinio,* published a year after *Hadrian,* was more colourful and had more popular appeal. On the book's half-title page he had printed: 'The author reserves U. S., serial, dramatic, and translation rights.')

'Corvo on Corvo' by Robin Barrow, *The Idler: An Entertainment,* Vol. 1, No. 2, Wheatley, Oxford, p. 7.

In the vein of a 'Review of Unwritten Books', Corvo here reviews *The Quest for Corvo,* recently republished by Penguin.

INDEX

Beauclerk—*cont.*
    Rolfe's complaints to Rome, 147-8
Beerbohm, Sir Max, 179
'Begging Letters' (Holmfield), 189-91, 410
Bellasis, Edward, 120
Benson, A. C., 263, 388, 389
Benson, E. F., 388
Benson, Robert Hugh, 243-4 249-52, 269-70, 315, 345; collaboration with Rolfe on St. Thomas book, 251-2, 258-9, 263-4, 265-6; denounced by Rolfe, 284, 297; in *The Desire and Pursuit*, 339-40; dissuaded from association with Rolfe, 263-4; financial aid to Rolfe through Pirie-Gordon, 286; and *Hadrian*, 249, 250, 387; and *In His Own Image*, 370, 387; Martindale's biography of, 388-9, 412; reluctance to aid Rolfe in Venice, 287; and Rolfe, xvi, 249-52, 263-4, 266, 387-90; and Rolfe as portrayed in *Initiation*, 389-90; and Rolfe's work, 245, 283-4; and the supernatural, 250; walking tour with Rolfe, 251; writings, 387, 389-90, 412, 428-9, 431
Bentley, John Francis, 123
Beresford, Lord Charles de la Poer, 101
Beurms, Fr. Francis, 20-1
Bierce, Ambrose, 203, 415
Blackwood's Magazine, 366
Borgia Genealogy, 222, 248, 252-3, 254, 380
Bourne, Bp. Francis, 263
Brown, Horatio, 286, 287, 315, 317, 364, 395-6; Rolfe asks his help, 290
Browning, Oscar, 248
Bull Against the Enemy of the Anglican Race, 191, 215, 418
Bute, J. P. C. Stuart, 3rd Marquess of, 17-19, 38-9, 120-1; in *Hadrian*, 21, 22

Callanan, Helena, 170
Campbell, Sir Gerald, 367, 368, 382-3, 421; letter to Herbert Rolfe, 371-2; on Rolfe, 381-2
Campbell, Mgr. James A., 43-4, 53-4, 411; expels Rolfe from Scots College, 47, 48, 49
Caraman, Philip, 388
Cardinal, The (Robinson), 377, 434-5
Carlile, Wilson: Rolfe's article on, 185
Carmont, Rev. John, 53-4
Carmont, Canon Robert: on C. D. McVarish, 50; on Rolfe at Scots College, 44-5, 46-8
Carpenter, Edward: *Towards Democracy*, 379
Castle, Cecil, 38, 62, 407; photographic model for Rolfe, 65, 66, 69
Catholic Church: and *Hadrian*, 262-3; and Modernism, 260-3
Catholic Church in Modern Scotland, The (Anson), 54
Catholic Controversy (Ryder), 15
Catholic Times, The, 161; reprint of Aberdeen Attack, 147, 161, 170
Cazenove, C. D., 339
Chambers, Robert William: *Outsiders: an Outline*, 246-7
Champion, Henry Hyde, 103 ff, 158-60, 167; in *Hadrian*, 110, 111; and Rolfe, 106, 108-9, 113, 121, 158-60, 167, 168
Chronicles of the House of Borgia, xxii, 7, 82, 83, 181-2, 191-5, 216, 375, 417-18; Harland's praise of, 195; payment for, 181, 192; Rolfe's denunciation of, 196-7, 221
Church of England: and ritual in 19th century, 14-15
Church of Scotland: unrest in 19th century, 52
Church Times, The, 161
Clark, Scotson, 72
Clarke, Fr. R. F., 24-5, 89

Hunter Blair—*cont.*
  Hadrian, 25; Rolfe's suspicions of his part in Aberdeen Attack, 82-3, 161-2

Ideal Content, An, see Don Renato
In His Own Image, 175-6, 185 ff., 209; De Zueleta's review, 4, 7, 189; Harland's comments, 187-8; homosexual taint in, 187-8, 388; Leslie's Introduction, 395; Martindale's comments, 370-1, 388
Initiation (Benson), 389-90
Irving, Sir Henry, 219, 220, 422

Jacobus, Mar, *see* Herford, Ulric Vernon
Jackson, Vincent H., 164
Jacobitism, xxv-xxvii
Jerome, Jerome K., 116, 167, 407-8
Johnson, Pamela Hansford: on *The Desire and Pursuit,* 304; *The Unspeakable Skipton,* 320, 435; on the Venice Letters, 304
Jones, Morgan Akin, 367
Jones, Mrs. Morgan Akin, 361-3, 422

Kains-Jackson, Charles, 38, 62-3, 156, 427; and the boy, 317; and Nicholson's publication of Rolfe's poem, 88; poem about Masson Fox, 318; and Rolfe's attempt to buy Gleeson White's property, 72-3; on Rolfe's painting, 78, 79, 375; on Rolfe's photography, 69; and Rolfe's relations with boys, 70

Lane, John, 7, 137, 146, 179, 181, 195, 202, 204, 290, 315, 420; and *In His Own Image,* 176, 185, 186; and *Nicholas Crabbe,* 245-6; in *Nicholas Crabbe,* 173-4, 176
Lanier, Henry Wysham, 146, 414

Layard, Lady: in *The Desire and Pursuit,* 338; Rolfe's behaviour at her funeral, 381-2
Leo XIII, Pope, 216, 217; *Rerum Novarum,* 108-9
Leslie, Sir Shane, xvi-xvii, 86, 372, 432; on *The Bull Against the Enemy of the Anglican Race,* 191; 'Frederick Baron Corvo', 75, 395, 413, 427; *Masquerades,* 1; and Rolfe's burial, 396-7; on the Venetian letters, 332
Littledale, Cmdr., 100
Littledale, Dr. R. F.: *Plain Reasons Against Joining the Church of Rome,* 15
Lockhart, Fr. William, 85, 95, 116
Looking Back (Douglas), 391-4, 416
Lowder, 'Father' Charles Fuge, 10-11
Luckock, R. M.: in *Hadrian,* 9
Luke, Sir Harry, xvii-xviii, 254, 270, 328, 422, 425; and the Order of Sanctissima Sophia, 256; and Rolfe, 377

Macdonald, Hugh, Bp. of Aberdeen, 89-90, 102, 163, 164; receives Rolfe into Franciscans Third Order Regular, 93; refusal to buy Rolfe's paintings, 100
Mackie, Fr., 55
McVarish, Charles Duncan, 45, 50-2, 54; press attack on, 51, 161-2
Martindale, C. C., 388; biography of R. H. Benson, 388-9, 412; and *In His Own Image,* 370-1
Meleager, 201-2, 207, 267; Rolfe on its publication, 369
Memories of a Misspent Youth (Richards), 255-6, 416
Menevia, Bp. of, *see* Mostyn, Francis, Bp. of Menevia
Menghini, Canon Charles, 53-4
Meredith, George: *Adventures of Harry Richmond,* 208-9